THE HISTORY OF
AHEPA
1922 – 2022

THE HISTORY OF AHEPA 1922–2022:
A CENTURY OF SERVICE

Alexander Kitroeff

With a Foreword by
Basil Mossaidis
AHEPA Executive Director

Holy Cross Orthodox Press
Brookline, Massachusetts

Copyright 2023 The American Hellenic
Educational Progressive Association (AHEPA)
Published by
Holy Cross Orthodox Press
Hellenic College, Inc.
50 Goddard Avenue
Brookline, MA 02445
ISBN 978-1-935317-95-1
All rights reserved.

**Publisher's Cataloging-in-Publication
(Provided by Cassidy Cataloguing Services, Inc.).**
Names: Kitroeff, Alexander, author. | Mossaidis, Basil, writer of foreword. |
    American Hellenic Educational Progressive Association, sponsoring body.
Title: The history of AHEPA 1922-2022 : a century of service / Alexander Kitroeff ;
    with a foreword by Basil Mossaidis, AHEPA Executive Director.
Other titles: History of American Hellenic Educational Progressive Association
    1922-2022.
Description: First edition. | Brookline, Massachusetts : Holy Cross Orthodox Press,
    [2023]
Identifiers: ISBN: 978-1-935317-95-1
Subjects: LCSH: American Hellenic Educational Progressive Association--History.
    | Greek Americans-- Societies, etc.--History. | Greek Americans--History. |
    Greek Americans--Ethnic identity. | Greeks--United States--History.
Classification: LCC: E184.G7 K58 2023 | DDC: 973/.04/893--dc23

Table of Contents

Foreword 6

Introduction 9

Part I 1922–1945
1. The Formative Years 1922–1928 15
2. Americanism and Hellenism in the 1930s 47
3. AHEPA & World War II 1940–1945 69

Part II 1946–1972
4. Cold War & Postwar Reconstruction 1946–1956 87
5. AHEPA Turns to Education 1957–1962 117
6. AHEPA Reaches Its 50th Anniversary 133

Part III 1973–1999
7. AHEPA & US Policy in the
   Eastern Mediterranean 1974–1980 167
8. AHEPA: A Bridge Between
   the United States & Greece 1981–1987 191
9. Honoring The Immigrant Roots 213
10. AHEPA Recalibrates 1993–1999 231

Part IV 2000–2022
11. AHEPA Enters the 21st Century 2000–2008 253
12. AHEPA Stands by the Homeland 2009–2014 287
13. AHEPA Stands by Hellenism & Orthodoxy 2015–2019 321
14. AHEPA Reaches Its Centenary 349

Endnotes 385

Foreword to the First Edition

Eight visionary men came together to create a fraternal Order and to promote its "objectives and principles: effect a perfect and harmonious understanding between ourselves and others..." Bold words for a group of salesmen who wanted to create an organization to help make Greek immigrants, good Americans. Who knew that on a hot day, June 26, 1922, these eight men would create an organization—the American Hellenic Educational Progressive Association—which eventually would span the world? Who knew in 1922 that this organization would thrive in turbulent decades and survive 100 years, promoting values and traditions of the immigrants who created it? The creation of this organization, this fraternity, was organic and original. Many organizations started from a chapter or a group and flourished into a national organization, but not this. AHEPA was invented at the national level and much like Johnny Appleseed spread its important message to communities and chapters across North America, Europe, Asia, and as far away as Australasia.

We honor our Mother Lodge: Harry Angelopoulos, John Angelopoulos, George Campbell, James Campbell, Nicholas D. Chotas, George A. Poulos, Speros Stamos, and James Vlass, who worked to make AHEPA flourish.

AHEPA has been through many challenging times. We assisted people in keeping their communities running during the depression of the 1930s. During World War II, AHEPA became an official issuer of World War II War Bonds, selling over $300 million (that is $5 billion today)! In the aftermath of World War II, AHEPA worked to create the "Greek War Relief" Association which raised hundreds of millions of dollars, building homes and sending food, clothes, and much needed necessities to the war-ravaged country of Greece.

In the 1950s and 60s AHEPA built hospitals and medical centers in Greece. We built statues and dedicated buildings to our ancestors, and we expanded our chapters into every city in America. In 1974 AHEPA led the charge to Washington, DC to fight the injustice in Cyprus. In the 1970s our youth program had thousands of dances raising hundreds of thousands of dollars in support of Special Olympics and other worthy causes. The AHEPA family worked to make our name and impact glow bright across the country and across the globe.

In the 1980s AHEPA donated millions in support of the youth, including $1 million to St. Basil's; we created and maintained the AHEPA Educational Foundation which awards scholarships; we created the AHEPA Housing Corporation. AHEPA Housing currently manages 96 facilities in the United States, providing safe and affordable homes for nearly 6,000 elderly residents. In 1986 AHEPA donated to the restoration of the Statue of Liberty. In 1990 AHEPA donated to the restoration of Ellis Island; over $1 million was raised and AHEPA was the FIRST organization to host an event on Ellis Island in 1991.

In 2001, AHEPA took the lead and raised $500,000 for 9/11 relief and assistance. We have raised nearly $1 billion since 1922 for aid to the United States and Greece. **AHEPA takes the lead and AHEPA Cares.** AHEPA worked throughout the 2000s to promote international peace in the Eastern Mediterranean and worked with the governments of Cyprus and Greece for peace in the sea and air which were being violated by the only aggressor nation in the region. In 2009 was the first ever visit of the Ecumenical Patriarch Bartholomew to AHEPA Headquarters. In 2010 the Order of AHEPA, under the auspices of the Cyprus Hellenic Affairs division, hosted for the first time EVER a conference bringing together the Greek, Cypriot and Israeli ambassadors. During the financial crisis in 2011 AHEPA donated millions of dollars to Greece in medical aid to hospitals through the IOCC and other international organizations.

In 2019 AHEPA donated $1 million to the restoration of the St. Nicholas Greek Orthodox Church and Shrine at Ground Zero. AHEPA continues to combat for the rights of all Hellenes and defends Hellenism daily. In 2020, we faced the COVID-19 pandemic and AHEPA fought back and served our communities. Our chapters are out in the field, feeding the frontline heroes, our doctors and nurses, firemen and EMTs. AHEPA proves that it is relevant today and our members know it.

We celebrate our 100th Anniversary this year and AHEPA has scheduled dinner events across the country, celebrating our "Centennial of Service," with the crescendo building up to our 100th Annual Supreme Convention in Disney World this summer. As we all start coming out, we invite you and your family to come to Disney World and spend a magical week with the AHEPA family to rekindle old friendships and forge new ones. We look to all of you to keep AHEPA alive another 100 years. We look to our youth and our new members to pick up the mantle of leadership to take us to another century.

The 100th Anniversary book is written by our friend Dr. Alexander Kitroeff, Professor Emeritus of History at Haverford College, and author of several books dealing with the history of the Greek diaspora in America and elsewhere. AHEPA would like to thank him for his dedication and assistance in the promotion of the AHEPA story. It has been an honor to work with Dr. Kitroeff and a pleasure to serve the Order of AHEPA.

In my capacity as Executive Director since 2002 and as the youth coordinator and assistant between 1991–1996, I have to say that this is a 28-year chapter of my life which I would never change, watching the greatness of our organization and witnessing the hard work of our members to promote AHEPA.

In this, our centenary year 2022, we were profoundly honored when Prime Minister of the Hellenic Republic Kyriakos Mitsotakis presented the Order of AHEPA with the Grand Commander of the Order of the Phoenix, the highest honor Greece bestows.

Basil Mossaidis
Executive Director

INTRODUCTION

To assess AHEPA's rich and diverse 100-year history is a challenge for any historian. Formed in 1922 to combat racism and xenophobia and to encourage Greek immigrants in the United States to become American, AHEPA could have become a victim of its own early success and not lasted very long after achieving its goals. Instead, it survived and flourished by adapting to the changing face of Greek America and helping it evolve throughout the 20th and early 21st centuries. Thus, in many ways, AHEPA's history is the history of the Greek experience in America. Greek Americans responded to AHEPA's call that they become integrated into American society, but faced a new set of challenges in the 1930s that required a sense of brotherhood and solidarity that AHEPA offered. The Order tempered its advocacy of Americanism and sought to retain its relevancy by invoking the ideals and values of the distant ancestors of the Greek immigrants, the ancient Greeks whose achievements influenced America's Founding Fathers. It was the beginning of a series of transformations AHEPA underwent in the decades that followed, while it also used the wide remit of its mission, to be progressive and to educate, in order to broaden its activities and, most importantly, acquire a women's auxiliary, the Daughters of Penelope, that grew into AHEPA's companion organization. As AHEPA marks its centenary its website lists its programs as being "Athletics, Veterans, Education,

Housing, Public Health, Hellenic Cultural Commission, and Public Policy," and that does not begin to capture the depth and range of initiatives that each topic represents. And while AHEPA's leadership seeks to coordinate the pursuit of all those goals, regional bodies and ultimately local chapters choose what activities they wish to focus upon. In addition to the range of its activities, the size of its membership, and its geographical spread, AHEPA also has three separate auxiliaries: the women's Daughters of Penelope, and the Maids of Athena and the Sons of Pericles for the youth. While these auxiliaries belong to AHEPA, they operate on their own and thus merit consideration as well.

This book offers a synopsis of AHEPA's history from 1922 and 2022. It traces its trajectory through its conventions and its major activities but does not claim to be a comprehensive record. There are too many events, domestic and international missions, awards and awardees to fit into this overview. It is written in a way that can tell AHEPA's story to its members and introduce AHEPA to the Greek American community, and to a wider readership in Greece and the diaspora. And hopefully it can function as a building block upon which others may probe deeper the Order's rich history. This book highlights AHEPA's leadership role in shaping the evolution of the Order and more broadly of Greek America. Toward that purpose it considers AHEPA's trajectory during those 100 years against the backdrop of the major developments in American society, the evolution of the Greek American community, and the changes that took place in Greece and the Eastern Mediterranean. This account is arranged chronologically as well as thematically. It treats AHEPA's history in consecutive periods that are divided according to AHEPA's principal objectives at the time.

In focusing on AHEPA's major efforts at any given historical moment, this book acknowledges the entire range of AHEPA programs and projects in the spheres of athletics, education, housing, public health, public policy, and veterans' support. Through those initiatives, many of which were which were innovative for the Greek American community, AHEPA played the role of catalyst for many progressive changes in Greek America's history. Being an overview, this book focuses primarily on the actions of the organization's leading national body and the decisions of the annual national conventions. Mention will be made of AHEPA's affiliated organizations, the Daughters of Penelope, the Sons of Pericles, and the Maids of Athena, as well as the role of local chapters and AHEPA in Canada, Greece, Cyprus, and Europe, but all these require—indeed deserve—their own separate studies to do justice to the breadth and depth of their initiatives. For several years now AHEPA has ceased referring to them as its "auxiliaries" and instead considers them part of "the AHEPA family." This confirms that they are too important to be summarily tagged on to the end of the story of AHEPA in the United States. Indeed, this book should be seen as an invitation to all those interested in exploring AHEPA's history locally, and the history of the Daughters of Penelope, the Sons of Pericles, and the Maids of Athena.

The first two parts of this book that cover AHEPA from 1922 to 1972 owe a huge debt to the book the then Executive Secretary George Leber compiled on the Order's 50th anniversary in 1972.[1] I have relied on his account of this period and incorporated many parts of it in my own narrative. Leber's account is a comprehensive recording of activities and names of officials, and one that stresses AHEPA's positive achievements and sidesteps the more controversial moments. I have supplemented Leber's account with information from a few other studies on aspects of AHEPA's history, several studies of the Greek experience in the United States, and my own research. In bringing these additional resources into the narrative, I have tried to go beyond Leber's account and lists of names and provide further information about those persons mentioned, and mention whether they were born in Greece or the United States and provide information about their background and professional activities. I used the same additional resources for the second 50 years of AHEPA's history, along with AHEPA's Yearbooks, its Magazine, its press releases, American, Canadian, Greek American and Greek newspaper reports, data from the AHEPA History Project, and my own Greek American history database. It includes notes taken with meetings I had with two former supreme presidents back in the 1980s, Dean Alfange and George Vournas, the latter thanks to an introduction by former AHEPA information director Elias Vlanton. I consulted the minutes of several previous conventions but could not do so systematically because of the bulk of the material. I was unable to consult AHEPA's records that are housed at the University of Minnesota's Archival

Collections because of the COVID-19 pandemic. I also learned a lot through speaking to several former supreme presidents and other leading Ahepans who kindly shared their views and experiences. They are too many to list here. For all the help I received, as the saying goes, all errors remain mine.

I kept footnotes to a minimum. Where quotation marks appear without a citation the text is either from Leber's book or from an official AHEPA news release. Hopefully this book will encourage Ahepans and historians to delve deeper than this overall survey has, with the help of those records and any other available sources.

I thank the Order of AHEPA for entrusting me with the task of writing this book. I was able to attend two supreme conventions and a governors' meeting and get a sense of the ways the Order and its members come together and work. AHEPA's small but busy headquarters in Washington, DC proved a most welcoming place for me to do most of my research on the Order's materials. Executive Director Basil Mossaidis was most generous with his time and shared his experiences and deep knowledge of AHEPA's history with a unique blend of authority, analytical clarity, and self-effacing humor, all of which inspired me and sustained me throughout this research and writing project.

An earlier version of this book was produced by the Hellenic American Union, Athens in 2022 in time for AHEPA's Supreme Convention of that year. Thanks are due to the President and his staff for their excellent work. For this updated and revised second edition of the book thanks go to the Very Reverend Dr. Anton C. Vrame and his team at Holy Cross Orthodox Press.

PART I 1922–1945

ORDER OF AHEPA
MOTHER LODGE

NICHOLAS D. CHOTAS
(Deceased)

JAMES CAMPBELL

S. J. STAMOS
(Deceased)

HARRY ANGELOPOULOS

GEORGE A. POLOS
(Deceased)

JOHN ANGELOPOULOS
(Deceased)

GEORGE CAMPBELL
(Deceased)

JAMES VLASS
(Deceased)

Chapter 1: The Formative Years 1922–1928

When a handful of Greek Americans gathered in the basement of a Greek Orthodox church in Atlanta to form the American Hellenic Educational Progressive Association, the AHEPA, on July 26, 1922, little could they imagine they were establishing what became the largest and most important Greek American secular institution for the next 100 years. The six, who were joined by another two to become the eight founders and Mother Lodge of AHEPA, were urgently focused on one thing: the need to find ways to defend the Greeks who had come to America from the threat of nativism and racism that had grown after the end of World War I, especially in the American South. Their plan was to promote the Americanization of the Greeks but to allow the organization a broad enough scope to not lose touch with their homeland's culture and to promote the values they saw embodied in its ancient civilization. They may have known their initiative was part of a long tradition of adaptability and resourcefulness that the Greeks have displayed through the ages. With their model being the legendary Odysseus, whom Homer endowed with cunning intelligence and versatility, the Greeks had overcome adversity especially when they had found themselves under foreign rule or when their independent nation state suffered from foreign intervention. As both a seafaring and diaspora-oriented people, the Greeks quickly learned that to survive on the high seas and on foreign lands they should not take anything for granted, think on their feet, and adjust their course to react to sudden changes in the prevailing winds or climates. And soon after World War I in the United States and in the American South in particular, the climate was changing and demanded a Greek response.

About 400,000 Greeks arrived in the United States between the 1890s and the early 1920s when strict quotas essentially put an end to the entry of immigrants from southeastern Europe. The exact number is hard to determine; there were a few hundred Greeks who had settled in America before the 1890s, while several thousand of those who arrived after 1890 returned to Greece after a stay of a few years. There were a few hundred Greek immigrants who had died before 1920, either because they had fallen in battle with the United States Armed Forces during World War I or they were victims of the deadly flu epidemic of 1918. The Greeks had arrived mainly at the tail end of the massive wave of transatlantic emigration from southeastern Europe, which is probably why many settled in New York, Chicago, the mill towns of New England, and the mining and steel towns of Pennsylvania and West Virginia. Very soon, thousands more spread out quickly throughout the rest of the United States, working along the railroad and the mines in Colorado and Utah and eventually reaching California and the Northwest. There was an early presence in Florida as well, with the arrival of sponge divers from the islands of the Aegean. The preference of the Greeks to be self-employed, if possible, made it even more likely one would soon find Greeks even in small towns not only on the East Coast and the Midwest but also out West and even in the South.

The wave of newcomers from southeastern Europe that arrived between the 1870s and World War I inherited the animus of nativism which had greeted immigrants from Ireland and elsewhere earlier in the 19th century. Nativist sentiment entailed a dynamic and more and more encompassing hostility and prejudice against foreigners that was amplified whenever economic downturns were thought to endanger the jobs of those already settled in the country, or whenever significantly large numbers of new arrivals were perceived as a threat to whatever was considered at the time as the American way of life. This xenophobic attitude was variously expressed by religiously motivated anti-Catholicism and anti-Semitism, an unfounded belief that the newcomers brought with them an ingrained criminality, or an assumption that by maintaining ties to their homelands they were disloyal to America and what it represented. And worst of all, a bigoted belief in white superiority meant that racist attitudes, actions, and policies targeted a wide range of immigrants, including "Mediterraneans" whom the spokesman of whiteness considered as being on the lowest civilizational rung of all Europeans.[2]

The Greeks were no exception to the widespread negative targeting of the immigrants from southeastern Europe. The incidents ranged from everyday insults on the street, job postings barring Greeks from applying, and newspaper articles recycling unfounded claims of Greek criminality, but also included several incidents of premeditated attacks on Greeks and their businesses. Such occurrences were usually in towns where there were small numbers of Greeks. The worst episode was an anti-Greek riot in South Omaha, Nebraska where most of the town's 1,300 Greeks worked in the meatpacking industry. A mob of 3,000 people attacked and destroyed the Greek quarter, forcing all the Greeks to flee to nearby Omaha. There had been other anti-Greek riots in Roanoke, Virginia in 1907 which caused the destruction of Greek businesses but there the authorities reacted and reassured the Greeks they would be protected. Smaller scale incidents also took place in Idaho and Montana. In some cases, newly arrived Greeks were used as strike-breakers, many times unknowingly, across the country, from New England to Utah, and this also gave rise to clashes fueled by xenophobia and racism.

Yet there were also many examples of the Greeks encountering positive attitudes, even admiration. In 1909 Grace Abbot, the activist and social worker, countered the accusation that Greeks had a propensity for criminality by explaining that many of their transgressions were due to misunderstandings because of language barriers, lack of knowledge of the prevailing rules and regulations, and disproportionate exposure to policemen on the beat because they operated pushcarts and other businesses in public places.[3] When those same pushcart owners managed to open their own stores and acquired the respectability the move entailed, city officials acknowledged their work ethic and contribution to the local economy. And when hundreds of Greeks enlisted in the US

Armed Forces to fight in World War I there was a spate of articles in newspapers across the country praising their commitment and loyalty to America. And by the same token the press endorsed Greece's territorial claims against the Ottoman Empire and reported on the depredations they faced in the hands of the Ottoman authorities. It was this social capital that the Greeks had accrued that functioned as a springboard enabling the Greeks to defend themselves when nativism reared its head after the end of World War I.

Spearheading and defining post-World War I nativism was the Ku Klux Klan, the white supremacist organization active in the 1860s and 1870s which was relaunched in 1915 in Atlanta. In its new guise, the Klan promoted nativism fused with nationalism, combining racism with a view that the American nation should be exclusively Anglo-Saxon in character, admitting only northern Europeans, "Nordics," into its vision of 100 percent Americanism. After the war it broadened its agenda even further. The migration of many blacks to northern states forced the Klan to seek out new enemies, and it rediscovered anti-Catholicism and even attacked Protestant whites for not living up the moral standards the organization supposedly espoused. Animating the Klan's anti-Catholicism and determination to regulate morals was a deep belief in a fundamentalist version of Protestantism. Thus by 1921 its targets included blacks, Catholics, foreigners, Jews, and even whites who committed transgressions of the Klan's view of the moral code.

The Greeks fell into the category of foreigner and were also in the Klan's crosshairs even though their relatively small numbers in the South attracted less attention than the Catholics. William Joseph Simmons, the Georgian who founded the Klan in 1915, writing soon after the elections in Greece resulted in a victory of the monarchists over the republicans, asked if the Greeks in their home country preferred the king, "how can we expect the Greek immigrants in the United States to enthuse over our republican institutions?" And he added that the Greeks came "to avail themselves of the opportunity to advance their material interests" and not, presumably, to contribute to the common good. He also suggested if Greece had been on the side of the Central Powers during World War I the Greek immigrants would have been disloyal to the United States. The Greeks, he added, along with the Hungarians, Italians, Germans, and Jews were a "mass" that "induces the vilest sort of boss rule" and were therefore unsuited to function properly in America's political system.[4]

The Klan's growing presence in Atlanta, with many state and local officials joining it and with its headquarters only a few blocks away from the Greek Orthodox church, meant that the Atlanta Greeks had to react in some way to defend themselves. Racist, xenophobic, and anti-Semitic words and deeds had been escalating in the city during the first two decades of the 20th century which affected the Greeks either directly or indirectly.[5] Naturally, it would have been unthinkable to confront the Klan directly given its influential presence in the city. A more subtle response was required to show that the Greeks were eligible and willing to join the American mainstream. And there would no better and safer way than to adopt the Klan's own language to protect the Greeks effectively. This tactical move, understand your enemy and act accordingly, which epitomized the agility of mind of Greek immigrants the world over, was at the core of the thinking that led to the creation of AHEPA.

AHEPA Is Born
The eight Greek Americans who founded AHEPA owned businesses, and their daily contact with customers and others in similar professions helped them understand that the Klan's influence was becoming pervasive in Atlanta and endangering the Greek presence. At the turn of the century, when the Greeks numbered a few hundreds, they had struggled against xenophobic attitudes, but they had persevered. Within a couple of decades their hard-earned upward social mobility had brought grudging acceptance by the Anglo elite and the city's press which echoed its views. By the 1920s the number of Greeks in the city was close to 1,000 and the most common businesses they ran were restaurants, fruit stores, and confectionary stores. They were becoming an integral part of the city's economy and were making their way up the social ladder. Part of that process entailed seeking to blend in as much as possible and to shorten or anglicize their last names, though they used the original Greek forms when registering with the local Greek Orthodox church.

One of AHEPA's founders, Harry Angelopoulos, described the prevailing climate in the city to a letter he sent his daughter many years later, in 1965. The Klan's view that the immigrants were corrupting the accepted norms of behavior and moral values meant that its members would react violently if they even heard someone using a foreign language. Persons could be assaulted and whipped and their stores could be vandalized. Their businesses could be easily subjected to boycotts and other acts of hostility. The city authorities meanwhile would not intervene, mostly because they shared those beliefs.[6] His view has been confirmed by studies of Atlanta's society and politics in that era. There was a strong anti-Catholic movement led by the Klan targeting alleged Catholic influence in the city's schools, and most city officials were either members of the Klan or tolerated its activities. There were public protests on the part of Catholics and Jews but there is no mention of representatives of the Greek Orthodox Church expressing any view publicly.[7]

Such was the suffocating atmosphere in Atlanta that persuaded eight Greek American business owners to establish AHEPA. At the first formal meeting, on July 26, 1922, Harry Angelopoulos and his brother John, James Campbell, Nicholas D. Chotas, George A. Polos (who had changed his last name from Nikolopoulos to Poulos and then to Polos), and James Vlass (who had changed his fist and last names from Dimitrios Vlassopoulos) set out the goals, the constitution, and the by-laws of AHEPA. While they waited for the granting of a charter, George Campbell and Speros J. Stamos joined and completed what was named as the eight member AHEPA Mother Lodge. Bearing in mind that the wave of Greeks who emigrated from the United States in the early 20th century were from Peloponnesos, it is not surprising that most AHEPA's founders were from that region of the country. James and George Campbell and John and Harry Angelopoulos were from the village of Divry in the Peloponnesian province of Elea, Chotas was from the same province, and Stamos was from near Argos in Peloponnesos. Vlass was from Ithaca, and Polos from central Greece. The Campbell brothers had arrived the United States in 1910 to join their uncle Leonidas who owned the first cinema in Atlanta.

The organization's purposes were outlined as follows: a) To advance and promote pure and undefiled Americanism among the Greeks in the United States, its Territories and Colonial possessions; b) To educate the Greeks in the matter of democracy, and in the matter of the government of the United States; c) To instill the deepest loyalty to the United States; d) To promote fraternal sociability; e) To practice benevolent aid among this nationality.⁸

Also present at the meeting was an Atlanta attorney, Carl F. Hutcheson, whom the founders invited. Hutcheson, Leber informs us, "was of great assistance to them in establishing the basic principles of the organization."⁹ His role was much more than that; he provided valuable cover for AHEPA, because he was connected to the Klan and active in Atlanta's public affairs. Hutcheson's advice in articulating the new association's goals, its constitution, and its by-laws helped the founders express their wish to promote Americanization, education, and loyalty to the United States among their fellow Greek immigrants in language that would not trigger the Klan's reaction. If the founders had not found the right way to express their goals, there was a danger of catastrophic consequences for the Greeks of Atlanta and elsewhere in the years to come. Even though the Klan's presence declined steadily in the mid-1920s, xenophobia remained. Hutcheson drew up the application to the State of Georgia to grant AHEPA a charter, and he was also instrumental in the decision to create AHEPA as a masonic style organization, which was another tactical move the founders took which would lend them legitimacy and allay suspicions that this was a foreign organization. The strategic choice of adopting a masonic structure made eminent sense at the time; it indicated that AHEPA was striving to join the American mainstream. But it inevitably created a great deal of misunderstanding among fellow Greek immigrants who were not familiar with that type of organization. Hutcheson was made an honorary member and retained his relationship with AHEPA. He was an honored guest at the national convention held in New Orleans in 1938 and delivered a speech entitled "State of AHEPA and the United States."¹⁰

There was another indirect source of firsthand information about the Klan that AHEPA's founders were able to exploit. According to a series of articles on AHEPA's history published by V. I. Chebithes, one of the Order's most important figures in the first four decades of its history, one of the Order's founders, George A. Polos, had done business with members of the Klan. Polos had been born in Karpenisi in Central Greece in about 1905 but had obviously assimilated enough so as not to be considered by them a suspicious foreigner. What he learned alarmed him but also made him realize the best way the

Greeks could protect themselves from potential trouble was to state their loyalty to America publicly. Polos himself had explained in an article that appeared in The Ahepan magazine in 1925 that "from my association with Greeks and Americans in the United States I perceived that the Greek element was really American at heart and the prejudiced opinion prevailing against it was due largely to a misunderstanding of the Greek rather than any reprehensible characteristic that was believed to exist." He became convinced that if the Greeks were organized in some sort of brotherhood they could accomplish great things. He then called a meeting of his Greek and American friends in the Greek school in Atlanta on July 26th, 1922." Polos therefore can be credited as the individual who conceived of the creation of AHEPA.[11]

The next meeting produced AHEPA's first president, Nicholas D. Chotas. He had been born in Lehená in northwestern Peloponnesos and had come to the United States in 1906, one of the peak years of emigration from Greece. Chotas was probably chosen because he was the only one of the founders who had experience in fraternal work; he was a leading member of the Fulton Lodge, one of the Masonic organizations in Atlanta. Chotas was the proprietor of the Capital City pharmacy. A newspaper notice announcing his marriage to Evstathia Sarafi in September 1922 mentioned that Chotas was "popular with a large circle of Greek and American friends" in Atlanta.[12] At that meeting James Campbell became Supreme Vice President and Harry Angelopoulos Supreme Secretary-Treasurer.

The Supreme Lodge, as the eight founders described themselves, embarked on an energetic effort to enhance AHEPA's organizational apparatus and held 10 meetings through September 1, 1922. A clear sign that the founders wished to allay any suspicions and make their support for Americanization clear was to adopt an emblem that included the Statue of Liberty and the American flag. And although they created an oath of membership in both English and Greek, they also decided that membership would not be restricted to Greeks in America. In the fall, thanks to the outreach its leaders engaged in beyond Georgia, subordinate lodges (i.e., chapters) began mushrooming throughout the South and the Eastern Seaboard as well. By October 1923 AHEPA had 32 subordinate lodges spread out over 16 states, with six each in Florida and North Carolina. It was a phenomenal increase, and this was only the beginning.

While AHEPA's creation was a pioneering event in the history of Greek America, it was part of a broader effort of recent immigrants to establish mutual benefit societies as well as to defend themselves against racism and xenophobia by becoming more integrated in American society. The Sons of Italy organization was established in 1905 to encourage Italian immigrants to assimilate. During the era of World War I the Ukrainian Women's Alliance in Chicago worked to encourage that group's women to become more active in both the ethnic and the wider community. Only a few weeks after AHEPA was established, Irish Catholics in Chicago formed the American Unity League to combat the Ku Klux Klan. Yet it is notable that of all those organizations AHEPA was the only one to establish itself in the South.

AHEPA's First Celebration of Greek Independence Day

In view of what we know about AHEPA's push for the Americanization of the Greek immigrants, it may be surprising to learn that the Order publicly celebrated the anniversary of Greek independence in Atlanta, in April 1923. There were over 500 persons in attendance, many of them from out of town. The dignitaries in attendance included George M. Napier, who was the Attorney General of Georgia and a Mason, and Atlanta Mayor Walter Sims, who would make a name for himself by initiating a plan for the city's airport that same year. At the event, children of the Greek Orthodox school sang the American national anthem and then, according to AHEPA officials, the first ever rendition of the Greek national anthem in English performed in the United States. The newspaper report of the event added that AHEPA's purpose was to promote better understanding between Greeks and American in the United States and that eight months after its founding it had spread to six southern states and numbered about 1,000 members. The presence of a choir from the Greek Orthodox church at such a public event with dignitaries attending suggests that the Orthodox church had managed not to be associated with the Catholics and risk being targeted.[13]

George Demeter Assumes a Leadership Role

In October 1923 AHEPA held its first National Convention (known then as a Convocation) in Atlanta, chaired by C. R. Nixon. A proposal to move the Order's Headquarters from Atlanta to Philadelphia caused such a heated debate that the delegates were asked to move their meeting away from the Piedmont Hotel because they were disturbing the other guests. The delegates moved to the roof garden of the nearby Cecil hotel "where they continued with undiminished fervor and vehemence."[14] A sign, maybe, that despite the drive toward Hellenization, the Ahepans could not completely forget their Hellenic roots. The proposal was eventually accepted because its proponents promised additional funding for AHEPA. The other issues decided upon were that the convention would elect Supreme Lodge officers, the first Supreme Lodge would be named "Mother Lodge," and all members of the Supreme Lodge would become ex officio members of the annual national conventions with the right to vote. The meeting elected New Yorker Hugh Neal Wells as Supreme President, John DeMoss Supreme Vice President, Soterios Retsinopoulos Supreme Secretary, Harry Coroneos Supreme Treasurer, and C. R. Nixon Supreme Counsellor. And Ben Davis, George Demeter, Arthur Greenwood, Charles H. Kirby and Gabriel M. Saliba were elected Supreme Governors. This administration proved short-lived however, because at a meeting of AHEPA's leaders in March 1924 it became apparent that there had been significant overspending of funds. The Supreme President and the Supreme Secretary stepped down.

The AHEPA governors were the leaders of particular geographical regions, and these would grow steadily throughout AHEPA's history. Over the years other bodies would be created to support the Supreme Lodge such as the Board of Trustees and Board of Auditors. As AHEPA adapted to its changing environment over time it would make any necessary changes to its organizational structure and its constitution but leave intact the original vision of its founders.

The Supreme Lodge held a vote to replace the Supreme President and elected George Demeter, who was nominated by George Polos. Demeter was born in Tropea, Arcadia in 1896 and arrived in the United States at a young age. He was a graduate of Harvard College and Boston University Law School and a World War I veteran and had organized the first AHEPA chapter in Boston. Demeter had been very deliberate in his intentions to become assimilated and lose his Greek accent as soon as possible. He went on to become a professor of law at Boston and Suffolk Universities and also served with distinction in the Massachusetts State Legislature.

Demeter would be Supreme President for only three months, but he accomplished a great deal in that time, steadying the Order and introducing several improvements and innovations that remained in place for a long time. He introduced the term "chapter" to the local AHEPA organizations, special regalia for the officers known as "jewels," and an installation ritual written and adapted exclusively for AHEPA. Although he was not reelected president Demeter remained an active Ahepan. He became nationally known when he published "Demeter's Manual of Parliamentary Law and Procedure: For the Legal Conduct of Business in All Deliberative Assemblies," which explained in simple and concise terms the standard rules of parliamentary law and illustrated its practical applications in every area of organizational procedure. AHEPA adopted that procedure at its 27th Supreme Convention that met in 1949 in Miami.[15]

As Supreme President, Demeter had referred to Greek politics as one of many Greek "traits" that ensured Greek organizations in America would fail and contrasting them to AHEPA's "American" character. He published his views in a special publication the Order produced for the 2nd Supreme Convention held in 1924 in Washington, DC. The tone reflects the sense of urgency that consumed AHEPA's leaders in the 1920s and that drove them to stress its American over its Greek character. He claimed that except for AHEPA, none of the one thousand Greek organizations that were formed in America either lasted very long or functioned properly. He then launched into a list of the causes and claimed that while the Greek obeys the laws of any nation, when it comes to those of his local Greek business or social organization: "In this respect," Demeter declared, "he is glaringly insubordinate... he is independent and indifferent... he will never acknowledge submission to authority... he will not carry out the instructions of his superior officers." But he would be loyal and obedient to the laws of an American organization. And Demeter went on, rubbing in his point. In his Greek organization, the Greek "fails to respond to any payments, he challenges his officers' judgement and humbles them, if he can he kills worthy purposes..." The reason for all this as well as political factionalism, was, in Demeter's opinion, a feeling of petty jealousy which characterized the Greek operating in a Greek organization. And reaching the apex of his critique, Demeter suggested that the Greek is jealous of the president of his organization and, "if he can't be the President, he won't have anyone else hold that position." And he concluded by saying "Thank God that the AHEPA is an American institution."[16]

Greek Politics in the 1920s

Demeter's words about Greek politics may have sounded harsh, and there is certainly a tone that reflects the views of an immigrant who was eager to underline that he had become an American. But those words were also prescient because a deep political polarization in Greece had made its way across the Atlantic and threatened the cohesion of Greek American organizations. Even the Greek Orthodox churches which were under the guidance of the Greek Orthodox Archdiocese of America, created in 1922, were being affected by political infighting.

The so-called national schism in Greece had erupted in 1915 when King Constantine, the head of state, and Eleftherios Venizelos, the prime minister, disagreed over Greece's alignment in World War I. The king forced Venizelos to step down, but following an Anglo-French intervention in Greece's affairs Venizelos was restored to power in 1917 and Greece entered the war on the side of the Anglo-French Entente, as did the United States that same year. The king made a comeback in 1920 by winning the elections but was forced out in 1922 after Greece's defeat in the Greco-Turkish war of 1919–1922. Those changes happened against the background of violent clashes between the supporters of both sides. The pro-Venizelos side proceeded to dominate Greek politics but the deep division between the supporters of Venizelos and the royalists remained and continued to poison political and social affairs in Greece but also in America. But it was the Archdiocese that suffered because it was closely associated with Greece and Greek culture, while AHEPA's American orientation, as Demeter pointed out, insulated it from political polarization.[17]

AHEPA Surges Led by V. I. Chebithes

AHEPA had to build on the work of Demeter and bolster its organizational structure and put its finances in order if it was not going to build on sand. On the eve of the 2nd Supreme Convention of 1924, out of the 2,790 members initiated there were 2,122 who belonged to active subordinate lodges, some lodges having already become inactive. And only 902 members had paid their annual dues. The decision to move the AHEPA Headquarters permanently to Washington, DC after Atlanta and a brief stint in Philadelphia reflected the organization's understanding that it had to acquire a better national coordination. And Washington had an active chapter with a president who was already showing a great deal of promise: V. I. Chebithes.

Next to its founders, the most influential force in AHEPA during the first two decades was Vasilios Isidorou Chebithes, who served as president between 1924 and 1927 and again between 1935 and 1940. In his first tenure as president, Chebithes helped AHEPA overcome its early difficulties and grow exponentially. One can confidently say that AHEPA grew into a big and influential organization thanks to the solid foundations that Chebithes created in this early period. He did so thanks to his boundless energy, dynamic leadership, and extraordinary speaking skills. Ahepans expressed their admiration and respect by referring to him affectionately as "V. I."

Chebithes was born in Greece, but his experiences after arriving in the United States as a teenager prepared him very well to assume the leadership of an organization that stood for the Americanization of Greek immigrants. Chebithes was born on the island of Icaria in 1892, the son of an Orthodox priest. After he first came to the United States in 1906 at the age of 14 and joined an uncle who traveled around to find work as painter, he was raised by Mr. and Mrs. Lemuel Gragg in Somerset a town in rural Kentucky. He attended Somerset High School and played football there. After graduating high school, he attended Centre College in Danville, Kentucky, where he won several oratorical and debating prizes, an early sign of one the attributes he would display later as a lawyer and an AHEPA member. He then moved to Washington, DC, where he worked for the government and attended George Washington Law School. He was a veteran of the First World War, serving overseas with Field Remount Squadron 326. He returned to Washington, DC and received his degree of Bachelor of Law from George Washington University in 1922, and in the same year he was admitted to the Washington Bar. In 1923 he became Commander of the American Veterans of Hellenic descent in the District, and he coordinated the ceremony held at the burial of Greek American World War I hero George Dilboy at Arlington National Cemetery on November 11, the anniversary of Armistice Day.[18]

In electing V. I. Chebithes as its Supreme President at the 3rd Supreme Convention held in September of 1924 in Washington, DC, AHEPA regained the initial momentum that its founders had generated in Atlanta in 1922. The others elected were Dr. Gabriel M. Saliba Supreme Vice President, Nicholas Chotas Supreme Secretary, Harry Coroneos Supreme Treasurer, C. R. Nixon Supreme Counsellor, Dr. C. Carusso Supreme Chaplain, and Nicholas G. V. Nestor Supreme Warden. The Supreme Governors elected were George Caranicholas, F. M. Witherspoon, Theodore Polemanakos, N. A. Loumos, P. P. Stathas, and George S. Smitzes. Chebithes embraced his responsibilities as leader with remarkable energy and fervor and within a year had visited 50 chapters (as the subordinate lodges became known), revived several that were on the brink of dissolution, and inspired the creation of 25 new chapters. What also ensured his success beyond his energy was his magnetic personality. The St. Louis Star described AHEPA's president as "a comparatively young man, of fine presence, perfect command of English, a clear thinker and an eloquent speaker." The Intelligencer Journal of Lancaster, Pennsylvania wrote that "Chebithes is a man possessed of a high education" and "is recognized as one of the high powers in Greek affairs in Washington, DC."[19]

More members meant more income, and this helped AHEPA address and overcome its financial difficulties and expand its activities. The publication of a 78-page magazine helped give the organization a more distinct understanding of itself and elaborated what AHEPA represented. Another even thicker publication that ran to 370 pages appeared in 1926, recording the activities of all the chapters across the nation. These were the forerunners of a significant series of publications that would follow in the decades to come, which included a magazine and special editions associated with national and regional conventions.

Recognizing the success of Chebithes' first term, AHEPA reelected him president at the 3rd Supreme Convention held in Chicago in 1925. The others elected were Nicholas A. Loumos, a Boston-based attorney, Supreme Vice President, Andrew Nickas Supreme Secretary, George J. Willias Supreme Treasurer, C. R. Nixon Supreme Counsellor, F. M. Witherspoon Supreme Chaplain, Arthur S. Stephos Supreme Warden, and Nicholas G. Psaki Supreme Archon Dialectis. The Supreme

Governors who were elected were Constantine J. Critzas, Theodore Polemanakos, Dr. S. D. Zaph, W. A. Ganfield, and Philip Stylianos. The chair of the convention's organizing committee was D. N. Delevois, a cousin of Greek American World War I hero George Dilboy, and the chair of the convention was Dean Alfange. AHEPA had reached the number of 65 chapters in total and had initiated 5,264 members since its inception.

Delegates reelected Chebithes Supreme President to a third term at the 4th Supreme Convention in Philadelphia in 1926. Also reelected were all the other senior officers of the Supreme Lodge. In between the Chicago and Philadelphia conventions 4,299 new members were initiated into the Order bringing the total number of members to 9,291. Devoting himself full time to his responsibilities as president, Chebithes visited 73 chapters throughout the country and established and organized 21 of the 35 new chapters. The fraternity's healthy finances enabled it to issue all members and chapters membership certificates, to mandate the regular publication of a magazine and to adopt an official "AHEPA Manual."

AHEPA & the White House

President Calvin Coolidge received a group of delegates of the 1924 Supreme Convention held in Washington, DC. The visit to the White House by members of the Supreme Lodge soon became an annual event and a wonderful photo opportunity for AHEPA to underscore its respectability and its character as a bona fide American institution. And this continued throughout the following decades. Carefully observing its nonpartisan character, AHEPA paid its respects equally to Democratic and Republican occupants of the White House. President Coolidge was an ideal leader through which this process would start positively. Coolidge believed that "Americanization" did not mean forcibly turning immigrants into natives and should instead be pursued through education designed to instruct new arrivals to the United States in the meaning of its laws and customs. Coolidge was therefore able to relate to AHEPA's goal, making Greek immigrants responsible American citizens.

The Successful Push toward Americanization

Sustaining a relentless campaign to persuade the Greek immigrants to Americanize was the most prominent achievement during

Chebithes' three-year tenure as president. Chebithes, the World War I veteran, believed that the war, by bringing the Greek immigrants into America's army, had brought about a major transformation in the mind of the Greek. Prior to the war, he believed, because the Greeks had only recently arrived in the United States, they had not had time to consider whether to remain there and their eyes were turned toward their homeland. However, "the end of the war found the Greek heart and soul for America. Whatever his ideas may have been before the war, he now feels he is part and parcel of this country... He may justly feel that he can stand upon equal footing with every other nationality in this country. The American flag has been baptized in Greek blood... our rights to American citizenship were purchased upon the field of carnage. The Greek taught the world the real meaning of patriotism. They are now Americans by choice, not by accident." And because of that, he added, "Today ninety per cent at least of our compatriots have definitely decided to remain in America permanently... rearing their children to be real Americans. This is the country where they will die—the country where their children will live."[20] It would be easy to think of Chebithes' analysis as an exaggerated version of the truth because there were as many if not more Greek immigrants still focused on their homeland and on preserving not only Greek culture but a Greek way of life in America. Yet we would do well to remember the prevailing circumstances at the time. Chebithes' claims were specifically designed to offer protection to the Greek immigrants at a time when the Klan was still very strong and had even spread its influence beyond the southern states. For example, in the wake of a contest for the position of mayor in Denver, Colorado in 1924, the Denver Post wrote that the Klan was "the largest, most cohesive and most efficiently organized political force in the state of Colorado today."[21] As it turned out, in Colorado and elsewhere, 1924 was the peak year of the Klan's influence, but that was not at all obvious at the time, nor did it mean that xenophobia would suddenly recede. Quite the opposite, it would linger well into the 1930s. For example, a major study on land values in Chicago that appeared in 1933 listed "races and nationalities" according to their favorable impact on neighborhoods. The Greeks along with the Russian Jews and southern Italians came last among the European ethnic groups.[22]

AHEPA could not confront either the Klan or the culture of xenophobia head on, so the best it could do, in Chebithes' view, was to overemphasize its belief in the virtues of Americanization and highlight the Greek immigrant's predisposition to becoming an American. By repeating that message whenever he spoke publicly, which was very often, the AHEPA president aimed at improving the image of the Greeks, who, in turn, would see that the best way to protect themselves from discrimination was to confirm that assertion through their actions. Thus, in his speeches at banquets organized by the local AHEPA chapters he was visiting, Chebithes addressed his comments not to the Greek immigrants directly, or even the AHEPA members, but instead to the local politicians and civic authorities were invited and often attended.

Almost always in attendance were reporters from local newspapers, coaxed there by the leaders of the local AHEPA chapters to be sure, but who were also on the lookout for local news to fill the columns of their small local newspaper. And judging by the frequency with which local chapters included local newspaper reports in their own reports to the annual convention, this happened very frequently. From the mid-1920s through the outbreak of World War II, local newspaper coverage of AHEPA's meetings and its push for Americanization increased steadily as Chebithes energetically crisscrossed the country. A news item on Chebithes' arrival in Montgomery, Alabama noted that AHEPA's main purpose was "to Americanize the Greeks of this country."[23] A newspaper report of a speech by Chebithes to AHEPA's chapter in Charlotte, North Carolina, in August 1925 was entitled "Assimilation is Need of Greeks—Should Stand Wholly for America While Living Here."[24] Good citizenship was a concomitant aim to Americanization. In October, a report about the establishment of an AHEPA chapter in Binghamton in upstate New York mentioned that Chebithes described AHEPA's purpose as being "to promote and encourage loyalty to the United States, allegiance to the constitution and traditions and obedience to the laws of the land."[25] Newspaper coverage of AHEPA and its commitment to Americanization also produced praise for the Greeks, demonstrating its effectiveness only a few years after being established in Atlanta. The Wilmington, Delaware Morning News commented in March 1926 that "rarely, indeed, have any Greeks in this country been accused of plotting against the national welfare or seeking to overthrow our form of government... they appreciate the opportunities the United States affords. And it must be said to their credit that the Greeks usually embrace these opportunities and succeed in business."[26] The words used in that commentary would have had a special resonance with readers at the time. That same year the ongoing controversial case of the two Italian anarchist immigrants, Nicola Saco and Bartolomeo Vanzetti, accused of murder and robbery in Massachusetts, had reached its peak publicity-wise with many claiming the two were convicted unfairly because they were foreign-born. The two were executed a year later. On the 50th anniversary of that event that was still considered the outcome of xenophobic prejudice, the Governor of Massachusetts Michael Dukakis, a Greek American, issued a proclamation declaring they had been tried and convicted unfairly.

AHEPA's Americanization Drive
As part of its commitment to the Americanization of the Greek immigrants, in the first years of its existence AHEPA prohibited the use of the Greek language, and while it projected its Christian identity it somewhat downplayed its ties with the Greek Orthodox faith even though locally Ahepans were active in their parishes. It also maintained initiation and other rituals that served to demonstrate its similarities with other masonic organizations in America. Not surprisingly perhaps all three of those practices could be easily misunderstood and cause alarm within the Greek American community which was anxious about preserving its ethnic identity. The English-only rule brought the most protests because the Greek language was and still is considered a cornerstone of Greek identity. The same applied to religion, even though AHEPA did not actively shun Greek Orthodoxy but merely signaled an openness to all Christian faiths, especially Protestantism, a tactic which served to distinguish the Greeks from Catholicism which was targeted by the Ku Klux Klan. AHEPA's critics ridiculed the rituals and the secretive nature of the organization. The ritual was a quite elaborate process; despite its secret nature AHEPA published the process in small pamphlets that could run to 50 pages long. What also motivated some of the attacks on AHEPA were clashes of personalities among Greek

Americans in a particular place and the behavior of some officials of the organization who found themselves in positions of power.[27]

The language question was the one that attracted the most debate within the organization and outside. Clearly Chebithes was persuaded that the use of English was a prerequisite for leading AHEPA members toward Americanization. And having to use English at chapter meetings was both an incentive for members to learn as well as a good way of practicing its use. The Greek language press and especially the two New York dailies, the Atlantis and the Ethnikos Kyrix, led the charge against the English-only rule. At first both papers mostly ignored AHEPA but whenever they did mention it was in a critical vein. And even though AHEPA preferred not to engage directly with its critics, there were occasions when some of its officials issued hard-hitting statements, so much so that the 3rd Supreme Convention that took place in Chicago in 1925 had to issue a statement that AHEPA was not officially opposed to the foreign language press in America. The press came out even more strongly against AHEPA following the successful 4th Supreme Convention held in Philadelphia in 1926 which drew nearly 1,000 Greek Americans.

At the convention in 1927 in Miami, Chebithes, who was completing his three-year tenure as president, revealed that AHEPA had asked the Greek press for its support when it was setting out, but the editors of the major newspapers had declined, doubting that an American-oriented organization could unite the Greeks. It may not have seemed so at the time, but within very few years the Greek language newspapers would be showcasing AHEPA's achievements.

The suggestions that AHEPA was turning its back on Greek Orthodoxy were also unfounded. AHEPA emphasized its Christian character but downplayed the Greek Orthodox faith of its members only as a tactical move. Thus AHEPA adopted what seemed to outsiders as contradictory policies in the mid-twenties. For example, the chapter in Manchester New Hampshire attended church in a body once a month, but alternated between going to Holy Trinity Greek Orthodox Church, the First Congregationalist Church, and the St. Paul Methodist Episcopal Church. At the same time, Greek Orthodox Bishop Philaretos (Ioannides) was a member of the local AHEPA chapter board of governors. Greek Orthodox Reverend Mark Petrakis, who son Harry would become a widely read novelist, was the AHEPA chapter treasurer. As for the Greek Orthodox Archdiocese of North and South America, the Church's governing body, AHEPA and its policies were the least of its problems, especially since local AHEPA chapters included prominent Greek Americans who were also active in parish life. It was not too much Americanness that concerned the Greek Orthodox Church but instead the fact that the deep political division in Greece between supporters of the king and supporters of the liberal politician Eleftherios Venizelos had carried over into community life and polarized parishes across the United States.

The third aspect of AHEPA's practices that drew negative comments were the masonic-style rituals. These were used at initiation ceremonies and during the meetings. These were enforced zealously in the 1920s. There was also an insistence on formal dress during official events including banquets. Such things were alien to the world the Greek immigrants had left behind, but played an important role in bolstering pride and a sense of self-worth among the Order's members who were first-generation businessmen and happy to find an environment that conferred upon them a sense of dignity. Thus, the rituals came in for criticism but not so much the formal wear, because all Greek immigrants hungered for the type of self-worth that came with changing from one's work clothes and wearing a tuxedo for an evening event.

"H" stands for Hellenic
AHEPA may have been overly fervent at times at promoting Americanism in its early years, but it did not pursue that policy by forsaking the cultural origins of its members. It promoted the culture of ancient Greece, and it was concerned with offering aid to Greece, even though the Americanization drive overshadowed those two important activities, which would become much more pronounced over the next decades. One of the earliest signs of AHEPA's attachment to ancient Greek civilization came in the multi-page volume prepared for the 1926 Supreme Convention. The third of the prefatory articles was entitled "Quintessence of Hellenic Contributions" and outlined the historical trajectory of the Hellenic people from the classical era to the present, laying stress on the achievements and contributions of the "Hellenic genius" in the classical era. Not once did the article mention the word "Greek," preferring instead to talk of Hellas and

Hellenes throughout the historical trajectory it described, which ended with the inhabitants of modern Hellas looking "to America and there they saw the land of opportunity—the country where Hellenism, with all its glory, might be revived and made to flourish and bless humanity as it had often done in day of yore." And "thither, came the most enterprising sons of modern Hellas. Here they determined to devote their energy and genius in the cultivation and perpetuation of the Hellenic ideals and to restart and establish their claim to the highest place among the most intellectual races of this age."[28]

The tactics are transparent: there is no mention of Greece, which is instead referred to as Hellas, and thus associated the Greek Americans with ancient, not modern, Greece. It was and is a legitimate claim in the sense that modern Greeks claim and certainly believe there is a continuity between those two eras, a concept known as the continuity of Hellenism, a cornerstone of modern Greek identity which was fashioned by thinkers in the 19th century. In the American context this claim had the additional value of insulating the Greeks from xenophobic hate by associating them with a culture widely regarded to be at the core of Western civilization. Recourse to and identification with ancient Hellas would become a recurring theme in the self-identification of not only AHEPA but of other Greek American organizations and individuals. Embracing a Hellenic rather than a Greek identity implied "forgetting" the Greek customs and character traits that produced violence and knifings as part of quarrels generated by vendettas or masculine pride, something that has been highlighted in Professor Yiorgos Anagnostou's study of Greek America in the 1920s. Moreover, as he has demonstrated, the "Hellenic" identity was associated with whiteness, since Ancient Hellenism was considered the foundation of Western civilization that white America saw as its model. This way of "proving" the Greeks were "white" was implied in the Order's goal of proving the compatibility between the Greek Americans, ancient Greek civilization, and American values.[29] The invocation of ancient Greece did not mean that AHEPA was turning its back on modern Greece, even at this early stage of its history when rampant xenophobia required an emphasis on Americanization. Newspaper items announcing the formation of AHEPA chapters, next to highlighting its purpose to Americanize the Greeks, also mentioned that it would work to create a better understanding of Greece in the United States. The chapter in Newark, New Jersey gave financial aid to the Greek American Institute, one of the earliest Greek language schools in the United States, which was located in the Bronx. And in 1926, Charalambos Simopoulos, the Greek ambassador to the United States, attended and spoke at an AHEPA banquet in Manhattan.[30]

The Sons of Pericles

Very soon after its establishment, AHEPA witnessed the emergence of an affiliated junior Order for young men in 1926. Eleven young Greeks, "with a spirit which equalled the spirit of their ancestors," conceived the idea of and organized the Sons of Pericles together with the aid of a few Ahepans from the Manchester AHEPA chapter. The 11 young men who were the first members and are the Mother Lodge Members of the Sons of Pericles are: Gregory Papagiotas, William Vasiliou, Christ Kourcoulis, Peter Kourides, Vasilios Hasiotis, Peter Clainos, William Chaloge, James Papadopoulos, Arthur Hasiotis, George Houliaras, and James Papademitriou. The first chapter named itself the "Queen City Chapter No. 1." Its first officers were installed on February 3, 1926. Within a short time, they had interested the Ahepans of Haverhill, Lynn, Lowell, Boston, Nashua, and Lawrence in establishing Sons of Pericles chapters in their cities. By the time the First National Convention of the Sons of Pericles was called to order in Lowell, Massachusetts, on September 12, 1927, there were 14 chapters in the fraternity. The convention saw the inauguration of a per capita payment to Headquarters, the selection of an emblem, and the creation of a uniform bookkeeping system. Achilles Poulos, of Washington, DC, was elected Supreme Archon Megistan and George Helis of New York City Supreme Megistan. At its 1928 National Convention in Detroit, Michigan, AHEPA officially recognized the Order Sons of Pericles organization as its Junior Order.

The Alfange Presidency

When V. I. Chebithes strongly endorsed Dean Alfange as new AHEPA president at the 5th Supreme Convention in 1927 in Miami, he knew his successor would build on the extraordinary success the Order had enjoyed during his own three-year tenure as president which was coming at an end. Born in Constantinople in 1897, Alfange moved to the United States with his parents at age five and grew up in the town of Utica in upstate New York. It was not quite as rural as Chebithes' hometown, but there were few Greeks and no Greek Orthodox church in the vicinity, which meant Alfange would become quickly assimilated. And like Chebithes he enlisted in the US Army during World War I, after that attended college and went on to receive a law degree from Columbia University, and then opened a practice in New York City.

Those elected along with Alfange at the Supreme Convention in 1927 were George Phillies Supreme Vice President, Achilles Catsonis, a Washington, DC lawyer, Supreme Secretary, George J. Willias Supreme Treasurer, and Philip Stylianos Supreme Counselor. The Supreme Governors elected were Alexander D. Varkas, James Veras, Philip D. Reppas, the Rev. S. Psathey, George S. Smitzes, C. R. Nixon, Parasco E. Volo, Constantine Theodrow, A. Petrillis Perry, N. C. Calogeras, and George Patterson. Attending the convention were 10 Supreme Lodge officers and 109 delegates representing 99 chapters.

Alfange pursued the goal of Americanization just as ably and passionately as Chebithes had, but in light of the mounting criticism of AHEPA from some Greek American quarters, he tempered the Americanization message by explicitly acknowledging AHEPA's Hellenic connection. The Supreme Convention in Miami earmarked funds to sponsor the establishment of Athens College in Greece, to support the "Manna Sanatorium" which was being established in Peloponnesos for the treatment of persons suffering from tuberculosis, and for research on the aid given by Americans to the Greeks during the 1821 War of Independence. Alfange eloquently expressed AHEPA's commitment to both Americanism and Hellenism in 1927 when he wrote that AHEPA had brought the Greeks together by eliminating their "provincialism, prejudice and fanaticism" and enabled them to see "the opportunities which result in fraternity and cooperation." Because "it is non-political. It is non-sectarian. It is fraternal and benevolent. It speaks the English language. It follows American methods. It vibrates with the spirit of progress. It has none of the earmarks of the Greek organizations of the past. This is this secret of its success." The Greek immigrants in America, Alfange said, did not need to be put "to sleep with lullabies of Greek patriotism, Greek language, Greek Orthodoxy. They were awake and had another needs that is why AHEPA was so successful, it reflected "the renaissance of the Greek people in America." To allay fears that this Americanism implied a repudiation of Hellenism Alfange pivoted and proclaimed: "The true Ahepan cherishes the deepest reverence for the land of his origin, its language, its history, and its traditions. He is proud of his noble heritage. He is proud of those mighty contributions which Greece has made to civilization. He has no use whatever for the Greek who will attempt to hide his nationality or belittle his native land. But he will not permit these sacred sentiments to be used as tools of exploitation."[31]

This passage from Alfange's article neatly summed up the way he continued Chebithes' legacy of continuing to push for the Americanization of Greek immigrants, but he also increased AHEPA's acknowledgement of its Hellenic heritage. This included a more open embrace of the Greek homeland, most notably with an excursion to Greece which became an annual affair. About 1,000 Ahepans and their families traveled to Greece in March 1928 on what Alfange, who led the trip, described as "the first time in the history of Hellenism in America that an organized group of nearly 1,000 men undertook as a unit to traverse 5,000 miles of water for the purpose of paying a visit of good will to the land of their origin." They received red carpet treatment by the government in Athens and thousands of Athenians turned out to greet them. Among the many events during the trip was a meeting with the President of the Hellenic Republic, Pavlos Coundouriotis. And the newspapers in Athens gave the visit extensive and very positive coverage. Alfange was right to emphasize that this was the first large scale organized visit by Greek Americans to their homeland. Not only did it become an annual fixture in AHEPA's calendar, it also inspired other Greek American organizations to do the same, a practice that began to cement the ties between Greeks and the Greeks in the United States.

In 1928, Theodore S. Agnew, the president of the AHEPA chapter in Baltimore, and father of Spiro, the future US vice president, gave a speech refuting the charges that AHEPA was against the Greek language and religion. It was one of the last occasions that a senior member of the Order had to make that point. That year there were many other examples of AHEPA's growing connection to Greece. Among the most important was offering relief funds for the victims of an earthquake that struck the towns of Corinth and Loutraki in

April 1928, killing 30 persons and destroying 3,000 houses leaving 15,000 inhabitants homeless. AHEPA's mobilization included an appeal issued by the mayor of Baltimore for city-wide contributions to AHEPA's drive. The wives and daughters of members of the AHEPA Longfellow chapter in Stark County, Ohio held a bazaar in which they sold their handmade linens, scarves, and shawls and raised $1,300.

At the 6th Supreme Convention in 1928 in Detroit, AHEPA presented the nearby city of Ypsilanti, Michigan with a bust of Demetrius Ypsilanti, the 1821 Greek War of Independence hero after whom the town had been named. The bust, which stood on a 12-foot-high pedestal, was made in Greece with the same Pentelic marble used to build the Parthenon. It was shipped to New York and traveled by rail to Detroit and on to Ypsilanti by truck. The unveiling of the bust took place during the Supreme Convention with the delegates traveling to Ypsilanti from Detroit. It was a half-day holiday for Ypsilanti, with a parade with three bands prior to the dedication at which Michigan Governor Fred Green was among the speakers.[32]

AHEPA in Canada

The number of Greeks in Canada before World War II was small; according to official figures there were 5,580 in 1941 and their total number had grown only slightly to 5,871. But as usually happens with official counts of Greeks in the diaspora their size was underestimated because a number of them had Ottoman or other countries' citizenship papers upon their arrival. In any case, the Greeks in Canada at the time also faced the need for an organization such as AHEPA. The first chapter was formed in Toronto in October 1928 and over the next few years there followed chapters in London, Ontario; Hamilton, Ontario; Ottawa; and Montreal as well as further west in Winnipeg, Saskatoon, Edmonton, Calgary, and Regina. More chapters would be formed after World War II when emigration from Greece increased exponentially. The focus of AHEPA's activity before the war was to encourage the assimilation of the Greeks into Canadian society. One newspaper noted that AHEPA was founded upon loyalty to Canada and editorialized at the time: "In the process of merging themselves into the life of Canada, the citizens of Greek origin are contributing much towards the enrichment of community life. There is room for diversity in Canada within the unified nation. So long as the residents from other countries do endeavor to become truly Canadian in spirit, setting up no barriers to separate themselves from fellow citizens they are an asset to this country. They should be encouraged to keep alive the best traditions, particularly of art, literature, and culture of the countries from whence they came. Life in Canada can surely be enriched by the high traditions of Greek culture."[33]

AHEPA's First National Banquet
By 1928 AHEPA's continuing growth was obvious, as was the Order's ability to stage public events locally wherever it acquired chapters. AHEPA extended its reach into western and northwestern states such as California, Nebraska, Iowa, and Utah. The meetings were well attended and local officials were usually present, and the extensive local press coverage of AHEPA events continued with the drive to promote citizenship featuring prominently. The report of the local chapter's annual banquet in 1928 was accompanied by a large photograph and appeared on the front page of a newspaper in Binghamton, New York. Local chapters began organizing picnics during the summer months. One held by the Wilmington, Delaware chapter attracted Ahepans from the surrounding states bringing the total to 300 persons, which included Supreme President Alfange.[34]

The most important public event AHEPA would stage in this period of early growth was on February 6, 1929, when held its first national banquet in Washington honoring the US Congress. The banquet was the brainchild of George C. Vournas, a Washington-based attorney and leading Ahepan who would serve as Supreme President in the 1940s. AHEPA's Bulletin of February 1929 declared: "The National Banquet held in Washington on February 6, 1929, will go down in the fraternity's history as one of the outstanding accomplishments of the fraternity. Needless to say, it will have the distinction of being the most important AHEPA function of the year. On that occasion seventy-five members of the United States Senate and House of Representatives, together with two-score of prominent journalists of national reputation, Governors, ex-Governors, governmental Department heads, and other prominent visitors, assembled at the Hotel Willard that night—the occasion of our first national banquet to do honor to the AHEPA. It was one of the most brilliant gatherings of the Nation's leaders which Washington had ever witnessed. To quote the words of a United States Senator who was present, 'There were never so many Senators and Representatives of different political faiths sitting together at the same table at the invitation of a third party.' The Supreme President (Alfange) in making the principal address of the evening, touched upon the significance of the occasion when he said, 'This affair tonight, brings to us an AHEPA climax—a rich fulfillment of our hopes and our aspirations.' And these words were true for that night it might be said that the United States of America was officially honoring the AHEPA—giving to it official recognition for its long period of faithful service and imparting to it encouragement to carry on the great work that it is propounding."

Indeed, 75 members of the United States Senate and the House of Representatives along with state governors and senior government officials attended, an extraordinary fact for an organization formed by Greek immigrants seven years earlier in Atlanta. AHEPA had gained the greatest recognition it could have hoped for from Washington's political elite. Supreme President Alfange rightly said in his address that the event "brings at an AHEPA climax—a rich fulfillment of our hopes and our aspirations." It was striking, for example, that Senator H. King of Utah, who acted as toastmaster at the banquet, had served a few years earlier on the Senate's Overmann Committee that investigated German and Russian Bolshevik activities during World War I and had been regarded as unfairly targeting certain immigrants. As he rose to assume his duties as toastmaster King "delivered an eloquent oration in which he lauded America's citizens of Hellenic extraction and signaled the AHEPA as the outstanding patriotic organization of the United States which is sponsored by citizens of foreign descent."[35]

Smaller banquets were held regularly if not annually by local chapters, and a banquet would become one of the highlights of the Supreme Conventions. These were perfect venues for speeches before invited guests at which AHEPA's best orators could present the Order's program, harp on its American values, and also bring its members together in a formal grand event. The National Banquet in Washington, DC honoring Congress was the greatest of all AHEPA banquets, an occasion when its most able speakers affirmed the Order's loyalty to America before an audience of senators and congressmen. The long list of important guests was yet more proof of AHEPA's increased standing in the eyes of mainstream America. The event remains one of the most important on AHEPA's calendar of activities. The emphasis on banquets was yet another way in which AHEPA's activities sought to inhabit an American cultural environment. More conventional Greek immigrant practices were to hold picnics in open spaces outside cities as a way to escape the claustrophobic urban environment and recreate the ambiance of rural Greece, as much as possible. Banquets were not part of the world the Greek immigrants had inhabited, even in the case of those who had originated in cities. Banqueting was a western European practice that was eagerly borrowed by the American bourgeoisie. Thomas Jefferson, who had served as ambassador in Paris, was responsible for continuing the practice of presidential banquets inaugurated by George Washington and introducing French-style menus with multiple courses. By organizing banquets in Washington, DC therefore, AHEPA was asserting its American identity in one more way.

In 1948 the name of the National Banquet was changed to "AHEPA Congressional Banquet" and President Harry Truman became the first US president to attend. In 2000 the name was changed again to "AHEPA Biennial Banquet." Since 1964 the event has featured the award of the highest honor AHEPA bestows, the Socrates Award, which recognizes prominent men and women who have emulated ancient Hellenic ideals. The awards that are part of these banquets and other major AHEPA events are also a sign of the Americanization of the Greeks in the United States, for such awards were not common in Greece.

There was another first for AHEPA in 1929, with the appearance of the first issue of The Ahepan magazine which was published in May. The masthead described it as: "The Ahepan, Illustrated National Monthly Magazine, the Official Organ of the American Hellenic Educational Progressive Association." It was dedicated to President Herbert Hoover, and the President's photograph was on the cover. The issue listed the location of the then 220 chapters of AHEPA, and carried several articles, editorials, and news of the chapter activities.

The Daughters of Penelope
The establishment of a women's organization affiliated with AHEPA, the Daughters of Penelope, signaled the early stages of Greek

American women's involvement in community and public affairs. Until then there were only local parish-based women's groups that engaged in charitable work and in some instances teaching as part of Greek Orthodox church life. In 1929 we have the emergence of the Daughters, the first national Greek women's organization thanks to the efforts of 25 women in San Francisco, all relatives of Ahepans, led by Alexandra Apostolides. As Leber puts it in an appendix to his history of AHEPA, these women "daringly assembled at the home of Dr. Emanuel Apostolides, who was the AHEPA Deputy Supreme Governor of District 21, for the purpose of establishing the Order, later to be known as the Daughters of Penelope. Filled with the ardent desire to create this great women's organization, inspired by the need and stimulated and encouraged by their friend AHEPA Supreme President V. I. Chebithes, Dr. Apostolides and his wife Alexandra proceeded to formulate their dreams into realities with their enthusiasm and hard work. Mrs. Apostolides envisioned a new beginning for first generation Greek American women. Up until this time, the wives and daughters of Ahepans had limited their activities to the sanctity of their homes and their church. Mrs. Apostolides proceeded to draft the basic principles of the organization which were to be an inspiration for all women. First, the foundation was structured on two strong ideals: To perpetuate the study of the American ideals and to encourage Hellenic study of the ancient Greek ideals. To merge the two, the best of two worlds were the aims of our founder. With this active idealism and our heritage, she felt we would be able to repay in some small measure this glorious country, land of our adoption, for its many blessings and many advantages to our families and ourselves." In 1934, AHEPA officially adopted the Daughters of Penelope as their senior Women's Auxiliary, and this was ratified the following year. In 1939 the Daughters would hold their first convention. Soon after, the civilian mobilization during World War II would present the Daughters of Penelope an opportunity to make their mark through their diligent work for the relief of Greece and in support of America's war effort.

The Maids of Athena
An organization of young women, the Maids of Athens, was created in 1930, and it would change its name to Maids of Athena in 1963. The

young women's order emerged thanks to the efforts and inspiration of Thomas D. Lentgis, of Seattle, Washington, Past Supreme Governor of the Order of AHEPA. The first chapter of the Maids of Athens was founded in Tacoma, Washington in July 1930 and was given the name "Sparta." Seven years passed and in November 1937 a Charter was granted to the 12 members of Sparta Chapter. At the same time, Charters were also granted to three other chapters: Alethea No. 2 of Seattle, Washington; Diana No. 3 of Portland, Oregon; and Ariadne No. 4 of Vancouver, British Columbia, Canada. By the end of 1937 there were 20 chapters with a total membership of 444. AHEPA introduced a program of reorganization in 1941, and by the 1950s the Maids were growing steadily.

Chapter 2:
Americanism and Hellenism in the 1930s

AHEPA's 7th Supreme Convention in Kansas City, Missouri in August 1929 was the first convention to be held west of the Mississippi River and was a sign of how AHEPA's westward influence was growing. And there was further proof of this the next year when the 8th Supreme Convention was held in San Francisco. In between those two conventions the United States had suffered the Wall Street Crash of 1929 and entered the decade known as the Great Depression. It brought a new and difficult reality for the Greeks in America, and a new phase in AHEPA's history, one of retrenchment and perseverance and ultimately survival and growth.

The 1930s were a decade of contradictions for the status of the Greeks in the United States. Nativist discrimination still existed but it ebbed significantly as the decade wore on. Aside from the manifest degree of self-proclaimed Americanization and assimilation on the part of Greek Americans, race as a category with all its negative implications began disappearing from American public discourse because of learning about the horrors of race-based Nazi ideology and practice. The concept of ethnicity began being used more commonly, and in that sense the whiteness of the Greeks ensured their greater acceptance. At the same time however, the economic difficulties the Great Depression brought on affected living standards and the activities of ethnic organizations that relied on members' contributions. And the diminished abilities of ethnic organizations to offer succor and support to the members meant that Greek Americans would turn to the New Deal programs enacted by President Franklin D. Roosevelt beginning in 1933 and in doing so were assimilated further into American society.[36]

Even though increased assimilation by way of the New Deal enhanced AHEPA's standing and justified its decade long crusade to persuade the Greek immigrants to become Americans, the 1930s posed serious challenges to the Order. Yet again, AHEPA demonstrated its ability to anticipate and adapt to the social changes unfolding in America. In the early part of the decade, after dealing with the issue of the use of the Greek language and the balance between Americanism and Hellenism, it turned toward the urgent problems caused by the Great Depression. Then, in 1935, AHEPA turned again to three-time Supreme President V. I. Chebithes who began an unprecedented five-year period as president. Chebithes' solution to boosting the Order's fortunes was to focus on programs that would benefit its members, and thus AHEPA acquired a mutual aid society dimension to its activities while continuing to campaign for the Americanization of the Greek immigrants and cultivating ties with Greece.

Americanism & Hellenism
With the election of George E. Phillies at the 7th Supreme Convention in 1929 in Kansas City, AHEPA gained another dynamic president. It had been one of the most difficult conventions in the Order's short history, because of an at times acrimonious and long confrontation over whether the Greek language should be permitted in its official business meetings. Two leading Ahepans and future presidents, George C. Vournas and Harry J. Booras, led the critique against the prohibition of using Greek and showed that it had cost the Order members especially in New England. Alfange and Chebithes defended the English-only policies and after a long debate carried the day. In the wake of this serious rift, itself of course a sign of the changing times the Order was experiencing, Phillies as the newly elected president had the responsibility of preventing the emergence of a debilitating division among the membership.

Phillies, like Alfange and Chebithes, had been in the United States for a long time, but having grown up in Buffalo amidst an active Greek Americanized community he was much less Americanized than his two predecessors. Phillies was born on May 15, 1886, in Stimagka, a village in northern Peloponnesos and came to the United States as a boy. In 1907 he was the founder and first secretary of the Greek community in Buffalo, and two years later he traveled to Greece where he married Urania Theodoracopoulou in Tripolis and returned with her to the United States. In 1915 he graduated from the University of Buffalo Law School and in 1916 he organized and became first president of the Greek-American Republican Club. In 1926 he became the secretary of the newly established William McKinley chapter of AHEPA in Buffalo; his brother Theophane was treasurer.[37]

The others elected to the Supreme Lodge along with Phillies were Peter G. Sikokis, from Chicago, Supreme Vice President; Achilles Catsonis, Supreme Secretary; John Govatos, Supreme Treasurer; George C. Vournas, Supreme Counsellor; and, as Supreme Governors, Harris J. Booras, John J. Manos, Arthur A. Karkalas, Rev. S. S. Spathey, John Theophiles, Constantine Pellias, P. J. Stamos, Parasco E. Volo, Stelianos Reckas, Michael D. Konomos, P. S. Marthakis, P. J. Andrews, and Dr. N. S. Checkos.

Phillies adopted a middle of the road attitude that managed to appease both sides of the debate. Soon after the Kansas City convention he published an article in the AHEPA magazine where he noted that "once more, and in the most categorical manner, we are declaring that writings tending to show that we are neglectful or antagonistic to our Mother language, either in practice, fact or form, are completely unfounded. Our avowed policy has been to teach the Greek language to those who need it and the English language to those who need it." 47 Though that statement did not address the issue of the language used in business meetings, it acknowledged its cultural significance. And during his two-year tenure as president AHEPA showed that it took its Hellenic dimension seriously by: highlighting the significance and value of classical Greek civilization; asserting that the modern Greeks including the immigrants to America were heirs of the classical civilization; supporting Greek language schools in America; and fourthly offering various forms of aid to Greece.

These goals were frequently overlapping and some of AHEPA's initiatives managed to address more than one of them. For example, in December 1929 the magazine carried a chapter of I Was Sent to Athens, a book in which Henry Morgenthau related his work as chairman of the League of Nations Commission that worked toward the settlement of the thousands of Greek refugees that had arrived in Greece in the 1920s after their brutal expulsion during the establishment of modern Turkey out of the ruins of the Ottoman Empire. Next to conveying a concern about the plight of the Greek refugees, Morgenthau's writing and his high regard for the Greeks also served AHEPA's aim of elevating the Greeks and comparing them with the ancient Greeks. Morgenthau noted that "It may help the Western World to better understand and better appreciate these worthy descendants of a glorious race. When the Greeks are mentioned in Europe and America it is too much the habit to dismiss them mentally as only another of 'those hopeless Balkan peoples.' The Greeks are, however, very different from the other peoples of the Balkans, and it is a grievous injustice to misunderstand these differences. First of all, the Greek has a passion for excellence and progress unique in that part of the world. Whenever he is poor or ignorant or backward, he is so against his will. Education is a passion universal among the Greeks, and parents there, as in America, will make every sacrifice to provide schooling for their children." He added: "Democracy is ingrained in the Greek." Clearly, an emphasis on the connection between the Greeks of the present and the ancient Greeks remained important in deflecting the lingering assertions of white racial superiority on the part of the nativists.

There were other signs of AHEPA's embrace of its Hellenic dimension during Phillies' tenure as Supreme President, which was extended for another year after he was reelected at the 8th Supreme Convention held in 1930 in Boston. There were 127 delegates in Boston, and Chebithes was elected chair. Delegates decided to amend the constitution to formalize AHEPA's expansion into Canada that was already underway. An AHEPA memorial plaque at the Tomb of the Unknown Soldier was approved; an AHEPA Veterans Unit was to be studied and put into action; San Francisco was honored as first place winner in the membership drive, and Lowell, Massachusetts was given second prize. The sum of $3,500 was appropriated for scholarships, and $1,500 for the Sons of Pericles. The following were elected as the Supreme Lodge for 1930–1931 along with Supreme President George E. Phillies. P. S. Marthakis, who was a high school math teacher from Salt Lake City, was elected Supreme Vice President. He had been born in Greece and came to the United States as an infant. His parents died while he was still young but that did not prevent him from educating himself, going to college and then earning a master's degree. The others elected were Achilles Catsonis, Supreme Secretary; Andrew Jarvis, Supreme Treasurer; Harris J. Booras, Supreme Counsellor; and the following Supreme Governors: George C. Eliades, George A. Stathes, Constantine G. Poulakos, Rev. S. S. Spathey, Dr. G. M. Saliba, Nicholas D. Chotas (Mother Lodge Member), C. R. Nixon, James T. Lekas, A. George N. Spannon, Michael D. Konomos, C. E. Athas, P. J. Andrews, and Dr. N. S. Checkos.

Several chapters, including those in Chicago, Lowell and Marlboro in Massachusetts, Phoenix, Arizona, and Pittsburgh offered aid to Greek schools. The program of a benefit dance held in Pittsburgh noted, "We have the dance for the benefit of the Greek Schools because AHEPA stands for education and in this instance of the Greek youth in our mother language. We wish to assist as much as we can the parents, the church, and the community in their efforts to teach our youth our mother language which they cannot learn from the city public schools which they attend. AHEPA fosters education, progress, and true Hellenism, it is fitting that it should do this." Chapters awarded scholarships to young Greek Americans based on contests of essays that focused on ancient Greece's contributions to civilization or on ancient Greek plays by Euripides and Sophocles. Many chapters held events to commemorate the centenary of Greece gaining its independence and sovereignty.

AHEPA's excursion to Greece in 1930 demonstrated how important these visits were for both the Order and for Greece itself. Making the trip on the SS Saturnia that sailed from New York in March were honored guests Senator William King and Mrs. King, and the Honorable Henry Morgenthau. Newspaper reports described the excursion as a "a potent embassy of goodwill from America to Greece." The standard greeting after arrival in Greece was "Long live America, long live Greece, and glory and honor to the AHEPA." Premier Eleftherios

Venizelos of Greece, Athens Mayor Spyros Mercouris, and Piraeus Mayor Takis Panayotopoulos all greeted the Ahepans on their arrival. The Akropolis newspaper welcomed the excursionists by noting in a front-page article: "They are being received with special joy because always and at every opportunity, even though they are far away and they left several decades ago, they never forgot their homeland and felt nostalgia for it. They always supported every national project, they contributed their money, they contributed armies of volunteers during the wars, they became apostles of philhellenism in the United States, their second country. The warmth with which the homeland welcomes them today is a small part of this free nation's debt towards them." Prime Minister Eleftherios Venizelos sent his own message welcoming AHEPA. When the SS Saturnia sailed into the bay of Phalero it was met by hydroplanes that dropped bouquets of flowers on and around the vessel.[38]

The next day Ahepans in full uniform held a parade through downtown Athens which ended at the municipality, where Mercouris, Phillies, and the US Ambassador to Greece Robert Skinner made speeches. There was a special meeting at the Greek Parliament that was addressed by Senator King. There were many other activities the excursionists undertook during their visit; these ranged from attending a play based on the ancient myth of Demeter and Persephone at the site of ancient Eleusis outside Athens, to watching a soccer match between the teams of Panathinaikos and Athinaikos played in their honor and sponsored by the mayor of Athens. During their visit the AHEPA excursionists donated $4,000 to the war orphans fund of Greece, and to the National Archaeological Museum.

AHEPA & the Greek Orthodox Archdiocese
The early 1930s witnessed the beginning of close relations between AHEPA and the Greek Orthodox Church's governing body, the Archdiocese. This came about thanks to the combined efforts of the Greek Orthodox Ecumenical Patriarchate, the Greek government, and the Greek Orthodox Church of Greece. They intervened in order to put an end to the disruption that the political polarization had brought to the Archdiocese in America. The head of the Church, Archbishop Alexandros, was identified with the pro-Venizelos side and there were several pro-royalist bishops who had come

from Greece with the express purpose of challenging his authority and offering legitimacy to the pro-royalist clerics and parishes. The "mother" Church of Greek Orthodoxy, the Ecumenical Patriarchate of Constantinople which had jurisdiction over the Church in the Americas, decided to intervene directly in 1930 to resolve the difficulties created by the political polarization. With the Greek government and the Church of Greece in agreement, the Patriarchate sent Metropolitan Damaskinos of Corinth as its "exarch" representative to the United States. Damaskinos had made a very good all-round impression on a visit in 1929 to solicit funds for the relief of the people in the Corinth area after the earthquake it had experienced, a campaign to which AHEPA had contributed. AHEPA members assisted Damaskinos in making contacts with the community and with officials in the United States. On this second visit that was focused on ecclesiastic issues, the metropolitan had the support of Greek Ambassador Simopoulos and the Greek language newspapers. Damaskinos' mission included visiting many parishes across America, and he both reached out to AHEPA and also local AHEPA chapters participated in his welcoming.[39]

Most significantly, Damaskinos attended AHEPA's Supreme Convention in September 1930 in Boston, and he conducted a service there in honor of AHEPA and also participated in the Dilboy commemoration. And when he visited several parishes AHEPA was there to welcome him. For example, when he arrived in in Akron, Ohio, John Petrou, the president of the community who welcomed him, was also an AHEPA member. At a banquet in his honor the Akron chapter of AHEPA's orchestra provided the music.[40] AHEPA's close relationship with Damaskinos paved the way for the Order to acquire a close and mutually beneficial relationship with the newly appointed Greek Orthodox Archbishop of North and South America Athenagoras. As a result of Damaskinos' efforts in 1930 calm began to be restored in the affairs of the Church, and he was recalled to Greece before the end of 1930. In February 1931, hundreds of Greek Americans including AHEPA members would welcome Athenagoras when he arrived in New York to take up his responsibilities as the new archbishop. AHEPA would support the archbishop as he oversaw the restructuring and rebuilding of the Church in America during a successful tenure that ended in 1948 when he became Ecumenical

Patriarch of Constantinople. One of the first things Athenagoras did was to visit the White House with AHEPA's help.

Honoring Greek American World War I Hero George Dilboy

The dedication of a monument to World War I hero George Dilboy in Sommerville, Massachusetts during AHEPA's 8th Supreme Convention that met in nearby Boston in 1930 was another sign that the Order was conscious and proud of both its American and Greek identities. Dilboy was an immigrant from Asia Minor who fought in the US Army in the war and met a heroic death. Dilboy was born in 1896 in the ethnically Greek town of Alatsata, present-day Alaçati on Turkey's Aegean coast, across from the island of Chios, and emigrated to the United States as a boy and became an American citizen. He went back to Greece briefly to fight in the Balkan Wars and soon after returning to the United States he enlisted in the US Army and served on the Mexican border in 1916. He reenlisted the following year when the United States entered World War I and went overseas with the 103rd Infantry. His death came in July 1926 on the battlefront in France when he singlehandedly charged and overcome a German machine gun post that had pinned down his unit, dying from the wounds he sustained as he charged the enemy machine gunners fully exposed with fixed bayonet. Dilboy received the US Congressional Medal of Honor for his actions. His body was taken back to Alatsata to be buried. Four years later Turkish forces entered the town at the conclusion of the Greco-Turkish war of 1919–1922 and desecrated his grave, prompting a sharp reaction from the United States and the return of his body across the Atlantic and his reburial in Arlington National Cemetery.

The monument, a bronze bust of Dilboy resting on a granite base, was erected in Sommerville where Dilboy had lived, in an elaborate and moving ceremony organized and funded by AHEPA. A crowd of 50,000 people watched the parade of veteran troops and the ceremony in front of the City Hall, which opened with music from a 40-piece military band and prayers offered by Greek Orthodox Bishop of Boston Joachim. Phillies delivered the dedicatory address followed by US Senator David I. Walsh of Massachusetts. As the Boston Globe put it, the senator's oration "was a eulogy of the contribution to civilization made by the Greek people through their art and literature and traditions. He went on to a eulogy of George

Dilboy, as typifying the continued contribution of the Greek race in modern times and emergencies." Following his address, the band played "America" and the Greek national anthem. The bishop offered a closing prayer, and there was more patriotic music, firing of guns, and four buglers sounded the "Taps" facing in the four directions of the compass. There followed a five-division parade through the town that passed by Dilboy's house, which was decorated with flags.[41]

George Dilboy's heroism, and even more importantly his embodiment of American and Greek values, became widely known when they were described in a syndicated column that appeared in newspapers across the United States. The author, Lieutenant Frank E. Hagan, made sure he mentioned Dilboy's ethnicity. At the beginning of the description of Dilboy's act of heroism, he wrote: "George Dilboy couldn't claim Mayflower ancestry nor a fighting heritage from Concord or Bunker Hill. He was a Greek immigrant boy, brought to this country by his father to escape persecution by the Turks six or seven years before the outbreak of the World war. But when the One Hundred and Third made an attack near Belleau on July 18, 1918, it was George Dilboy who raced forward under the fire of German snipers and machine gunners on a railroad embankment, throwing hand grenade after hand grenade until he silenced the enemy's fire..." This column was carried by newspapers across the United States and was yet another step in raising the profile and the pride of the Greek immigrants.[42]

AHEPA's Relief Work
By the 1930s the effects of the Wall Street Crash of 1929 were being felt across the country and within the Greek American community, and AHEPA mobilized. "Our Relief Work" is the title of a short editorial in The Ahepan magazine of December 1930, a time when the Great Depression was taking strong hold of the country: "What a grand, good work we are doing. Ahepans feed 15,000 needy each day. How? Well, many restaurant proprietors are Greeks, and a true Ahepan is his brother's keeper, and this is signally true now when our country feels the pressure of economic depression. To mention one instance: In Chicago a Grand Charity Ball is to be given December 29th when ten AHEPA Chapters, and many Greek societies unite with an objective to raise $50,000, stirred to action by the fact that in that

city alone 400 destitute Greek families ask assistance. Thanks to the Ahepans who set forth the idea—let each restaurant feed a certain number. The torch has been passed on, and all over our land our Greeks are feeding the needy, irrespective of nationality. We salute you—many of whom are naturalized citizens. You are showing the true American spirit."

There was another important AHEPA initiative in 1930, this one reflecting AHEPA's commitment to honoring a connection that Greece shared with the United States when it had offered relief to the Greeks during the Greek War of Independence in the 1820s. The AHEPA magazine reported on the presentation of the State Flags of the United States to the government of Greece on that country's 100th anniversary of its independence from Turkey. American Legionnaires carried the State Flags to Greece, and all States of the Union were represented. Maude Howe Elliott, daughter of Dr. Samuel Gridley Howe, was Honorary Chairman of the Excursion of the American Legion to Greece which left for Greece on August 15, 1930. Howe was Surgeon General of the Greek armed forces between 1929 and 1931, and prior to that he was the best-known American philhellene, who had fought with the Greeks during the 1821 revolution that resulted in Greece's independence. That was also the occasion of the unveiling of a monument in Athens in honor of those Americans who helped Greece during that War of Independence, and the Greek government also donated land in Athens to the American Legion for its American Legion Memorial and Community Center. The cornerstone for the building was laid during the ceremonies in Athens.

The 9th Supreme Convention, 1931, San Francisco

The 9th Supreme Convention was held in San Francisco in August 1931 with 169 delegates present and James Veras as chair. Veras had served for several years as Supreme Counselor and was the owner of a confectionary store in Dunmore, Pennsylvania which he had acquired after working there as an employee soon after he emigrated from Greece. Among the convention's resolutions were a decision that AHEPA be represented in the George Washington Bicentennial Celebration, as well as in the Flag Day Pageant to be held in Washington in June 1932 and that the Florida AHEPA chapters participate in the annual Epiphany Day ceremonies at Tarpon Springs, Florida. No one knew it at the time, but this was another "first" for AHEPA because soon the celebration in Tarpon Springs would become not only an important occasion for Greek Orthodoxy in America but also an important event in the annual calendar of Greek America.

The convention was rightfully mostly concerned with the need to study and refute the findings of the Wickersham Commission Report. Appointed by President Herbert Hoover in May 1929, pursuant to an act of Congress, the members of the Commission were charged with the responsibility of "studying exhaustively the entire problem of the enforcement of our laws and the improvement of our judicial system, including the special problem and abuses growing out of the prohibition laws." The Commission was chaired by George W. Wickersham and under his leadership the Commission pursued its studies under 11 headings: namely, Prohibition, Delinquency, Criminal Justice and the Foreign Born, Lawlessness in Law Enforcement, Penal Institutions, Probations, and Parole. Its findings became known in June 1931. One of the conclusions of the report was that "the Greek element in America is criminally inclined." The AHEPA convention appointed its own committee, which came out with a comprehensive report and a resolution, adopted by the convention, condemning the report as being inaccurate and untrue, and the convention action was sent to the President in the form of a resolution.

The new Supreme Lodge elected by the convention for 1931–1932 was: Harris J. Booras, a Boston attorney, as Supreme President; Theodore Andronicos from San Francisco, Supreme Vice President; Achilles Catsonis, Supreme Secretary; Andrew Jarvis, Supreme Treasurer; Soterios Nicholson, Supreme Counsellor; C. R. Nixon, Supreme Governor; Peter G. Sikokis, Supreme Governor. Booras, the new Supreme President, would become one of the great figures in AHEPA's history. He would be reelected as Supreme President the next year to a two-year term, and he would serve as Supreme President again in 1945 and 1946. Character-wise he was the opposite of Chebithes, more reserved, rhetorically eloquent but more direct in his speeches. And he maintained close ties to the homeland and was especially active in the aid AHEPA would offer to hospitals in Greece, and led several projects designed to erect statues of ancient Greek heroes in Sparta and Thermopylae.

New York Governor Franklin Roosevelt Joins AHEPA

In March 1931, members of AHEPA's Delphi chapter went to Albany, New York to meet with Governor Franklin Roosevelt and perform his induction ceremony into AHEPA. Two years later, Roosevelt became President of the United States. A new era opened for the country, one in which the "New Deal" would greatly benefit Greek Americans. Roosevelt had been persuaded to join AHEPA by Ulius L. Amoss, who had worked with the YMCA in Greece and had then formed a "Friendship with Greece" committee to raise funds for the YMCA facilities in Greece. Through that committee, Amoss had met Alfange and learned about AHEPA. Roosevelt's involvement in the committee led Amoss, who aside from his philanthropic work was also involved in political activities, to suggest that Roosevelt might gain support from Greek Americans if he joined AHEPA. For its part, AHEPA was very eager to recruit American elected officials as members of the Order, albeit in an honorary capacity, and had already registered many as members. Thus, AHEPA was honored by Roosevelt's agreement. Following the initiation ceremony in 1931, Roosevelt remained a dues-paying member of AHEPA up to the time of his death in 1945, including of course the years he served as President of the United States.[43]

Weathering the Great Depression 1932–1934

The Order's 10th Supreme Convention was held in Baltimore, Maryland, in August 1932, with a total of 168 delegates and D. G. Michalopoulos, a Chicago attorney, as chairman. Among the accomplishments of the convention in Baltimore were a $5,000 donation to the Hellenic Institute sponsored by Archbishop Athenagoras of North and South America; donations to Tuberculosis Relief and the Sons of Pericles; and a $3,000 loan to the Detroit chapters. Legislative action of the convention included a decision that Supreme Conventions would only be held once in every two years, and an increase of the term of Supreme Lodge Officers to two years. The newly-elected Supreme Lodge officers elected for a two-year term were: Harris J. Booras, Supreme President; P. S. Marthakis, Supreme Vice President; Achilles Catsonis, Supreme Secretary; George L. Pappas, Supreme Treasurer; George C. Vournas, Supreme Counsellor; C. E. Athas, Supreme Governor; and Robert Katson, Supreme Governor. The economic depression which engulfed the entire country led the new Supreme Lodge to make several decisions concerning debts, and these included the cancellation of all debts owed by members to their chapters for delinquent chapter dues; cancellation of debts owed by the chapters to the Supreme Lodge, if chapters were unable to meet them; the offering of complete reinstatement back into the fraternity for suspended members upon payment of only $1.00; and a reduced initiation fee for membership of only $10.00 for newly-initiated members. There was no Supreme Convention in 1933 in order not to burden the Order and its members.

In 1933, the Hellenic Institute at Pomfret, Connecticut opened on an estate purchased by the Greek Archdiocese of North and South America, under the direction of Archbishop Athenagoras. The Order of AHEPA, through the Supreme Lodge and its chapters, contributed more than $10,000 toward the purchase. Within a short while, the school was renamed the Theological School of Pomfret, and became the Greek Orthodox Church's first theological school in America. In 1946, the school would be moved to Brookline, Massachusetts. In 1966, Holy Cross expanded its undergraduate division into a full four-year liberal arts college named Hellenic College, which opened in 1968.

In 1934, the Sixth AHEPA Easter Excursion to Greece arrived in Athens in March, under the command of Supreme President Harris Booras. One of the highlights of the Excursion was the visit of the excursionists to the AHEPA Agricultural School, at Velos, Corinth, when the school was dedicated by Prime Minister Panayotis Tsaldaris, with members of his cabinet, and American Minister Lincoln Mac Veagh. More than 20,000 local citizens attended the ceremonies. A new agricultural school is functioning presently on the original site.

The 11th Supreme Convention of AHEPA was held in Columbus, Ohio in August 1934 with James Veras again as chair. Archbishop Athenagoras was at the opening session; the day before he dedicated the Greek Orthodox church in Columbus. Among the convention's resolutions was that "a Ladies Auxiliary be adopted by the Order of AHEPA, and that the matter of name and other questions be settled by the Auxiliary and the AHEPA Supreme Lodge." The newly elected Supreme Lodge officers for the fiscal year 1934–1935 were: Achilles Catsonis, Supreme President; George E. Johnson, Supreme Vice

President; Constantine G. Economou, Supreme Secretary; Peter W. Katsafanas, Supreme Treasurer; George Eliades, Supreme Counsellor; Arthur Peponis, Supreme Governor; Peter Boudoures, Supreme Governor.

The Five-Year Chebithes Presidency 1935–1940
AHEPA turned to three-time Supreme President V. I. Chebithes in 1935 and elected him again as the head of the Order; it was hoping that this leading personality would be able to address the negative effects the Depression had on the organization itself and on the Greeks in America, and to find ways to solve them and move AHEPA ahead. He did not disappoint. In what was a defining feature of an AHEPA leader, Chebithes managed to balance between three major goals. He continued the push toward Americanization but also deepened AHEPA's ties with the homeland. And at the same time, he took charge of the initiatives that were already underway to offer relief to members and the wider Greek American community who were facing difficulties. His election in 1935 inaugurated a five-year period in which he stayed at the helm and managed to steer AHEPA forward.

While focused on the growing needs of the membership, Chebithes also had to carefully navigate through the difficulties presented by the political turbulence that was occurring in Greece at the time. The royalist side won the elections of 1933 bringing an end to Venizelos' tenure in office, but tensions remained; there was a failed coup by pro-Venizelist military officers in 1935 and later that year the monarchy was restored, with George II, the son of Constantine who had died in exile soon after stepping down in 1922, ascending the throne. With political tensions continuing, even though Venizelos passed away in early 1936, General Ioannis Metaxas established a dictatorship in August of that year, a move that was supported by the king. Throughout these events, AHEPA, true to its non-political attitude, maintained good relations with whoever was in power in Athens. In any case, AHEPA's annual visit was very warmly welcomed by all Greek political factions.

The 12th Supreme Convention, at which Chebithes was elected Supreme President again, was held in Chicago in 1935 and was chaired by Constantine A. Tsangadas, an attorney from Detroit. Those elected to the Supreme Lodge were V. I. Chebithes, Supreme

President; Constantine A. Tsangadas, Supreme Vice President; Constantine G. Economou, Supreme Secretary; Charles Preketes, a restaurant owner in Ann Arbor, Michigan, Supreme Treasurer; D. G. Michalopoulos, a Chicago attorney, Supreme Counsellor, George K. Demopulos, Supreme Governor; Thomas D. Lentgis, Supreme Governor. Among the convention's decisions were to reduce the number of administrative districts the Order maintained; it gave the Supreme Lodge authority and control over Auxiliary organizations; it passed a resolution condemning as Un-American "all communistic, fascistic and other subversive propaganda and activities"; and established "Americanism Committees" in the districts. That decision was the first example of AHEPA's stand against the rise of Nazism and fascism which was taking place in Europe. Within the next years AHEPA would also condemn the acts of anti-Semitism suffered by the Jews in Europe.

In March 1936, the AHEPA Supreme Lodge visited President Franklin D. Roosevelt at the White House, where the President greeted them and posed for a photograph. The visit to the White House to meet with and be photographed with the President had become a regular annual occurrence. In the previous month the AHEPA National Banquet was held in Washington, DC with more than 100 members of Congress present as guests of the fraternity. Among the speakers were: Secretary of War George H. Dern, US Senator William H. King of Utah, and Supreme President V. I. Chebithes. More than 600 persons attended the event, chaired by Past Supreme Counsellor George C. Vournas; Past Supreme President Dean Alfange was toastmaster.

It was at the 13th Supreme Convention that was held in St. Paul, Minnesota, in 1936 that a major decision was taken to adopt the AHEPA Silver District Sanatorium in Albuquerque, New Mexico as an AHEPA national project. The convention, chaired by A. A. Pantelis, a Chicago attorney, featured a convention parade with 2,500 marchers. Chebithes was reelected Supreme President; the other members who were elected to the Supreme Lodge were D. G. Michalopoulos, Supreme Vice President; Constantine G. Economou, Supreme Secretary; August Rogokos, Supreme Treasurer; Andrew J. Dritsas, Supreme Counsellor; Thomas D. Lentgis, Supreme Governor; and Speros J. Cosmos, Supreme Governor.

Albuquerque was chosen because at the time there was a strong belief in the healing powers of high-altitude dry desert air and sunshine ideal for those suffering from tuberculosis, a disease that was on the rise at the time because many Americans and Greek Americans were living in poor and unsanitary living conditions. The facility AHEPA acquired was built in 1916, already existed as a sanatorium, and had been used by several Protestant churches over the years. AHEPA worked toward raising funds to improve the facility. Among the countless fundraising events, one stands out: former boxing champion Jack Dempsey refereed a series of benefit boxing matches that took place to raise money. There was an entire dedication week arranged around the sanatorium's official opening on March 25, Greek Independence Day, which began with an inspection and blessings offered by Archbishop Athenagoras. The Ethnikos Kyrix hailed the opening of the sanatorium and described AHEPA as "the mother and sister" of all Greeks who were facing misfortune. The AHEPA magazine issues of those years gave extensive coverage to the fundraising, the preparations, and the operation of the sanatorium.[44]

AHEPA took several additional important steps toward addressing the needs of its members at its 14th Supreme Convention in Syracuse, New York in August 1937. The convention decided that discussions be held with other Hellenic groups for the purpose of the unification of Hellenic organizations to better serve community needs, and that the Supreme Lodge be authorized to accept contributions toward the purchase of property in Florida for the establishment of a national home for orphans or old men, or both, in Pinellas County. It also decided to appoint a Supreme Governor of Canada. The convention was chaired by Achilles Catsonis, Chebithes was reelected, and the following members were elected to the Supreme Lodge: Van A. Nomikos, Supreme Vice President; C. G. Economou, Supreme Secretary; John F. Davis, Supreme Treasurer; A. A. Pantelis, Supreme Counsellor; C. G. Paris, Supreme Governor; Peter Boudoures, Supreme Governor. Also, the following three members of the Sanatorium Board were elected: John A. Manta, Chris E. Athas, and Harris Booras.

The AHEPA National Banquet was held in Washington, DC in 1938, under the chairmanship of Dr. Harry S. Sembekos of Washington, with co-chairman Helen Peratino. Toastmaster was Supreme Counsellor A. A. Pantelis, and speakers were Sons of Pericles Supreme President

Christ J. Petrou, US Representative Everett M. Dirksen of Illinois, Senator William King of Utah, Paul V. McNutt, American High Commissioner of the Philippine Islands, and Supreme President V. I. Chebithes.

> berlain when he revealed that no German refugee has been deported from the United States as a public charge since the beginning of the Hitler regime.
>
> **American Greeks Condemn Persecution.** Recently the Ahepa Society, composed of Americans of Greek descent, met in national convention in New Orleans. Ahepa stands for American Hellenic Educational and Progressive Association. The delegates stood in horror before the facts of anti-Jewish treatment today, and passed a resolution "condemning the inhuman and cruel persecution of a race and faith which has given so much to the world," and congratulating the American government for launching the movement to ameliorate the lot of refugees. "Members of Ahepa and American citizens of Greek descent in general are bound to their co-citizens of the Hebrew faith with manifold ties," declared the resolution, which described Jews as "a loyal, law-abiding and valuable element in the political, economic, cultural, and scientific fields of the nation."

> **SPAIN**
>
> **Loyalists Repeal 1492.** A striking example of the difference between democracy and Fascism was seen last

> by B'nai Grand Lo(constituted rights and munity pr(
>
> **Terror S** Semites c crimes dur others: th old synago ish boycot all Jewish mentary s Yorker na 30 Jews an ish shops tacked Je the Lwow Jewish pu schools; a linski, not
>
> **Black S** German Je of 1933 are Jewry tod: resigning fore they controlled for Jewish

The long list of goals set by the 15th Supreme Convention of the Order was held in New Orleans, Louisiana in August of 1938 attests to the organization's dynamism and the fact it had regained the ability to pursue both an international as well as a domestic agenda. And the pinnacle of its programmatic statements is by far its condemnation of anti-Semitism in Europe. By that time anti-Semitic decrees had been promulgated in Germany and extended into Austria when Hitler's forces incorporated it into the Third Reich. A few months after the AHEPA convention the situation worsened with the gruesome actions during Kristallnacht (Night of Broken Glass), the anti-Jewish pogrom in Germany and Austria. The list of goals reads as follows: Plans were initiated to assess the feasibility the formation of a federation of Greek organizations throughout the country for the purpose of dealing with charitable and educational problems of all Greek Americans; chapters were directed to appoint an Americanization Committee; the Athletics program was expanded through the holding of annual AHEPA Olympiads, which would become a very important and popular activity; satisfaction was expressed with the progress of the Maids of Athens, the junior girls' auxiliary; the AHEPA scholarship program was continued; the annual excursion to Greece the following year began being planned; a Sons of Pericles Excursion to Greece for 1939 was approved; AHEPA requested that Italy return to Greece the ethnically Greek Dodecanese Islands which Italy had taken from Turkey in 1922 under the pretext that they were to be turned over to Greece; a resolution was passed calling for the Greek immigration quota to the United States be increased; AHEPA condemned any and all individuals and organizations "particularly communistic" whose intent may be to undermine or destroy the American Constitution or curtail the liberties guaranteed to every citizen under the Constitution; AHEPA condemned the persecution of the Jews by certain governments of Europe and congratulated the American government for its humanitarian stand on the matter; the convention favored the discontinuance of any local or national beauty contests within AHEPA, but not necessarily popularity contests; all Past Supreme Presidents of the fraternity were allowed a full vote as a voting delegate to all future Supreme Conventions; the sum of $1,000 was donated to the Pomfret Theological School; and a "United Hellenic Charities" organization was established. AHEPA's condemnation of anti-Semitism was the first of several initiatives the Order or its individual members would take in expressing their solidarity with Jewish Americans.

The convention, which was chaired by P. S. Marthakis, elected the following Supreme Lodge for the fiscal year 1938–1939: V. I. Chebithes,

Supreme President; Van A. Nomikos, Supreme Vice President; Louis P. Maniatis, Supreme Secretary; John Zazas, Supreme Treasurer; A. A. Pantelis, Supreme Counsellor; James G. Dikeou, Supreme Governor; George E. Loucas, Supreme Governor. Constantine Halikas was appointed Special Canadian Supreme Governor. The AHEPA Silver District Sanatorium Board of Directors who were appointed were: John L. Manta, Chairman; Chris E. Athas, Vice Chairman; Anthony G. Pavlantos, Treasurer; James Ipiotis; Dr. S. D. Zaph; George Kisciras; and Theodore Anderson, with Supreme President Chebithes and Supreme Governor Dikeou also as members of that board.

By the time AHEPA held its 16th Supreme Convention in August 1939 Europe was teetering on the brink of war. Germany had occupied Czechoslovakia and less than a week after the convention ended Germany attacked Poland, which signaled the beginning of the war. The convention was held in Providence, Rhode Island and chaired by Alexander D. Varkas, an attorney from Belmont, Massachusetts. Somewhat optimistically, the convention agreed the annual excursion to Greece should take place the following year. Thinking more practically, it established the office of national Executive Secretary at the Headquarters in Washington, DC, to assume the duties previously undertaken by the Supreme Secretary. The new Supreme Lodge elected for the year 1939–1940 was: V. I. Chebithes, Supreme President for his fifth consecutive term, Van A. Nomikos, Supreme Vice President; Louis P. Maniatis, Supreme Secretary; John G. Zazas, Supreme Treasurer; Constantine G. Economou, Supreme Counsellor; George E. Loucas, Supreme Governor; George Papaeleas, Supreme Governor. John L. Manta, Dr. S. D. Zaph, and Chris E. Athas were reelected to the Sanatorium Board of Directors.

During the Providence convention, AHEPA dedicated its memorial to Dr. Samuel Gridley Howe, the American philhellene of the Greek Revolutionary War of 1821, at Brown University. The memorial was a base of granite upon which rested a flagpole, the flagpole once a mast of an America Cup defender. Howe was a graduate of Brown University. Mrs. Maud Howe Elliott, surviving daughter of Samuel Gridley Howe, attended the ceremony, as did many university, city, and state officials. The First National Olympiad of AHEPA was held at the Providence convention, and competition was held between young American athletes of Greek descent in track and field events, under the direction of Van A. Nomikos, national director of athletics, and assistant athletic director Peter Clentzos of California, who had participated in the Los Angeles Olympics of 1932 as a member of the Greek national team. This was the forerunner of a continuous line of annual AHEPA Olympiads held every year thereafter at Supreme Conventions for many years.

When AHEPA turned to Chebithes in the mid-1930s it was looking for a new lease on life which it richly deserved and which it gained. It had managed to balance so well in between the need for the Greeks to Americanize and for them to retain their Greek roots, but the Depression threatened not the existence but certainly the well-being of the organization. AHEPA's membership had dropped off and a fresh approach was needed if AHEPA was to rally the Greek American community around its program again. Chebithes sought to revitalize the organization by emphasizing its character as a mutual-benefit society. Real estate property was purchased for the purpose of creating an old people's home and an orphanage. Sponsoring education and offering other social services to the membership were the order of the day. AHEPA thus recast its role into one that was going to preserve "Hellenism" in the United States from the ills of the Depression. It did not do it singlehandedly—it was Roosevelt's New Deal policies that helped the most—but AHEPA's contributions were very important for its members and the wider Greek American community. And it was about to enter another challenging decade that lay ahead in a much stronger position than it had entered the 1930s.[45]

The First National Convention of the Daughters of Penelope

The First National Convention of the Order of Daughters of Penelope, Senior Women's Auxiliary, was also held in conjunction with the AHEPA Convention in 1939. It was a major step taken 10 years after the establishment of the Daughters and signaled its ongoing growth. By then, there were 95 chapters and 5,000 members. The convention was presided over by Alexandra Apostolides from San Francisco, the organization's founder, the vice chairman was Froso Xenides, the secretary was Catherine Katopes, and the assistant secretary was Alexandra Lamberson. The convention reflected a degree of self-governance the Daughters had achieved during their decade-long existence through their energetic efforts. AHEPA's convention had given final official recognition to the Daughters of Penelope as a "senior auxiliary" of the Order of AHEPA. In light of this, the Daughters proceeded to adopt a new constitution and by-laws. The purpose of the organization, it stated, was promoting the intellectual, social and ethnical interests of its members, perpetuating good fellowship among its members, and disseminating American Hellenic culture. The eligibility of membership was limited to wives, daughters, sisters (including "half-sisters" and sisters-in-law), nieces, and goddaughters of members of AHEPA in good standing. From this modest but significant beginning, which reflects the conventional wisdom of the 1930s, the Daughters of Penelope grew steadily gaining stature and importance. The present-day aims of the Daughters reflect that growth. These consist of the following: To encourage and promote loyalty to the United States of America or to another country in which a chapter exists; to encourage the interest of its members in the duties of citizenship and a further participation in the larger life of their country as well as in the philanthropic, social, political, and civic life of their respective communities; to cultivate the ideals and traditions of Hellenism as our best contribution to the development of America or to another country in which a chapter exists; to promote opportunities of education; to cooperate by precept and example in furthering the purposes and ideals of the AHEPA family; to promote the welfare of the Junior Order of the Daughters of Penelope, the Order of the Maids of Athena. At the end of the convention Alexandra Apostolides was reelected as Grand President, Estelle Eliades from Washington, DC as Grand Vice President, Marie Zuras, also from Washington, DC, as Grand Secretary, Theodora Mangas Anderson from Indiana as Grand Treasurer, and Mrs. Simeon Agnos from Kansas City and Josephine Pandel from Los Angeles as Grand Governors.

Chapter 3: AHEPA & World War II 1940–1945

AHEPA was able to play an important role supporting both the United States and Greece during World War II thanks to the balance between Americanism and Hellenism that it had forged by the late 1930s. Its role during that period was one of the Order's finest hours. Greece entered World War II on October 28 when dictator Ioannis Metaxas refused to capitulate to Italy and the entire Greek people rallied to the country's defense. Greece's heroic stance was met with admiration from the entire democratic world including the United States where government officials and the media showered the Greeks with well-deserved praise. AHEPA led the effort to offer support to Greece during its successful defense against Italy's attack. After Nazi Germany also attacked Greece and thanks to its overwhelming power occupied the entire country by the end of May 1941, AHEPA continued to work toward providing much needed relief to the Greek people. Six months later the United States entered the war. As had been the case in World War I, the United States and Greece were fighting on the same side in the name of democracy.

America's entry into the war in 1941 brought new attitudes toward the new immigrants, including the Greeks, which had been changing and now improved even further. In battling fascism and Nazism, American spokesmen portrayed the United States as a nation whose values were antithetical to its enemies. This meant that if totalitarianism demanded conformity, mocked freedom, and preached racial hatred then Americans were surely plural and instinctively democratic. While this theory did not quite apply in practice to all groups, it functioned as an open invitation to southern and eastern European immigrants to feel fully American. This new climate operated beneficially for all southern and eastern European immigrants and Greece's particular role in World War II meant that the Greeks would be made twice as welcome into mainstream America. The admiration Americans had for Greece when it rejected Italy's attempt to subdue it was expressed by many American newspapers and evoked in a New York Times editorial entitled "The Hour of Greece" on October 29. It noted: "The Greeks in this hour, outnumbered as they are, poor in the instruments of modern war, remember and defend the glory that was Greece. They recognize at once that this is a fight for independence of all small nations... their instant determination to prove worthy of their ancestors of their freedom vindicates the heroic tradition of Marathon, Thermopylae and Salamis." In the next few months, the American media continued to shower Greece with praise because of the extraordinary achievement of the Greek armies in pushing the Italian forces back over the Albanian border and deep into Albanian territory.

The Greek Americans responded to America's greater acceptance by joining the US Armed Forces in droves, continuing to raise funds for relief for Greece, and joining the campaign to sell US government War Bonds. AHEPA was the driving force in those efforts. It raised more than $253 million for US War Bonds during World War II, for which AHEPA was named an official Issuing Agent for United States War Bonds by the Department of the Treasury, an honor that no other civic organization was able to achieve at the time.

In terms of AHEPA's history, therefore, the war years were a period of sustained aid offered to Greece via the Greek War Relief Association, and to America's war effort through its members who enlisted in the military and through the War Bonds sales and purchases. There were several aspects to the aid: the period from October 28 when Greece made its heroic entry into the war until the Axis occupied Greece entirely by the end of May 1941, the difficult period under Axis rule that ended in October 1944, and the years America fought, from 1941 to 1945.

OXI! Greece Enters World War II

Greece had not yet entered the war when AHEPA held its 17th Supreme Convention in Seattle in August 1940, but the war's rumblings were visible on the horizon. The possibility of war took up a great deal of the discussions on the floor of the convention and in the hallways outside. As one local newspaper reported during the convention: "Two thousand members of the Order of AHEPA (The American Hellenic Progressive Educational Association) resumed national business sessions today disturbed by war-like developments involving Greece, homeland of their forefathers."[46] The convention issued resolutions endorsing the efforts of Congress to bolster the defenses of America, urging complete preparedness of men and arms, regardless of cost or sacrifice, reaffirming AHEPA's faith in and loyalty to America, and pledging the support of the entire Order of any legislation enacted to preserve the American philosophy of life; issued resolutions rededicating the Order and its members to the principles of democracy and human freedom, renouncing tyranny and despotism, and urging immediate aid to England in her struggle against the dictatorships; it established an AHEPA Board of Education to find ways and means of assisting the schools; issued a resolution urging the establishment of a Federal Department of Education; it inserted into the AHEPA Ritual the requirement that all members initiated into the Order must recite the Pledge of Allegiance to America; it donated $1,000 to the Pomfret Theological School, in addition to individual contributions of $1,000 made by members during the convention; it donated $1,000 to the Hellenic Red Cross.

The convention authorized the new Supreme Lodge to conduct a campaign among chapters and members to raise funds for the people of Greece, who were momentarily expecting to be invaded by Italy, following months of one provocation after another by Italy against Greece by air against Greek warships and shipping. Only days before the Convention met an Italian submarine had torpedoed the Greek cruiser Elli while it was berthed at the island of Tinos to participate in the August 15 Greek Orthodox celebrations of the Dormition of the Virgin Mary. And with an eye to America's role, the convention endorsed an oral resolution favoring conscription. As George Vournas explained to delegates, the United States should not have to rely only on volunteers; for war it required an organized and trained military.[47]

Archbishop Athenagoras, who was on a four month visit to Greek Orthodox churches in the western United States, attended the AHEPA Convention in Seattle and offered prayers for peace. As the Seattle convention ended, delegates elected the following new Supreme Lodge for fiscal year 1940–1941: Van A. Nomikos, Supreme President; George C. Vournas, Supreme Vice President; Peter T. Kourides, Supreme Secretary; Charles Davis Kotsilibas, Supreme Treasurer; Daniel Pananicles, Supreme Counsellor; Charles N. Diamond, Supreme Governor; George Kisciras, Supreme Governor. Nomikos, an owner of a chain of movie theatres in Chicago, had served as vice president for three terms from 1937 through 1940 and had also been National Director of Athletics. Upon being elected Nomikos told delegates that "at this convention we have reaffirmed our allegiance to the United States, and we stand ready to sacrifice not only our wealth but our lives in the defense of the government of the United States—the government which most closely approaches that of the first democracy, our motherland."[48]

As soon as Metaxas, expressing the sentiments of all Greeks, rejected Italy's ultimatum with a resounding "Oxi" (No) on October 28 and entered the war, Nomikos met with Archbishop Athenagoras and other Greek American leaders and formed the Greek War Relief Association to aid Greece. The other Greek American leaders who joined AHEPA's Supreme President in establishing the GWRA were prominent community members, including Spyros S. Skouras, the president of Twentieth Century Fox, who became the GWRA's national president. William Hellis, who owned oil drills in Louisiana, was vice president, and Kyriakos Tsolainos, a Wall Street stockbroker who would also serve as Chairman of the Trustees of Athens College in Greece, was GWRA's national secretary.[49]

The GWRA also enlisted the support of several prominent and respected Americans, to strengthen the organization's appeal and stature. They included Harold S. Vanderbilt who owned several railway companies, and Helen Huntington Astor whose husband was a well-known businessman and philanthropist. This brought other notable American philanthropists, academics, Hollywood actors, and singers in contact with the GWRA. The actors and singers were active in organizing performances and appeals through the radio that raised funds for Greece. It was another indication of the admiration that Greece's wartime struggles had gained throughout the United States.

Greece's fighting spirit forced Italy back over the Greco-Albanian border from where they had launched their attack. American newspapers featured the heroics of the Greek people on their front pages, praising their courage. In January Metaxas died, but by then the Greek people had taken the war effort into their own hands. In the five-month period between the Italian attack and the German invasion of Greece in April 1941, the GWRA had sent $3,766,000 to Greece. These funds were used to supply civilians with food, heating fuel, clothing, and medical attention, as well as outfitting ambulances, the construction of bomb-proof shelters, the creation of refugee workshops, and the support of distressed families of slain soldiers. AHEPA's local chapters bore the brunt of organizing fundraising events throughout the United States.

Vournas Statement About Italian Americans
Supreme Vice President Vournas made multiple public appearances in the name of the Greek War Relief Association. In the speeches he made, aside from pleading for help for Greece, he spoke up in defense of German and Italian Americans. Vournas said that Hitler and Mussolini were dictators who did not represent their people, much less Americans of German and Italian descent who were loyal US citizens and opponents of the regimes in their home countries. Vournas' statement that "the true American spirit can be best displayed by Americans of Greek descent by extending a helping hand to their fellow Americans of Italian descent against prejudices that may follow from Mussolini's actions" was widely reported and received very favorable comments in newspapers throughout the United States.[50]

Humanitarian Aid to Occupied Greece
When the 18th Supreme Convention was held in Cincinnati, Ohio during the week of August 17-23, 1941, Greece had fallen under Axis control following Germany's attack in April which concluded by the end of May with the fall of Crete. This meant that the GWRA now switched its activities toward offering humanitarian aid to Greece, something that became urgent as the harshness of the occupation became apparent, especially during the winter of 1941–1942. Seeking

to rally a broader number of Greek Americans on the side of Greece, AHEPA sponsored a Pan-Hellenic Congress during its convention, inviting delegates from all other Greek American associations to attend to discuss matters of common interest. AHEPA had not gone along with an earlier initiative to form a "National Committee for the Restoration of Greece" because it wished for such an organization to be free of the control of the Greek government which was slowly transitioning from the Metaxas regime and be more authentically representative of the Greek Americans.[51] The first session of the Pan-Hellenic Congress was held on Monday evening, August 18. Besides delegates of the Order of AHEPA, the Congress included delegates from the following other associations: Pan-Cretan Association; Pan-Arcadians; Pan-Epirotai; Pan-Icariaki; and miscellaneous societies, churches, and communities. Ultimately, despite the presence of 461 delegates from Greek American organizations throughout the United States, this federated body was unable to function effectively and AHEPA went back to working through the GWRA.

The 18th Supreme Convention opened with a religious service and a sermon from Archbishop Athenagoras at Cincinnati's Holy Trinity Church. The delegates called upon chapters nearest army posts, in cooperation with their local Greek Orthodox clergy, see to it that religious services and counsel were made available to Greek Orthodox youth in the service of their country; it decided that the dues payments of any Ahepan inducted in the armed services of the United States be suspended for the period of his service; it established definite guidelines for the administration of the Maids of Athena; it decided that all AHEPA chapters cooperate with and aid in every possible manner the local civilian defense officials; it proclaimed that all-out aid by the United States be given to those countries fighting aggression; it endorsed the work of the Fight for Freedom committee in their efforts to secure all-out aid for England and her allies. Also, the convention initiated a five-year program under which funds would be raised, and invested in US War Bonds, to be used in the reconstruction of Greece after the conclusion of the war, for the rebuilding of hospitals, orphanages, schools, churches, and historical landmarks, which might be destroyed or damaged by the invaders of Greece, such drive to be known as the American Hellenic Drive for the Defense of America, and the Reconstruction of Greece. It also decided that each chapter purchase a minimum of $100 in US Defense Bonds, and it donated $1,000 to the Pomfret Theological School, $2,000 to the Dilboy Memorial at Hines, Illinois, and $2,000 to the Tarpon Springs Greek Orthodox church.

The convention was chaired by John P. Harritos, a prominent Ohio Ahepan who had been active on the Greek American Patriotic Committee. That committee had worked to refute charges of Greek immigrant criminality in the United States in the 1930s. Speakers included Sam Rayburn, the Speaker of the US House of Representatives; Spyros Skouras, the national president of the GWRA; and Homer R. Davis, president of the American College in Athens and member of the GWRA's administrative committee, who reported the distribution to Greece of aid of the value of $6 million collected by the GWRA. Another speaker at the convention was the controversial figure of Kostas Kotzias, who had served as mayor of Athens and then as a minister of the Metaxas dictatorial regime between 1936 and 1940 and whose presence in the United States after the dissolution of the Metaxas regime had drawn considerable criticism. In order to reassure the audience he condemned Nazism and fascism. Kotzias was reelected mayor and parliamentary deputy in Greece after the war. Fears that politicians or others might be trying to continue the policies of Metaxas led to a misunderstanding over the creation of a Church-based youth organization, whose acronym in Greek was EON, because that was also the acronym of the differently named youth organization that Metaxas had established.[52]

The main speaker at the convention's banquet was Senator Claude Pepper of Florida, a liberal who turned conservative later in his political career and who was an outspoken supporter of the union of the Italian-controlled Dodecanese Islands with Greece in the 1940s. A few months later AHEPA would act on behalf of Greek American Dodecaneseans and persuaded the US Attorney General not to intern them as Italian citizens. Pepper made a passionate speech entitled "The Bastille of Tyranny is Falling" which was broadcast nationally. He castigated Nazism, lauded American democratic values, and said the new order that would be coming would be made up of old traditional values. V. I. Chebithes was the toastmaster and in attendance were Archbishop Athenagoras and Greek Ambassador Cimon Diamantopoulos.

After a long 18-hour session which debated the candidacies for Supreme President of Nomikos and Vournas, the convention elected the following Supreme Lodge Officers for fiscal year 1941–1942: Van A. Nomikos, Supreme President; George C. Vournas, Supreme Vice President; Stephen S. Scopas, Supreme Secretary; Charles Davis Kotsilibas, Supreme Treasurer; George E. Loucas, Supreme Counsellor; Tom Semos, Supreme Governor; George Kisciras, Supreme Governor.

Reports from occupied Greece indicated that the Axis forces were confiscating foodstuffs for use of their own armies and that the Greek population was suffering from severe food shortages. In the fall of 1941 Greece and especially Athens was suffering from a famine, and as winter approached daily deaths rose to 400 and even higher according to the Red Cross. This made the GWRA and AHEPA's efforts to raise funds for Greece even more urgent. While AHEPA chapters across the country engaged in fundraising activities, the GWRA had to deal with the problem of an Allied naval blockade of Greek sea ports which meant relief could not reach Greece. In February 1942 the GWRA's pressure persuaded the US government to oblige the reluctant British to relax their embargo and allow vessels from neutral Turkey to reach Piraeus with food supplies bought by the monies raised in the United States.

AHEPA Hosts the King and the Prime Minister
When Crete fell to the German forces in May 1941, King George II, prime minister Emmanuel Tsouderos, government ministers, and units of the Greek army and navy escaped south to Egypt, which was under British control and a major Allied base of operations in the Mediterranean. The exiled government and the military remained in Egypt; the king travelled on to London. In June 1942 the king and the prime minster made a two and a half week visit to the United States, going to Washington, DC, Philadelphia, and New York City. The purpose of the visit was to thank the United States and the Greek Americans for their support and strengthen the ties between the two countries. AHEPA held a banquet in honor of the king and the prime minister at the Astor Hotel with 2,000 guests. It was one of the very few occasions during the visit that both George II and Tsouderos spoke in Greek, and The Ahepan magazine published both speeches in the original. Chebithes was the toastmaster and Supreme President

Nomikos welcomed the honored guests and other dignitaries.

The visit was very successful, but the months that followed would prove increasingly difficult especially for the king because there were increasing concerns that he had not done enough to distance himself from the Metaxas regime. Those concerns were shared by a number of leading Greek Americans, including AHEPA's George Vournas and Basil Vlavianos, the Ethnikos Kyrix newspaper owner from 1940 to 1947. Much stronger feelings against the king existed in Greece, especially the largest resistance group, the left-wing EAM/ELAS. There would be several changes of prime minister during the war, and when Greece was liberated from Axis rule it was considered prudent that while the exiled government, which had become more representative of all Greek political factions, could return, King George II should bide his time in London awaiting political developments.

AHEPA's 20th Anniversary
AHEPA held its 1942 convention in September, in Atlanta, Georgia in honor of its founding in that city in 1922. The gathering was of course less of a celebration and more of a recommitment to AHEPA's backing for America's war effort and its support for Greece through providing much needed food supplies. Nonetheless, there was much to be proud of as AHEPA reached its 20th anniversary, because AHEPA and Greek immigrants more generally were now not only fully considered as Americans, but their virtues were also publicly praised. At the time the convention was getting under way, an Atlanta Constitution columnist, Ralph McGill, wrote: "There are no finer citizens who have come to our country to become citizens than the Greeks. They turn out to be good, substantial essentially patriotic and loyal. You do not read of any Greeks who have been found to be spies against this country. You do not read of any Greek saboteurs. You do not read of any Greeks who serve the enemy. You may read that of the men of most any nation. But not the Greeks." And then he added praise, noting that he liked the way the Greeks got into business, they obeyed the laws and paid their taxes without complaining or evading them. While much of that sentiment reflected the recognition of the Greeks after Greece entered the war on the side of the Allies, the columnist also reserved special praise for AHEPA's role in helping the Greeks

integrate into America. "The members of AHEPA have made a fine contribution to Americanism and to the Americanization of the Greeks who have come to this country… they and their people and their church are a very real asset. They are conservative, honest, and loyal people. They work hard and they make a very real contribution in citizenship." And he concluded his paean by praising Greece for fighting against the Axis. It was a welcome that would have heartened all the delegates who arrived in Atlanta for the convention.[53]

The convention, which opened with a special service officiated by Archbishop Athenagoras, was chaired by former Supreme President Harris J. Booras. In his opening remarks Booras delivered a blistering attack on Germany's use of the category of race and called for the elimination of the concept. The convention passed resolutions of appreciation to the governments of the United States, Great Britain, Canada, and Sweden, for furnishing food, clothing, and medical supplies to the people of Greece. The convention inaugurated a drive to collect funds for the establishment of a home for orphaned children of Greece, as well as to work towards placing those orphans in various homes in the United States, and, if possible, create several units for those children in various locations. In addition, the convention voted to suspend the holding of Supreme Conventions for the duration of the war and passed a resolution pledging solemn support of the government of the United States in every phase of the war effort, including a donation of $650 for radio broadcasts requested by the US Government Office of Facts and Figures. Other decisions included a call to all AHEPA chapters to invest at least 10% of their treasuries in US Defense Bonds; a pledge to continue full support for the GWRA; and it thanked the movie industry for its support of the GWRA.

Supreme Lodge officers elected by the 1942 Atlanta Supreme Convention were: George C. Vournas, Supreme President; Charles Davis Kotsilibas, a businessman from Worcester, Massachusetts, Supreme Vice President; Stephen Scopas, Supreme Secretary; John F. Davis, Supreme Treasurer; Leo Lamberson, Supreme Counsellor; William A. Vasiliou, Supreme Governor; Constantine J. Critzas, Supreme Governor. The election of 45-year-old George Vournas demonstrated that AHEPA was not averse to choosing an outspoken liberal as its leader. Vournas, who was born in the village of Isari in Arcadia, Peloponnesos arrived in the United States at age 17. He settled in Maryland and worked as a bootblack gradually making his way to become a respected Washington, DC attorney. Upon his election Vournas stated that "Greek Americans will continue their wholehearted support of the nation's efforts to bring the war to a quick close."[54]

AHEPA & FDR

As part of the United States' encouragement of the push toward Americanization, AHEPA had been granted the right to an annual visit to the White House and a photo opportunity with the President. While this was always a cordial occasion, AHEPA established a particularly friendly relationship with Franklin Delano Roosevelt who served as the 32nd president of the United States from 1933 to 1945. FDR, as he was known, had become a member of AHEPA's Delphi Chapter 25 in 1931 when he was Governor of New York, and he maintained his membership to the day of his death. AHEPA visited Roosevelt regularly at the White House and he had often sent messages to the Order on special occasions. Under Supreme President Vournas AHEPA cemented the close relationship even further when in March 1943 it presented FDR with a huge bust of himself, the work of sculptor and painter Walter Russel. The bust, which rests on a tall square of red granite, was unveiled in the courtyard of the FDR Library in Hyde Park, New York in 1945. AHEPA would go on to establish a close connection with FDR's successor, President Harry Truman, and to a lesser extent with the next president, Dwight Eisenhower.[55]

The three US Presidents who were members of AHEPA were Roosevelt, Truman, and Gerald Ford.

The National Conference of 1943

Since the Atlanta Supreme Convention voted to suspend Supreme Conventions for the duration of the war, it was decided that the convention elect a Supreme Lodge for the ensuing year, and "that for the duration of the emergency the powers now exercised by this Supreme Convention shall be vested in a conference composed of the Supreme Lodge, the Past Supreme Presidents, and the District Governors, which shall convene in Washington, DC on the third Monday of August as provided for in the Constitution." This action gave the forthcoming conference to be held in Washington, DC, the full powers of a Supreme Convention.

The National Conference was held in Washington, DC for two days, August 16-17, 1943. Supreme President George C. Vournas was absent because he was on military duty in North Africa and was replaced by Acting Supreme President Charles Davis Kotsilibas; Constantine T. Gulas was elected chairman of the conference. On the question of the status of the Supreme Lodge, the Conference affirmed the ruling of the Supreme Counsellor that the Supreme Lodge elected at the 1942 convention would serve in office for the "duration," and until the next regular Supreme Convention of the Order. The term "duration" was then defined to mean "until the day of the cessation of hostilities in the European theatre of war." It was further stated that the suspension of annual conventions had been necessary and proper because of the transportation problem, travel regulations, hotel accommodations, and a desire to help the war effort of the country, which was uppermost in the minds of the delegates of the 1942 Atlanta convention. The meeting decided by ruling that the limited powers of the Conference would be those powers which were not of a legislative nature, and which did not change or amend any of the provisions of the Constitution and by-laws of the Order or any of its convention mandates. It was ruled that the Conference did have the right and power to set the annual Budget of the fraternity, establish war emergency projects, hold membership drives, and pass resolutions for the good of the Order and the promotion of the welfare of the fraternity.

Vournas & the OSS
Supreme President Vournas was very active as well as outspoken during his tenure as president between 1942 and 1945. Ulious Amoss, who had persuaded Roosevelt to join AHEPA back in 1931, had become a senior member of the Office of Strategic Services, a new intelligence agency Roosevelt had created. Amoss recruited Vournas and requested that during his visit to AHEPA chapters across the country he identify young men who could join a military unit of Greek American volunteers who were being trained to eventually fight in Greece. The unit became official when the President issued an executive order in 1943 establishing the 122nd Infantry Battalion, the number 122 being chosen because that year was the 122nd anniversary of the Greek Revolution of 1821. A Vournas recruit,

Peter (Panagiotis) Clainos, a founding member of the Sons of Pericles and a West Point graduate, became the battalion's commander. The battalion grew to the size of a regiment; some of its members went on to the OSS, but most were absorbed into regular army units. Vournas himself travelled to Greece and Egypt where the Allies had their Eastern Mediterranean headquarters. But ultimately, he was considered to be too outspoken against the king and unsuitable for clandestine operations so he returned to the United States to resume his responsibilities as AHEPA's Supreme President.[56]

The 2nd & 3rd National Conferences & Greece's Liberation

The second National Conference of the AHEPA was held in Washington, DC on August 21–22, 1944, Supreme President George C. Vournas safely back and in attendance. Nicholas C. Giovan chaired the conference. Giovan, a Chicagoan, was active in the Order in the 1940s, but he was not a typical AHEPA member. An engineer whose father had founded the earliest ice cream companies in Chicago went on to become a speed boat champion. The work of the Conference consisted of approving a budget; approving the AHEPA War Service Units program with its component parts, the AHEPA War Bond Drive, the American Red Cross Drive, the Greek War Relief Association Drives, the National War Chest Fund, and blood donor campaigns; and recommending that these activities be intensified during the coming year. The Conference also approved a plan calling for the establishment of a Scientific and Historical Research Bureau under the AHEPA War Service Units, whose purpose would be the collecting and disseminating of scientific information helpful to the cause of Greece and the Greek people. Among resolutions passed were: That immediately following declaration of peace, AHEPA schedule a series of excursions to Greece so that members with families in Greece be able to visit that country; that the Supreme Lodge take steps to secure from the US government permission for orphan children of Greece to enter the United States, and that a survey be taken of the fraternity to find sponsors for these children for adoption; that Greece be selected as the initial and first member from smaller nations to the Council of Nations; that an expression of thanks be given to Senator Pepper of Florida for his support of the return of the Dodecanese Islands to Greece; that $1,000 be donated to Pomfret Theological School, and $500 to the West Palm Beach chapter for the three Greek orphans sponsored by the chapter. The conference adjourned with the incumbent Supreme Lodge serving until the next conference or Supreme Convention, depending on the status of the war.

Several weeks after the second National Conference concluded, Greece was liberated from Axis rule when the German armies hastily left in October 1944. They left behind them a country which had been utterly devasted and was also deeply polarized between the political right and the communists and their left-wing allies, who had managed to make significant advances thanks to the role they played in the resistance movement. The polarization came to a head in December 1944 when street fighting broke out for a month in Athens, as Greek army units supported by British forces clashed with and ultimately defeated left-wing guerrilla fighters. An uneasy truce between the two sides was established in early 1945.

The third National Conference was held in Washington, DC on August 20–22, 1945. The Conference resolved: to undertake to assist Greece in every way possible in the proper attainment of her just and meritorious national demands and to do so in ways that were consistent with the rules and regulations of the US government; to obtain volunteer college men and women of Greek extraction to go to Greece to aid in its rehabilitation, and to invite Greek students to America; to express to the Council of Foreign Ministers of the great powers in behalf of the rights and the claims of Greece and its people; to pursue the policy of Supreme President Vournas as to the matter of immigration, so that 2/6 of the German quota be assigned to Greece; to transfer the title of the AHEPA Sanatorium from the Silver District Sanatorium Corporation to the Order of AHEPA. The Conference also approved that a National AHEPA Hospital be established and sponsored by AHEPA in Greece, since it was evident that Greece was sorely in need of such institutions following World War II. The resolution sent to the Council of Foreign Ministers of the great powers requested that, in view of its just rights, Greece be awarded due reparations, the annexation of Epirus, the Dodecanese Islands, and Cyprus, and the rectification of the Bulgarian boundary to provide maximum security for Greece. It was the first of many actions AHEPA would be taking in the years to come in support of Greek national claims, and the number and breadth of the decisions reflected the urgency the members of the Order felt in assisting the homeland.

Elections were held for a new Supreme Lodge. Opposition had been brewing against Vournas, both because of his continued tenure as president and his anti-royalist public stance. Chebithes published a 45-page pamphlet entitled "AHEPA Under Dictatorship" with an exhaustive critique of what he considered Vournas' authoritarianism.[57] The new Supreme Lodge elected for the year 1945–1946 was made up of: Harris J. Booras, who had served as Supreme President in the 1930s, was elected Supreme President; Frank E. Pofanti, a businessman from Chicago, Supreme Vice President; Leo J. Lamberson, Supreme Secretary; C. G. Paris, Supreme Treasurer; Stephen S. Scopas, Supreme Counsellor; George Cotsakis, Supreme Governor; and Nicholas Economou, Supreme Governor. Arthur H. Laios continued as national Executive Secretary at the Washington, DC Headquarters. During the National Conference luncheon, Ted Gamble of the US War Finance department paid tribute to the Order by stating there was no organized group in America who had done a better job in the sale and promotion of War Bonds than the Order of AHEPA.

On the anniversary of the Greek Revolution, March 25, 1945, the Supreme Lodge went to the White House and made President Truman an honorary member of AHEPA. He joined the chapter in Kansas. This was symbolic of the long rise of the Order during its almost 25-year existence. The stature that AHEPA had achieved in just under 25 years of existence is nothing less than remarkable if one considers the difficult circumstances Greek Americans were faced with the early 1920s. AHEPA had contributed mightily to helping them go from being victims of xenophobia to becoming respected American citizens. A significant step had been realized thanks to the sacrificial and voluntary work of thousands of its members across the country.

Part II 1946–1972

Chapter 4:
Cold War & Postwar Reconstruction 1946–1956

As the guns of World War II finally grew silent and peace returned, AHEPA and the Greek American community emerged as a respected and integral part of American society. AHEPA could claim a great deal of credit for this as well as the way it offered aid to Greece during the wartime era through the Greek War Relief Association. Now, a new world was taking shape, and AHEPA needed to adapt and respond to those changes if it was to maintain its role as the major Greek American institution next to the Greek Orthodox Church. What needed to be done quickly became apparent, thanks to the emergence of the Cold War that involved both the United States and Greece. Domestically, along with other European ethnic organizations, AHEPA reiterated its loyalty to America and its Cold War goals, thus claiming a place in the American mainstream. In terms of foreign policy, the significant role the United States began to play in Greece in the postwar era offered AHEPA a wonderful opportunity to serve both America and its homeland in the same breath in help for postwar reconstruction. AHEPA also stood by the homeland through its support for the union of the Aegean Dodecanese Islands with Greece in the immediate postwar era, and for the union of Cyprus with Greece in the 1950s. Another issue that AHEPA was monitoring throughout the 1950s was the lingering matter of the determination of the frontier line between Greece and its northern borders, including Greek claims on Northern Epirus, the region in southern Albania inhabited by a large Greek ethnic element.

Even as Greece began the task of rebuilding its ruined infrastructure, it first had to confront a communist insurgency that developed into a civil war fought between 1946 and 1949 mainly in the northern mountainous part of the country. It was the result of the collapse of the uneasy truce that had been established in early 1945. Observers have put the blame on both sides, citing instances of violence inflicted from either side that escalated while the right-wing leaning governments proved unable or unwilling to control the situation. In 1946 the communist party, which still retained the large following it had acquired during the war, decided to abstain from the national elections citing the victimization of its supporters. This paved the way for the government to hold a referendum on whether King George II should return from exile. The result, as expected, was an overwhelming approval. Yet this last phase of his reign was short-lived because he died in April of 1947 and was succeeded by his son Paul. But meanwhile, the communist forces amassed in the northern part of the country launched attacks on the army and the police and very soon the country sank into a fully-fledged civil war.

The civil war triggered direct US involvement in Greece and brought the two countries closer together. After Britain announced as of March 1947 it would no longer provide military and economic assistance to the Greek government in its growing conflict with communist forces challenging its authority and claiming to defend left-wing Greeks from persecution, President Truman asked Congress to support the Greek government and provide assistance for Turkey because of its border with the Soviet Union. Congress' approval led to what became known as the Truman Doctrine. Congress duly appropriated financial aid to support the economies and militaries of Greece and Turkey. This would prove crucial in determining the outcome of the Greek civil war in favor of the government forces. A few years later, both the United States and Greece solidified their diplomatic and military alliance when they both joined the North Atlantic Treaty Organization (NATO).

AHEPA at 25: Setting the Agenda for the Next Decade

In July 1947 AHEPA celebrated its silver or 25th anniversary with a gathering of about 300 members hosted by the Order's Mother Lodge in Atlanta. The meeting paid tribute to the founders Harry Angel, James Campbell, Nick Chotas, Spiros J. Stamos, and James Vlass, all of whom were present. Within 25 years from its founding in Atlanta AHEPA had grown to an organization with over 40,000 members and almost 400 chapters around the country along with women's, young men's, and young women's auxiliaries. It was an extraordinary achievement. The July-August 1947 issue of The Ahepan magazine was a "silver jubilee edition" that commemorated the 25th anniversary. Its contents included a summary of the Order's history that concluded with the following assessment: "The AHEPA can look back on its accomplishments with pride... it has spent millions of dollars on charitable causes... it has sought out and championed every cause that elevates man to the exalted position he should occupy on earth, as intended by our Lord and Maker; it has sponsored education in its broadest aspects and has devotedly fought against movements intended to stop the progress of the world and thus we can look to this AHEPA of ours which now consists of 369 chapters in the United States and Canada, and sincerely say it has rendered 25 years of constructive service."[58]

The 25th anniversary event came in between the first two conventions AHEPA held in the postwar era in 1946 and 1947, which discussed its future in a new era and pointed to the broad range of domestic and international initiatives the Order was contemplating. On the domestic front there were measures to bolster AHEPA's anti-communist image and to offer privileges to returning war veterans, which was also a way it could bolster its membership. The international initiatives included aiding Greece directly by building medical facilities, supporting Greece's territorial claims, and, in a move that would consume a great deal of its energies, push for a greater number of Greeks to immigrate to the United States. Legislation on relaxing immigration rules would be enacted in 1948 but there was growing debate in the years leading up to that, and AHEPA was involved. The idea was that populations that endured wartime conditions would benefit from the opportunity to emigrate to the United States, especially where reconstruction was proceeding slowly. AHEPA would be centrally involved in a succession of measures gradually introduced by the US Congress in the next few years that opened the way for the immigration to the United States of Europeans, including Greeks, whose lives had been affected by war.

In 1946, the 24th Supreme Convention was held in Baltimore, Maryland during the week of August 22-28 with Nicholas Giovan as chair. Aside from the presence of Supreme Lodge members, Mother Lodge members, Past Supreme Presidents, and district governors, there were 312 chapter delegates attending the Baltimore Convention. General Alexandros Papagos, the Marshall of the Greek Army, who was touring the United States, was the convention's honored guest and was made an honorary life member. In his speech Papagos discussed Greece's claims at the upcoming post-World War II Peace Conference in Paris, which included the union of the Dodecanese Islands with Greece, an extension of Greece's northern borders to include Northern Epirus in the southern part of Albania, and moving the Greek-Bulgarian border northwards. Papagos became prime minister following the national elections of 1952 and served until his death in 1955, when he was succeeded by Constantine Karamanlis, whose first two consecutive terms in office lasted until 1963. AHEPA had already mobilized around those issues. It had formed a "Justice for Greece" committee with several other Greek American organizations in 1945. The committee's leader was Past Supreme President of AHEPA George Phillies. The committee sought to draw support from both Greek Americans and American friends of Greece through direct contacts and an extensive public relations program.[59]

When the AHEPA Supreme Convention got down to business, Supreme Vice President Frank E. Pofanti, who had been named as one of several Ahepan champion bond salesmen during the war, stated that the two most important issues on the agenda were the hospital program for Greece and support for Greece's claims at the upcoming Paris Peace Conference. The range of decisions taken at the Baltimore convention showed AHEPA's vision for its evolution in the postwar era. There was an extension of special initiation fees for returning veterans and a decision to support all pending congressional legislation and future legislation for the benefit of veterans of World War II. With a view to bolstering the Order's membership, the convention decided to increase the number of Supreme Governors to four, stating that one of the Supreme Governors would be from Canada, and it limited the number of terms of a Supreme President to two terms. With regard to AHEPA's support of Greece, the convention left the scheduling of an excursion to Greece in 1948 to the discretion of the Supreme Lodge; it mandated that the Justice for Greece Committee that was focused on the union of the Dodecanese with Greece be continued for the ensuing year and that all chapters give full support to the Committee even though the; it instructed the Immigration Committee to advocate a change of quota laws to the government and that the Greek quota be increased; it decided that the AHEPA Hospitals in Greece program be continued. And the convention agreed with the Greek War Relief's proposal to match on a 50-50 basis in money or material in kind any amount of money raised by AHEPA through its hospital drive, that such monies to be used for hospitals in Greece, and that the Greek War Relief should execute the physical end of this agreement for administrative and technical services. There was a closely contested election for Supreme President at the Baltimore convention between the incumbent Harris Booras and Louisiana oilman and racetrack owner William G. Helis. Booras won narrowly, but in a gesture of reconciling the two sides it was decided that Helis should become Vice President. The others who were elected were Nicholas Giovan as Supreme Secretary; Aristides Georgiades, Supreme Treasurer; Zack T. Ritsos, a lawyer from Chicago, Supreme Counsellor; T. Bass, Supreme Governor; William Petros, Supreme Governor.[60]

On April 1, 1947, AHEPA held its first postwar excursion to Greece, which was also the first airborne one. Twenty-four members, headed by Supreme President Booras, flew to Athens from Boston in a Trans World Airlines plane. The trip took 30 hours with three stopovers. King George of Greece died while the plane was en route, and the Ahepans attended the coronation of the new King Paul after their arrival in Athens. The Ahepans were enthusiastically received by the people of Greece and given several receptions and visited with King Paul. They also laid the cornerstone for the AHEPA hospital in Athens, and the cornerstone for the AHEPA hospital in Thessaloniki. The civil war hostilities were occurring further north and mainly in the mountainous regions.

The following year, the 25th Supreme Convention was held in Los Angeles during the week of August 17–23, 1947, with 333 chapter delegates attending. The convention was taking place a few months after the announcement of the Truman Doctrine and a great deal of the convention was taken up by statements of AHEPA's support. Archbishop Athenagoras told delegates that of all political systems in the world, America's political system was the closest to ancient Greek democracy. The members of the new Supreme Lodge who were elected were: William G. Helis, Supreme President; John G. Thevos, Supreme Vice President; Peter L. Bell, Supreme Secretary; Aristides Georgiades, Supreme Treasurer; Zack Ritsos, Supreme Counsellor; Peter N. Derzis, Supreme Governor; George Bezaitis, Supreme Governor; James J. Starr, Supreme Governor; Tim Bass, Supreme Governor. William G. Helis, the new Supreme President, was one of the most prominent Greek Americans of his era. He was a millionaire oilman based in Louisiana who had also served as president of the Greek War Relief Association. Helis had emigrated from the village of Tropaia in Arcadia and arrived in the United States in 1904 at the age of 17. Aside from his business acumen he was known for his love of horse racing and called "The Golden Greek of Turf." He retained close ties with Greece, where he and his son invested in drilling before World War II, and he became a friend of King Paul of Greece. He was decorated by Greece and named Honorary Consul in New Orleans. Helis was outspoken when it came to recounting the core Greek American narrative of the Greeks having arrived with no money and not knowing the language but having done well, and he was certainly an example of that immigrant success story. He blended it with public affirmations of loyalty to America and condemnation of communism, and portrayed aid to Greece as a way of proving the superiority of life in America and a way of "stopping communism in its tracks," as he put it. This was very typical of the language organizations such as AHEPA used at a time when the Cold War was getting underway. Another development in that era was the beginning of the civil rights movement. Although Greek Americans were not directly involved, it is notable that the first issue of The Ahepan magazine in 1948 published an article condemning racism by Walter White, the Executive Secretary of the National Association of Colored People.

The 26th Supreme Convention, 1948, Detroit

AHEPA held its 26th Supreme Convention during the week of August 15–21, 1948, in Detroit, Michigan, where there were 423 chapter delegates in attendance. The convention decided that the Supreme Lodge have authority to hold an excursion to Greece in 1949 if conditions permitted—in fact very soon AHEPA was able to resume its annual excursions to Greece which continued throughout the 1950s; to establish an AHEPA Job Placement Bureau for veterans; that a student loan fund be established; to try to effect a summer program in Greece for members of the AHEPA family between the ages of 18 and 30, the expenses to be derived from voluntary contributions from chapters; that the Districts issue monthly or bi-monthly publications for their respective memberships; that all colleges and universities be encouraged to offer Greek language courses; that a Public Relations Committee be established by the Supreme Lodge, and chapter public relations councils be also established; raised the Per Capita Tax to $5 per year per member; that the chapters be asked to give financial aid to the people on the island of Lefkada. This extraordinary range of goals the convention set is emblematic of the way AHEPA, throughout its history, has adopted the widest possible lens in addressing issues important to Greek Americans. The following were elected as the new Supreme Lodge: William G. Helis, Supreme President; John G. Thevos, Supreme Vice President; Peter L. Bell, Supreme Secretary; James J. Starr, Supreme Treasurer; A. A. Pantelis, Supreme Counsellor; Peter Grammar, a confectionery store owner from St. Catherine's near Niagara Falls, Supreme Governor for Canada; Peter Derzis, Supreme Governor; George Bezaitis, Supreme Governor; Charles N. Diamond, Supreme Governor.

In 1948, two AHEPA Health Centers were created in Greece, a quick implementation of a decision taken at the 1947 convention in Los Angeles. It mandated the creation of health centers that had been envisioned by the Greek War Relief Association in the provinces. They would be built in Chrysoupolis in northern Greece; Ierapetra on Crete; Kalavryta, Meligala in Peloponnesos; and Paramythia in Epirus. There was also one at Thebes that was completed and ready for use around the time the Ierapetra AHEPA Health Center in Crete was dedicated in late November of 1948. Those centers were eventually absorbed by the Greek public health system and AHEPA's contributions have receded in memory. But in 2022, Iordanis Vlachopoulos, who as a young boy received treatment at the Chrysoupolis health center, published an account of the history of that center, which was inaugurated in March of 1948. He writes that the architectural design of those centers was assigned to a Greek American architectural company, Kokkinis and Lyras, and that everything to the last screw was imported from the United States. The medical equipment was state of the art. Sadly, the author reports, when his sister was born there in 1954 the center was almost an empty hulk because the authorities deemed it appropriate to move all the medical equipment to the hospital of the nearby town of Kavala. Whether this was done with AHEPA's approval or not is not known. But this story invites further research on the creation and functioning of the other health centers that were constructed at the time.[61]

AHEPA & the Displaced Persons Act of 1948

In 1948 the US Congress approved the Displaced Persons Act which authorized for a limited period the admission into the United States of 200,000 certain European displaced persons (DPs) for permanent residence. This immigration program emerged from the enormous need to handle millions of displaced persons in Europe at the end of World War II. President Truman signed the Act reluctantly because he considered it too restrictive. One strong objection was that it took away previous immigration quota places from others already on quota waiting lists, and simply transferred these places to DPs, and did this forwardly for as many years as needed by DPs (mortgaging the future years' places). Another strong objection was that the details of the Act caused it to discriminate against Jewish DPs very heavily. Greece, which had been seriously afflicted by the war and the civil war, was affected by the restrictive quotas imposed in 1924. Realizing the need for the Act to be amended to allow greater numbers of Greeks to be entitled to enter the United States, AHEPA joined the efforts that began in Congress to relax the restrictions of the Act. Supreme President Helis submitted a detailed memorandum to congressional hearings that were held in March 1949, requesting that 50,000 persons from Greece be allowed to enter the United States. AHEPA's memorandum mentioned the responsibilities felt by Greek Americans, noting: "Every American of Greek extraction is deeply conscious of his obligations as an American citizen. He feels with equal keenness his duty to his family and his blood relations. It is for both of these reasons that the Greek-Americans are unanimously behind this effort to amend the Displaced Persons law. The Greek-Americans want to support the Greek refugees who come to America. As patriotic Americans they see no reason why Americans of non-Greek extraction should be asked or expected to support Greek refugees. To the extent that these displaced persons are permitted to come to America there will be a lessening of the tax burden on other Americans and a reduction in the emergency relief problem in Greece."[62]

The memorandum reflects the way AHEPA represented and spoke for all Greek Americans. Among the many ethnic and religious institutions that were submitting memoranda to Congress, AHEPA's was the only Greek American voice. Its tone also evokes the sincere feelings of goodwill that defined the Order's involvement in the effort to enable as many Greeks as possible to escape the war-torn circumstances in the homeland and start a new life in the United States. Unfortunately, toward the end of the decade certain individuals would be accused of corrupt practices, especially with the transfer of Greek children without families to American parents. Those abuses were grave and injurious to many children. But they should in no way detract from the well-meaning involvement of AHEPA in improving the lives of many Greeks.

Allowing more Greeks to enter the United States was one of the main issues at the 27th Supreme Convention that was held in Miami, Florida, during the week of August 15–21, 1949. It was also the subject that the Daughters of Penelope were promoting. The convention was chaired by John K. Douglas, and there 224 chapter delegates in attendance. Bishop Germanos Polyzoides of New York, the Acting Archbishop, offered the invocation. Archbishop Athenagoras was already installed as Ecumenical Patriarch of Constantinople in Istanbul after his election in 1948 and Bishop Germanos was the Acting Archbishop pending the election of Athenagoras' successor. He performed the first service of the new Greek Orthodox church in Miami, St. Sophia, on Sunday, the day before the AHEPA convention opened. On that Sunday the Miami Herald devoted an entire page to discussing the convention and the new church under a banner headline that read "Welcome AHEPA" in Greek.[63] The convention issued a resolution urging the Senate and the House of Representatives to take immediate and favorable action on an amendment to the Displaced Persons Act of 1948 so as to permit at least 50,000 Greek orphans, and other refugees in Greece who have been driven from their homes as a result of the communist war, to enter the United States during the years 1949 and 1950 under the provisions of the Displaced Persons Act and without regard to the existing Quota of Limitations on Greek Immigration. The convention also decided that a permanent National Immigration Committee be appointed by the Supreme Lodge. In addition, and somewhat differently from working toward helping Greeks emigrate to the United States, the Convention also endorsed the work of the Foster Parent Plan for War Children and urged chapters and members to work for and with the plan, which involved Americans sponsoring children abroad, in other words supporting them while they remained in their own countries.

The other highlights of the convention included the announcement that the US Treasury Department had made Savings Bonds Awards to both the Order of AHEPA, and the Daughters of Penelope; the decision that the final title of the AHEPA Sanatorium be given to the Supreme Lodge of the Order of AHEPA, and that neither the whole property nor any part of it be sold, or leased for longer than five years, without vote of the Supreme Convention; and the election of Chris Athas, a pharmacist from Salt Lake City, George E. Johnson, and John Manta as Directors of the AHEPA Sanatorium property. The delegates elected John G. Thevos Supreme President. At 37 years old, the new president was young in age for such a position, though he did not lack experience as a dedicated member of AHEPA and had already served in several key positions. Thevos' age was noted by V. I. Chebithes, who spoke at a dinner held in honor of the newly elected Supreme President in his home state of New Jersey. Chebithes remarked that AHEPA was entering "a young man's era" and that it expected a lot from the second generation of leaders.[64] Thevos, who at the time was a Board of Education Commissioner in New Jersey and who was reelected for a second term as Supreme President, would justify Chebithes' expectations through his work toward revitalizing moribund AHEPA chapters and creating new ones, working toward and fostering friendship between the United States and Greece, for which he was decorated twice by Greece. And it was Thevos who, later on, originally conceived of and proposed the erection of a statue of President Truman in Athens.[65] The others who were elected were Constantine G. Economou from Youngstown, Ohio, who had served in many senior positions in the Order, Supreme Vice President; Peter Derzis, Supreme Secretary; Charles Preketes, Supreme Treasurer; Peter L. Bell, Supreme Counsellor; Pantelis B. Lambros, Supreme Governor; Constantine P. Verinis, Supreme Governor; Peter Grammar, Supreme Governor for Canada.

In 1949 Past District Governor Anthony Aroney visited the AHEPA chapters in Australia and reported to the Supreme Lodge that there were six chapters in the states of Queensland and New South Wales and seven chapters in the formative stage in the state of Victoria, in western and southern Australia.

Meanwhile up in the mountains of northern Greece the last battles of the civil war were being fought until the war officially concluded at the end of August 1949. It left Greece with additional devastation and loss of life, along with a deep and visceral right versus left polarization that would remain for a very long time.

AHEPA and the Cypriot Struggle for "Enosis" with Greece

In January 1950 the Greek population in Cyprus, 82% of the total number of inhabitants of the island, held a referendum on the proposition that Cyprus achieve union (enosis) with Greece. The result was that 97.7% approved the proposition. The event kick-started the struggle of the Greek Cypriots to end British colonial rule on the island and satisfy their longstanding demand for Cyprus to become incorporated into Greece. On April 1, 1955, the struggle became militant with the EOKA organization launching a guerilla war against the British. Throughout this period AHEPA rallied to the side of the Greek Cypriots. Even before the referendum, with Greek Cypriot agitation on the rise, the Supreme Convention in 1948 urged the United States to support the demands of the people of Cyprus for the return of the island to Greece. In August 1950, the 28th Supreme Convention stated that AHEPA favored a means of achieving union of the Island of Cyprus with Greece and that the matter should be placed on the agenda of the Congress and the United Nations. The following year the Supreme Convention decided that the Cyprus Committee that had been formed continue its work to achieve annexation of Cyprus to Greece. The 32nd Supreme Convention in 1954 decided that AHEPA would petition the United Nations to vote in favor of incorporation and unification of Cyprus with Greece. Following the 1954 Supreme Convention, AHEPA formed a National Advisory Board of the Justice for Cyprus Committee. It was composed of more than 150 members of Congress and 21 state governors.

Following the outbreak of the armed struggle led by EOKA the situation in Cyprus became even more critical. In 1956, the British government ordered the arrest and exile of Archbishop Makarios of Cyprus, and this action brought down protests from throughout the world. AHEPA requested that government leaders to seek an amicable and just solution to the Cyprus problem. That same year, the Justice for Cyprus Committee became permanent and AHEPA also requested the assistance of the United States government toward the solution of the Cyprus question and granting the Greek Cypriots their right of self-determination.

The 28th Supreme Convention, 1950, Cleveland
The 28th Supreme Convention was held in Cleveland, Ohio during the week of August 14–20, 1950, and the following were elected convention officers: Louis J. Dukas, Chairman; in addition, there were 294 chapter delegates in attendance. The convention approved the following: that AHEPA express its appreciation to the Save the Children Federation for its work, and that all members and chapters support this program; that the historic Macedonian borderline of Greece be safeguarded for the protection of Macedonia and of Greece; that the AHEPA Florida Property in Pinellas County, Florida be offered for lease either for farming, cattle grazing or cattle raising, or citrus farming; to continue the scholarship funds under the supervision of the Supreme Lodge; to urge the Congress and the United Nations to clearly establish the boundaries of Northern Epirus and reaffirm the Greek territorial jurisdiction thereof; to authorize and direct the new Supreme Lodge to implement the action of Congress of allowing 10,000 Greek persons and orphans to enter the United States by establishing an AHEPA Displaced Persons Board of nine members, and

appropriating $10,000 for the operation of the Board; appropriated $2,000 for the relocation of the AHEPA bust of President Roosevelt to a more suitable site at Hyde Park; appropriated $5,000 as a donation to St. Basil's Academy, Garrison, New York; appropriated $500 as a donation to the American Friends of the Blind in Greece, Inc.; raised $600 from the floor of the convention as a donation to the New Orleans Holy Trinity Church; and elected the following to the AHEPA Displaced Persons Committee: Louis Dukas, a New York attorney; George A. Polos (Mother Lodge member); Nick Copanos, a restaurant owner in Ohio; Chris Anton, Charles N. Diamond, James Veras, George Papanicolas, Leo Ypsilanti. The elections for the new Supreme Lodge were contested. John Thevos defeated Constantine (Gus) Economou in the vote for Supreme President; Leo J. Lamberson defeated Peter Bell in the vote for Supreme Vice President; Zack Ritsos defeated James Dikea in the vote for Supreme Secretary; George T. Geroulis defeated Charles Preketes in the vote for Supreme Treasurer. The others who were elected were William D. Belroy, Supreme Counsellor; Nick Jamson, Supreme Governor; Socrates V. Sekles, Supreme Governor; Peter V. Paulus, Supreme Governor; Stanley Galanos, a restaurant owner in Ottawa, Supreme Governor of Canada.

President Truman sent a message to the Cleveland convention: "Greece, the ancient homeland of members of AHEPA and their forebears, has long been the battleground of freedom. Through the centuries, as in more recent years, Greece has learned that only through constant struggle can those freedoms be maintained which are the basis of all our happiness as Americans. A few years ago, the proud Hellenic people met and overcame a totalitarian assault on their freedom comparable with the attempted enslavement of Korea which the world witnesses today. Soon after the war ended five years ago it became apparent that one powerful nation did not want world recovery and would not respect the freedom of small nations. Our own country by wholehearted support of the United Nations bore witness to its faith in freedom. We backed our choice with deeds. Besides supporting the U.N., we carried out a practical program of European recovery and military assistance in the common defense of free nations. The field for service today in the cause of world peace and justice in the world is limitless. May I, as my message to the convention in Cleveland, express the hope that AHEPA will again dedicate itself by word and deed to the cause of liberty with peace and justice to all nations." AHEPA maintained its close ties with President Truman and continued its annual visits to the White House to meet with the president.

The AHEPA Displaced Persons Committee Moves into Gear
Herve J. L'Heureux, Chief of the Visa Division, US State Department in Washington, addressed the Cleveland convention, and explained the provisions of the amendment to the Displaced Persons Act allowing for the entry of 10,000 Greek refugees into the United States. US General James A. Van Fleet, who directed the successful war against communist guerrillas in Greece, as head of American aid to Greece, also spoke to the convention. It must be noted that only American advisors were on the scene in Greece during the civil war, and that no American soldiers or American service men took any active part in the fighting. In his address, General Van Fleet said: "Whether by cold or hot war, communism must be destroyed and the sooner the better. Communism is a ruthless enemy; it plays no rules. We have seen in Greece that the communists even shot their own wounded. Greece set an example to the world what a courageous people can do to defeat communism. It was first in Greece that the line of Western civilization was held in bloody war against world communism." The AHEPA Displaced Persons Committee immediately went to work after the convention and sent instructions to all chapters and members on procedures, requesting that chapters obtain sponsors for the Greek refugees who would provide employment, living quarters, and the necessary funds to bring the refugees to the United States. It was pointed out that the Order of AHEPA had been designated as "an arm of the government of the United States in administering the resettlement of 10,000 Greek refugees."

US Attorney General J. Howard McGrath wrote to AHEPA on its AHEPA Displaced Persons Committee: "It is organizations such as AHEPA that have been instrumental in making this (Displaced Persons Act) humanitarian activity possible; and it is organizations such as yours, together with Federal and State Commissions, volunteer local agencies and patriotic individual sponsors, working in team-like fashion, that have been doing the magnificent job with the newcomers that American society desired. As service to mankind has ever been the guiding spirit of your organization, I know the members of the Order of AHEPA will meet this important challenge by happily and ably doing their part of the work that is essential in making the Displaced Persons movement a complete success." The AHEPA Displaced Persons Committee was certified as a voluntary agency by the Advisory Committee on Voluntary Foreign Aid of the United States government. The Certificate of Registration issued on November 17, 1950, reads: "This is to certify that Order of AHEPA Displaced Persons Committee is accepted for registration with the Advisory Committee on Voluntary Foreign Aid of the Department of State, effective November 15, 1950, and is assigned Registration No. VFA 058. Registration No. VFA 058 shall remain valid under the terms of 'Acceptance and Termination' in the Conditions of Agency Registration issued September 1, 1948, or any amendments thereto, and until the termination date as established by the Displaced Persons Act of 1948, as amended by Public Law 555- 8lsL Congress." Besides the AHEPA office at Washington, DC, the committee also opened an office at the New York Port of Entry and set its goal of bringing 10,000 Greek refugees to the United States before the deadline of June 30, 1951, as set by the law itself.[66]

Taking a Stand Against Communism

In the late 1940s and early 1950s the United States witnessed the rise of McCarthyism, in a wave of unsubstantiated allegations of the existence of subversives and traitors in the United States secretly working for the cause of communism. The new "Red Scare" is known to have alarmed members of European ethnic groups whose homelands had experienced post-World War II active communist movements with or without the imposition of Soviet rule. The response of those groups was loudly proclaiming their loyalty to the United States and their implacable rejection of anything that could be deemed communist or socialist. This continued at least until the mid-1950s when the main propagator, Senator Joseph McCarthy, was censured by the Senate and the fears he had generated began to subside.

The Greek Americans were no exception to the pattern of reactions among European ethnic groups, and this was shown especially by the anti-communist proclamations at the 29th Supreme Convention was held in Minneapolis, Minnesota, in August of 1951. Chaired by Van A. Nomikos, the proceedings included 322 chapter delegates in attendance. The convention emphasized AHEPA's opposition to communism and any other "ism" which threatened the American way of life and the dignity and freedom of the individual, and repeated the Order's protests at the removal of 28,000 Greek children from Greece by communists during the Greek civil war and called upon the United Nations and all other parties for their return to Greece. The convention also established a permanent National AHEPA Hospitals Committee for Greece and named Past Supreme President Harris Booras as permanent Chairman for his "work as author and moving spirit in the success of the program"; it continued the scholarship program; it mandated the Supreme Lodge seek bids for the sale of the Florida Property, and seek a more suitable property near Tarpon Springs, Florida for the creation of a Rest Home for the Aged; that the Sunday before Memorial Day be set aside for memorial services for departed members; and it raised the age limit for members of the Sons of Pericles to 25 years. Chairman George Polos of the AHEPA Displaced Persons Committee reported that the committee had completed its goal of resettlement of 10,000 displaced persons from Greece to the United States, and that more than 40,000 had filed for refugee status in Greece. He also reported that efforts were being mainly pushed for the resettlement of Greek orphans which was a major area of relief in Greece. The red tape, processing, and securing of visas had proved to be an enormous task, which necessitated offices of the committee in Greece, as well as in the United States. The committee was also endeavoring to get Congress to pass another bill to allow an additional number of displaced persons to come to the United States from Greece. On the question of the original Displaced Persons Act of 1948, it was noted that the United States allowed 300,000 displaced persons to come to America within a short period of time, but up to the end of 1950, Greeks were not included in the legislation. A critic of this lack of consideration of the Greeks stated: "We have the greatest respect and compunction for all of these people. They were or are displaced as the victims of religious and political persecution. But, outside of the Polish people, few if any of these people were participants in and victims of active warfare on America's side. They did not lose their homes, their property and their loved ones while fighting and resisting the enemy as America's allies. The Greeks did. And therein lies the difference and the greatest injustice to America's staunchest, most dependable, and faithful ally. We shall always wonder and will ever be mystified as to why the special groups that sponsored this Displaced Persons legislation through Congress failed to include a Greek quota in the law. The Order of AHEPA, to rectify this mistake, sponsored, and the United States Congress gave Greece a ten thousand quota for 1951."

The new Supreme Lodge elected included Peter L. Bell, an attorney from Worcester, Massachusetts, Supreme President; Anthony Aroney, Supreme Vice President; Constantine Verinis, Supreme Secretary; George Geroulis, Supreme Treasurer; Louis J. Dukas, Supreme Counsellor; Socrates V. Sekles, Supreme Governor; John A. Kiamos, Supreme Governor; Tom Ralles, Supreme Governor; Stanley Galanos, Supreme Governor for Canada.

The 10th National Biennial Banquet honoring the Congress of the United States was held in Washington on March 24, 1952, at the Statler Hotel. George Cazana was chairman, and Past Supreme President John G. Thevos was toastmaster. The Greek-born Cazana was a somewhat unusual choice as chair of an AHEPA banquet because he was a well-known promoter of sports events, especially wrestling. One of the wrestlers with whom Cazana had a close relationship was Greek American George Zaharias, the husband of the legendary athlete Babe Didrikson Zaharias.[67] Principal speakers were US Secretary of the Interior Chapman, US Senator Charles Tobey of New Hampshire, Commissioner of Immigration Argyle MacKay, and Secretary of Agriculture Charles F. Brannan. Two awards were given that night to outstanding Greek Americans, Spyros P. Skouras for his services as President of the Greek War Relief Association, and Dr. George Papanicolaou of Cornell University for his discoveries in methods of detecting cancer in its early stages.

The 30th Supreme Convention, 1952, Washington, DC
The 30th Supreme Convention was held in Washington, DC during the week of August 17–23, 1952, and was chaired by Stephen S. Scopas and included 412 chapter delegates in attendance. Mandates of the convention were: setting the National Advisory Board of the Sons of Pericles at seven members, with the AHEPA Supreme Vice President

to automatically be the Chairman; to establish a National AHEPA Education Week each year the last week of January; to continue the National athletic program as set up in previous years, with Chapter, District and National tournaments and competitions; a request that the official AHEPA fez be worn at all AHEPA functions; a request that chapters sponsor annual social functions with all proceeds to be donated to the orphanage and school at St. Basil's Academy in Garrison, New York; the election of a new AHEPA Displaced Persons Committee consisting of Harris J. Booras, John G. Thevos, and C. G. Paris; and giving the Supreme Lodge the right to lease the Albuquerque Sanatorium land for up to 30 years.

The new Supreme Lodge members elected by the Washington convention were Peter L. Bell, Supreme President; Stephen S. Scopas, Supreme Vice President; Constantine Verinis, Supreme Secretary; Stephen L. Berdalis, Supreme Treasurer; Louis J. Dukas, Supreme Counsellor; Speros A. Versis, Supreme Governor; Peter Kourmoules, Supreme Governor; Speros J. Zepatos, Supreme Governor; Chris D. Tsipuras of Montreal, Supreme Governor for Canada.

President Truman sent the following message to the convention: "Meeting in the nation's capital has special significance for our Order, which is deeply devoted to increasing the friendship between the people of Greece and of the United States. I doubt if this friendship has ever been at a higher level than it is today. With our help the people of Greece have made great forward strides in recovering from the ravages of war and have withstood the attempts of communist imperialism to destroy Greece itself. This friendship is symbolized in Korea where Greek and American soldiers are fighting side by side in defense of the highest principles of justice and freedom. We must never forget that we owe the concept of democracy—even the word itself—to the ancient Greeks. Love of freedom lives on in the soul of the Greek people. It is perpetuated in the political institutions the Greece of antiquity gave to the entire modern world. You have my best wishes for a most successful and enjoyable convention."[68]

AHEPA and President Eisenhower
Truman's message to the 1952 convention was his last as president because following the November 1952 elections Dwight D. Eisenhower became the 34th President of the United States. He would be

reelected to a second term in 1956. At the inaugural parade for Eisenhower held in Washington, DC in January 1953, the fraternity sponsored an AHEPA Float, and the motto on the float was: "AHEPA Promoting Citizenship." The project was initiated by Ahepan George Papanicolas of Washington, DC, and was paid for with contributions from members of the Order. The Supreme Lodge's first visit to the White House to meet the President took place in March 1953 and was repeated every year.

Alfange's Creed

Past Supreme President Dean Alfange was one of the most important figures in AHEPA in the 1920s and the 1930s and was also well-known for his political activities. He ran for New York State Governor on the American Labor Party ticket in 1942 against Thomas E. Dewey, and was a strong advocate of the New Deal and a great admirer of Franklin D. Roosevelt. During World War II Alfange was an outspoken advocate for US aid to Greece and he was also the Vice Chairman of the Emergency Committee to Save the Jewish People of Europe. He made speeches for aid to the Jews against the Nazis, and at a hearing before the Foreign Affairs Committee in the House of Representatives submitted a plan to save the Jews in Europe. After World War II he became chairman of the Committee to Arm the Jewish State, a group aimed at lifting the arms embargo on Palestine. Alfange was instrumental in the formation of the Liberal Party in 1944 when the American Labor Party split between pro-communist and anti-communist factions. However, crossing party lines, Alfange held nominations or appointments from Democrats and Republicans as well as the Liberal and American Labor Party. As early as 1954 he expressed opposition to the American policy of military aid to the French government in Indo-China, his position being one based on anti-colonialism. This position continued throughout America's involvement in the Viet Nam conflict.

In 1952 Alfange authored a few lines which he entitled "My Creed," which received widespread use and was quoted many times in publications over the succeeding years: "I do not choose to be a common man. It is my right to be uncommon—if I can. I seek opportunity—not security. I do not wish to be a kept citizen, humbled and dulled by having the state look after me. I want to take the calculated risk; to dream and to build, to fail and to succeed. I refuse to barter incentive for a dole. I prefer the challenges of life to the guaranteed existence, the thrill of fulfilment to the stale calm of utopia. I will not trade my freedom for beneficence nor my dignity for a handout. I will never cower before any master nor bend to any threat. It is my heritage to stand erect, proud, and unafraid; to think and act for myself, enjoy the benefit of my creations and to face the world boldly and say, this I have done. All this is what it means to be an American."

The Knights of Thermopylae

Past Supreme President Harris J. Booras organized a group of donors, the "Knights of Thermopylae," for the purpose of erecting a monument at Thermopylae commemorating the stand of Leonidas and 300 Spartans in 480 BC against the invading forces of Emperor Xerxes of Persia. It was an idea by George Dousmanis, a citizen of Sparta in Greece, but there had been no way to raise enough funds until Booras got involved. Another statue of the lawgiver Lycurgus was to be unveiled in Sparta. Membership in the organization was limited to 300 persons. The "Knights" traveled to Greece for the ceremonies associated with both unveilings, which took place with a great deal of pomp in July 1955, during which the 16-foot bronze statue was unveiled. The names of the 300 Greek Americans whose donations funded the creation of the statue appeared on the back side of the stone base but because of their Greek names some visitors were confused and thought those were the names of the Spartan fighters. The names were replaced by a plaque in Greek and in English that reads: "Original donation by George Dousmanis of Sparta completed in 1955 at the expense of a foundation of 300 Americans of Hellenic origin and on the initiative of Harry J. Booras."

Earthquake Aid to Greece

In the early 1950s Greece was struck by a succession of devastating earthquakes. The first occurred in early August 1953 on the Ionian islands off the western coast of mainland Greece. The islands of Cephalonia, Zakynthos and Ithaca were leveled and up to 800 people lost their lives. From the 33,300 buildings of these three islands, 27,659 were completely destroyed. The second earthquake hit in 1954 in Thessaly in central Greece, killing 25 persons and destroying 6,559 buildings. The third big earthquake hit the town of Volos, also in Thessaly, and destroyed one in four houses in the city and damaged 80% of all buildings. A few days after the first of those earthquakes, in August 1953, AHEPA held its 31st Supreme Convention in Houston, Texas during the week of August 16–22, 1953. It was chaired by George Epaminondas Johnson, whose name was originally Joanides. He had been born in Greece, had arrived in the United States in 1910, and became a successful restauranter in Sacramento.[69] There were 348 chapter delegates in attendance. The first decision the convention took was to address the needs caused by the earthquake in the Ionian islands. The convention immediately raised $20,252.00 for aid and relief to the people of the islands, with a drive to begin immediately among the chapters to raise additional funds, as well as food and clothing to be sent to the islands.

The other decisions the Houston convention took were the establishment of a Supreme Board of Trustees of seven members, two of whom were to be the Supreme President and the Supreme Treasurer, with the responsibility of managing and directing all national projects of AHEPA, such as the AHEPA Sanatorium, the National Home Fund, the Florida Property, and future national projects, with authority to buy, sell, transfer, rent, lease, and mortgage all real and personal property designated as belonging to a national project or projects, with the respective funds to be kept in a separate account under their jurisdiction. In addition, the Trustees were given the administration of the AHEPA Scholarship Loan Fund, with future grants to be only on a loan basis, to be repaid after graduation. The convention also initiated an immediate drive to raise funds for a Boys' Dormitory at St. Basil's Academy, Garrison, New York to be designated as the AHEPA Dormitory. It also raised the annual Per Capita Tax for each member from $5.00 to $6.00 and renamed the AHEPA Displaced Persons Committee as the AHEPA Refugee Committee.

The new Supreme Lodge elected Leo J. Lamberson, an attorney from Indiana, as Supreme President. The other elected officers were Stephen S. Scopas, Supreme Vice President; for the office of Supreme Secretary there was a tied vote, and with the consent of the convention, each candidate agreed to serve six months in office, therefore Peter Kourmoules was Supreme Secretary for the first six months of the fiscal year, and George Nick George was Supreme Secretary for the last six months; John A. Kiamos, Supreme Treasurer; John T. Laskaris, Supreme Counsellor; James P. Mazarakos, Supreme Governor; Andrew C. Angelson, Supreme Governor; James Millas, Supreme Governor; Chris Tsipuras, Supreme Governor for Canada. The new Supreme Board of Trustees chair was Chris Athas, a businessman from Salt Lake City.

King Paul and Queen Frederica of Greece

President Eisenhower invited King Paul and Queen Frederica of Greece on a state visit to the United States in 1953. They arrived in October and toured the country for four weeks. They visited the Hyde Park estate of the late President Franklin D. Roosevelt, where they laid a wreath at the President's grave, and visited the AHEPA Bust of the late President. The Poughkeepsie, New York AHEPA and Daughters chapters held special ceremonies for the visiting couple. Just prior to their return to Greece, King Paul and Queen Frederica held a meeting with the Supreme Lodge in New York City. The king and queen also met with AHEPA representatives in Athens during several of the Order's annual excursions to Greece. Two years earlier, during the 12th AHEPA Excursion to Greece in 1951, with Past Supreme President V. I. Chebithes as Commander, the Excursionists attended the dedication of the AHEPA Hospital at Salonika on May 14, with the king and queen of Greece and many other government officials.

The Refugee Act of 1953

The new US Refugee Relief Act of 1953 that replaced the 1952 Act included visas to 214,000 special non-quota immigrants, among which were visas for 15,000 Greek refugees who were residing in Greece on the date the act became law, and for 2,000 visas to Greeks who were relatives of citizens or permanent residents of the United States. The Act defined a refugee as any person in a country or area which is neither communist nor communist-dominated, who, because of persecution or fear of persecution, natural calamity, or military operations, is out of his place of usual abode and unable to return to it, who has not firmly resettled, and who is in urgent need of assistance for the essentials of life or for transportation. The Act also allowed an additional 4,000 special non-quota immigrant visas to eligible orphans under 10 years of age who had been adopted abroad or who were to be adopted in the United States by citizens of the United States and their spouses. The first Greek to enter the United States was 12-year old Stamatoula Roumanis on January 1, 1954. She was reunited with her parents, who had arrived in the United States in 1948 and operated a hotel in Denver, Colorado. New York Ahepans and members of the Daughters of Penelope were at the airport to welcome the new arrival. That same month, the State Department recognized the AHEPA Relief Committee as a Voluntary Agency under the Refugee Relief Act of 1953.

AHEPA's other activities over the following months included the 11th National Biennial Banquet honoring the Congress of the United States held in Washington in March, and the AHEPA Excursion to Greece departed on April 1, with Past Supreme President Van A. Nomikos as commander. The Excursion committee raised more than $4,000 on board ship, which was donated to the Queen Frederica's Fund, the Patriarchate Fund, and the Agricultural School for the Blind in Greece. An AHEPA Greek Independence Day banquet was held in New York City at the Waldorf-Astoria, with Spyros P. Skouras as toastmaster.

The 32nd Supreme Convention, 1954, Pittsburgh
The 32nd Supreme Convention was held August 15–21, 1954, in Pittsburgh, Pennsylvania. It was the first time in its history that AHEPA was holding its Supreme Convention in that city. It was chaired by New York attorney Peter T. Kourides, and there were 356 chapter delegates in attendance. The convention made the following decisions: Appointed former Olympic athlete Peter Clentzos again as National Director of Athletics; it decided that the project for St. Basil's Academy be named the AHEPA Hall for Boys, and would be built on a site acceptable to AHEPA at a cost not to exceed $500,000; it expressed AHEPA's support for the repeal of the Immigration and Nationality Act as creating inequities and containing undesirable discriminatory provisions; it decided that AHEPA go on record as endorsing the coordinated movement of the National Service Organization to combat juvenile delinquency and offer AHEPA's services in this movement; it decided that AHEPA undertake to conduct a general drive through the chapters and membership in the United States and Canada to raise funds for the purpose of rendering

relief to the earthquake sufferers and victims of Thessaly. During the convention Past Supreme Treasurer James J. Starr presented an official Olympic torch, which was used at the Olympic Games in 1948 in London, England, to the AHEPA Athletic Department for use in future AHEPA Olympiads.

After a closely fought election that was reported in the local newspapers covering the convention, Stephen S. Scopas defeated Steve Manta in the contest for Supreme President. Scopas, a New York attorney, was a former Supreme President of the Sons of Pericles. The other officers who were elected were: Constantine Verinis, Supreme Vice President; Constantine Gatsos, Supreme Secretary; Socrates V. Sekles, Supreme Treasurer; George Papanicolas, Supreme Counsellor; Louis G. Manesiotis, Supreme Governor; George J. Pappas, Sr., Supreme Governor; Gust Rakus, Supreme Governor; Nick Kogos, a restaurant owner from Vancouver, Supreme Governor for Canada. The AHEPA Refugee Relief Committee elected was: Past Supreme Presidents Leo. J. Lamberson and Van A. Nomikos, Louis J. Dukas, Supreme President Stephen S. Scopas, and Supreme Treasurer Socrates V. Sekles.

The Earthquake in Volos, 1955
A major earthquake in the span of a few years struck Greece, this time the city of Volos, on April 27, 1955. This was the third earthquake within almost months, the other two being in the Ionian Islands and Thessaly. AHEPA immediately started a "Greek Earthquake Committee" to raise funds and supplies to be sent to the sufferers. The Volos earthquake made 35,000 people homeless and damaged or destroyed 90% of all the homes and buildings in the city. The AHEPA Excursionists were in Greece at the time, and Supreme President Scopas and his committee visited Volos very soon after the earthquake. In June AHEPA in conjunction with the Archdiocese began a national fundraising campaign to assist the rebuilding of the town of Volos.

Harry Agganis
The entire sports world was shocked, and more so the Greek American communities of the United States, at the news of the death of Harry Agganis, the "Golden Greek", on June 27, 1955, at age 26. Just when he had entered the threshold of becoming one of the greatest stars of professional baseball, a sudden illness and death overtook him.

Aristotle George "Harry" Agganis was a college football player and professional baseball player who played as a first baseman from 1954 to 1955 for the Boston Red Sox. Born in Lynn, Massachusetts, to Greek immigrants, Georgios Agganis and Georgia Papalimperis, Agganis first gained notice as a college football player at Boston University, becoming its first student named All-American. He passed up a professional career in football to play his favorite sport, baseball, close to his hometown. In 1955, Agganis became gravely ill early in the season and was hospitalized for two weeks for pneumonia. He rejoined the Red Sox for a single week before being hospitalized with a viral infection. After showing some signs of recovery, he died of a pulmonary embolism on June 27.[70] Shortly after the death of Harry Agganis, the Order of AHEPA instituted the "Harry Agganis Award" given annually by the fraternity to the outstanding American athlete of Greek descent. Awardees included not only players but also coaches and broadcasters. The first winner of the award was Alex Aronis, a place kicker for the United States Naval Academy football team. He was a three-year letterwinner on the football team. He was part of the "Team Named Desire" squad that defeated Mississippi in the 1955 Sugar Bowl, 21-0. After graduating that year, he served as a Navy chaplain and was deployed on the USS Missouri, the ship where Japan signed its surrender following World War II.

The 33rd Supreme Convention, 1955, San Francisco

The 33rd Supreme Convention was held in San Francisco, during the week of August 14–20, 1955. It was chaired by George J. Margoles and there were 370 chapter delegates in attendance. A San Francisco Examiner editorial welcomed AHEPA to town, noting that it lived up to its beliefs in good citizenship, education, and non-partisanship in politics and was not sectarian in religion. As proof it cited AHEPA's sale of $200,000 worth of War Bonds during World War II and its aid to Greece, aid for Florida and Mississippi hurricane and flood victims, relief for refugees in the Near East, and help to victims of earthquakes in Greece. It also pointed out AHEPA's generous support of the Salvation Army, the YMCA, the Boy Scouts, the Red Cross, and of students through scholarships.[71]

The opening of the convention, as was customary in the 1950s, opened with a church service which was officiated by Archbishop

Michael. The Archbishop had succeeded Athenagoras in December 1949 and led the Archdiocese until his death in 1958, a period which witnessed close relations between AHEPA and the Greek Orthodox Church in America. The delegates took action on the following: Favored the adoption of Senate Bill No. 1206 for a new immigration and nationality law, that all unused immigration quotas be pooled and supported the extension of the expiration date of the Refugee Relief Act to December 31, 1960 and raising the age limit of orphans from 10 years to 16 years of age. Other decisions were to continue and complete the drive for the AHEPA School for Boys at St. Basil's Academy; an expression of best wishes to George Christopher on his candidacy for the office of Mayor of San Francisco (in which he would be successful); that the Pledge of Allegiance and Salute to the Flag of the United States be incorporated into the AHEPA Ritual for the opening of meetings. The new Supreme Lodge the convention produced was made up of: New York attorney Stephen S. Scopas, who was reelected Supreme President; the other officers elected were Constantine Verinis, Supreme Vice President; Gregory M. Pahules, Supreme Secretary; George A. Bezaitis, Supreme Treasurer; Ernest E. Dematatis, Supreme Counsellor; Louis G. Manesiotis, Supreme Governor; Anthony C. Lingon, Supreme Governor; James Frangos, Supreme Governor; Nick Kogos, Supreme Governor for Canada. Chris Athas continued as the Supreme Board of Trustees chair.

Mutual Aid Initiatives

In the same way AHEPA moved toward including mutual benefits programs in the 1930s to shore up and increase its membership, it did the same in the 1950s. A Scholarship Trust and Loan Fund got under way. Persons eligible for the Loan Fund for scholastic work were members in good standing of AHEPA, Daughters of Penelope, Sons of Pericles, and Maids of Athena, and non-members who were endorsed for such scholastic loans by a chapter of AHEPA. The loans were to bear 4% interest after graduation and were repayable to the Trust by payments of 10% one year after graduation, and 40% four years after graduation. The first two contributors to the loan fund were Past Supreme President Van A. Nomikos with $1,000 and George Harold Pappas, Atlanta, Georgia, with $500. This loan fund continued for almost 12 years, when it was reorganized by the 1966 convention, and reverted thereafter to an outright scholarship grant fund, instead of a loan. Also, a Fraternal Benefit Society was incorporated in December 1955 and began operations, offering a wide variety of insurance to members of AHEPA. Despite hopeful and ambitious plans, the insurance program lasted only for about two years, failing to sell sufficient insurance to maintain the program, and it was soon abolished, and the policies in force turned over to commercial insurance companies. In his history of the Order's first 50 years, George Leber wondered whether if that same program had been put into effect at least 25 or 30 years earlier, when the fraternity was in its first years of operation, it would have succeeded, since the fraternity would have been identified with an insurance program and enrolling new members into the insurance program would have been much simpler. Leber was equally unimpressed with the AHEPA Family Protective Fund insurance plan which would offer members insurance. It was adopted in 1956. This hastily developed insurance program, he noted, which was set up as annual term insurance, lasted only two years and was abolished at the 1958 convention since its insurance benefit payments soon outstripped its premium income—the failure to establish either age limits or health conditions doomed it to early failure and financial losses to the fraternity.

1956: The Abolition of the AHEPA Refugee Relief Committee
On the morning of Thursday, August 16, 1956, Past Supreme President Leo Lamberson took the floor at AHEPA's 34th Supreme Convention that was being held in New York City, chaired by John G. Thevos and in the presence of 424 chapter delegates. Lamberson was presenting the report of the Order's Refugee Relief Committee that had been appointed at the previous year's Supreme Convention in San Francisco with a mandate to push hard to persuade Congress to extend the existing deadlines that would enable Greeks to enter the United States as refugees. A day later, the convention decided to abolish the AHEPA Refugee Relief Committee and dispose of all pending cases as soon as possible. It was an astounding about turn whose reasons are unclear from the convention's minutes and which remained unexplained in The Ahepan magazine's Fall issue that reported on all that had gone on in the Supreme Convention. With the help of revelations that came to light later, it is now known

that the Refugee Relief Committee had become a law unto itself and was pursuing the refugee cause with an unjustified zeal and with a troubling treatment of the considerable financial implications associated with its activities. There had been growing complaints that greatly concerned many AHEPA's members.

That day Lamberson spoke in a crusading tone about the need to try and achieve legislative cover to bring more Greek refugees into the country. He also spoke at length because for technical reasons his committee's report had not been ready in time to be included in the convention's Yearbook given to all delegates upon their arrival. Lamberson took up a great deal of time urging delegates to contact their congressmen and senators and put pressure on them to support the extension of the deadlines which would cut off the entry of refugees from Greece. He felt sure many would agree despite the existence of unemployment in parts of the United States. And he made a special plea for the allocation of visas for 500 orphans from Greece. There were no questions after he finished speaking because the convention had appointed its own Refugee Relief Committee which would "go into" the operations of the regular committee and report later, an arrangement that indicated the underlying concerns with those operations. Indeed, an attempt to ask Lamberson about the numbers of orphans his committee was dealing with and whether he could produce financial records was not allowed to proceed because of the pending report of the Convention's committee. And the next day, based on that report the convention decided to disband the AHEPA Refugee Relief Committee.

Officially, the liquidation of the AHEPA Refugee Relief Committee was being completed because the Refugee Relief Act of 1953 terminated on December 31, 1956. The committee's report showed that 32,980 applicants from Greece had been filed with the State Department; that 19,054 of these had obtained visas for admission to the United States; 2,183 visas had been denied; 23 were still in process; and 11,919 were on the waiting list. The only hope at the time for those on the waiting list was that the law would be extended after January 1, 1957 by Congress. But this was not going to be end of the story. The issues that caused many members to express concerns about the conduct of members of the refugee committee were shelved in order to preserve the Order's unity and public good standing. But within a few years the American legal system would respond and investigate the entire system of adoptions that had gone on in the 1950s and the way certain individuals, including leading members of AHEPA, had conducted themselves while the Committee was operating, but also afterward, acting on their own.

The 1950s were a yet another moment in the Order's history in which it was expanding its activities in other to shore up and increase its membership. Its involvement in the Cypriot cause was noble as was its concern for the Greeks of Istanbul who had suffered a horrific pogrom in September of 1955. But aside from offering aid in the way it did with earthquakes in Greece, there was little it could do. The era when ethnic groups would be able to shape or try to shape US foreign policy had not arrived yet. Thus, the campaign to bring persons from Greece, including children who were either orphans or whose families were unable to keep them, over to the United States became an example of goodwill and noble sentiments that went too far. For some it became an obsession, for others a "job" for which they expected compensation. The very idea that there were "refugees" in Greece seven years after the end of the civil war and when postwar reconstruction was successful thanks to the Marshall Plan was stretching reality. And Greeks were able to finally emigrate to other countries, such as Australia, Canada, and Germany, and did so in the thousands.

The New York convention was busy on many other fronts. It reelected Peter Clentzos as National Athletic Director; it decided to award contracts for the AHEPA School for Boys at St. Basil's Academy just as soon as possible—most certainly a bright spot in all of AHEPA's initiatives; it changed the title of Supreme Governor for Canada to that of 2nd Supreme Vice President; and it amended the Constitution so that a member of either the Canadian or Bahamian jurisdiction could become Supreme President (it had previously been limited to a member of American citizenship). The new Supreme President who was elected, John L. Manta (Mantas or Mantakoudis) from Icaria, was a building contractor and movie theatre businessman based in Chicago, who had begun in the profession by painting bridges in St. Louis. Manta, whom the Ethnikos Kyrix newspaper described as having the appearance of an imposing tall weather-beaten sea captain rather than a businessman, had single-handedly covered the expenses for Greece's participation in the Chicago World's Fair held from 1933 to 1934.[72] The others elected were Peter T. Kourides, Supreme Vice President; George Nick George, Supreme Secretary; George A. Bezaitis, Supreme Treasurer; Gregory Lagakos, Supreme Counsellor; Stephen C. Andreadis, Supreme Governor; George J. Brotsis, Supreme Governor; Dr. Nicholas H. Despotopulos, Supreme Governor; George D. Vlassis, 2nd Supreme Vice President, Canadian Jurisdiction. Vlassis, a former teacher, had served for many years as information officer in the Greek embassy in Ottawa and was the author of a book on the Greeks in Canada.

Chris Athas continued as the Supreme Board of Trustees chair.

Historian Theodore Saloutos described the 1950s as Greek America's "Age of Respectability" because thanks to the assimilation of many of the Greek-born and the upward social mobility of themselves and their better educated children, the Greek Americans were not only a respected part of America but also of the middle class. And a great deal of that success was thanks to AHEPA's efforts since 1922. And considering that achievement AHEPA was turning to other activities and widening the scope of its initiatives continuously—not all of its projects would be entirely successful, but the forward momentum in the post-World War II era was unmistakable.

Chapter 5: AHEPA Turns to Education 1957–1962

AHEPA's commemoration of its 40th anniversary in 1962 brought a new beginning for the Order. The late 1950s and early 1960s were a period when AHEPA paused to reconsider its activities and refurbished its internal organizational structures with a view of ensuring greater accountability of its officers and enabling greater oversight by its members. The intensity with which AHEPA had worked to ensure greater numbers of Greeks could emigrate to the United States and especially its pursuit of enabling more and more adoptions and the financial implications therein had clearly veered out of control. Demands for investigations of the finances of the Order's refugee program from within, followed by public investigations of the program meant to bring children over by a court in New York, cast a shadow over what had been originally a charitable motivation. The source of the divisions that coursed through AHEPA in the late 1950s was due to different views about the refugee relief work and the abolition of the committee in 1956. No doubt some were motivated by an overriding sense of compassion that made them overlook the difficulties and irregularities that had plagued the program. The ambivalence within the Order's ranks unfortunately meant that a few current or former officials were still indirectly or directly active in procuring orphans from Greece for a few more years.

Out of the debates and differing opinions on how to proceed a new dynamic was born, expressed by the crystallization of two groups that represented a new alignment within AHEPA, and some observers spoke about the end of the earlier pro-Booras and pro-Chebithes tendencies. The first of those two new formations was the AHEPA First Party and the other was New Horizons. It is difficult to pinpoint the differences between the two; as was often the case in organizations such as AHEPA, internal differences reflected groups that identified with strong leadership figures and therefore personality rather than ideology or politics was what made members choose one over the other. Judging by their respective attitudes to the problems generated by the refugee and orphan programs, AHEPA First favored a "don't rock the boat" approach while New Horizons pushed for greater accountability and transparency. AHEPA First describes the victory of its candidate for Supreme President, Constantine Verinis, in 1957 as an "upset." Verinis was reelected the following year and another AHEPA First candidate George Loucas the year after that. But in 1960 it was the turn of the New Horizons group to elect the president.

All this did not mean that AHEPA did not continue with the other programs it had been pursuing in the post-World War II era. It continued its advocacy of increasing the quotas of Greeks allowed to emigrate to the United States even though it had it suspended its work in connection with bringing orphans from Greece to the United States. Another area of AHEPA initiatives was its support for the Greek American community and specifically the Greek Orthodox Archdiocese's St. Basil's Academy. Thirdly, the Order sustained its commitment to the support of Greece and Cyprus. Indeed, developments in Cyprus during that time would absorb a great deal of AHEPA's energies. The struggle of the Greek Cypriots for union with Greece that had begun in earnest in 1955 eventually led to a compromise. The London and Zurich Agreements signed between Greece, Turkey, the United Kingdom, and the leaders of the Greek Cypriot and Turkish Cypriot communities paved the way for the proclamation of an independent Cyprus in August 1960. AHEPA remained on the side of the Greek Cypriots throughout that process and beyond. Next to the ongoing engagement with the Cyprus issue, AHEPA turned toward the issue of education and the promotion of

Hellenic culture in America. This issue became a regular feature of the Supreme Conventions between 1957 and 1962.

The 1957 & 1958 Conventions

The 35th Supreme Convention held in St. Louis and the one the following year that was held in Boston charted the changes AHEPA would undergo over the next few years. The St. Louis convention, co-chaired by Louis J. Dukas and Anthony Kollias and with 343 chapter delegates in attendance, addressed issues relating to the membership by deciding that all insurance programs be grouped under one administrative head; the delegate representation at Supreme Conventions for chapters be increased by basing such representation on total number of paid members in each chapter for the current year; and it directed the new Supreme Lodge to appoint a national executive secretary at Headquarters because the office had been vacant for 15 months. The convention also reaffirmed AHEPA's stand on self-determination for the people of Cyprus. As incumbent Supreme President Manta stated that the people of Cyprus deserved the right to choose a government of their own choice. The US Secretary of Labor James P. Mitchell, known as the social conscience of the Republican Party thanks to his concern for workers, was one of the main speakers at the convention's banquet along with future Michigan Governor G. Mennen Williams, a civil rights advocate.[73]

At the St. Louis convention delegates elected Constantine P. Verinis of New Haven, Connecticut. Verinis, known as Gus to his family and friends, was one of four brothers, including James Angelo Verinis who became a famous airman during World War II. Their father Peter was born in the village of Agios Petros in Arcadia in Peloponessos and moved to the United States soon after he married Diamanto Proestakis, settling in New Haven. Airman Verinis told an interviewer: "My family came to America from Greece just after they got married. All their four sons were born here. We spoke Greek at home... Dad owned and operated an ice-cream store. That's all he ever did."[74] Constantine Verinis worked at Coclin Tobbaco Company, which sold cigarettes, candy, and vending machines in the New Haven area; its founder was another Greek immigrant whose original name was Aristomenis Kokkaliadis. Verinis was the father of two Greek adoptees.[75] The other officers who were elected were George

E. Loucas, Supreme Vice President; George D. Vlassis, Supreme Vice President of Canada; Kimon A. Doukas, Supreme Secretary; Stephen Andreadis, Supreme Treasurer; Gregory Lagakos, Supreme Counsellor; Peter Kouchalakos, Supreme Governor; Michael Colias, Supreme Governor; William C. Karnaze, Supreme Governor. Chris E. Athas continued as chairman of the Supreme Board of Trustees and John C. Mandros, a salesman for the Greek American business Lacas Coffee, was elected Athletic Director.

The two major events between the 1957 and the 1958 Supreme Conventions were the 13th National Banquet honoring the US Congress in Washington, DC on March 16, 1958, at the Sheraton Park Hotel, and the excursion to Greece. Banquet chairman was John A. Vlachos, and toastmaster was John M. Manos. Speakers were Ahepan Paul H. Douglas, US Senator from Illinois; and US Senator William A. Purtell of Connecticut. The 1958 Excursion to Greece sailed on March 18 on board the SS Queen Frederica, with commander Peter T. Kourides, Supreme Vice President; Vice Commanders William D. Belroy and William Vasiliou; and Past Grand President Poppy Mitchell as head of the Daughters contingent, and Sons of Pericles Supreme President Thomas Cholakis. Supreme President Verinis also accompanied the excursionists. Leading this excursion was one of the last full-time engagements with AHEPA for Peter Kourides, one of the founding members of the Sons of Pericles, who went on to serve as an AHEPA Supreme Lodge member with great distinction. Kourides would become the personal counsel to Archbishop Iakovos in 1959 and the Archbishop's most trusted advisor, a position he held throughout Iakovos' tenure that ended in 1996.

The 36th Supreme Convention, 1958, Boston

The 36th Supreme Convention was held in Boston, during the week of August 17–23, 1958, and it opened with a service held at the Holy Cross Theological School in the Boston suburb of Brookline. Past Supreme President Harris J. Booras, who was chair the last time AHEPA met there in 1930, was the administrative director of the 1958 convention. The Boston Globe newspaper which carried reports of the convention's activity throughout the week was especially fascinated by AHEPA's evening barbecue event held at the Suffolk Downs racetrack. It humorously informed its readers that about

2,500 Greeks and their descendants attended and consumed 3,000 pounds of shish kebab, as well as 6,000 pounds of Greek olives and 700 pounds of cheese. The grilling of the meat, it went on to explain, required two tons of charcoal and the work of 125 persons.[76]

When it got down to business the convention decided to request that the US government and the United Nations bring about self-determination for the people of Cyprus; it approved the establishment of AHEPA chapters in Greece, for the first time, limiting their membership however to only those who were already members of AHEPA and had moved residence to Greece; it raised the annual Per Capita Tax per member to be paid to Headquarters by chapters to $6.50 per year; and it abolished the Family Protective Fund, which had shown steady losses since its inception. The delegates reelected Constantine Verinis as Supreme President, and George E. Loucas, Supreme Vice President. The other officers elected were Edward Ghikadis of Toronto, Supreme Vice President of Canada; Kimon A. Doukas, Supreme Secretary; Michael J. Vrotsos, Supreme Treasurer; John G. Plumides, Supreme Counsellor; Peter Kouchalakos, Supreme Governor; George J. Papademas, Supreme Governor; Paul Koken, Supreme Governor. John Mandros was elected National Athletic Director. The Supreme Board of Trustees acquired a new chair, Ernest E. Dematatis, of Washington, DC.

A month after the convention, George J. Leber was appointed the new national Executive Secretary of the fraternity and took office on September 22, 1958. Born in Wichita, Kansas, he graduated from the local university and served in the Naval Reserves during World War II. He had previously served the fraternity as national Executive Secretary of the Sons of Pericles (1937–1942) and as Managing Editor of The Ahepan magazine. Leber was the author of the history of AHEPA's first 50 years. Leber remained as Executive Secretary until his death in 1976.

The 1959 Excursion to Greece

The 1959 Excursion to Greece departed in April headed by commander Socrates V. Sekles and vice commander Aristides Georgiades. There was a message of President Dwight D. Eisenhower for the excursioners: "It was good to learn of the plans for the 1959 AHEPA Excursion to Greece. This is a fine example of the work your organization is doing in strengthening the historic bonds which unite the citizens of our country and Greece. To those who are taking part in this Excursion, I send a hearty 'bon voyage' and best wishes for a pleasant and meaningful visit. I know that each one of them will be an effective ambassador in carrying to the Greek people the good will and friendship of us all." During the visit to Greece, the AHEPA Preventorion, a type of sanatorium, in Volos, was dedicated. It had been started in 1955 by funds solicited for aid to the Volos earthquake sufferers and the Order contributed $18,500 toward this project. Later that year Archbishop Iakovos of the Greek Orthodox Church of North and South America dedicated the AHEPA Boys' Dormitory at St. Basil's Academy on June 14, 1959.

Scopas Under Scrutiny
On May 5, 1959, the New York Times reported that New York city magistrate and lawyer Stephen Scopas was arrested and accused of selling Greek children in a black market for babies. In one of the two counts that Scopas was being accused of, his co-defendants were Brooklyn lawyer Jacob Cohen and Leo J. Lamberson, who was described as a South Bend, Indiana lawyer. The article did not mention that both Scopas and Lamberson were former AHEPA Supreme Presidents, and the Order was saved, momentarily at least, a great deal of embarrassment. According to the article, Scopas was accused of selling 30 children to couples in the New York metropolitan area and was said to have violated the law "by assertedly accepting payment for placing the children; and for placing them out for adoption without being authorized to do so" and that some children went to couples who were not fit to be parents.[77] The time span of those activities that was being addressed began in late 1956, and this technically saved AHEPA more embarrassment because it had disbanded its Refugee Relief Committee that handled the arrival of children, due to concerns of financial wrongdoings.

What happened next has been meticulously pieced together in a book length study by Professor Gonda Van Steen. The cases did not go to trial, for lack of sufficient evidence, and the defendants were released. By June 1960, Scopas had petitioned for the charges to be dismissed which was granted. It was then that the public prosecutor initiated an appeal (through the Court of Appeals of the State of

New York). The cases of People v. Scopas and People v. Scopas and Cohen became enmeshed in interpretations of the law. Ultimately, in March 1962, however, the Appeals Court upheld the earlier dismissal of the charges. Key to this failure to criminally prosecute Scopas and his affiliates was that all their adoptions were proven to have been completed in Greece. In other words, the legality of the adoptions completed in Greece, pursuant to Greek law, could not be challenged. This ruling of course raises the worrying issue of how much monitoring there was on AHEPA's part on the adoption of Greek children that it had brokered throughout the 1950s.[78]

Reading through Van Steen's study, one realizes that one of AHEPA's well-meaning and ambitious programs did not work out well and the organization dropped it and moved on. Advocating for refugees was one thing but bringing infants over from Greece for adoption was an entirely more complex operation which became even more challenging especially when it managed to be recognized as a private adoption agency. The least of the criticisms leveled against those in AHEPA who were directly involved was that they did not follow up the placement of a child with any subsequent monitoring by qualified social workers. At worst, some members allowed greed to replace the original goodwill. It must be said also that Scopas continued to maintain his innocence and remained active in AHEPA until his death in 1999.[79]

The 37th Supreme Convention, 1959, Hollywood, California

The 37th Supreme Convention met during the week of August 16-22, 1959, in Hollywood, California, and was chaired by John Manos. There were 390 chapter delegates in attendance. At the convention's banquet, San Francisco Mayor George Christopher was presented with the AHEPA public service award, and Nicholas C. Christophilos of the US Radiation Laboratory at Livermore in California received the science award. Both awards were made for the first time. The speakers at the banquet included Alexis S. Liatis, Greece's ambassador to the United States, who spoke about how AHEPA had built a bridge between Greece and the United States, and the Rev. Leonidas C. Contos, the dean of the Saint Sophia Greek Orthodox Cathedral in Los Angeles.[80] President Dwight D. Eisenhower sent the following message to the convention: "It is a pleasure to send greetings to those attending the 37th Supreme Convention of the Order of AHEPA. The members of AHEPA are ever mindful of the rich heritage shared by the United States and Greece. As they seek to strengthen the bonds which unite our two countries, and as they advance the principles of Democracy which we together hold in high regard, they add much to the life of the free world."

The convention decided that an Excursion to Greece be held in 1960, as well as excursions to the Patriarchate in Constantinople, and to Cyprus; that Ahepans renew their Oath of Allegiance to the Flag of the United States, and express AHEPA's aversion to the purposes of international communism and to organizations whose purposes were foreign to those of America; it endorsed the efforts of the Hellenic people of Epirus in their effort to become free and have the right of self-determination; it decided that all Ahepans cooperate fully with their local blood banks; it established a Standing Committee for the Good of the Order, composed of current District Governors in attendance at conventions; it called for a study of the feasibility of holding a future Supreme Convention in Greece; it changed the title of the "Board of Trustees" to "Supreme Board of Trustees." The delegates elected George E. Loucas as Supreme President. He was an attorney in West Virginia. He had held numerous positions in AHEPA and other organizations and had served one term in the House of Delegates in West Virginia. Upon his election to the office of Supreme President he spoke about the need for AHEPA to speak out on behalf of more Greek Americans and represent their interests. The other members of the new Supreme Lodge whom the convention elected were: Kimon A. Doukas, Supreme Vice President; Edward Ghikadis, Supreme Vice President for Canada; John G. Plumides, Supreme Secretary; Dr. N. S. Nicholas, Supreme Treasurer; Nicholas A. Loumos, Supreme Counsellor; William P. Tsaffaras, Supreme Governor; John Mercury, Supreme Governor; William G. Nicas, Supreme Governor. Nicholas Laskaris was elected National Athletic Director. The chair of the Supreme Board of Trustees was Sam S. Nakos. Nakos, who was born in Corfu, was a well-known beer distributor and real estate investor in Birmingham Alabama where he had established a foundation for educational and charitable purposes. He had donated a statue of Hippocrates to the University of Alabama.

A New Decade

In 1960, the 14th National Biennial Banquet was held in Washington, DC at the Statler Hilton Hotel. Chairman was John T. Pappas, and William D. Belroy toastmaster. Among the speakers were Secretary of State Christian A. Herter, Speaker of the House of Representatives Sam Rayburn, and Congressman John Brademas, who was the first Greek American elected to Congress in the 20th century. A Democrat, he had won the race for the congressional seat in Indiana's Third District in 1958. White House Special Counsel David W. Kendall brought a message from President Eisenhower. The banquet was covered by the US Information Agency and the Voice of America, both of whom sent news photos, articles, and radio broadcasts to Greece.

The 1960 Excursion to Greece left on March 21, from New York City, with Supreme President George E. Loucas heading the committee of Supreme Vice President of Canada Edward Ghikadis, Past Supreme President Dean Alfange, and Daughters, Sons, and Maids presidents Emily Tamaras, Frank J. Manta, and Denise Tomaras. The 1960 Excursion carried more than 750 cartons of American books to Greece, representing more than 25,000 volumes, which were distributed by the excursionists to libraries in Greece, as a contribution of AHEPA to President Eisenhower's People-to-People Program. The volumes included children's books, American history, government, science, education and encyclopedias. Congressman Brademas called the AHEPA Excursion to Greece a People-to-People program in remarks he inserted in the Congressional Record: "These Americans serve as individual diplomats from Main Street, U.S.A."

On Memorial Day, 1960, AHEPA held its second wreath-laying ceremonies at Arlington National Cemetery in Washington, at the Tomb of the Unknown Soldier, and decorated graves of Greek American veterans, including that of Past Supreme President V. I. Chebithes, who died in 1959. Supreme Trustee Ernest E. Dematatis represented the Supreme Lodge at the ceremonies. The wreath-laying ceremony became one of AHEPA's regular annual activities.

The 38th Supreme Convention, 1960, Montreal

The 38th Supreme Convention was held in Montreal during the week of August 14–20, 1960; it was chaired by Leo E. Ypsilanti and there were 485 chapter delegates in attendance. This was the first Supreme Convention to be held in Canada and the occasion was marked by warm welcoming messages from Canadian prime minister John Diefenbaker and Montreal's Mayor Sarto Fournier. Iakovos, the newly installed Archbishop of North and South America, also arrived in order to formally open the convention's proceedings, and he also officiated at the new Greek Orthodox Cathedral on Cote St. Catherine Road. Also attending the convention was Greece's ambassador to Canada, J. D. Callergis.[81]

The choice of holding the convention in Montreal reflected the growth of AHEPA all over Canada. There were about 16,000 Greek Canadians living in Montreal in 1960, about a third of the total Greek population of Canada. The largest number had arrived in Canada after World War II. But the first AHEPA chapter in Montreal was formed as early as 1930, in the Mount Royal district of the city. The main speakers at the convention's banquet were Congressman John Brademas and Bishop Athenagoras of Boston. Brademas spoke about the values of democratic freedom that were being challenged internationally. He said that Greek Americans had a special responsibility to be involved in public life and urged AHEPA to encourage the younger generation to be involved especially because Greece was the birthplace of democracy. The bishop spoke about the need for Christians around the world to be united.[82] The promotion of education, which was especially prevalent in this phase of AHEPA's history, was featured prominently at the convention. The AHEPA national awards committee announced the success of the AHEPA medal for scholastic excellence which went to the top student of local Greek school graduating classes. Other initiatives taken during and after the convention included the inauguration of the Greek Classics program in 1960, which entailed offering a seven-volume set of the complete Greek Drama, the Greek Historians, the Dialogues of Plato, and the Works of Aristotle, to all chapters for purchase and presentation to their local city, college, and high school libraries. Hundreds of complete sets were purchased by AHEPA chapters from Headquarters over the next 12 years and presented to libraries throughout the United States and Canada, as an incentive for continued study of these classics by high school and college students. The AHEPA Headquarters also reprinted "The Holy Liturgy of the Greek Orthodox Church" which was offered for sale at cost to AHEPA chapters for presentation to local churches and youth groups. The booklet was originally published by the Sons of Pericles in 1939, written by George J. Leber and John Chrysostom, and several thousand booklets were distributed by AHEPA chapters in 1960 and 1961.

The new Supreme President elected was Nicholas Coffinas, an attorney who had established a law firm in Brooklyn with his brother Gustav. Nicholas and his brother were the sons of Greek immigrants George and Mary Coffinas. The other Supreme Lodge members elected were John G. Plumides, Supreme Vice President; George Adamakos, a restaurant owner in Montreal, Supreme Vice President of Canada; Nicholas J. Chirekos, Supreme Secretary; Gust J. Herouvis, Supreme Treasurer; John M. Manos, Supreme Counsellor; William Tsaffaras, Supreme Governor; George J. Brotsis, Supreme Governor; James Kostopulos, Supreme Governor. Nicholas T. Laskaris was elected Supreme Athletic Director. Sam S. Nakos continued as the chair of the Supreme Board of Trustees.

The 1961 AHEPA Excursion to Greece arrived in Piraeus on March 24. Past Supreme Governor James Mazarakos was commander of the group, and his committee consisted of James Argyros, Supreme Trustee Gus Nicholas, Daughters Grand President Evelyn Semos, Sons Supreme President John Cholakis, and Maids Grand President Despina Bilides. Dr. Michael Rethis of the College of Emporia, Emporia, Kansas, moved to that school from Tufts University, and started plans to offer a program of modern Greek studies, including modern elementary Greek, modern Greek literature, and courses in special studies of ancient Greece. More than 20,000 American books were shipped to Greece by AHEPA on the SS Queen Frederica in March 1961 for distribution to libraries in Greece by the Greek-American Cultural Institute of Athens. Also in Greece, the Daughters of Penelope chapter in Athens started construction of the Penelopean Shelter for Teen Age Girls in early 1961. In Canada, the First AHEPA National Canadian Banquet was held in Ottawa, in June 1961. It was given in honor of Prime Minister John G. Diefenbaker of Canada and the Canadian Parliament. Members of Canada's Parliament and government officials also attended, as well as the AHEPA Supreme Lodge and members and officers of AHEPA. Peter Kotsonas was the banquet chairman, and Supreme President Nicholas Coffinas was toastmaster. Prime Minister Diefenbaker was the principal speaker of the evening.

The 39th Supreme Convention, 1961, Miami Beach
The 39th Supreme Convention was held in Miami Beach, Florida, during the week of August 13-19. It was the third time AHEPA was holding its convention in Miami. The proceedings opened with a liturgy officiated by Archbishop Iakovos. The "World Committee on Employment of the Handicapped" presented its award "The Book of Golden Deeds" to AHEPA for services rendered by Ahepans in the employment of handicapped people. The award read: "The Book of Golden Deeds, the Mark A. Light Memorial Award presented in recognition of Exceptional and Continuous Service to the Cause for Creating Equal Opportunity in employment for the Handicapped. To the Order of AHEPA." Other important moments of the convention included the honoring of retired General James Van Fleet, who as lieutenant general in 1948 was the head of the Joint US Military Advisory Group that administered the military aid to Greece provided by the Truman Doctrine, and which ensured the victory of the government forces in the Greek civil war.

The theme of promoting education was present in one of the convention's resolutions, which called on American high schools and colleges to offer courses in modern Greek. The presentation of the "Greek Classics" to local high school and college libraries rapidly gained momentum in 1960 and 1961, with presentations in all sections of the country. More than 150 of the 7-volume sets were presented within the first 12 months. The American Farm School and Anatolia College, both in Salonika, Greece, received $300 AHEPA Scholarship Awards. A drive was started in January 1962 for the purchase of CARE Tool Kits to be given by AHEPA to students of vocational trade schools in Greece. These included: Sewing Machines, Woodworking, Electricians, Metal Workers, Needle Trades, Masons, Auto Mechanics, and Basic Plumber's Kits. Each "Kit" contained the basic tools needed for vocational students upon their graduation from trade school. Chapters and members were urged to contribute funds for the purchase of the kits, to be shipped to Greece. Andrew Fasseas of Chicago was National Chairman of the drive. Local chapters also mobilized over the issue of education. AHEPA District 20, Southern

California, gave support to "The Greek Heritage" course of 12 lectures given at the Extension Division of the University of California at Los Angeles under the direction of Dr. Theodore Saloutos, professor of history at the school. Among subjects offered in the lectures were: modern and Byzantine Greek history, Greek religion, ancient and Byzantine art, Greek democracy in action, Greek literature, Greek music, Greek drama, the Greek people in the United States, and the American influence on Greece. There were also resolutions relating to George Papanikolaou, the Greek American physician who was a pioneer in early cancer detection and the inventor of the "Pap" test. Papanikolaou had missed selection for the Nobel Prize for Medicine by one vote, and AHEPA requested he be considered again by the Committee for the award. The Order also expressed its appreciation that the Miami Cancer Institute was renamed "The Dr. Papanicolaou Cancer Research Institute at Miami."

The other resolutions included one expressing the view that the Parthenon Marbles, taken from Greece in the early 1800s by Lord Elgin of England and placed in the British Museum, be returned to Greece; that a Committee on Americanism be created; that Northern Epirus be liberated; and that an AHEPA chapter be established in Athens, Greece. The convention also raised the annual Per Capita Tax for members to $7.00 per year. The Miami Beach convention also decided appropriate ceremonies should be held at New Smyrna Beach, Florida, to commemorate the First Landing of Greeks in the New World in the year 1768, and first steps were taken to approve a future Supreme Convention in Athens, Greece. The new Supreme Lodge elected at the Miami Beach convention was made up of: Nicholas Coffinas, Supreme President (reelected); George J. Margoles, Supreme Vice President; Nicholas J. Chirekos, Supreme Secretary; Panayes G. Dikeou, Supreme Treasurer; John M. Manos, Supreme Counsellor; Peter Kotsonas, a hotel owner in Montreal, Supreme Vice President of Canada; Toby Caragian, Supreme Governor; James Kostopulos, Supreme Governor; Mike Costas, Supreme Governor; Sam Nakis, Supreme Governor; Peter Caravoulias, Supreme Governor. Nicholas T. Laskaris was elected Supreme Athletic Director. The Supreme Board of Trustees chair was Ernest E. Dematatis.

The 15th National Biennial Banquet, 1962

The 15th National Biennial Banquet honoring the Congress of the United States was held on March 19 in Washington, DC at the Sheraton Park Hotel. Chairman was Tom Ross, and Supreme Secretary Nicholas J. Chirekos was the toastmaster. Principal speakers were: US Senator Hugh Scott of Pennsylvania; US Senator Gale McGee of Wyoming; Edward R. Murrow, Director of the US Department of Information; and Mike Manatos, Administrative Assistant to President Kennedy, who read the new President's message to the banquet. Mike N. Manatos was the first American of Greek descent to be appointed to the staff of the White House. He was appointed by President John F. Kennedy as an Administrative Assistant to the President of the United States and assumed his new duties in the White House in February 1961. Manatos had become an Ahepan in 1933 at age 18 in Wyoming.

Other events in 1962 included the annual wreath-laying at Arlington National Cemetery's Tomb of the Unknown Soldier on Memorial Day, 1962. AHEPA wreaths were also placed on the graves of Greek American veterans buried at Arlington Cemetery. Also, tool kits and sewing machines that the Order of AHEPA distributed in Greece in 1962 were given to the National Boys' Orphanages, American Farm School Vocational Orphanages, Royal National Foundation Vocational Schools, Girls' Vocational Schools, Rural Youth Clubs, Homemaking Schools, Church Girls' Orphanages, and an institute for disabled persons. The newly completed AHEPA School at St. Basil's Academy in Garrison, New York was dedicated in June 1962 with a large group of Ahepans and their families in attendance, as well as church leaders. The AHEPA School was completed at a cost of $245,000, and with the previously completed AHEPA Hall for Boys which was built at a cost of $90,000, the AHEPA projects at the Academy represented a total cost of $335,000.

The 40th Supreme Convention, 1962, Chicago

The 40th Supreme Convention was held in Chicago, Illinois, during the week of August 19–25, 1962, marking the convention's return to the city after 27 years. The 1962 convention was chaired by Louis J. Dukas and there were 613 chapter delegates registered. The convention's banquet was an extraordinary affair because it featured feisty speeches by both former US President Harry Truman and Arizona Senator Barry Goldwater, a well-known conservative Republican. They each claimed that the ancient Greeks were aligned with the values they espoused. Both politicians received huge ovations by the attendees. Archbishop Iakovos also spoke at the banquet.[83] The convention took the following decisions: it expressed support of pending legislation in Congress to increase immigration from Greece; approved membership of AHEPA into the American Immigration and Citizenship Conference; stated that AHEPA disapproved and condemned any and all discriminatory acts by friendly governments against the United States nationals and interest, and respectfully petitioned the US government to withhold any and all aid of any nature, form, or description to such governments under the 1962 or subsequent Appropriations Acts until such time as discriminatory actions were effectively removed or just compensation had been made; that the inclusion of Byzantine History be made in the curriculum of the public schools; it authorized the Supreme Board of Trustees to subdivide the Florida Property into a section to be an Old Age tract, and the balance of the property to be sold as lots for housing. It also selected Athens as the venue of the 1965 Supreme Convention.

The following new Supreme Lodge was then elected: George J. Margoles, Supreme President; Nicholas J. Chirekos, Supreme Vice President; Louis G. Manesiotis, Supreme Secretary; Panayes G. Dikeou, Supreme Treasurer; Peter C. Charuhas, Supreme Counsellor; George Prahales-Panos of Montreal, Supreme Vice President of Canada; Gus Cherevas, Supreme Governor; Mike Costas, Supreme Governor; Chris Anton, Supreme Governor; Arthur Lagadinos, Supreme Governor; Nick Smyrnis, Supreme Governor. Angelo F. Mavrigan was elected Supreme Athletic Director. The new Supreme President, George J. Margoles, was a graduate of Yale Law School and was an attorney in New Haven, Connecticut where he also had business interests.

Education continued to be a focus. A special survey was undertaken by the AHEPA Headquarters during the year on the number of courses offered in universities and colleges on Hellenic culture. The results were published in a special report by Supreme Vice President Nicholas J. Chirekos, which listed the schools offering courses in Greek language, history, and drama, as an aid to students seeking such learning. The report also included facts on AHEPA's scholarship programs over the years. The booklet was entitled "AHEPA's Educational and Scholarship Programs." It was an apposite symbol of AHEPA's focus on education in that period, in the words of Supreme President Chirekos in The Ahepan magazine in 1963, a focus on the "E" for education. The years that followed would bring an additional focus which we could describe as one on the "H" for Hellenic in AHEPA.

Chapter 6: AHEPA Reaches Its 50th Anniversary

As AHEPA approached its 50th anniversary in 1972 it contributed toward strengthening the ties between the United States and Greece. This process began with the unveiling of President Truman's statue in Athens in May 1963 and continued with two Supreme Conventions held in Athens, in 1965 and 1970. Throughout this period the annual excursion to Greece continued and there were additional visits to Athens by AHEPA officials who were a part of the US delegations that travelled to Greece. The momentum AHEPA's orientation with Greece had acquired meant that it continued after 1967 when a military coup d'état in April led to the establishment of a dictatorship in Greece. A lack of judgement on the part of the Order's leadership led it to believe in the dictators' claims that they were restoring law and order and would eventually also restore democracy in Greece. The election of Richard Nixon as president in 1968, with his Greek American running mate Spiro Agnew being elected Vice President, and their administration's support of the regime in Athens was another factor that contributed to AHEPA's misplaced trust in the dictatorship. Throughout this period AHEPA also continued its cordial and respectful relations with the presidency and visited the White House annually. Naturally, from the time Nixon chose Agnew as his running mate in the summer of 1968, and especially after the election, Agnew, whose father was an Ahepan, featured as a guest in several AHEPA events. AHEPA continued the annual wreath-laying ceremony at Arlington National Cemetery in Washington, DC, at the Tomb of the Unknown Soldier, at which graves of Greek American veterans were also decorated.

The Truman Statue in Athens

In early 1962 AHEPA announced it would be erecting a statue of President Truman in Athens. Sculptor Felix W. de Weldon, internationally known for his Iwo Jima Statue in Washington, DC, began work on the statue. In expressing its reasons for the erection of a statue to President Turman, AHEPA published this statement: "Under the circumstances of the conditions then existent in Greece, (in 1947) the outcome of the struggle between the Communists and the Greek government would have been doubtful had not the United States come to the assistance of Greece. With the logistic support of the United States, the Greek Army was reorganized and managed, after three years of bitter warfare, to crush the Communist rebellion in September 1949. The economic assistance of the United States to Greece was mainly used for keeping the economy going on a day-to-day basis and caring for the homeless and jobless refugees of war-stricken areas, which at one time reached the alarming proportions of 1/10 of the population of the country, or 700,000 persons. The 'Truman Doctrine' not only saved the country of Greece from communistic control, but also furnished the necessary economic aid for a starving, homeless and war-stricken people. In 1950, the country of Greece finally embarked upon a comprehensive plan of economic reconstruction and started on the final road to recovery. The effect of the economic and technological assistance from the United States upon the Greek economy can best be judged by stating that without this aid, Greece would most likely not be a free nation today. The Order of AHEPA, desiring to pay tribute to the 'Truman Doctrine' and to President Truman for the life-giving and critical aid given Greece, has undertaken the AHEPA Truman Memorial, as a commemorative gesture of international friendship and good-will between the two countries."

On May 29, 1963, the AHEPA-funded statue of President Truman was dedicated in Athens with great pomp. The bronze statue, twice life size, was said to have cost about $100,000. It featured the President holding a scroll that represented the Truman Doctrine, the 1947 legislation that led to the United States supporting the government forces during the Greek civil war. Prime Minister Karamanlis was present and offered remarks, as did Supreme President Margoles and Archbishop Iakovos, who also officiated in a service along with Chrysostomos, the Archbishop of Athens and Greece. US Ambassador to Greece Henry Lambouisse and Mayor of Athens Angelos Tsoukalas also spoke. A military band played the national anthems of both countries while a large throng of spectators surrounded the statue. The event was front-page news the next day in all major Greek newspapers.

Truman, then 79 years old, was physically unable to travel to Greece for the celebration. But two years later he was presented an original model of the statue at a luncheon and ceremony at the Truman Library in Independence, Missouri. National and local officers, and members of AHEPA attended, as well as representatives of the Greek government. President Lyndon B. Johnson's message to the ceremony was: "I am delighted to participate in AHEPA's splendid tribute to my cherished friend and our distinguished former President Harry Truman. The handsomely wrought statue which you dedicate will serve as a fitting symbol of profound and common gratitude to a statesman who honorably defended and exalted the high ideals and traditional love of freedom of Greece. Emblematic of the ties of friendship and cooperation between our two nations, it will always be an inspiring memento of the past and a magnificent monument to human freedom."

The 41st Supreme Convention, 1963, San Diego
The 41st Supreme Convention was held in San Diego, California during the week of August 11–17, 1963. It was chaired by William Tsaffaras, with 268 chapter delegates in attendance. The 1963 San Diego convention was the first Supreme Convention under the direct supervision and responsibility of the Supreme Lodge, the Supreme Board of Trustees, and the Executive Secretary, by amendment of the Constitution at the 1960 Montreal convention. President John F. Kennedy sent the convention the following message: "It gives me great pleasure to extend greetings to the members of AHEPA on the occasion of your Supreme Convention. Your ancestors gave to all

Western Civilization its first idea of human freedom by giving the world not just the word for, but the very concept of, democracy. Their descendants who have come to these shores have contributed much to the rich cultural traditions of this Nation. American democracy has been defended on battlefields throughout the world by men—many of them in your Order—whose ancestors defended the cause at Marathon and Thermopylae. Thus, the United States owes a unique debt to you just as you enjoy a unique heritage as the heirs alike of Socrates and Jefferson. With best wishes for continued good fortune in all your endeavors." Tragically, the President was assassinated in November. Only three weeks before his death, President Kennedy gave an interview in which he referred to the definition of the Greeks for happiness: "It is full use of your powers along lines of excellence." Vice President Lyndon B. Johnson succeeded to the presidency, and one of his first acts was to reappoint Ahepan Mike N. Manatos as Administrative Assistant to the President.

Action was taken by the San Diego convention on the following: it approved the report of the special committee on the feasibility of a Supreme Convention to be held in Athens, Greece in 1965, and directed the Supreme Lodge and Supreme Board of Trustees to proceed with all arrangements; it endorsed pending legislation designed to protect all minorities in the United States regardless of race, religion, or national origin, to achieve for all groups and people full and complete equality in education, employment, and housing; supported a stronger scholarship program; created the new elective office of District Athletic Director; and created an AHEPA Publication Board.

At the Grand Banquet the main speakers were Archbishop Iakovos and Stanley Mosk, the Attorney General of California. Upon his inauguration in 1959, Mosk became the first Jewish American to serve as a statewide executive branch officer in California and was reelected by a large margin in 1962. Mosk established the Attorney General's Civil Rights Division and successfully fought to force the Professional Golfers' Association of America to amend its by-laws denying access to minority golfers. He was an early supporter of John F. Kennedy. At the Grand Banquet, George E. Loucas, Past Supreme President, was honored as the recipient of the Cross of the Commander of the Royal Order of the Phoenix by the Greek government for his many services to the peoples of Greece and the United States.

The new Supreme Lodge members elected were: John G. Plumides, Supreme President; Nicholas J. Chirekos, Supreme Vice President; Nick Smyrnis, Supreme Secretary; Xenophon K. Microutsicos, Supreme Treasurer; Theodore Alexander Bardy, Supreme Counsellor; George Prahales-Panos, Supreme Vice President of Canada; Harry C. Boosalis, Supreme Governor; George Dimas, Supreme Governor; Gus G. Gatseos, Supreme Governor; Nick T. Georges, Supreme Governor; John G. Kaplanis, Supreme Governor; James G. Petheriotes, Supreme Governor. Pete G. Pasvantis was elected Supreme Athletic Director. The new Supreme Board of Trustees chair was Socrates V. Sekles, a restaurant owner from Michigan. The Supreme President and the other officers were elected unanimously, and this heralded a new era of unity for AHEPA. The new Supreme President, John Plumides, was born in North Carolina; both his parents were members of AHEPA and at the time of his election he was an attorney practicing in Charlotte, North Carolina. Plumides was the first Supreme President in AHEPA's history to be born and raised in the South.

AHEPA at the White House

One of Plumides' first duties as Supreme President was to attend ceremonies on September 11, 1963, at the United Nations in New York City where US Ambassador to the United Nations Adlai Stevenson presented a donation of $500,000 from the United States to the United Nations to be used as assistance for refugees in Greece. The funds were to be used for housing, medical, and subsistence requirements, and for resettlement of refugees. Besides government officials, Congressman Brademas and Presidential Administrative Assistant Mike Manatos also attended. In January 1964 Plumides attended a special White House Conference on Immigration on January 13, 1964 at the White House, as the representative of Americans of Greek descent. The conference was attended by 40 national leaders of labor, ethnic, and social groups for a seminar discussion on immigration laws and how they should be revised for a more equitable application to those nations with small quotas. The same month Plumides and his wife attended the White House luncheon given by President and Mrs. Lyndon B. Johnson for Her Majesty Queen Frederica of Greece.

In June 1964, several leading Ahepans attended the White House Luncheon given by President Lyndon B. Johnson in honor of visiting Greek Prime Minister Georgios Papandreou. They included Supreme President John Plumides, Executive Secretary George J. Leber, Past Supreme President George C. Vournas, Past Supreme Vice President George E. Johnson, Gregory G. Lagakos, Spyros Skouras, Justice Theodore Souris, and Peter Agris. Also, when King Paul of Greece died in March 1964, President Lyndon B. Johnson's personal representatives to the funeral included several Ahepans. The delegation was composed of former President Harry S. Truman, Mrs. Johnson, Archbishop Iakovos, Supreme President John Plumides, Judge John Pappas, Congressman Brademas, Presidential Special Assistant Mike Manatos, and Past Supreme President George C. Vournas. Except for Mrs. Johnson, all members of the American official representatives to the funeral were members of the Order of AHEPA, undoubtedly a signal honor to the fraternity's place in all aspects of American life.

AHEPA's First Socratic Award

The 1964 AHEPA National Banquet honoring the US Congress was held on March 16, 1964 and featured the first presentation of the new AHEPA Socratic Award to Henry R. Luce, Editorial Chairman of LIFE and TIME magazines, in appreciation and recognition of the series of articles published in LIFE magazine in 1963 entitled "The Miracle of Greece."

The articles depicted the contributions of ancient Greece to modern civilization and the Western world, and it was for this dissemination of Hellenic culture and Hellenic ideals to the peoples of the world, that AHEPA made this award to Mr. Luce. In its editorial page, LIFE magazine Managing Editor George P. Hunt wrote: "The greatest thrill for an editor is to be seized with a great theme. Speaking in Washington last week to a gathering of a thousand Americans of Greek descent, Editor-in-Chief Henry R. Luce was referring to LIFE's 1963 series The Miracle of Greece. For the series, Luce was presented the first Socratic Award from the Order of AHEPA—The American Hellenic Educational Progressive Association—which was founded in 1922 to educate in the English language and the American way the thousands of Greeks who emigrated to the United States after World War I and the Turkish invasion of 1922. Supreme President of the Order John Plumides made the presentation to a standing ovation of the men of AHEPA and members of its Auxiliaries—the Daughters of Penelope, the Sons of Pericles and the Maids of Athena. 'In the 20th Century,' Luce ended his acceptance speech, 'we have a little bit of the feeling of what it must have been like in the time of Pericles. The challenge is to create an American civilization based on the idea of Greece—the expansion of knowledge, music, culture, universities. For 200 years the American people have been faithful to one dominant purpose, namely, to the establishment of a form of government. That purpose has now been fulfilled, and we are at present seized by a broader challenge, namely, the shaping of a civilization. We will meet that broader challenge, too. We will succeed in creating the first modern, technological, prosperous, humane and reverent civilization—2,500 years after Pericles. Pursue excellence rather than mediocrity—that is what the Greek community is saying to us today."

Besides Henry R. Luce, principal speakers at the 1964 banquet were US Senator Kenneth B. Keating of New York, Congressman Brademas, and US Senator Sam Ervin of North Carolina. Banquet chairman was John J. Charuhas, and toastmaster was Supreme President John Plumides. Two hundred and four members of the US Congress attended that evening. In his message President Lyndon B. Johnson stated AHEPA was an "American organization, an association of American citizens of Hellenic descent which constantly propounds and follows the ideals and principles of the American heritage. The Order of AHEPA blends the cultural heritage of both America and Greece, which has served to help maintain the close bonds between these two countries."

The AHEPA Socratic Award was a bust done in bronze, about 3/4 life size, of the ancient Greek philosopher Socrates, accompanied by a scroll. From 1964 onwards, the award was given every two years, on the occasion of the AHEPA National Banquets honoring the US Congress. In the 1990s the award was renamed the Order of AHEPA Socrates Award. A full list of the recipients is available on AHEPA's website and that of the AHEPA History Project which includes a more detailed narrative.[84]

Crisis on Cyprus

To overcome the unworkable constitution of Cyprus that gave the Turkish minority veto power over any government decision, President Makarios presented an alternative plan in late 1963. It which was rejected by the Turkish side, and this triggered Greek-Turkish ethnic clashes on the island which escalated in 1964 and culminated in an attack by Turkish warplanes. Thus, the situation on Cyprus was the major issue that concerned AHEPA that year. The 42nd Supreme Convention was held in Toronto, Canada during the week of August 16–22, 1964, chaired by Charles J. Panagopoulos, with 403 chapter delegates in attendance. It was AHEPA's second Supreme Convention to be held in Canada, and the first in Toronto. Several resolutions were passed on Cyprus. One of them noted "That Whereas Turkey, a recipient of U.S. Military and Economic Aid in excess of Three Billion Dollars did, on August 8, 1964, embark upon acts of aggression against the defenseless people of Cyprus, using U.S. made planes, rockets, air bombs and military equipment and supplies of all types, in clear violation of Sections 505 and 506 of the Foreign Assistance Act of 1961, as amended in 1962, and Whereas such aggression caused the deaths of innocent civilians, women, and children, and the destruction of peaceful towns and villages, including churches, and the government of Turkey has taken no action to redress and mitigate the suffering and repair the damage inflicted by such wrongful acts, Therefore be it resolved that the President of the United States be petitioned to suspend all economic and military aid to Turkey and be petitioned to espouse, on behalf of the United States, the establishment of a branch of the International Court under the United Nations and cite the Government of Turkey and such persons who participated in the Cyprus Aggression to said court for proper trial; That a full-page advertisement be published in the New York Times on Sunday (August 23) stating the stand of AHEPA on the Cyprus Question and also featuring the statements of U.S. Senators and Congressmen who supported the position of AHEPA in this matter." Another resolution condemned the action Turkey took in retaliation in expelling Christians from Turkey and confiscating their properties without compensation, as being arbitrary, unjust, and uncivilized, and condemned Turkey's action in persecuting the Ecumenical Patriarchate of Constantinople and in exiling certain members of the Patriarchate, which was another anti-Greek measure taken by Turkish authorities.

Other decisions taken included the adoption of an insurance program, changing the name of the Junior Order of Maids of Athens to "Maids of Athena," and the appropriation of $5,000 to be donated to the Columbia Cancer Clinic for a Cobalt radiation machine for the King Paul General Hospital in Greece. A special moment of the convention was the appearance of Miss Corinna Tsopei of Greece, selected as Miss Universe at the Miami Beach contest that year. She attended most of the convention functions and was also honored with events by the City of Toronto. The convention also featured the first AHEPA family debutantes' presentation during convention week. The new Supreme Lodge elected was: Nicholas J. Chirekos, a restaurant owner in Illinois, Supreme President; Kimon A. Doukas, Supreme Vice President; Gus Cherevas, Supreme Secretary; Gust Rakus, Supreme Treasurer; George S. Stratigos, Supreme Counsellor; Nicholas Liaskos of Montreal, Supreme Vice President of Canada; Peter H. Cardiges, Supreme Governor; Gus G. County, Jr., Supreme Governor; Charles M. Georgeson, Supreme Governor; J. William Holmes, Supreme Governor;

George T. Poolitsan, Supreme Governor; William G. Poulos, Supreme Governor. Andy Panos was elected Supreme Athletic Director. The new Supreme Board of Trustees chair was Socrates V. Sekles.

For the rest of the year, the Cyprus issue, which was the subject of negotiations aimed to defuse the tension, was foremost in the minds of Ahepans. The November 1964 issue of The Ahepan magazine was almost entirely devoted to the Cyprus Question, with a historical background of the island and events leading up to the current crisis in 1964, as well as statements from members of Congress on the situation. It was mailed to every newspaper, library, and government official in the United States, as well as to city and state officials. AHEPA also published a special reprint of the book The Blight of Asia by George Horton, former US Consul in Smyrna during the destruction of the city in 1922, and several thousand complimentary copies were also mailed to government officials and prominent citizens throughout the United States. This book deals with the atrocities of the Turkish Army during the burning of Smyrna and with the long history of Turkish massacres against Christianity.

AHEPA's engagement with both those issues continued in 1965. A policy statement on Cyprus noted: "Since the first outbreak of difficulties in Cyprus [in August, 1964 when Turkish planes attacked Greek-populated areas of the island], the Order of AHEPA has taken an intense interest in the problems besetting the Greek population of Cyprus. We have recognized the just position of the Greek population of Cyprus and have made every effort towards informing not only the American government, its officials, and the American public, but even the world, of the validity and justness of the stand taken by the Cypriot Greek... This is not the first time that the AHEPA has taken an active part in the affairs of Cyprus. In the year of 1955 the Order of AHEPA formed a Justice for Cyprus Committee which strongly endorsed the Cypriot struggle for independence, and which helped form favorable American opinion during that Cypriot struggle... The AHEPA is now deeply concerned with the goal of the Cypriot Greeks in seeking a just solution to their problem. The fraternity has strongly advocated 'self-determination' for the peoples of Cyprus and our position has been made known to American officials. During the past several months, we have received strong letters of support in our stand from almost 200 Members of the United States Congress... The

AHEPA has protested strongly to our government for the rashness and incredible acts of the Turkish government against both Cyprus and the Greeks in Constantinople during these past few months. Members of the AHEPA throughout the United States and Canada have sent letters and telegrams of protest to their government officials and to the President of the United States... Full page advertisements were published in August and September 1964, in the New York Times, carrying the letters of endorsement that the AHEPA received from U.S. Congressmen. These advertisements were also published in the International editions of the Times. The Committee and AHEPA Supreme Lodge participated in briefings with the U.S. Department of State on different occasions on the Cyprus Question."

AHEPA also issued a statement on the protection of minorities in both Cyprus and Turkey, which noted: "The rights of the Turkish minority in Cyprus and the rights of the Greek minority in Constantinople should be upheld and guaranteed by a United Nations Mission which will have the right to inspect and check into all conditions affecting these minorities in both of these troubled areas. The Mission should submit periodical reports of its findings to the United Nations Organization and to the press of the world. We advocate the creation of such a Mission." And with regard to the Ecumenical Patriarchate, which was also under pressure by the Turkish authorities, AHEPA pointed out: "The See of Constantinople was established by the Apostle St. Andrew. Its Primate is accepted as the symbolic head of all Eastern Orthodox Christian Churches. Even the Ottoman Sultans allowed the Ecumenical Patriarchate to exercise its churchly and religious functions. Today, in the twentieth century, the Hierarchy and Clergy of this ancient institution are being persecuted and exiled without as much as a protest from the Christian Nations of the West. The same United Nations Mission should have the responsibility to constantly review and examine the treatment of the Ecumenical Patriarchate by the Turkish Government so that there will be no persecution or interference by the Turks in the proper and free exercise of the churchly and religious functions of this seat of Eastern Orthodoxy. The United Nations Mission should also be required to make periodical reports on this subject matter to the United Nations and the world news media."

The 43rd Supreme Convention, 1965, Athens, Greece

After a great deal of debate AHEPA agreed to hold its first ever Supreme Convention in Athens during the week of August 7–13, 1965, and despite the travel distances required for attendance, it proved to be the fraternity's most spectacular and best-attended convention in history to that point. The Post Office of Greece issued a special AHEPA Stamp (6 Drachmas) in honor of the convention. The membership's response was remarkable, despite the distances and travel times involved. Fifty AHEPA charter flights left the United States for Greece during the spring and summer of 1965. The first flights left in late March, and the last returning flight came back in late September 1965. The duration of the charters was from a minimum stay of two weeks, up to a maximum stay of six months. More than 8,000 members and their families took part in those jet flights. An additional 4,500 members and their families travelled to Greece either on AHEPA steamship excursions, or on other non-AHEPA flights. The huge numbers involved, the inadequacy of the available facilities in Athens, and close relatives in Greece wishing to participate meant that there were constant problems of overcrowding. However, despite these problems which had no solution, the convention was highly successful, for, as many put it, "Just being able to be in, and visit, Greece, is more than worth the trip." What was also remarkable about the big attendance in Athens was that beginning in July, Greece descended into a political crisis because of the resignation of Prime Minister Georgios Papandreou following a clash with the young King Constantine, who had replaced his father, the late King Paul. The crisis meant a series of demonstrations in the streets of Athens in protest of what was seen as the king's unacceptable dismissal of the country's elected prime minister. Indeed, the unrest never really subsided and would lead to the colonels' coup in 1967. But Ahepans seemed unfazed both by the news before they traveled and by the demonstration and the occasional use of tear gas by the police during their stay in Greece.

The social events of the Athens convention were rich and varied. They included an opening ceremony at the newly constructed open-air theatre on Lycabettus Hill where crowds were turned away after the 3,500 seats were filled, creating a monstrous traffic jam. Greek officials attended a liturgy at the Athens Cathedral, after which an

AHEPA processional marched to the Greek Tomb of the Unknown Soldier and to the Monument of the American Philhellenes of the Greek Revolutionary War of 1821, where AHEPA wreaths were laid. There was a "Festival of the Greek Armed Forces" at the Athens Stadium, with more than 65,000 people present, a capacity crowd. The festival was in honor of AHEPA, and featured Greek folk dancers from all parts of Greece, floats, exhibits of gymnastics, and a representation of the ancient Panathenea Procession. Toward the end of the week AHEPA hosted a banquet in honor of the Greek government officials at the Grande Bretagne Hotel, and a Farewell Dance was held on the same evening at the Athens Hilton. The king and queen of Greece also gave a special audience to the officers of AHEPA.

The business sessions were held at the Athens Hilton, the convention chair was Peter G. Batsakis, and there were 750 chapter delegates in attendance, or an overall total of 802 voting delegates at this convention, the largest voting delegation in the history of the Order.

The major decisions included a demand for self-determination for Cyprus, and stated opposition to any partition of Cyprus into Greek and Turkish enclaves; a reaffirmation of AHEPA's stand against communism; a demand for religious freedom for the Greek Orthodox Christians living in Turkey; approval of the progress of the new AHEPA Group Insurance Plan; an expression of appreciation for the US government CARE program for Greek charitable institutions of the distribution of surplus food commodities; an expression of appreciation and gratitude to Mrs. Joseph Gale Ramsay III, of Minneapolis, Minnesota, for bringing to the United States eighteen Greek children for open heart surgery at the University Hospital in Minneapolis; a demand for the return of Northern Epirus to Greece; an affirmation of AHEPA's support of America's foreign policy in Viet Nam; and an approval for the sale of the Albuquerque Property.

The new Supreme lodge was elected unanimously: Kimon A. Doukas, Supreme President; Xenophon K. Microutsicos, Supreme Vice President; Peter H. Cardiges, Supreme Secretary; Gus Cherevas, Supreme Treasurer; William Tsaffaras, Supreme Counsellor; Chris Zakos, a business owner and Rotarian from Kingston, Ontario, Supreme Vice President of Canada; George P. Dikeou, Supreme Governor; Charles A. Alexander, Supreme Governor; Christopher

Ekonomou, Supreme Governor; Gus G. County, Jr., Supreme Governor; Andy Panos, Supreme Governor; Peter J. Chimoures, Supreme Governor. John Paulos was elected Supreme Athletic Director. The new Supreme Board of Trustees chair was Gust J. Herouvis from Ohio.

The new Supreme President, Kimon A. Doukas of New York City, was born in Asia Minor and arrived in the United States in 1922. He received a Doctor of Jurisprudence degree from New York University and a Doctor of Philosophy degree in public law and government from Columbia University. He was the author of several studies on public enterprises. Doukas' unanimous election was evidence of a period of unity that had been established at that time, thanks to the efforts of John G. Thevos, a Past Supreme President who at the time was a prosecutor in New Jersey and Delaware. For his services Thevos was named AHEPA's Man of the Year in 1965.

The Immigration Act of 1965

One of Supreme President Doukas' first responsibilities was to attend, with the AHEPA officers, a ceremony at which President Lyndon B. Johnson signed the Immigration and Nationality Act of 1965 at the Statue of Liberty. This law was an important milestone in American immigration history. It ended the "national origins formula" that had been in place since the 1920s. From 1924 until 1965, following passage of the National Origins Act of 1924, a person's place of birth often determined his or her ability to immigrate legally into the United States. Numerical limits, often called quotas, were assigned to each country. Immigration laws favored people from northern and western Europe over those from southern and eastern Europe, Asia, and Africa. Those quotas deliberately limited immigration from countries according to their immigration to the United States in 1890, at which time there was very little immigration from any of the Mediterranean or eastern European nations. President Johnson said, in signing the bill: "It repairs a deep and painful flaw in the fabric of American justice. It corrects a cruel and enduring wrong in the conduct of the American Nation. It will make us truer to ourselves as a country and as a people. It will strengthen us in a hundred unseen ways."

The changes in the immigration laws of 1965 brought a bigger influx of immigrants from Asia and Latin America compared to that from southeastern Europe and the Mediterranean, but there was a significant increase of arrivals from Greece between 1965 and 1974, when emigration flows decreased. According to the US Census of 1980 there were 211,000 persons born in Greece in the United States, compared to 159,000 in 1960. In 1980 there were also almost 9,000 persons in the United States who had been born on Cyprus. Taking into account the numbers that had entered since World War II thanks to the Displaced Persons Act and other allowances, a total of about 200,000 persons from Greece and Cyprus had immigrated into the United States between 1945 and 1980. Most had settled either in or around New York City or other big cities such as Boston, Chicago, and Philadelphia. The immediate effects were not felt by AHEPA because the Greek-born immigrants gravitated toward the "topika somateia," the associations of persons from a common geographic origin, but their American-born offspring were more likely to join AHEPA.

The 17th AHEPA National Banquet, 1966
The 17th AHEPA National Banquet honoring the US Congress was held on March 14, 1966, at the Sheraton Park Hotel, and the main speaker of the evening was Ahepan Hubert H. Humphrey, Vice President of the United States. The recipient of the AHEPA Socratic Award was President Lyndon B. Johnson, and the award was received on his behalf by Presidential Assistant Mike N. Manatos. In his message to the banquet, President Johnson said: "The Order of AHEPA has adhered to the highest traditions of democratic citizenship." Besides Vice President Humphrey, speakers were US Senator Philip Hart of Michigan and US Representative Donald Fraser of Minnesota, a congressman who would become very active over the issue of defending human rights around the world. Chairman of the banquet was Anthony E. Manuel, and the toastmaster was Judge Gregory G. Lagakos.

The 44th Supreme Convention, 1966, Washington, DC
The 44th Supreme Convention was held in Washington, DC during the week of August 14–20, 1966 and was chaired by Past Supreme President Constantine Verinis. President Lyndon B. Johnson sent the following message: "For many decades the Order of AHEPA has championed the rebirth and growth on American soil of the democratic traditions of ancient Greece. Your dedication to the ideals

and aspirations of your forebears has enriched your contributions to our nation and enhanced our common legacy as Americans. As you meet for your forty-fourth convention, I extend warmest gratitude and good wishes. Let the time-tested heritage of your ancestors inspire you to sustained achievement. And let this gathering be a living reminder of the glory of ancient Greece and a lasting tribute to the glory of modern America." Thirty-three Senators and 91 Congressmen inserted special remarks in the Congressional Record about the Order of AHEPA and the convention to such an extent that these were all incorporated into a special booklet for distribution to the membership. Vice President Hubert H. Humphrey was the principal speaker at the convention grand banquet. Among the convention's decisions were: another resolution on Cyprus, seeking a peaceful and lasting solution of its problems, and the principle of self-determination; a protest of the actions of Turkey in harassing and persecuting Greek Orthodox Christians and the Ecumenical Patriarchate; approval of the US government actions in Viet Nam; mandating the Supreme Lodge to arrange for proper commemoration of the 200th Anniversary of the First Landing of Greeks in the New World at New Smyrna, Florida; the establishment of the AHEPA Educational Foundation as a means of granting scholastic aid, and abolishment of the Student Loan Program, which funds were incorporated into the new Foundation; and mandated that an annual AHEPA Youth Program in Greece be established. The new Supreme Lodge elected was: Kimon A. Doukas, Supreme President (reelected); Andrew Fasseas, Supreme Vice President; Nick Kogos, Supreme Vice President of Canada; Gus Cherevas, Supreme Secretary; Gus G. County, Jr., Supreme Treasurer; Charles J. Panagopoulos, Supreme Counsellor; George J. Cavalaris, Supreme Governor; Peter J. Chimoures, Supreme Governor; Angelo Chouramanis, Supreme Governor; George P. Dikeou, Supreme Governor; James Scofield, Supreme Governor; Stephen J. Pechewlys, Supreme Governor. John J. Paulos was elected Supreme Athletic Director. The new Supreme Board of Trustees chair again was Gust J. Herouvis.

The 45th Supreme Convention, 1967, Dallas, Texas
The 45th Supreme Convention was held in Dallas, Texas during the week of August 20–26, 1967. It was chaired by Sam Nakis and there

were 501 chapter delegates in attendance. As was the case the previous year, President Johnson sent a congratulatory message to the convention. The convention demanded that the people of Cyprus be given self-determination; stated that AHEPA gave its full support to the United States government policy in Viet Nam; and decided that $10,000 be donated to His Holiness Patriarch Athenagoras of Constantinople for his travels to other seats of Orthodoxy in Europe and for his official visit to Pope Paul in Rome.

The new Supreme Lodge elected for fiscal year 1967–1968 was: Andrew Fasseas, Supreme President; Gus Cherevas, Supreme Vice President; Alfred G. Vonetes, a political consultant, Supreme Secretary; Gus G. County, Jr., Supreme Treasurer; Charles J. Panagopoulos, Supreme Counsellor; John N. Stratas, Supreme Vice President of Canada; Thomas Chase, Supreme Governor; Angelo Mountanos, Supreme Governor; James Scofield, Supreme Governor; Michael T. Thames, Supreme Governor. John Paulos was elected Supreme Athletic Director. The Supreme Board of Trustees chair was Panayes G. Dikeou from Colorado. The new Supreme President, Andrew Fasseas, was born in Sparta in Greece and had arrived in the United States in 1914. He had served as director of the Illinois Department of Revenue until 1960, and owned two bilingual newspapers in Chicago, the Greek Press and the Greek Star which merged in 1966. He was Republican and an outspoken anti-communist who had visited Greece several times offering aid designed to improve the transportation network around Sparta. At the time of his election, he was a board member of a savings company and a bank in Chicago.

In October 1967, the AHEPA Supreme Lodge issued a statement through Supreme President Andrew Fasseas, on the Order's attitude toward the dictatorial regime in Greece and toward efforts that were being made in Congress to restrict the sale of arms to Greece until the restoration of democracy: "The Order of AHEPA is composed, in great part, of Americans of Greek descent. It is non-sectarian in religion and non-partisan in politics. AHEPA's members are proud and happy that our country and Greece always have been allies and friends… since World War II Greece has been a faithful ally of the United States. She is a valued and loyal member of NATO. Greece supplies the bases in the Middle East for the United States 6th Fleet and American forces required in that part of the world in order to contain Communism.

The best interests of our country require that Greece become and remain economically sound, and militarily strong... the Order of AHEPA therefore urges that the United States continue its military and economic aid and assistance to Greece. Many of our officers and members have recently visited Greece. They have found that law and order prevail and that conditions for visitors and tourists are most pleasant... if a European came to the United States and told the American people what type of government we should have, or whom to elect as President, we would rightfully reject it as an unwarranted interference with our internal politics... the members of the Order of AHEPA feel that the type of government in Greece is a matter that concerns the Greek people only. As Americans, our only concern is that whatever Greek government Greece has should keep Greece as a member of NATO and a faithful ally of the United States." It should be noted that not all Ahepans were supportive or even tolerant of the regime in Athens, and Past Supreme President George Vournas was among those who made their criticisms publicly.

The 18th National Biennial Banquet

The 18th National Biennial Banquet honoring the Congress of the United States was held at the Washington Hilton Hotel in Washington in March 1968. US Senator Everett M. Dirksen of Illinois was the recipient of the AHEPA Socratic Award for his public services to his city, state, and country. Principal speakers were Senator Dirksen, US Attorney General Ramsey Clark, Maryland State Governor Spiro T. Agnew, and Greek American Congressmen Brademas, Nick Galifianakis, and Peter N. Kyros. Banquet chairman was Alfred Vonetes and toastmaster was Peter G. Batsakis.

The Monument to the New Smyrna Settlement of 1768

On May 4, 1968, AHEPA dedicated the monument it erected at New Smyrna Beach, Florida, to commemorate the 200th anniversary of the first landing of Greeks on American soil. They were more than 400 Greek colonists who came to America as indentured servants with Andrew Turnbull. They arrived in 1768 after a difficult transatlantic crossing that cost many lives, only to encounter no infrastructure and perilous living conditions. About a third of them survived after they made their way north to St. Augustine. The AHEPA Memorial plaque and monument ceremony attracted a large crowd at the city of New Smyrna Beach, Florida, on the Atlantic ocean, with officials of the state, county, and city present. Governor Claude R. Kirk, Jr. of Florida spoke and participated at the unveiling of the plaque. Attention was focused on the New Smyrna Bicentennial Day celebration by nationwide newspaper stories, Voice of America broadcasts to Greece, United States Information Agency coverage, a Congressional Resolution, messages from President Johnson and Vice President Humphrey, and a statewide proclamation of the day from Governor Kirk. Supreme President Fasseas and Grand Secretary Joanna Panagopoulos headed the AHEPA and Daughters of Penelope contingents, and Metropolitan Germanos was chief celebrant for the Greek Orthodox Church. Supreme Governor Scofield, chairman of the National AHEPA New Smyrna Bicentennial Celebration, was master of ceremonies for the dedication, Counsellor Stathatos of the Greek Embassy represented the government of Greece, and District Governor Angelo P. Demos of Florida represented his District. Governor Kirk accepted the monument and plaque for the state, and Mayor Robert C. Patillo accepted on behalf of the citizens of New Smyrna Beach, Florida. Greek costumed dancing groups from St. Petersburg and Tarpon Springs performed Greek folk dances. Congressman Brademas introduced House Resolution 774 in the House of Representatives to commemorate the 200th anniversary, and Governor Kirk of Florida proclaimed May 4, 1968, as New Smyrna Beach Bicentennial Day.

The 46th Supreme Convention, 1968, New York City
The 46th Supreme Convention was held in New York City during the week of August 18-24, 1968. It was chaired by John Plumides and there were 661 chapter delegates attending the convention, making a total of 716 voting delegates in all. The convention took the following steps: endorsed the project of "Glasses for the Eyes of Greece," the furnishing of eyeglasses to the needy; recommended that chapters sponsor the program of sending letters and packages to servicemen overseas; adopted an Educational Program for Students in Greece during the summer, under the auspices of Anatolia College at Salonika, Greece; and honored Alexander Demit of Brooklyn, New York Chapter 41, who was the oldest living Ahepan at age 100. Spiro T. Agnew, Governor of Maryland, who had been recently nominated

at the Republican National Convention as the party's candidate for Vice President of the United States, made a brief appearance at the convention. The new Supreme Lodge elected was composed of: Gus Cherevas of Queens, New York, Supreme President; A. T. Tsoumas, Supreme Vice President; Louis Yankou, a real estate and insurance businessman from Toronto, Supreme Vice President of Canada; Gus G. County, Jr., Supreme Secretary; Peter G. Chingos, Supreme Treasurer; William Zacharellis, Supreme Counsellor; Christ J. Kallos, Supreme Governor; Angelo T. Mountanos, Supreme Governor; Michael Skarlos, Supreme Governor, Nicholas J. Stroumtsos, Supreme Governor; Paul Yphantes, Supreme Governor. Lee G. Rallis was elected Supreme Athletic Director. The new Supreme Board of Trustees chair was Panayes G. Dikeou.

The AHEPA-Anatolia College Summer Scholarship Program
Immediately following the convention, Supreme President Cherevas scheduled a meeting in each of the 24 AHEPA Districts for the purpose of informing the membership about the new "AHEPA-Anatolia

College Summer Scholarship Program" for the Sons of Pericles and Maids of Athena for 1969. The program included eight weeks in Greece, for students between the ages of 15–18, with six weeks at the school in Salonika, and two weeks of tours in Greece. The program was set up for a total of 100 students, with a student quota for each AHEPA District. Courses at the school covered Greek language, Greek heritage, Greek history, and modern Greek institutions, as well as arts and crafts, sports, and recreation. AHEPA's first summer programs in Greece proved to be a success. One hundred and five students and chaperones arrived in Greece on July 4, 1969, to take part in the AHEPA-Anatolia College Summer Scholarship Program and were met on arrival by Deputy Prime Minister of Greece Constantinos Vovolinis and Athens Mayor Demetrios Ritsos, both of whom were appointed by the colonels' regime, and a large welcoming program. An additional 144 students and chaperones began arriving the following day from the United States, to take part in the "AHEPA Youth Summer in Greece Program," a five-week study and tour program. A total of 249 students and chaperones visited Greece in the summer of 1969, the first of an annual AHEPA program in Greece for high school students. These students represented 48 states of the country.

The 47th Supreme Convention, 1969, Minneapolis
The 47th Supreme Convention was held in Minneapolis, Minnesota, during the week of August 17–23, 1969. The convention was chaired by Past Supreme President George E. Loucas. Speaking at the convention, outgoing Supreme President Cherevas, echoing AHEPA's misinformed attitude toward the Greek junta, said he had no basis on which to criticize the government in Athens and had the highest praise for the officials he met in Athens, an indirect response to the negative picture of the regime that several American newspapers had presented over the previous months.[85] The main speaker was former Vice President of the United States Hubert Humphrey. Archbishop Iakovos and Athens Mayor Demetrios Ritsos were present at the convention; the mayor was cheered after he gave a short speech. There were a small anti-junta protests outside the hotel where the business meetings were being held and during the convention's sports events. The major decisions the convention took concerned the Order's inner workings. The new Supreme Lodge members who were elected were: Louis G. Manesiotis,

Supreme President; Sam Nakis, Supreme Vice President; Louis Yankou, Supreme Vice President of Canada; Dr. Michael N. Spirtos, Supreme Secretary; Peter Kouchalakos, Supreme Treasurer; Lee G. Rallis, Supreme Counsellor; John P. Angelson, Supreme Governor; Nick C. Demeris, Supreme Governor; George Laskaros, Supreme Governor; John E. Maniatis, Supreme Governor; Tommie Sotiriou, Supreme Governor; Steve Tsagaris, Supreme Governor. Dr. Monthe N. Kofos was elected Supreme Athletic Director. Kofos, who was born and raised in Vermont and was an optometrist in Marlborough, Massachusetts, would remain as the Athletic Director through his death in 2008, a period in which he created a rich and robust athletic program. The new Supreme Board of Trustees chair was Peter Derzis, a retired colonel of the US Army who worked as a broker in the Washington, DC area. The new Supreme President, Louis Manesiotis, was born in Pittsburgh in 1918, served in the US Navy during World War II, and then became a successful painting contractor.

Spiro Agnew

Richard Nixon's victory in the presidential elections of 1968 meant that Spiro Agnew became Vice President of the United States. They were both reelected in the next elections in 1972. This was obviously a very important development for the Greek American community, with one of its members being elected to the highest political office in the United States. While Agnew's resignation in October 1973 after being investigated on suspicion of criminal conspiracy, bribery, extortion, and tax fraud has tarnished his own reputation and the way Greek Americans regarded him subsequently, AHEPA's overflowing pride following his election in 1968 is perfectly understandable. Whether that pride was also fueled at least among some Ahepans by an additional attraction to Vice President Agnew's outspoken conservatism would be more difficult to establish. In any case, from 1969 onwards and through his resignation Agnew was honored in several ways at AHEPA events. Most notably, in 1970 Agnew was the recipient of the Socratic Award at the 19th AHEPA National Banquet honoring the Congress of the United States in Washington, DC in March. In his remarks prior to the presentation of the Socratic Award to Agnew, Supreme President Manesiotis quoted from an address that Theodore S. Agnew, the Vice President's father, had made in 1928, as follows: "AHEPA also is worthy of the fate which awaits her, because she cherishes in her heart the sweet longing, the tender hope and aspires to the honor of one day seeing in the White House a son of hers, one of her members who'll be proud of his Greek origin." Theodore S. Agnew apparently delivered these prophetic words in 1928, when he was President of Baltimore, Maryland Chapter 30, and the prophecy had come almost true when his son, Spiro T. Agnew was elected Vice President of the United States. More than 1,400 persons were present in the banquet hall, making that the largest AHEPA National Banquet of all time. Vice President Agnew was the principal speaker of the evening, and other major speakers included US Senator Philip A. Hart of Michigan, US Representative Gerald R. Ford of Michigan, and Supreme President Manesiotis. George J. Apuchis served as the banquet chairman, and the toastmaster was Joseph S. Bambacus, a Richmond lawyer who had been US Attorney for the Eastern District of Virginia from 1958 to 1961, and who was a special assistant to Attorney General Robert F. Kennedy in the early 1960s.

AHEPA Returns to Athens
The 48th Supreme Convention was held in Athens, Greece during the week of August 1-8, 1970. It was chaired by James Mazarakos and there were 549 chapter voting delegates in attendance, or a total of 593 voting delegates in all. AHEPA again offered a variety of charter and group flights to the convention, and an estimated 6,000 persons attended, about half the total of the 1965 meeting in Athens. Convention events included about the same schedule as that of the 1965 meeting, with the exception that AHEPA Track and Field and Basketball teams were sent to Greece for the convention by the fraternity who participated in meets and games with Greek teams. Peter Clentzos was director of the AHEPA sports teams, which acquitted themselves favorably against top ranking Greek teams. As in 1965, the Greek government proved to be an excellent host in conjunction with the City of Athens, and the Cambas Winery and Metaxas Company hosted functions for the visiting Ahepans and their families. Also, as in 1965, the highlight of the convention was the Festival at the huge Athens Stadium, which was filled to capacity with Ahepans and Athenians to witness the celebration given in honor of AHEPA.

The 1970 AHEPA Educational Journey to Greece program for high school students of the AHEPA family attracted 126 students and chaperones who made the 30-day visit to Greece. The program coincided with the 1970 Supreme Convention, so that the students could spend a few days participating in convention events. Dr. Peter V. Paulus was National Chairman of the 1970 program, which was under the jurisdiction of the AHEPA Educational Foundation Board, and the Royal National Foundation of Greece was in charge of housing and travel arrangements for the program.

The convention decided that the newly-named "AHEPA Educational Journey to Greece" student summer programs in Greece be continued annually; it called on the US government to enter into discussions for compensation to American and Greek citizens whose property had been confiscated by the Turkish government; it decided that the fraternity participate in the annual memorial services at the Cathedral of the Pines at Rindge, New Hampshire that honored military personnel and civilians who had served in the war; and that the fraternity strongly support the teaching of the Greek language, and support Greek schools in the United States. The new Supreme Lodge elected was made up of: Louis G. Manesiotis, who was reelected Supreme President; Sam Nakis, Supreme Vice President; John E. Hadzipetros, Supreme Vice President of Canada; Michael Spirtos, Supreme Secretary; William Tsaffaras, Supreme Treasurer; Michael G. Plumides, Supreme Counsellor; A. Steve Betzelos, Supreme Governor; Emanuel J. Bouzis, Supreme Governor; Theodore Caras, Supreme Governor; Gregory J. Despinakis, Supreme Governor; Andrew A. Papaminas, Supreme Governor; Stephen Parnassa, Supreme Governor. Monthe Kofos was elected Supreme Athletic Director. Peter Derzis continued as Supreme Board of Trustees chair.

The other major Greek American convention that year, the 1970 Biennial Clergy-Laity Congress of the Greek Orthodox Church of North and South America, honored the Order of AHEPA during its meeting by scheduling its final luncheon as "Salute to AHEPA Luncheon."

The 150th Anniversary of the Greek Revolution of 1821

The year 1971 was the 150th anniversary of the outbreak of the Greek war of independence, also known as the Greek Revolution, and AHEPA mounted several initiatives to honor the event. AHEPA issued a medallion commemorating the 150th anniversary of Greek independence. The front side of the medal depicted the Metropolites Palaion Patron Germanos at Patras on March 25, 1821, with Greek military chieftains, proclaiming the start of the Greek Revolution against Ottoman rule. The reverse side depicted the American Philhellenes Monument in Athens, Greece, erected in memory of the many Americans who aided and fought with Greek soldiers against the Ottoman armies during the period of 1821–1830. The medals were struck by the Franklin Mint in pure gold, pure silver, and bronze. Solid gold medallions were presented to President Nixon at the White House, and to Prime Minister (dictator) George Papadopoulos of Greece, in Athens, during 1971. The medals were also struck in sterling silver and bronze. A third gold medallion was presented to Agnew in March 1972. AHEPA published a 52-page booklet in February 1971, on the 1821 Greek War of Independence, in commemoration of the 150th anniversary of that struggle for independence, entitled "The 1821 Greek War of Independence and America's Contributions to the Greek Cause." Written by George J. Leber, Executive Secretary of AHEPA, the book enjoyed a wide distribution throughout the country. Besides giving a brief history of the War of Independence against Turkey, the book also chronicled America's assistance to Greece in those years.

Also in 1971, then Supreme Treasurer William Tsaffaras went to Athens, Greece, taking with him the US state flags and state governors' proclamations on the 150th Anniversary of the Greek War of Independence, which he presented on behalf of the states and AHEPA to the people of Greece. The state flags and proclamations were properly displayed during the many celebrations of Greece during its 150th anniversary events, as a gesture of friendship between the people of the United States and Greece. The state flags and proclamations were gathered by AHEPA chapters in the various states, and read: "Do Hereby Proclaim March 25, 1971, as Greek Independence Day, and extend all good wishes to the people of Greece on this their 150th Anniversary of Independence from foreign rule and invite all citizens of the State to celebrate with the people of Greece their Anniversary of Independence." The proclamations were signed by the governors of the states.

The 49th Supreme Convention, 1971, Los Angeles
The 49th Supreme Convention was held in Los Angeles, California during the week of August 15–21, 1971. The chair was Past Supreme President Stephen Scopas, and there were 382 chapter voting delegates attending the convention. The convention called for Cyprus to remain a unitary and sovereign state free from foreign interference consistent with the principles of self-determination, as espoused by the United Nations and the Nixon administration; it declared that Hellenic art treasures taken to various parts of the world be returned to their rightful place, Greece; and called on districts and chapters make appropriate awards to persons in the fields of art, culture, and education, especially as they might relate to Greek heritage and culture. It requested that the US Post Office department issue an AHEPA Stamp in commemoration of AHEPA's 50th anniversary in 1972; it decided that an Educational Journey to Greece be again held in 1972; it endorsed the annual Memorial Services to Greek American dead at Rindge, New Hampshire, Cathedral of the Pines; it decided to study the feasibility of Hellenic Chairs at major universities; it decided to study the possibilities of making the new University to be established at Patras, Greece a cooperative American Hellenic university; it declared its intention to investigate the conditions of Greeks in the Soviet Union and the conditions of Greek Orthodox refugees in Jordan and the West Bank; and it decided to cooperate with and assist the United States Olympic Committee for the 1972 Olympic Games.

Only a few days before AHEPA gathered in Los Angeles for the 49th Supreme Convention the US House of Representatives voted to discontinue military aid to Greece. The reasons were that a majority in the House wished to express their disapproval of the regime in Athens, which after four years of dictatorial rule had not acted on its promises to restore democracy and continued to hold political prisoners, many of whom had been tortured according to several observers. The Nixon administration had argued instead that cutting off aid to Greece would destabilize NATO's presence in the Eastern Mediterranean. AHEPA, "as loyal and patriotic American citizens" and "as representatives of almost two million Americans of Greek descent," echoed the administration's positions and deplored the House's vote. The resolution was adopted unanimously.[86]

The new Supreme Lodge elected at the Los Angeles Supreme Convention was: Sam Nakis, Supreme President; Michael Spirtos, Supreme Vice President; Dinos Lambrou, a developer from Vancouver, Supreme Vice President of Canada; William Tsaffaras, Supreme Secretary; William G. Chirgotis, Supreme Treasurer; Dennis J. Livadas, Supreme Counsellor; A. Steve Betzelos, Supreme Governor; Peter J. Georges, Supreme Governor; George A. Heropoulos, Supreme Governor; Sam Platis, Supreme Governor; John G. Speliopoulos, Supreme Governor; Nicholas Zannetos, Supreme Governor. Monthe Kofos, who was reelected Supreme Athletic Director, announced the establishment of the William G. Chirgotis Collegiate Athletic Award to be given annually to an outstanding athlete of Greek descent from colleges and universities, which meant that future awards of the Harry Agganis Award would be only to professional athletes of Greek descent. A full list of the Agganis Award winners is available on AHEPA's website.[87] The Supreme Board of Trustees chair again was Peter Derzis. The new Supreme Vice President, Sam E. Nakis, a St. Louis businessman, was born in Lowell, Massachusetts in 1916. He served with John Connally, the former governor of Texas, as vice chairman of Democrats for Nixon, a national political group promoting the reelection of Nixon and Agnew. Nakis traveled to Athens and presented scroll copies of the AHEPA Resolution on US Military Aid to Greece to Prime Minister George Papadopoulos of Greece, and to Vice Premier Stylianos Pattakos.

A Socratic Award to the Ecumenical Patriarch
The 20th National Banquet honoring the US Congress was held in Washington, DC on March 13, and His Holiness Athenagoras I, Ecumenical Patriarch of Constantinople, spiritual leader of Eastern Orthodoxy, was named as the recipient of the 1972 AHEPA Socratic Award in recognition of 18 years as Archbishop of the Greek Orthodox Church of North and South America, and 24 years as Ecumenical Patriarch. He was unable to attend due to physical health and age, and the award was received on his behalf by His Eminence Archbishop Iakovos. Banquet chairman was John N. Deoudes, a businessman from Bethesda, Maryland, who like many Ahepans had a close association with the Greek Orthodox Church. Deoudes was a founding member of St. George Greek Orthodox Church in Bethesda and in Ocean City,

Maryland, and was a past president of the parish council at the Saint Sophia Greek Orthodox Cathedral of Washington. The toastmaster was John M. Manos, who at the time was a judge at the Ohio Court of Appeals and later on would receive AHEPA's Solon Award. In 1976 President Gerald Ford appointed Manos to the United States District Court for the Northern District of Ohio. Banquet speakers included the new US Secretary of Commerce, Peter G. Peterson, who was the child of Greek immigrants in Nebraska; Greek Foreign Undersecretary Dimitrios Tsakonas, US Senator Robert Taft, Jr., Archbishop Iakovos, Congressman Brademas, Supreme President Sam Nakis, Daughters Grand President Helen J. Beldecos, Maids Grand President Katherine Triantafillou, and Sons Supreme President Deno J. Krillies.

Cooley's Anemia

At the March meetings of the Supreme and Grand Lodges of AHEPA and its Auxiliaries, endorsement was given to the Cooley's Anemia (Thalassemia) Foundation for the purpose of supporting efforts to combat this hereditary disease of the blood which affects persons whose ancestors were natives of Greece, Italy, Turkey, southern France, and northern Africa. Cooley's Anemia, also called Mediterranean Anemia or Thalassemia, is inherited according to Mendelian laws, and the severe form known as Thalassemia Major occurs in a child born of parents who are both carriers of the disease. The fraternity immediately began publishing information on Cooley's Anemia to its membership, since information on the disease was not commonly known. Persons may carry the minor traits of the disease without suffering any ill effects, but two such persons with minor traits who marry, may bear a child who will emerge with Thalassemia Major, which is usually fatal. One quarter of the children of such a marriage of two persons with minor traits can be expected to have the severe form of the disease. The fraternity also urged support of federal funding legislation for research. Supreme Vice President Michael Spirtos, a physician, was appointed as national chairman of the AHEPA Committee on Cooley's Anemia.

AHEPA Reaches 50

To mark its 50th anniversary AHEPA returned to the city where it had been established, Atlanta, where it had also met to mark its 20th anniversary 30 years earlier, in 1942. The convention began with Archbishop Iakovos officiating at a liturgy at Atlanta's Greek Orthodox Church of the Annunciation on Sunday, August 20. At a banquet held after the service, Supreme President Sam Nakis praised Iakovos and criticized the Turkish government's decision not to allow the Archbishop to attend the funeral of Ecumenical Patriarch Athenagoras held in Istanbul after his death on July 7, 1972. In his opening speech at the convention Nakis spoke about the need for AHEPA to pay more attention to its youth policies and return to the concept of an "AHEPA family." He spoke about the Order needing to not rest on its laurels and realize it was entering a new era in which its leaders should become more aware of the needs of the members.

There was both a celebratory but also a somewhat politically partisan atmosphere at the Grand Banquet, which was extremely well attended. The main speakers were Secretary of State William Rogers, the Governor of Georgia Jimmy Carter, Atlanta Mayor Sam Massell, and North Carolina Congressman Nick Galifianakis, who was a candidate in the Senate race in his state. A few weeks earlier, Senator George McGovern, who was the Democratic nominee in the upcoming presidential election in November 1972, had pledged to halt American aid to Greece if he became president. This was inevitably discussed widely among delegates and when Supreme President Nakis arrived in Atlanta prior to the convention he spoke publicly about the need for US aid to Greece to continue. Rogers, speaking at the banquet, said it would not be correct for the United States to apply pressure on Greece to effect a change of government; he criticized the Democratic foreign policy positions and praised President Nixon's policy, eliciting frequent bursts of applause from his audience. At one point banquet chair John E. Skandalakis told Galifianakis: "Brother Nick, we wish you well locally, but for heaven's sake not nationally."[88] Nakis himself came in for praise for the work he had done to persuade members of the US Senate not to endorse the House of Representatives vote to ban military aid to Greece and there was displeasure expressed toward those in AHEPA and the Greek American community who had supported the ban to military aid to Greece. There was one strong voice criticizing the Greek regime and the attitude of the AHEPA leadership toward the colonels, and that belonged to Past Supreme President George Vournas. He issued a 10-page letter to the delegates at the Atlanta convention. It opened by discussing AHEPA's history and all its important achievements and then went on to suggest that the Order's goals and values were incompatible with what the junta represented.[89]

Going beyond the political situation in Greece, there was also a great deal of discussion of all the anniversary events that were taking place throughout the country and the popularity of the several mementos the Order had produced, including a Jim Beam decanter. And perhaps fitting of the overall climate of reflection on the past and looking forward to the future most of the decisions taken where about constitutional changes and the inner workings of the Order. Appropriately considering AHEPA's longstanding commitment to promoting sports, the anniversary convention included AHEPA's 27th annual Olympiad which opened as usual with the running of the Olympic torch.

The delegates elected Michael N. Spirtos Supreme President, William Tsaffaras Supreme Vice President, Supreme Vice President of Canada Dinos Lambrou, Supreme Secretary William Chirgotis, Supreme Treasurer Dr. Peter V. Paulus, Supreme Counsellor Gustav Coffinas. The Supreme Governors elected were Alex C. Booras, Nicholas P. Levendis, William Mackrides, Peter Pavoris, and Peter T. Stathes, and Monthe Kofos was reelected Supreme Athletic Director. Peter Derzis continued as chair of the Board of Trustees. The new Supreme President, Michael Spirtos, was a physician based in California. He was born in 1915 on the island of Calymnos when it was still under Italian rule, had arrived in New York with his family in 1920, and had first become active in AHEPA in Indiana.

AHEPA marked its golden anniversary the same year the Greek Orthodox Archdiocese of North and South America was marking its own 50th anniversary. The Archdiocese's tribute to AHEPA underscored the significance of that occasion: "The Greek Orthodox People of this hemisphere gratefully saluted the ORDER OF AHEPA, last August, as this great creation of its Mother Lodge and inspired pioneer members returned to Atlanta, Georgia, to joyfully celebrate its Golden Jubilee Anniversary. The church expresses warm wishes to AHEPA… for attaining its half-century mark with a distinguished record of manifesting its nine objectives by supporting and sponsoring many projects on the national and international level. On Sunday, August 20, 1972, Archbishop Iakovos, celebrated the Divine Liturgy at

Atlanta's Annunciation Cathedral, where he invested the five living Mother Lodge Members as Archons of the venerable Ecumenical Patriarchate, awarding also to them the Archdiocesan medal of St. Paul. Through these men, the Archbishop conferred honor upon each AHEPAN, who has served on the Supreme, District and Chapter level. We must ever look forward to the year 2022, when a century of service shall be completed. This journey into the next five decades must be patterned to offer a lasting contribution to the ultimate fashioning of our life-style as people of God in this pluralistic society. New orientations, drawn from the wellsprings of our traditions, are more than imperative."[90]

Part III 1973–1999

Chapter 7: AHEPA & US Policy in the Eastern Mediterranean 1974–1980

On July 20, 1974, Turkish armed forces launched a military invasion of Cyprus which resulted in Turkey illegally occupying about a third of its territory within a month. The events triggered a series of major changes not only for Cyprus but also Greece, where the military dictators stepped down and handed over power to the politicians whom they had banned from public life since 1967. That moment ushered in a new era in AHEPA's history as well. Partially distracted by the Watergate crisis and Richard Nixon's resignation in early August, but primarily wishing to preserve its ties to Turkey, the US government appeared to stand by and do very little to reverse the unfolding tragedy in Cyprus where many Greek Cypriots lost their lives, and thousands were forced to flee their homes and seek refuge in the southern part of the island. In response, the Greek American community launched a massive campaign to force the United States to intervene. AHEPA was front and center of that effort, while also managing to maintain the wide range of projects it was already pursuing.

The Greek American community's mobilization led to the creation of the Greek American Lobby based in Washington, DC and, thanks mainly to AHEPA, also with a presence across the United States. The lobby was made up of legislators, led by the so-called "gang of four" Senator Thomas Eagleton and Congressmen John Brademas, Joseph Rosenthal, and Paul Sarbanes, all of them Democrats, and was supported by AHEPA, locally formed Greek American committees, and the Greek American community writ large. Sarbanes, the son of Greek immigrants who owned a diner in Maryland, had been elected to the US Congress in 1970 and would go on to become a US Senator in 1976. He maintained a close relationship with AHEPA throughout his career on Capitol Hill. The work of the four during the fight for the embargo was supported by Greek American newspapers and radio stations. The lobby's success came when Congress voted for an embargo of US arms sales to Turkey that was implemented from 1975 to 1978. Throughout that period and onwards, AHEPA played a foremost role. It provided the necessary resources to Washington, DC Eugene Rossides, of Greek Cypriot origin, to form a lobbying organization, the American Hellenic Institute – Political Action Committee (AHI-PAC). AHEPA also mobilized in Washington while its members across the country became active, many of them joining Justice for Cyprus committees formed locally. AHEPA's work within the Greek American lobby involved informing the White House, Congress, and the American public about the situation in Cyprus, its incompatibility with American values, the rule of law, and national interests, and the suffering of the displaced Greek Cypriot refugees, was one of the Order's finest hours.

Michael Spirtos Speaks Up

In 1973, more than a year before the Cyprus crisis and the collapse of the dictatorship in Greece, AHEPA's Supreme President Michael Spirtos became the first Supreme President to speak up in favor of democracy in Greece during the seven-year rule of the military dictatorship. He was scheduled to travel to Greece in January to present dictator Papadopoulos with a medal commemorating AHEPA's 50th anniversary. A small group of businessmen and retired Greek military officers who were working against the dictatorship in the United States persuaded Spirtos that he should also visit the exiled King Constantine in Rome and present him also with a medal. The king, after initially going along with the colonels' coup in April 1967, had changed his mind and attempted a counter coup in December of that year. The plan failed and the king was forced into exile. He became part of conversations held outside Greece by the country's exiled political leaders about how democracy would be restored. For AHEPA to contact him was a sign that it was not entirely committed to supporting the regime. Spirtos was persuaded to visit the king and present him with a similar medal after meeting with Papadopoulos in Athens. At the time Spirtos was in Athens in early 1973, student anti-junta demonstrations had broken out and when he met Henry Tasca, the US ambassador to Greece, Tasca told Spirtos that very few people in the country were supporting the regime. When Spirtos returned, he issued a press release about his trip that listed his meeting, and which included mention of the visit with Constantine. Spirtos' personal statement included a reminder that AHEPA was a "non-political and non-partisan brotherhood," but it ended with what was a significant expression of support for the restoration of democracy in Greece: "One stated policy of particular interest to all Americans of Greek descent is the wish of the United States to see Greece return to democratic rule as soon as possible. The present Greek government has also expressed its desire for the reestablishment of democracy in Greece both through public statements and privately to Ambassador Henry Tasca. For all the above reasons I can only express my disappointment that I have not seen any real movement towards constitutional rule during the current year. I consider it my duty as an American, and as a member of AHEPA, to speak in support of the democratic ideal and call upon all fellow Greeks in positions of leadership to rise to the level of political maturity demanded by sacred Greek tradition concerning our participation in the community."[91]

There was however, mounting opposition to Spirtos' actions and words from within the Board of Trustees, and his next move, to invite King Constantine to the next convention. The Board ultimately had its way and the king after accepting initially decided to decline the invitation. Newspaper reports cited fears that the king might use the occasion to criticize the dictatorship and embarrass the Nixon administration that had lent it its support.[92]

The 51st Supreme Convention that met that year in Hollywood, Florida went on without King Constantine, but Spirtos' report contained the essence of the critique of the regime he had expressed after his visit. But there were objections expressed by several delegates and the wording was diluted in its final approved version. Nonetheless, thanks to Spirtos, AHEPA is on record as distancing itself from the dictatorial regime in Athens. A few weeks earlier Archbishop Iakovos had done so, describing it as "tyrannical." At that Supreme Convention the new elected Supreme President was William Tsaffaras. One of eight children of Greek immigrants Peter and Angelique Tsaffaras, the new Supreme President had been born in 1914 in Lowell, Massachusetts, and practiced law. The other members of the Supreme Lodge who were elected were Supreme Vice President William Chirgotis, Supreme Secretary Peter S. Kouchalakos, Supreme Treasurer Theodore N. Vombrack, and Supreme Counsellor Judge Thomas C. Yeotis. The Supreme Governors elected were Charles T. Adams, Peter W. G. Caylas, John Diamantakos, Thomas J. Pappas, Gust A. Saros, and Teddy C. Tzavellas; Monthe Kofos was reelected Supreme Athletic Director. Peter Derzis was to serve as chairman of the Board of Trustees, and Stephen L. Berdalis and Thomas Cavalaris as vice chairmen.

In what would turn out to be a somewhat ironic choice of principal speaker, then Vice President Gerald Ford had delivered the main address at AHEPA's 21st National Congressional Banquet held on March 25, 1974. Earlier that day the Supreme Lodge had visited President Nixon at the White House. Six months later Ford would replace Nixon at the White House and be facing the demands of the Greek lobby including AHEPA. In the days just before the banquet in March, the Supreme Lodge had held a three-day meeting in Washington, DC to discuss the wide-ranging activities the Order was taking that year. Those included the educational journey to Greece, the membership drive, the Cooley's Anemia project, and the Save-A-Heart Program. Those initiatives would continue in the months that followed, but the primary focus became the effort to persuade Congress to take steps to address the situation on Cyprus.

AHEPA Mobilizes
In the wake of Turkey's invasion of Cyprus, Supreme President Tsaffaras called a meeting of all presidents in DC where they met on July 23 and 24 and formed the "Congress of American Organizations" for the purpose of grouping together all Greek American associations to join in supporting Cyprus. Funds were to be raised for national

newspaper advertising, for releases to the members of Congress and the press, and other initiatives including relief for the refugees. AHEPA had called for a similar form of coordinated action in 1940 when Greece entered World War II. Ultimately, rather than working under an umbrella group, Greek Americans formed several different organizations all of which undertook the various tasks. For example, Eugene Rossides, a Washington, DC lawyer who had served in an Undersecretary position in Nixon's first administration, formed, with AHEPA's support, an organization specifically focused on lobbying Congress, the American Hellenic Institute (AHI). Rossides quickly became the key figure of the Greek American lobbying effort. Archbishop Iakovos meanwhile undertook several initiatives. As the unofficial spokesman of the Greek American community in the eyes of many, he started having meetings at the State Department and the White House. The Archdiocese launched a national campaign to provide relief to the Greek Cypriot refugees through its parishes nationwide. A little later, as the lobbying activities grew, Archbishop Iakovos formed his own lobbying group, the United Hellenic American Congress, which was based in Chicago and headed by the industrialist Andrew Athens. In New York, the Panhellenic Emergency Committee formed to coordinate the activities of the many topika somateia, the organizations representing persons from the same area of Greece, that were headquartered there, mostly in Astoria. And throughout the country, Greek Americans formed Cyprus solidarity committees designed to persuade their congressmen to act to reverse Turkey's actions and to solicit the support of the local press.

AHEPA itself undertook a lobbying and public information campaign, as well as raising funds for the relief of the refugees. The Order also collaborated closely with AHI, the Archdiocese, and the other Greek American organizations. And AHEPA members throughout the country became active through their local chapters and parishes and played a leadership role in the regional solidarity with Cyprus committees. Very soon, lobbying of Congress crystallized in the demand of an arms embargo on US arms sales to Turkey. Greek American Congressmen John Brademas and Paul Sarbanes led the effort, along with Congressman Jim Rosenthal and Senator Thomas Eagleton. Other Greek American congressmen, L. A. "Skip" Bafalis, Peter Kyros, and Gus Yatron were also involved. President Gerald

Ford, who had replaced Nixon because of Watergate, and Henry Kissinger whom he retained as Secretary of States and National Security Advisor, rejected the idea of the embargo, invoking issues of US security interests in the Eastern Mediterranean. If there was an irony to many of the same Greek Americans who had opposed sanctions on the Greek colonels in the name of security concerns now demanding that those same concerns be bypassed in the case of Turkey, this was not the time for anyone to raise that point.

With Greek American activity picking up pace rapidly AHEPA's national convention that met in Boston in the second half of August was one of the most intense and emotional meetings in the Order's history. Prior to that President William Tsaffaras had met with Joseph J. Sisco, the Under Secretary for Political Affairs of the State Department, on August 7 and had presented AHEPA's request for immediate action of the United States to put a stop to and reverse Turkey's actions. The next day the president informed members he hoped the meeting "will bring fruitful results on the American government." His optimism was misplaced because by the time AHEPA met in Boston in a week's time, not only had nothing had been done on the part of the White House and the State Department, but also Turkey had extended its reach and occupied an entire third of Cyprus' territory.

The 52nd Supreme Convention, 1974, Boston
Given the situation in Cyprus, AHEPA's 52nd Supreme Convention that opened in Boston on August 18th, 1974, was one of the most emotional and important in the Order's history as well as one of the best-attended in terms of attendance by national and local political leaders. Just prior to the convention an AHEPA delegation had traveled to Greece and met Prime Minister Constantine Karamanlis, who had been installed when the colonels' regime handed power back to the politicians in July. Upon the return of the delegation Supreme President William Tsaffaras stated that it was clear US policy was tilting toward Turkey and the traditional goodwill of the Greek people toward the United States was running out.[93] In Boston, a bipartisan AHEPA committee worked on the resolutions that would be put to a vote at the convention, and a Cyprus rally was combined with an already planned music event on the first

day of the proceedings. The speakers on that first day included Congressmen John Brademas and Paul Sarbanes who condemned the invasion of Cyprus by Turkey and criticized US policy. The other speakers that day included Massachusetts gubernatorial candidate Mike Dukakis. The State Department sent the US ambassador to Greece, Jack Kubisch, to address the convention. Over the following days mobilization around the Cyprus cause was combined with church services and social events. George Douris, who had chaired the 1973 Supreme Convention, chaired at Boston as well. At the Grand Banquet, the main speaker was the Greek Minister for Culture and Sciences Constantinos Tsatsos, who mentioned that Greece felt abandoned by NATO and that Greece sought peace with justice and honor. Archbishop Iakovos also spoke. An AHEPA Justice for Cyprus Committee was formed during the convention and its members traveled down to New York for a meeting with United Nations officials. Later that week another delegation met with Secretary of State Henry Kissinger in Washington, DC for an hour—Kissinger was generally considered the key figure who was shaping US foreign policy during the Cyprus crisis.

The delegates at the Convention elected William G. Chirgotis as Supreme President. Born in Piraeus in 1909, Chirgotis arrived in the United States with his family in 1919. After graduating from the Pratt Institute School of Architecture in 1940 he quickly established himself as one of the country's leading architects. He had designed the plaza around the statue of President Truman donated by AHEPA and erected in Athens in 1963. Chirgotis and Peter Derzis, who was elected Supreme Vice President, were both candidates put forward by the AHEPA First party. The others who were elected to the Supreme Lodge were Jean Pierre Van Eck, a businessman in Edmonton, as Supreme Vice President of Canada, A. Steve Betzelos Supreme Secretary, John T. Pappas Supreme Treasurer, Dennis Livadas Supreme Counselor. The Supreme Governors who were elected were Eli Chinonis, Andrew Liatos, Matthew Melonas, Thomas J. Pappas, Gust A. Satos, and Peter N. Stamas, and Monthe Kofos was reelected Supreme Athletic Director. Also, Nick N. Smyrnis was to serve as chairman of the Supreme Board of Trustees and George A. Bexaitis as first vice chairman.

The First Moves on the Cyprus Front

At the end of September 1974 AHEPA held a cocktail reception in honor of Cyprus' Archbishop Makarios and Greek Foreign Minister George Mavros in New York City. Two days later, on September 29, a Humanitarian Mission to Cyprus, led by Supreme President Tsaffaras and the president of the Justice for Cyprus Committee, John Plumides, flew to the Eastern Mediterranean. Traveling with them were Coordinator George Douris, Past Supreme Presidents Peter Bell and William Tsaffaras, Past Supreme Governor Scofield, and two aides to the committee, Archie Mavromatis and Peter Sideris. The delegation visited Greece where it met with Prime Minister Karamanlis, Foreign Minister George Mavros, and US Ambassador Kubisch. In Cyprus it met with Acting President Clerides, Turkish Vice President Rauf Denktash, and US Ambassador to Cyprus William R. Crawford. In his report following the eight-day fact finding mission, Chirgotis bluntly stated in his report that "what we witnessed during this short but productive period was something we never expected to find in the 20th century. Seeing is believing—and we saw 234,000 refugees living in tents, others under trees, on the beaches, in the city streets. We saw doctors examining children in tents that would make M.A.S.H.'s medical tents look like modern hospital facilities. We witnessed children slowly dying due to a lack of medicine and proper facilities to stop diarrhea and dehydration. We saw a baby left on a blanket unattended, the father captured by the Turks, the mother frantically seeking to find her other two infant children."[94]

The realization that AHEPA was faced by an enormous task, because it had to work both to shape US foreign policy in the Eastern Mediterranean and to offer humanitarian aid to Cyprus, received some encouragement thanks to a small victory on Capitol Hill. Thanks to the efforts of the Greek American lobby, Congress compelled the administration to accept tough conditions on military aid to Turkey, despite two presidential vetoes. It was a momentous event for both Congress and the Greek American community, which would be superseded a year later by an even greater success, the imposition of the embargo. But for now, this small victory was very encouraging because it also represented the lobby's successful negotiations of Capitol Hill's intricate legislative process. AHEPA had been sending a stream of "mailgrams" to its members explaining the process and highlighting the right moves. And the Order was also generous in its praise of all those who led the effort. Its announcement mentioned: "We cannot praise too highly, or thank sufficiently, our good Brother Eugene T. Rossides and his staff, for leading the way throughout the Cyprus situation; he was always on top of the issues, and we followed his recommendations at all times. He was a tireless worker, and he has the fraternity's full thanks for his efforts. Special thanks are also due Andy Manatos on Senator Eagleton's staff on Capitol Hill and Leon Stavrou, Past Supreme Governor of the Sons of Pericles for their unstinting efforts."[95]

The national media in the United States was reporting even more frequently on the actions and the achievements of the Greek American lobby and crediting the contributions of AHEPA. An article in the Washington Post that appeared in October 1974 mentioned: "Unlike the Jewish community, which has politically sensitized and mobilized on Israel's behalf for a long time, Greek-Americans had to organize themselves from scratch. The backbone was the Order of AHEPA, organized in 1922 to make American citizens out of Greek immigrants, and now a nonprofit charitable, civic and educational organization with about 1,100 chapters... Justice for Cyprus committees were organized in the AHEPA chapters around the nation. Each time a congressional action on Turkish aid impended, AHEPA Headquarters here contacted members and the word was spread. The Greek-Americans wrote, called, telegraphed, and occasionally personally visited their congressmen and senators."[96] The persistence of Congress led to a final effort in December 1974 to impose the arms embargo on Turkey. The Senate approved an amendment calling for an end of arms sales and military aid to Turkey unless the president could reach a diplomatic solution by December 10, 1974. When President Ford failed to break the impasse by the specified date, the embargo went into effect on February 5, 1975.

The year 1974, that brought the tragedy of Cyprus, was a turning point in AHEPA's history. Its response to the Cyprus crisis catapulted the Order on to a higher plane than before. Its leaders and members displayed a profound sense of purpose and an organizational level that served its ambitious goals and propelled the Greek American lobby forward. It was also a turning point in a different way. In August of that year, George A. Polos, one of the founders of AHEPA passed away, at age 84. As a member of the Order's "Mother Lodge" he had been instrumental in bringing together about 1,300 members who met at the first Supreme Convention in 1923. In the short span of a year another two founders had passed away, John Angelopoulos and Nicholas Chotas. This meant that only two of the eight founders were still living, James Campbell and John Angelopoulos. AHEPA was steadily being deprived of the inspirational presence of its pioneer leaders.

1975: Balancing Between International & Domestic Responsibilities
In 1975 AHEPA held its 53rd Supreme Convention in Cincinnati, Ohio, returning there for the first time since holding its 18th convention in that city in 1941. With the embargo in place beginning in January 1975, AHEPA was able to redirect some of its attention away from the international sphere and address its duties in the areas of philanthropy, civic responsibility, and the welfare of its members. Indeed, the beginning of the year saw AHEPA dealing with a range of issues, including arrangements for Easter and educational trips to Greece, setting the dates for the annual fundraising drive for the Cooley's Anemia Fund, and announcing the swearing in as member of newly elected Massachusetts Governor Michael Dukakis.

Among the domestic programs that Supreme President Chirgotis managed to attend were the Save-A-Heart Program and dealing with AHEPA's property in Pinellas County, Florida, even though the Cyprus issue took up a lot of his energy. The Save-A-Heart program had begun in 1974 when AHEPA pledged to raise $50,000 annually to assist the Loma Linda University School of Medicine Heart Surgery Team, which had an affiliation with Evangelismos Hospital in Athens, to assist in the performance of open heart surgery. While the program met with early success, it became clear that funds could be put to better use to enable Evangelismos to acquire a new heart surgery theatre and replace the old heart lung machine, and this became AHEPA's new policy.[97] The Florida Property, as it became known, had a long history that dated back to the late 1930s when Supreme President Chebithes began initiating projects that would benefit the Order's members. It was the 14th Supreme Convention in 1937 that authorized the purchase of 349 acres in Florida for the purpose of constructing a national home for orphans or one for old persons. The war years that ensued prevented any movement in that direction and at the 28th Supreme Convention in 1950 there was a proposal that the property be leased for farming or cattle grazing. From the late 1950s onwards Pinellas County and the surrounding area experienced a housing boom and in 1961 the Supreme Lodge had asked Chirgotis to prepare a report on the ways AHEPA could make the best use out of the property which was still underdeveloped. Fourteen years later, Chirgotis as Supreme President set the wheels in motion, pointing out the original validity of his initial assessment and the obstacles that had prevented the Order taking any immediate steps to implement his proposals. Now, with those hurdles cleared, AHEPA retained 72 acres and sold the rest of the property at a profit of just over $3 million. The property it retained, Chirgotis recommended it be used primarily for constructing residential family lots, as well as units for multi-family high density residential use and a public park.[98]

Those positive developments on the domestic front notwithstanding, the Cyprus crisis and the embargo dominated the proceedings at the Cincinnati convention. In the previous few months AHEPA had rejected an approach from the White House requesting that it cease to support the Turkish arms embargo. And in a visit to Athens which included a meeting with Prime Minister Karamanlis, AHEPA had expressed its continued commitment to doing everything in its powers to achieve the withdrawal of Turkish troops from Cyprus and to continuing its efforts to provide relief to the internal refugee problem in Cyprus that Turkey's invasion had created. At the convention AHEPA's Justice for Cyprus Committee held a special session and heard speeches from Texas Senator Lloyd Bentsen and Congressmen Paul Sarbanes and Mario Biaggi of New York as well as Cyprus' ambassador Nicos Dimitriou. Most speakers referred to the White House and other sources of pressure on AHEPA and stressed the need for the Order to stay the course on the embargo. References were also made to the presidential elections that would take place in the United States the following year. In the words of a reporter from a local paper the tone of most speeches "gave the normally middle-of-the-road, non-political organization a decided tilt away from the Administration of Gerald Ford. Virtually all speakers, politicians and AHEPA leaders alike, railed against Ford and Secretary of State

Henry Kissinger for their abortive attempts to resume military aid to Turkey before Cyprus is neutralized and in contravention of what Congress voted." [99]

The AHEPA elections at the Cincinnati convention were a closely contested affair with three candidates running for the post of Supreme President: Chirgotis, the incumbent who was the candidate of the AHEPA First party; Xenophon K. Microutsicos, the United AHEPA Party candidate; and former Supreme President Spirtos, who was the candidate of the New and Living AHEPA Party. Spirtos withdrew before the vote and backed Microutsicos, creating a very close race. In the end, Chirgotis was reelected after receiving 249½ votes with Microutsicos receiving 231 votes.[100]

America's Bicentennial in 1976

AHEPA was the first Greek American organization to mobilize around the need to take part in the nation's Bicentennial celebration in 1976. Preparations began in 1972 when George E. Perry (Pierratos), who worked in the Library of Congress, noticed that plans for the upcoming centennial that involved the library made no mention of the Greek American community and contacted AHEPA. George Leber, the Executive Secretary, immediately formed a working group that included Perry and Professors Dimitrios G. Kousoulas and Theodore Saloutos. At AHEPA's 1972 Convention Perry informed Archbishop Iakovos of AHEPA's plans and a few months later the Archdiocese formed its own Bicentennial committee. AHEPA's working group became an official committee that was headed by Perry, who would become an active member of an organization called the Ethnic Employees of the Library of Congress, which was dedicated to promoting non-discriminatory treatment of ethnic and racial minorities at the library. Two more distinguished Greek American academics, Peter Topping and Stephen G. Xydis, joined the committee. It was Perry who conceived of a wide range of activities AHEPA could undertake in connection to the Bicentennial, and he advocated for showcasing how the Greeks had adapted to America but also how they had contributed to their adopted country as well.

The Bicentennial committee's far-reaching agenda and its wide scope reflected the assertiveness and strength that AHEPA possessed as it moved forward having celebrated the half century of its existence. The principal event the committee envisioned was an exhibition of Greek art treasures to be held in the United States, and travel from the National Gallery in Washington, DC to the Museum of Fine Arts in Boston, the Field Museum of Natural History in Chicago, the Municipal Gallery of Art in Los Angeles, and the Metropolitan Museum in New York City. The committee also proposed a similar "Treasures of Cyprus" exhibition. The committee had also obtained an agreement with the Smithsonian Museum for another exhibit on Greek and American art that would also travel to 10 or 12 major American cities.

Additional initiatives the committee proposed were the publication of a collection of essays on the Greeks in America; a series of pamphlets on topics such as AHEPA's 50th anniversary, Greek Americans in politics, and America and the Greek Revolution of 1821; and a series of public lectures on Greek American subjects. In localities across the United States there existed memorials commemorating events or personalities prominent in the history of Greek-American relations. The committee suggested there could be wreath-laying ceremonies by the local AHEPA chapters. Those memorials included the AHEPA monuments at New Smyrna Beach, Florida commemorating the landing of Greeks in America in 1768; at Brown University in Providence, Rhode Island in honor of Samuel Gridley Howe; at Ypsilanti, Michigan in honor of General Dimitrios Ypsilanti; at Sommerville, Massachusetts in honor of George Dilboy; and the AHEPA commissioned sculptures honoring Presidents Franklin D. Roosevelt and Harry S. Truman. The committee also produced a list of 14 American and Greek personalities it deemed worthy of being honored by Greek Americans in connection with the Bicentennial.

This ambitious agenda that AHEPA's Bicentennial Celebration produced was only partially fulfilled because by 1976 the Order was focused on assisting the lobbying campaign over the Cyprus crisis. By 1976 government officials had been made aware of AHEPA's importance. A memorandum issued within the State Department in July listed the foreign policy issues that were likely to play a role in the upcoming presidential election in November. It mentioned AHEPA by name, speculating: "The current stalemate offers Carter an opportunity to charge a lack of effective leadership on the part of the Administration. While he is severely limited in offering specific alternatives, he can attempt to attract the support of AHEPA, other interested Greek Americans, and the liberal community at large, by reminding those groups of Administration insensitivity to their concerns at the outset of the crisis."[101]

Yet AHEPA managed to couple the Cyprus crisis with the Bicentennial when it drafted an announcement about Cyprus that appeared a full or half page advertisement in newspapers throughout the country. The banner headline read: "More than ever in this bicentennial year, America must stand up for Justice, Morality and the Rule of Law in its foreign policy." Also, many chapters were marking their 50th anniversary that year and understandably perhaps were involved in holding events designed to help them increase their membership locally. Among those chapters were Hancock Chapter 103 in Weirton, Virginia and the Tri-City Chapter 103 in Illinois and Iowa, while several even older chapters honored those who had reached their 50th year as members.

The Bicentennial Celebrations

The celebrations that took place in 1976 were during the weekend of April 3–5 in Washington, DC. The three-day program began with the opening of the AHEPA Bicentennial Exhibit at the Washington Hilton Hotel. The dedication ceremony was held in honor of George Leber, the Order's Executive Secretary, who had passed away in January 1976. The exhibit consisted of 25 large panels that covered the contributions of Greece to Western civilization, Greek immigration to the United States, and the contribution of Greek Americans to America. Following the dedication Professor Theodore Saloutos spoke about the exhibit. The other major event was the 22nd AHEPA National Banquet honoring the US Congress. It was the Order's most important social event of the year with more than 1,500 persons in attendance, among them 25 US Senators and about a third of the total number of members of the House of Representatives.

The highlight of the evening was an address by President Ford who praised the long friendship of Greece with the United States, and also praised the contributions of the Greek immigrants to the United States. Ford also described Greece's Prime Minister Constantine Karamanlis as an outstanding leader of the free world. The evening's principal honor, the Socratic Award, was to be presented to Karamanlis, but he was unable to travel to the United States because of the prevailing conditions in Greece. The Socratic awards to the Senate and Congress were accepted respectively by Senator Thomas F. Eagleton of Missouri, who was one of the main pillars of the lobbying efforts on Capitol Hill, and by Congressman Dante B. Fascell of Florida, who was also a supporter of the Turkish arms embargo. The one sour note of the evening was that Ford did not make any mention of Cyprus in his speech and Chirgotis would note that in his report to the 1976 Supreme Convention later that year. This was a time when the embargo on Turkey was in force. Out of respect to the President, in his remarks that evening Tsaffaras also did not refer to Cyprus. But the following day he sent the president a letter thanking him for honoring AHEPA with his presence at the banquet but adding: "The applause, and general expression of love, respect and devotion to you as President of our country, should not be understood as implying approval of the policies of your Administration toward Greece and Turkey. The members of AHEPA are united in condemning those policies. We consider them utterly detrimental to the American interests in the area, diametrically opposed to American ideals, and profoundly unjust and unfair to the people of Greece and Cyprus." Chirgotis went on to cite the history of Greece and America's staunch alliances and friendship. He acknowledged the significance of the US military bases on Turkish soil but disputed their relative importance compared to what bases in Greece could offer, adding that Greece, unlike Turkey, was not trying to blackmail the United States. Before closing with a request for a meeting between AHEPA's expert and President Ford, Tsaffaras also noted forcefully that even if the importance of the bases on Turkey were as big as some persons claimed, "it can never be as great as the importance of the moral issue involved and the devotion of people of goodwill throughout the world for whom the mishandling of Greece and Cyprus has a tremendous symbolic meaning."[102]

The 54th Supreme Convention, 1976, Houston

AHEPA held its 54th Supreme Convention in August 1976 in Houston, which at the time was the fastest growing city in the United States. One of outgoing Supreme President Chirgotis' last responsibilities was to present Peter Agris, the founder and publisher of The Hellenic Chronicle, the Boston-based English language weekly newspaper. As was the case at the convention the previous year, the speakers, who included Massachusetts Governor Dukakis, castigated the Ford administration's inertia over Cyprus. A resolution echoing those sentiments was endorsed by the Democratic party candidate in the November election, Jimmy Carter, and his running mate Walter Mondale sent a message to AHEPA saying he was proud of his efforts in the Senate in support of the embargo.

In the elections for the new officers, Xenophon Microutsicos, who narrowly missed being elected the previous year, was successful in his bid to become Supreme President. His victory over AHEPA First candidate Derzis was the narrowest possible, with 248½ votes to 247. Born in Greece in 1912, Microutsicos arrived in the United States with his family in 1920; his parents were from the town of Aigio in Peloponnesos. He lived in Trenton, New Jersey where he owned Banker Insurance Agency and Trenton Travel Service. The other elected members of the Supreme Lodge were Peter V. Paulus, Supreme Vice President; Anthony Demakos from London, Ontario, Supreme Vice President for Canada; George P. Gabriel, Supreme Secretary; Paul A. Karras, Supreme Treasurer. The Supreme Governors elected were Dr. James G. Demopoulos, Frank J. Francis, Fred Iconos, Stephen Johnson, Costas E. Pavlou, Emmanuel S. Zaphiriou, Supreme Governor for Canada Jean Pierre Van Eck; Monthe Kofos was reelected Athletic Director. A. T. Tsoumas would be the new chair of the Board of Trustees and Anthony G. Poulos the first vice chairman.

The new Supreme Lodge picked up where the previous one had left off on the Cyprus issue and AHEPA continued its initiatives seamlessly. In September, Democratic party candidate Jimmy Carter met with the AHEPA leadership to outline his foreign policy goals, which included a commitment to human rights and less emphasis on the unprincipled "realpolitik" that Kissinger had pursued and as a result had not applied pressure on Turkey. That same day Carter met with a wider group of Greek American leaders including AHEPA, and the next day he and his running mate Walter Mondale issued a policy statement that noted: "The policy of the Ford Administration of tilting away from Greece and Cyprus has proved a disaster for NATO and for American security interests in the Eastern Mediterranean... peace must be based upon the United Nations General Assembly Resolution... calling among other things for the removal of all foreign military forces from Cyprus." Carter repeated those points in October just prior to the presidential election. These statements fueled a wave of optimism and even enthusiasm which swept over the Greek American community and AHEPA members. It appeared that if elected, Carter would end Turkey's occupation of the northern part of Cyprus and pursue a foreign policy in the Eastern Mediterranean based on the rule of law.[103]

In October AHEPA published a full-page advertisement in major newspapers linking the values of the Bicentennial with the need to resolve the Cyprus situation with respect to human rights and fairness to its victims. In November Carter was elected president and this triggered even greater optimism among Greek Americans as well as in Greece and Cyprus that a just solution to the crisis was at hand.

The 55th Supreme Convention, 1977, New Orleans
By the time AHEPA held its 55th Supreme Convention in August 1977 in New Orleans, all the optimism and enthusiasm Carter's election generated had evaporated and in its place were growing concerns that the new administration was continuing its predecessor's pro-Turkish tilt. Upon taking office Carter forgot his prior commitments to AHEPA and the Greek American community and allowed his National Security Advisor Zbigniew Brzezinski to pursue a "realpolitik" approach to the situation in the Eastern Mediterranean, which boiled down to appeasing Turkey and eventually working toward lifting the arms embargo. The Cyprus issue dominated the business sessions of the convention, burdened with the sad note of the news that Cyprus' President Makarios had passed away in Nicosia a few days earlier. AHEPA would attend a memorial service held there to honor the great leader.

In the elections for the Supreme President, Peter N. Derzis was victorious over the incumbent Xenophon Microutsicos. Derzis was born in Birmingham, Alabama, received a degree in business administration, and then served in the Army as an intelligence officer achieving the rank of colonel. Upon his retirement from military service, he joined a stock brokerage firm. The other officers elected were Peter V. Paulus, Supreme Vice President; Nicholas Zambus, a realtor in Vancouver, Supreme Vice President for Canada; Gustav Coffinas, Supreme Secretary; James G. Petheriotes, Supreme Treasurer; George S. Stratigos, Supreme Counsellor. The Supreme Governors elected were John C. Argoudelis, John N. Deoudes, George A. Granitsas, Dr. Andrew Karantinos, Steve Moskos, Nick G. Paras, and Leo Polydoropoulos, Supreme Governor of Canada; Monthe Kofos was reelected Supreme Athletic Director.

Timothy J. Maniatis was appointed Executive Director of AHEPA in 1977 and he stayed in that position for 15 years. He was born in Pittsfield, Massachusetts, the son of Greek immigrants; his father owned a restaurant. Maniatis received his Bachelor of Science degree in economics from Illinois Wesleyan University, continued his education at Tufts and Harvard Universities, and received his MBA from Boston University in 1966. After his long service as AHEPA's executive director he would go on to become an organizer of events held by the Greek Orthodox Archdiocese and other Greek American organizations.

The End of the Embargo

The increasing concerns about Carter's foreign policy led to meeting in November 1977 in Washington, DC between Vice President Mondale and a small number of Greek American leaders including Supreme President Derzis and Archbishop Iakovos. The Greek Americans expressed their frustration at the administration's inertia, and Mondale acknowledged their impatience was justified. Toward the end of the meeting President Carter entered the room and in the conversation that ensued he asked for everyone's understanding about why he could discuss the developments of the Cyprus question publicly. After several months of silence from Washington, in early April 1978 the New York Times newspaper broke the news that Carter wished to lift the embargo. AHEPA's statement when the news was confirmed was summarized in the title "President Carter Betrays the Greek-Americans and the People of Greece and Cyprus."

What ensued was a bitterly fought battle over the lifting of the arms embargo from early April to August 1, 1978. AHEPA along with the other Greek American organizations relaunched the mobilization they had achieved in 1974, but Carter was gradually eroding support for the embargo in Congress. He held a meeting at the White House in June 1978 at which he invited Greek American leaders to try and explain the logic of his policies. When the audience spoke, he was roundly criticized and Supreme President Derzis remined him that he was reneging on his earlier promises. He added that while Carter supported human rights in the rest of the world, he was neglecting to do so in Cyprus.[104]

In the end Carter was able to prevail. The Senate voted 57 to 42 to repeal the embargo. The fight in the House of Representatives was more closely contested, but on August 1 the final vote was 208 to 205 in support of repealing the embargo. It was an end of an era for the Greek American lobby and AHEPA's efforts, but by no means the end. Indeed AHEPA emerged with a great deal of experience and know how that would serve it very well in the next round of involvement in US foreign policy in the Eastern Mediterranean.

The 56th Supreme Convention, 1978, Miami Beach
Without losing its focus on Cyprus after the lifting of the embargo, AHEPA addressed other issues at the 1978 convention. But outgoing Supreme President Derzis made sure his opening speech emphasized AHEPA's continued commitment to resolving the Cyprus crisis based on the principles of the rule of law. The other issues AHEPA would discuss in Miami Beach included the Save-A-Heart program, now oriented toward erecting a surgical theatre and intensive care unit at Evangelismos Hospital, Athens. Delegates also authorized appropriation of $160,000 toward construction of a new $600,000 dormitory to house 100 boys at St. Basil's Academy. Several of the reports submitted at the Supreme Convention mentioned the need for greater unity within AHEPA's ranks, suggesting the organization continued to experience internal tensions based on personal or political differences, which makes its achievements during the same time more significant.

At the 1978 convention delegates elected Dr. Peter V. Paulus, a chemist based in Cleveland with a PhD from the University of Cincinnati, as its new Supreme President, succeeding Derzis, who did not seek reelection. Paulus, like many other Ahepans, played a leadership role in the work of the Greek War Relief Association during World War II. After the war he pursued a distinguished career in the plastics industry. He led a sweep of AHEPA First candidates to victory, defeating Nicholas L. Strike. Gregory Lagakos, who was elected Vice President, led an equally distinguished career. The son of Greek immigrants, he was born and raised in Camden, New Jersey. He practiced law in Philadelphia and served as a judge on the County Court of Philadelphia and the Common Pleas Court. The other elected officers were: Leo Polydoropoulos of Windsor, Ontario as Supreme Vice President for Canada; Elias Chinonis, Supreme Secretary; T. J. Bouras, Supreme Treasurer; James P. Fusscas, Supreme Counsellor. The Supreme Governors who were elected were Pete J. Caras, Dr. Andrew Karantinos, Tassos Kellaris, William G. Rotas, John Samos, Dr. Leo F. Sarivalas, and Nicholas Zambus; Monthe Kofos was reelected Supreme Athletic Director.

In the wake of the lifting of the Turkish arms embargo earlier that year, Congress was considering the extent to which aid to Turkey would be resumed, and AHEPA was very busy in the months after the convention informing members of Congress of the ongoing situation in Cyprus. Efforts were also made to increase the membership in Canada, and some headway was made in that respect in British Columbia.

The 57th Supreme Convention, 1979 San Francisco
The Yearbook of 1979 produced for the 57th Supreme Convention that was held in San Francisco included photographs of an AHEPA delegation's meeting with Prime Minister Karamanlis and the model of a new dormitory at St. Basil's Academy which was the Order's

new fundraising project. It was an appropriate reflection of AHEPA's dual international and domestic orientation. And in yet another reflection of the Order's standing, outgoing Supreme President Paulus reported an improvement in the relations between AHEPA chapters and parish priests across the country. But most of his report was devoted to AHEPA's trips to Greece the past year, suggesting the traditional Easter trip be eliminated because of increased travel opportunities, as well as its meetings in Washington, DC with policy makers. The Supreme President clarified that AHEPA did not function in a diplomatic capacity in all those encounters but as a conduit of information between its members and policy makers and vice versa. At the 1979 convention delegates honored longtime Supreme Athletic Director Monthe Kofos by naming two golf tournaments after him. Since assuming his position in 1969 Kofos had upgraded AHEPA's sports programs in many creative ways, including visits to Greece by AHEPA's basketball team.

Delegates elected Nick Smyrnis as Supreme President. Born in Indianapolis, Smyrnis received an AB degree from Butler University. During World War II he joined the Army and served 32 months overseas in the Pacific, achieving the rank of First Sergeant. For his many years of public service, he received several honors, including the Silver Cross of the Phoenix by the government of Greece (1965), Kentucky Colonel (1966), and Ahepan of the Year (1974). He worked in commercial-industrial real estate, including sales, leasing, and developing. Smyrnis would go down in AHEPA history not only as a two-time Supreme President but also as the co-founder and first President of AHEPA National Housing Corporation, which he helped establish in 1983 to provide affordable apartment communities for over 5,500 low-income seniors nationwide. He was also an original founder and first President/CEO of AHEPA Management Company, created to provide property management services for affordable senior apartment communities.

The other elected officials were Gustav Coffinas, Supreme Vice President; Gus Kolitsas, Supreme Vice President of Canada; Charles P. Tsaffaras, Supreme Secretary; Pete J. Papageorge, Supreme Treasurer; George J. Charles, Supreme Counsellor. The Supreme Governors who were elected were Chris W. Caragianis, Clifford T. G. Geanopulos, George G. Papuchis, Harry Siafaris, Spero Theros, George J. Yioulios, and Anthony Demakos, Supreme Governor of Canada; Monthe Kofos was reelected Supreme Athletic Director.

While AHEPA continued to pursue a solution to the Cyprus crisis and despite its earlier conflicts with President Carter, it maintained a respectful relationship with the White House. In one of his last appearances before a Greek American audience, at AHEPA's banquet in Washington, DC in February 1980, Carter received a considerably warmer welcome than he had two years ago during the struggle over the embargo. In 1980 he spoke about Greece becoming the permanent site for the Olympic Games. AHEPA's banquet was an appropriate venue to make such a suggestion.

AHEPA Achieves Unity

AHEPA's involvement with the Olympic Games has been a means through which the Order honors its Hellenic heritage. In early 1980 President Carter called for a boycott of the Olympic Games that were scheduled to be held that summer in Moscow. The reason was the Soviet invasion of Afghanistan. Carter spoke about the boycott at AHEPA's 24th Congressional Banquet in February 1980, and the Order responded enthusiastically. At that moment, Greece's Prime Minister Konstantinos Karamanlis reissued his call for Greece to become the permanent venue of the Olympic Games. AHEPA also endorsed the proposal and Carter himself spoke of it at the AHEPA Banquet, and this was reported nationally across the United States. In the words of the New York Times, "The President drew enthusiastic applause when he once again spoke for the withdrawal from the Games, in a talk before 1,000 members of the Order of AHEPA, the American Hellenic Progressive Association. 'Wouldn't it be wonderful' Mr. Carter told the crowd of Greek Americans, gathered at the Washington Sheraton Hotel, 'if we had a permanent Summer Olympic site in Greece?'"[105]

Earlier that year Supreme President Nick Smyrnis had traveled to Greece as part of the 15-member US presidential delegation to the Olympic Torch Ceremony, staged at ancient Olympia for the purpose of transmitting the flame that would burn during the Winter Olympic Games at Lake Placid, New York in early February. It was the first delegation ever to escort the flame from ancient Olympia to the United States. There were several official and social events that took place in Athens in honor of the delegation, followed by the torch lighting ceremony at Olympia.[106]

The issues relating to US policy in the Eastern Mediterranean were an important element of the business sessions of the 58th Supreme Convention which met in Washington, DC in August 1980. AHEPA's Cyprus and Aegean committee reported on a successful trip to Greece, Cyprus, and the Ecumenical Patriarchate in November 1979. The delegation was received warmly in all three venues and discussions revolved among other things around the refugee situation in Cyprus, anti-American sentiments in Greece, and US relations with Turkey.

The most important moment of the 58th Supreme Convention in 1980 came on the days of the election. To preserve the bipartisan character of the Supreme Board of Trustees, member Steve A. Manta was nominated to run against incumbent Nick Smyrnis. But Manta declined and called for the unanimous election of Smyrnis in the name of establishing unity among all groups within the Order. His suggestion was accepted, a sign that AHEPA could overcome internal rivalries and present a united front. The other elected officers were Gustav Coffinas, Supreme Vice President; James S. Anas, a businessman from Ontario, as Supreme Vice President of Canada, who would serve another two year term in that position in 1994-1995; Gregory J. Despinakis, Supreme Secretary; Chris Caragianis, Supreme Treasurer; George J. Charles, Supreme Counsellor. The Supreme Governors elected were Andrew T. Banis, William T. Dillas, Anthony Mamais, Arthur G. Saridakis, Gus Stefanadis, Spero Theros, and Gus Vlahos; Monthe Kofos was reelected Supreme Athletic Director and Louis P. Logas National Sons Advisor. For the next year, Peter H. Cardiges would serve as chairman of the Supreme Board of Trustees and George P. Gabriel as first vice chairman.

In the weeks and months following the Supreme Convention the country was swept up by the upcoming presidential election which pitted the incumbent Jimmy Carter against Ronald Reagan. This time Carter did not receive unconditional Greek American support, especially because of his lifting of the Turkish arms embargo in 1978. Instead, the community voted according to its preference for one of the two major parties. AHEPA members voted along the same lines, and a few played a prominent role in the campaigns. John Plumides was active for the Democratic Party while the National Committee of Greek American Voters for Reagan & Bush had as its spokesman Peter Derzis, of Virginia, a Past Supreme President. The members of the committee included Past Supreme Presidents William Chirgotis, Gustav Coffinas, and Leo Lamberson. Reagan's victory in November 1980 and his reelection in 1984 would set the United States on a new course in its history, and the same applied to AHEPA.

CHAPTER 8: AHEPA: A BRIDGE BETWEEN THE UNITED STATES AND GREECE 1981–1987

Speaking at a conference entitled "Irreconcilable Differences? American Foreign Policy and Greek National Interests" organized by AHEPA in early 1985, Richard Haas, the US Deputy Assistant Secretary for European and Canadian Affairs, said: "AHEPA deserves our congratulations for sponsoring a conference on so important a topic, and I will direct most of my remarks to this question. AHEPA has a key role to play. Your close contact with the Greek people and understanding of both countries provides an important bond of friendship and trust. No group is more qualified to explain our perspective in Greece or the Greek perspective here than you. None can doubt your sincere concern for good US-Greek relations. You have represented a large segment of the American public's views on these issues responsibly and thoughtfully. We admire what your organization has done and continues to do to foster greater understanding and better relations. This conference is a fine example of your timely and perceptive efforts. I personally have appreciated AHEPA's dialogue with the Administration. I ask for your continued help toward the goals we share—better relations between the United States and Greece, better relations among the countries of the region, peaceful resolution of differences, and a uniting of effort to meet our common challenges and aspirations."[107] Haas' praise of

AHEPA appears to be more than polite praise for his hosts; he did, after all, agree to speak at AHEPA's event. It speaks to the huge and tactful effort AHEPA made throughout the 1980s to bridge the gulf between the Republican administration of Ronald Reagan and the PASOK socialist party government of Andreas Papandreou which was openly critical of the longstanding alliance between the United States and Greece. It was a difficult era in US-Greek relations which made AHEPA's role as a bridge between the two countries difficult but also especially valuable. Among its many concrete contributions during the 1980s, this role as a bridge between America and Greece may have been AHEPA's greatest achievement during that period.

The measure of AHEPA's achievement can be appreciated if one considers that a big part of Greek American lobbying or advocacy initiatives focused less on persuading the United States to change its policy toward Greece and focused instead on trying to persuade Athens to be more accommodating toward Washington. It was a phenomenon that Professor Van Coufoudakis aptly named "reverse influence phenomenon" and was the outcome of Greek American disapproval of the strong anti-American rhetoric adopted by Andreas Papandreou through at least the mid-1980s, after which he moderated his stance. This reversal was also because many Greek American leaders felt an affinity toward Ronald Reagan, either because they themselves were Republicans or because they were disappointed with the Carter administration's failure to live up to its promises to take concrete steps to resolve the situation on Cyprus, or both. Many AHEPA leaders felt the same way. In 1986 AHEPA awarded its coveted Socratic Award to Reagan. Prior to the 1980 elections, which pitted Reagan against incumbent president Jimmy Carter, leading Greek Americans formed the National Committee of Greek American Voters for Reagan and Bush. Its spokesman was AHEPA Past Supreme President Peter Derzis and its members included Past Supreme Presidents William Chirgotis and Leo Lamberson, as well as Gustav Coffinas who would be elected Supreme President in 1981. In its declaration, the committee cited Greek American disappointment with Carter, and it also cited what it considered other policy failures on the domestic front. Nonetheless, AHEPA maintained correct and close relations with the PASOK government in Athens throughout Papandreou's tenure in office between 1981 and 1989.[108]

Balancing between Reagan and Papandreou was not easy for AHEPA, and there were reports of inevitable internal tensions in the organization that had already existed and which it was trying to overcome. There was progress on that front beginning in the early 1980s with less internal friction and greater unanimity in the selection of the Order's officers. This enabled AHEPA to successfully pursue several other goals in the 1980s. AHEPA was also especially active over the Cyprus issue, which entered a new and difficult phase. AHEPA was also at the forefront of a very special process that underlined the mainstream status of Greek America, the Democratic Party's choice of Massachusetts Governor Mike Dukakis, a second-generation Greek American, as its nominee in the 1988 presidential election. AHEPA was honored by both Dukakis and his opponent Vice President George H. Bush in the run up to the elections. Dukakis was the keynote speaker at AHEPA's 65th Supreme Convention in Miami in August 1988. And that same month Bush cited the Order of AHEPA as one of the "Thousand Points of Light," which he said brightened and diversified America through a "Nation of Community," in his acceptance speech for the presidential nomination at the Republican National Convention in New Orleans in 1988.

AHEPA in Canada

In 1981 the Supreme Convention was held in Toronto. A highlight of the convention week included reaching the $51 million fund drive goal for the new AHEPA Hall for Boys at St. Basil's Academy. During the AHEPA Hall for Boys luncheon on August 11, over $75,000 was pledged toward the establishment of a Hall for Boys maintenance fund. The fund was to be used for future repairs and upkeep of the three new dormitories that would be completed by October of that year. Louis G. Manesiotis, the fund drive chairman and Past Supreme President, said that erecting those buildings was truly AHEPA's finest hour. The Toronto convention went on record urging the United States and Canada to use their good offices to bring about a peaceful settlement of the Cyprus problem by asking the Turkish government to withdraw its troops.

At the convention's banquet the chairman was Spiro Gadoutsis of Toronto, an owner of a real estate firm, the invocation was offered by His Grace Bishop Sotiros Athanassoulas of the Greek Orthodox

Diocese of Toronto, and the toastmaster was James Anas of Hamilton, Supreme Vice President of AHEPA in Canada and an executive in the restaurant business. Speakers included Joseph Clark, the head of the Progressive Conservative Party of Canada; the Greek Ambassador to Canada, Emmanuel Megalokomonos; Toronto Mayor Arthur Eggleton; Louis Yankou, general chairman of the convention and president of Yorktown Real Estate and Insurance Ltd.; Senator Paul Sarbanes; and the main speaker was outgoing Supreme President Smyrnis. At the convention's conclusion Gustav (Gus) Coffinas was unanimously elected Supreme President. Other elected officers were Peter Kouchalakos, Supreme Vice President; James S. Anas, Supreme Vice President of Canada; Nick C. Demeris, Supreme Secretary; James Mazarakos, Supreme Treasurer; George Charles, Supreme Counsellor. John Economou, Mike Giannirakis, Nick Jannetides, George Athans and Harry J. Pulos were elected Supreme Governors; Monthe Kofos was reelected Supreme Athletic Director.

The new Supreme President, attorney Gus Coffinas, was born and raised in Brooklyn, New York, was educated in the public schools of New York City, and completed the St. Constantine Cathedral Greek American Afternoon School. He graduated from St. John's University and St. John's School of Law. During World War II he served with distinction in the US Air Force for three years in the European theatre of operations. Coffinas was one of the founders of the A. Fantis Parochial School, the first Greek Orthodox parochial grammar school in the Brooklyn borough of New York City, which opened in 1963. The school was affiliated with St. Constantine Cathedral, of which Coffinas was member of the Board of Trustees for many years. He began his career as an attorney in 1952 with his older brother, Nicholas Coffinas, a Past Supreme President of AHEPA. Gus Coffinas had been elected Supreme Vice President of AHEPA in 1978 and held that office for two consecutive years.

The Toronto convention also mandated the appointment of a nine-person Board of Directors whose responsibility would be to make recommendations to the Supreme Lodge, the Supreme Convention, and the Supreme Board of Trustees concerning all aspects of the fraternity, its policy, program, and purpose. Its members, all of them Past Supreme Presidents, were William Chirgotis, Nicholas Coffinas, Peter Derzis, Louis Manesiotis, George Margoles, Peter V. Paulus,

John Ploumides, Michael Spirtos, and John Thevos. Gus Coffinas and George P. Gabriel, chairman of the Supreme Board of Trustees, were named ex officio members.

AHEPA at 60

The year 1982 marked the 60th anniversary of AHEPA and the 60th Supreme Convention met in Atlanta, as it had on the 50th anniversary 10 years earlier. It was a momentous year for another reason, because AHEPA had to deal with the first ever socialist, center-left government in Greece. The first meeting with newly elected Prime Minister Andreas Papandreou came in April 1982 during the Order's trip to Greece. Supreme President Coffinas, in his report that was published in the 1972 Yearbook, mentioned that AHEPA was honored to meet with the prime minister for a full hour in a private session and then to host him in a two-hour luncheon held in his honor at the King George Hotel in Athens. It was a good start to what would prove a challenging relationship, especially when Papandreou ramped up his criticisms of US foreign policy in the run up to the 1985 elections, after which his attitude became more moderate. By maintaining its regular annual trip to Greece and its meetings with government officials, AHEPA was the only one of all the Greek American organizations that helped keep open the lines of communication between Washington, DC and Athens. While AHEPA's regularly scheduled events may seem somewhat repetitive and routine and even staid to some observers, the benefits of the annual trip to Greece proved invaluable throughout the 1980s.

Several months before AHEPA met in Atlanta to commemorate its 60th anniversary, the Greek Orthodox Archdiocese of North and South America had honored AHEPA's 60-year history at its Cathedral Ball in New York City. At the convention the theme was Hellenism's legacy to America, but it was the new phase in the relations with the homeland that was on many delegates' minds. There were also, as always, internal issues to resolve. Supreme President Coffinas mentioned that "the political unity of the last few years has brough about some problems, as many Brothers who once viewed each other with suspicion have only slowly learned to work together," and he called on members of the Order to work toward eradicating that lingering distrust.[109]

The issue of retaining its members and expanding their numbers was a perennial one for AHEPA, and it featured at its 60th year convention. As of December 31, 1981, the membership stood at 27,691, with 2,333 new members and 1,141 reinstated during the past year. In his report, Coffinas mentioned AHEPA lost 15% of its membership annually and had to address that phenomenon as well as the reasons why "the youth" were not joining the Order.

The speakers at the Grand Banquet that took place at the Atlanta Hilton on August 19 included Margarita Papandreou, the spouse of the Greek prime minister, who spoke as his personal emissary. She mentioned how much she had in common with AHEPA members because she was both American and Greek, and expressed the view that the ties between the Greeks of Greece and the Greeks in the United States were very strong and that the Greek Americans would assist Greece in its hour of need. She added that the new government in Athens was trying to create conditions in which Greek Americans and all Greeks abroad could contribute through their organizational, administrative, scientific, and entrepreneurial skills and know how, either individually or through their organizations. Another speaker at the banquet was the newly appointed deputy foreign minister for affairs of the Greeks abroad, Asimakis Fotilas, who described the newly established government department in Greece as proof of the government's commitment to establishing close ties with the Greeks abroad. The other speakers at the banquet included Archbishop Iakovos; George Sioris, Minister-Counselor of the Greek Embassy in Washington; Cyprus Ambassador to the United States Andreas Jacovides; Chris Chiames, Supreme President of the Sons of Pericles; Alexandra Tarabicos, Grand President of the Maids of Athena; Mrs. Sonja Stefanadis, Grand President of the Daughters of Penelope; as well as outgoing Supreme President Gustav Coffinas and Peter Kouchalakos, the Supreme Vice President of AHEPA who was elected Supreme President at the conclusion of the convention. Along with Peter Kouchalakos the other officials who were elected in Atlanta were Peter H. Cardiges, Supreme Vice President; Cleo Zambetis, Supreme Secretary; George J. Brotis, Supreme Treasurer; John Parker, Supreme Counsellor, and Supreme Governors Charles Dekas of New Jersey, and John M. Cholakis of New York.

AHEPA was active over the Cyprus issue following the convention in Atlanta, reacting to the Reagan administration's push to persuade Congress to allot more aid to Turkey. AHEPA launched a campaign urging Greek Americans to contact Congress and oppose the proposed $934 million aid give away to Turkey, which would upset the 7:10 aid ratio to Greece and Turkey. Supreme President Kouchalakos, a lifelong teacher and a licensed psychologist in Florida who was born to Greek immigrants in Lowell, Massachusetts, proved to be an effective witness when called to submit statements before the Subcommittee on Europe and the Middle East of the Committee on Foreign Affairs of the US House of Representatives. Speaking on Capitol Hill on March 14, 1983, Kouchalakos began with a carefully worded but strong critique of US foreign policy in the Eastern Mediterranean, pointing out its inconsistencies in dealing with the two main issues in the area, which he identified as the tension between Greece and Turkey and Turkey's ongoing occupation of the northern part of Cyprus. He went on to say: "In November [1982] I met with Greek Prime Minister Andreas Papandreou and urged him—as an American citizen and a person of Hellenic descent—to keep the American bases in Greece. I believe the Prime Minister is a reasonable man, and from our conversations my impression was that in the interests of United States-Greek relations, the last thing he wants to do is close the American bases. But he takes the Turkish threat seriously. If Papandreou continues to feel that the security of Greece is imperiled and that the United States is unwilling to recognize its responsibility in helping find a solution, I think that closing the bases is an option he might exercise. American leadership in the area is needed." Kouchalakos outlined AHEPA's criticisms of US foreign policy and sought to explain why Greece was feeling insecure by saying: "A poignant example of ill-advised diplomacy was evidenced by President Reagan's recent letter to Greek Prime Minister Papandreou. The President stated in his letter that the United States, in the context of a new agreement, would "seek increased levels of security assistance on a par with Turkey only if there is a resolution of the current negotiations over the US bases. This policy does not provide for stability in the area, but only increases Greek feelings of insecurity." The Supreme President concluded his remarks by making several specific policy recommendations, suggesting that the United States must "(1) Take immediate, positive action toward the Turkish withdrawal of troops from Cyprus, and for a permanent resolution of that conflict. (2) Make an immediate affirmation of Greece's territorial integrity, and inform both Greece and Turkey that the use of force to settle conflicts by either country would severely and permanently alter our relationship with them. (3) Maintain aid to Turkey, Greece and Cyprus at current levels until stability reigns in the area."[110]

The 61st Supreme Convention, 1983, Chicago

AHEPA held its 61st Supreme Convention from August 7–14, 1983, in Chicago. About 1,500 Ahepans and friends attended the Grand Banquet, held on August 11, and highlights included speeches by Senators Charles Percy and Paul Sarbanes; Illinois Lt. Governor George Ryan; Minister-Counsellor George Sioris of the Greek Embassy in Washington; Andreas Jacovides, Ambassador of Cyprus to the United States; and Archbishop Iakovos. Senator Sarbanes thanked AHEPA for the efforts of its members concerning the maintenance of the 7:10 ratio of military assistance for Greece and Turkey. He referred to the "crucial role of AHEPA ... which brought a favorable response on the part of the Congress and helped to make possible the base agreement" that had been recently signed between Greece and the United States. Ambassador Iakovides expressed his appreciation for AHEPA's support of the cause of restoring justice to Cyprus. The remarks of Richard Burt, the Assistant Secretary of State for Europe, whose airplane was grounded in Washington, were conveyed to the audience." Speeches were also given by the four outgoing presidents Supreme President Peter Kouchalakos, Daughters of Penelope President Maria Spirtos, Maids of Athena President Daphne Papamichael, and Sons of Pericles President Chris Chiames. William P. Tavoulareas, Chairman of the Board of the Mobil Corporation, was presented with AHEPA's Aristotelian Award. Tavoulareas, a son of a Greek and Italian immigrant couple, was born in Brooklyn and studied law. He worked his way up from an accountant to becoming president of Mobil.

At the conclusion of its national Convention in Chicago, AHEPA elected Peter Cardiges as Supreme President; Cleo Zambetis, Supreme Vice President; Leo Polydoropoulos, Supreme Vice President of

Canada; Charles Georgeson, Supreme Secretary; John N. Deoudes, Supreme Treasurer; and Phillip Frangos, Supreme Counsellor. Serving as Supreme Governors were Gus Moshos, Gus Constantine, Jerome Kaler, Andrew Stamboulidis, John Cholakis, Ted Patouhas, E. P. (Terry) Mitchell, and Gus Gekas. Monthe Kofos was reelected as Supreme Athletic Director. New Supreme President Cardiges, who was born in Pennsylvania, coincidentally in 1922 and only a few days after AHEPA was established in Atlanta, owned an insurance agency. His family had helped the foundation of the Greek Orthodox Church in Mount Lebanon, Pennsylvania in the 1960s, when Greeks began moving out of Pittsburgh and into the suburbs.

A New Crisis in Cyprus

Only a few months after being elected Supreme President, Cardiges had to deal with a new crisis that erupted in Cyprus following the unilateral declaration of the so-called Turkish Republic of Northern Cyprus in November 1983. Cardiges led several AHEPA initiatives. These included letters sent to President Reagan and Secretary of State George P. Schultz urging the Administration to publicly disavow the Turkish Cypriot unilateral declaration of independence, and letters sent to the ambassadors of countries that had troops on Cyprus as part of the United Nations peace keeping force, urging their governments not to recognize the Turkish Cypriot republic. AHEPA also sent a telegram of support to President Kyprianou of Cyprus. AHEPA also contacted all members of Congress, and Cardiges met with leaders of other Greek American organizations and pledged that all AHEPA resources would be put to work toward ensuring an independent and unified Cyprus.[111] In January 1984 an AHEPA delegation visited Greece and met with President Konstantinos Karamanlis and Prime Minister Papandreou. In Athens Cardiges announced that AHEPA had created a pamphlet that responded to false Turkish claims about the situation on Cyprus and that it was being distributed to 100,000 Greek Americans.

AHEPA organized a two-day conference on the Cyprus issue at the end of January 1984 at which several important American policy and opinion makers spoke, including Senator Paul Tsongas, the Greek American who served as US Senator for Massachusetts from 1979 to 1985, and several Congressmen. Another speaker was

Leslie Gelb, a New York Times journalist who had served as Assistant Secretary of State in the Carter administration between 1977–1979. Gelb struck a note of pragmatism, expressing his view that the Reagan administration was unlikely to put pressure on Turkey and that the declaration of the Turkish Republic of Northern Cyprus required a robust diplomatic response on Greece's part. Former Mayor of San Francisco George Christopher addressed comments about the Papandreou administration being the source of American unwillingness to act. He asked what had the US government done about Cyprus in the seven years prior to PASOK coming to power. In doing so, Christopher reflected the sense of many attendees during the two-day gathering AHEPA hosted in Washington, DC.

Christopher was the keynote speaker at AHEPA's Congressional Banquet that year held in March, and the Cyprus issue was touched upon by several speakers that evening. Senator Tsongas, who was the recipient of the Periclean Award, castigated the inaction of both Republican and Democratic party administrations over Cyprus. The evening was then given over to humor thanks to comedian Bob Hope, the recipient of the Socratic Award, who opened his acceptance speech by noting that he was indebted to Greek mythology because it helped him fill in his tax declarations.[112]

The 62nd Supreme Convention, 1984, Miami Beach

The Cyprus issue was prominently discussed at AHEPA's 62nd Supreme Convention in 1984 in Miami Beach, Florida. A number of dignitaries and AHEPA friends attended the ceremonies marking the beginning of the Supreme Convention on August 19. The opening began with a blessing offered by Archbishop Iakovos and Bishop John of Atlanta. General chairman George Heropoulos welcomed the conventioneers to Miami Beach, while Greek Consul Thrasyvoulos Stamatopoulos called AHEPA "a primary instrument of Hellenism worldwide." His Eminence Archbishop Iakovos spoke of his deep love for "my brothers and sisters in the AHEPA. "In the last 25 years we have gone the distance together," he concluded, and "none of you has deserted me while I was trying to be of service to you." He added that Patriarch Demetrios I "is expecting to greet the new leadership of the AHEPA" very soon. He then outlined the dramatic decline of the Greek population in Turkey and the current plight of the Ecumenical Patriarchate.

The highlight of the welcoming was the presence of Congressman Claude Pepper, the chairman of the House Rules Committee and a friend of AHEPA for over 45 years. In 1946 he was the author of the Senate resolution urging that the Dodecanese Islands be returned to Greece. Pepper told the Ahepans he hoped to be able to say, in some not-too-distant day in the future, that he had something to do with the resolution that had the effect of making the invading Turks get out of Cyprus. In other parts of his speech he made the comment the entire free world would be forever indebted to Greece as the mother of democracy, and that people in America were proud of the Greek people who have been a continuation of the great Greek influence on civilization, phrases often heard on such occasions. Outgoing AHEPA Supreme President Cardiges told those gathered that Greek Americans were a solid part of the societies of North America while they foster our spiritual links with Hellas. He hoped Greek Americans would always maintain the critical balance between the past and the present and continue to weld their Hellenic spirit with American reality. To a great extent all such speeches at AHEPA conventions touch on the same themes year in year out; those words are nonetheless a sign that AHEPA was comfortable in invoking both Americanism and its Hellenic heritage in the 1980s.

At the 1984 Supreme Convention AHEPA elected Cleo Zambetis of Canfield, Ohio, as Supreme President. The other elected officials were George P. Gabriel, Supreme Vice- President; Dimitrios Bonnis, a businessman from Vancouver who had been born in Nemea in Peloponnesos, as Supreme Vice-President of Canada; Charles Georgeson, Supreme Secretary; Angelo T. Mountanos, Supreme Treasurer; and Phillip T. Frangos, Supreme Counsellor. The Supreme Governors elected were Gus A. Constantine, Gus Gekas, John J. Maniatis, Steve Manta, Andrew Manos, E. Perry Mitchel, Solon Petrides, and John Prokos. Monthe Kofos was reelected as Supreme Athletic Director. The chairman of the Sons National Advisory Board was Chris Economides. The new AHEPA Supreme President, Cleo Zambetis, was born in Samos, Greece in 1925. At the time of his election, he had been in business for 34 years and was President of Camco Painting Service, Inc. of Youngstown, Ohio, an international painting contracting firm. A 25-year member of AHEPA, he had been elected to several offices of Lincoln Chapter 89 in Youngstown, Ohio and had served as Supreme Secretary from 1982–1983, and as Supreme Vice President the year before he was elected Supreme President. He was a founder of the Greek Orthodox Church of Archangel Michael in Campbell, Ohio, had served on the board of St. John's Church in Youngstown, and was a grand benefactor of the League of Greek Orthodox Stewards "Logos". After attending Youngstown University in Business Administration, Zambetis served with the US Navy in the Pacific during World War II and was a life member of the Disabled American Veterans. Upon his election, echoing the convention's theme "Building with a Hellenic Vision," Zambetis said that he would emphasize an expansion of AHEPA's educational programs, greater involvement in cultural affairs, and a promotion of Hellenism and Americanism. Concerning education, Zambetis announced the dates of both AHEPA student programs in Greece, the Journey to Greece for high school students and the AHEPA Anatolia Summer College in Greece program. Regarding the Olympics, Zambetis stated he would appoint a fact-finding committee to continue AHEPA's effort to return the Olympics to Greece because the Order felt the return of the Games would not only improve international athletic competition, but also the standing of Greece within the world community.

The Supreme President also stressed AHEPA's continued support for the creation of an AHEPA Cooley's Anemia Endowment Fund to further medical research. He mentioned that relations with other Greek American organizations were strong and that relations between the AHEPA and the Greek Orthodox Church had never been better, and that AHEPA was going to host a testimonial in honor of the 25th anniversary of the enthronement of Archbishop Iakovos in September in Washington, DC. Referring to AHEPA's focus on housing, he stated that the total federal commitment to the four AHEPA-sponsored housing projects was standing at over $10 million and the apartment complexes in St. Louis, Missouri, Indianapolis, Indiana, Hartford, Connecticut, and Mobile, Alabama would bring in government subsidies over the next 20 years totaling over $30 million, and that seven additional projects were pending at the Department of Housing and Urban Development (HUD). Zambetis also expressed his great pleasure that the three other organizations that comprise the AHEPA family—the Daughters of Penelope, the Maids of Athena, and the Sons of Pericles—had also embarked on active programs for the coming year. In the next two months the Daughters would be dedicating a swimming pool for the children of St. Basil's Academy in Garrison, New York, the Sons of Pericles would help to sponsor the Greek team to the winter Special Olympics in March, and the Maids of Athena were continuing to raise funds for heart operations for children from Greece.

The Supreme Convention Banquet in Miami Beach
About 1,200 Ahepans and friends attended the Grand Banquet on August 22, during AHEPA's 62nd Convention in Miami Beach, Florida. The guests were welcomed by banquet chairman Gus Kotzamanis, and the toastmaster was George J. Charles, a past AHEPA Supreme Counsellor from Washington, DC. Highlights included speeches by the Chairman of the House Foreign Affairs Committee, Dante Fascell; Cyprus Ambassador Andreas Jacovides; Greek Ambassador Alexander Philon; and outgoing Supreme President Peter H. Cardiges. A message sent by Congresswoman Geraldine Ferraro, who was unable to attend, was read to the audience. Alex G. Spanos, head of one of the largest construction businesses in the United States, was presented with AHEPA's Aristotelian Award. Prior to presenting the award to Spanos, the audience was entertained with a 20-minute audio-visual presentation narrated by Telly Savalas on Spanos' life accomplishments. President Cardiges introduced Spanos, saying he "is a man whose belief in the values of America are unbending and unswerving, and because he is a man who believes and loves America, he has dedicated the rewards of his most exceptional career to making this country a better place in which to live." He then presented Spanos a hand-painted scroll and bust of Aristotle.

Spanos responded by saying: "Being an Ahepan and a Greek American, I am particularly pleased to receive this award." He then reviewed the struggles of Greek Americans for social equality, noting: "Under the best and worst of circumstances, we were dedicated to reach that which was beyond our grasp. As immigrants to this country, we made a home for ourselves under adverse circumstances, as citizens of this country, we generously contributed our skills and resources to better the quality of life in our communities and aid those who were in need. As individuals we dedicate ourselves to excel in our professional endeavors. I believe that if our past is any indication of what we can do, then I confidently say that we can do no less in the future." Among the many philanthropic activities of Alex Spanos had been support of cultural exhibits from Greece, including the notable Alexander the Great collection, and he had made several large donations to his alma mater, the University of the Pacific.

Ambassador Alexander Philon then read messages from Greek President Constantine Karamanlis, Prime Minister Andreas Papandreou, Foreign Minister Yiannis Haralambopoulos, and the Secretary-General for Greeks Abroad, M. Papastavrou. President Karamanlis wrote: "As members of AHEPA, loyal and responsible citizens of your new homeland, you have always stood by the country of your origin and given your support for its causes. It is a contribution which is recognized and honored by the nation." "Your long tradition of service to the homeland and your constant eagerness to respond whenever your country calls," wrote Prime Minister Papandreou, "constitute for us an example to refer to and a basis for support in the truly difficult struggle to protect and defend our precious heritage."

Andreas Jacovides, Ambassador of Cyprus to the United States, said that AHEPA had been uniquely successful in enhancing the position of Americans of Greek origin in the United States and it had been supporting the cause of Cyprus. He spoke of ominous new developments on Cyprus, which was facing a relentless and ruthless opponent, with important allies in the American establishment and a well-oiled public relations machine. AHEPA's longstanding principle that aid to Turkey must be contingent on real progress for a Cyprus settlement, the ambassador said, was correct first since, in its occupation of Cyprus, Turkey was illegally using American-supplied arms and was spending hundreds of millions of dollars every year maintaining its army of occupation in Cyprus, and while it did so it was effectively being subsidized by US military and economic aid.

The next speaker, Congressman Dante Fascell, said he agreed with what the ambassador had said and added that the Cyprus issue was not solely a Hellenic concern, because it involved human rights, democracy, fair play, rule of law, justice, common sense, and the courage to stand up in support of those values. Congress, Fascell said, had to take the lead and retain a balance in terms of money provided and to reduce the proposed level of foreign aid to Turkey by at least $250 million as a first step and a message to Turkey. Fascell said there was grave concern in Congress concerning the Turkish Cypriot declaration of independence, and the key to continued, equitable assistance to Turkey had to be focusing on the issue of Cyprus. Following the discussion of the Cyprus issue, Bishop John of Atlanta read a message by Archbishop Iakovos, who was then at the Republican National Convention in Dallas. The Archbishop stated he looked forward to working with AHEPA in harmony for the good of the Order of AHEPA and for the benefit of the Greek Orthodox Church and for the future generations to come. AHEPA Supreme Vice President Zambetis then spoke of the accomplishments of President Cardiges during the last 12 months, saying that he made the difference between an average AHEPA year and an outstanding AHEPA year, and he presented Cardiges with a plaque on behalf of the entire Supreme Lodge. Speeches were also made by outgoing Supreme President Cardiges, Daughters President Elaine Kevgas, Maids of Athena President Kukla Andros, and Sons of Pericles President Peter A. Pappas.

Addressing International, Domestic and Internal Needs
At its 63rd Supreme Convention held in Boston in 1985, AHEPA, as it had several times in its history, moved to strike the right balance between its domestic and international commitments and the need to cater to its own internal health and development. Supreme Governor Steve Manta mentioned in his report that in his view the Order spent too much time and resources on external and international areas and much less on retaining and recruiting new members, about $5,000 compared to $75,000. He added pointedly, "If this trend keeps up, we will become a group of tired old men who, like successful businessmen who neglect their families, find their success meaningless because there is no one behind them who can appreciate the work that was done and build upon it."[113] Manta urged the convention to address the issue of its growth and development over the next five years and consider recruitment among recent immigrants from Greece but also third and fourth generation Greek Americans.

Supreme President Zambetis addressed the membership issue at the conclusion of his report. He presented data that showed over the previous five years AHEPA had averaged 21,730 paid members a year. On December 31, 1984, the number stood at 21,522. These were small numbers, Zambetis suggested, compared to the one million or so

Americans of Hellenic descent in the United States. He put forward several ideas of how the number of members could be increased, including making it easier to join, streamlining the initiation ceremony, creating a chapter-at-large for those members who could not attend meetings, an emphasis on reinstating delinquent members, and regular billing of members. The rest of his reports covered the broad range of AHEPA activities. Most notably Zambetis reported on AHEPA's actions on the issues of Greece, Cyprus, and the Ecumenical Patriarchate, which included a meeting with President Turgut Ozal of Turkey. He also spoke about the National Housing Corporation and groundbreaking and construction at three sites in Indianapolis, Hartford, Connecticut, and Mobile, Alabama and commended the leadership shown in that area by Past Supreme President Nick Smyrnis. Other items in the Supreme President's report were a journey to Greece of young Greek American students, the formation of a committee to participate in the broader movement aiming at making Greece the permanent site of the Olympic Games, and the acquisition of new headquarters in Washington, DC. And he concluded his report echoing what all AHEPA Supreme Presidents have said, that the moral satisfaction he received serving in that position made the long hours he served trivial, and that he was departing as a debtor to the Fraternity.[114]

The convention elected George Gabriel as Supreme President; Charles M. Georgeson as Supreme Vice President; Dimi Bonis, Supreme Vice President of Canada; Nicholas Strike, Supreme Secretary; John N. Economou, Supreme Treasurer; and John D. Sakona, Supreme Counsellor. The Supreme Governors elected were Andrew Banis, Peter Dress, Alexander T. Lafkas, Dr. Theodore T. Perros, Thomas G. Rakus, C. Peter Strath, Lambros A. Svingos, and George S. Venturatos. Monthe Kofos was reelected National Athletic Director and Chris Economides Jr. National Advisor for the Sons of Pericles. The new Supreme President George Gabriel was a 28-year veteran of the Order; his most recent position was that of Supreme Vice President. At the time of his election as Supreme President, Gabriel, a graduate of Columbia University and a registered engineer, was president of a minerals and chemical company in Pennsylvania, his home state. Gabriel was a Mason and a Shriner and past president of St. Nicholas Greek Orthodox Church in Bethlehem, Pennsylvania.

One of the first initiatives that Gabriel took was over the issue of membership. In September 1985 he presented the Supreme Lodge with an action plan that proposed holding a series of national workshops for the entire AHEPA family with the theme "Working Together – Membership is Leadership." This led to nine such regional workshops that took place during the next months in which members of AHEPA, the Daughters of Penelope, the Sons of Pericles, and the Maids of Athena brainstormed over ways their members could be empowered and their organizations expand, retain members, and generally imbue everyone with a greater sense of purpose. The Daughters of Penelope, led by Grand President Lillian Demitry, cooperated closely with AHEPA in organizing the workshops. Throughout Gabriel's year long tenure AHEPA's Cooley's Anemia and Housing programs showed considerable progress. And as part of its role as a bridge between the United States and Greece AHEPA made an important 10-day trip to Greece, Cyprus, and the Ecumenical Patriarchate in December 1985. The visit included a meeting with Greek Prime Minister Andreas Papandreou, who throughout the previous months had been accused by the American media of being too anti-American, including the New York Times whose editorial admonished his "Yankee baiting." In April, the same newspaper reported that Greek Americans were bitterly divided over Papandreou's attitude toward Greece's relations with the United States. AHEPA nonetheless stood firm in its policy of trying to facilitate communication lines between the two countries and stay away from positions that reflected any preferences among the political parties in Greece.[115]

A Bridge Once More

A threatened reduction in US aid to Cyprus in 1986 was averted, which was another moment when the Greek American lobbying and AHEPA's advocacy became especially active. The Cyprus issue featured prominently at AHEPA's 1986 64th Supreme Convention Grand Banquet on Thursday, August 14, the highlight of the Convention in Miami. Among the dignitaries attending the banquet were Nebraska gubernatorial candidate Helen Boosalis; Alexander Philon, Minister-Counsellor of the Embassy of Greece; Andreas Jacovides, Ambassador of Cyprus to the United States; and Nicholas Veliotes, a recently retired career foreign service officer and president of the Association of American Publishers. Veliotes, born to Greek immigrant parents in California, had a famous brother, the Rock & Roll Hall of Famer Johnny Otis. The banquet opened with an invocation offered by the Very Reverend Demosthenes Nekras. After dinner toastmaster Gus Gekas introduced the Grand President of the Maids of Athena, Mary Varvaris, who outlined her organization's progress by comparing their activities in 1962, the year she was born, with their current projects. Sons of Pericles Supreme President George Dariotis also spoke about the Sons of Pericles and their achievements in the last 60 years.

Ambassador Philon noted that "one of the main tasks that AHEPA has undertaken and continues to pursue with great dedication is to play an active role in strengthening the ties that bind Greece and the United States and to encourage friendship and cooperation between the two countries, which they have traditionally had since their independence—ties that are more emotional and that go deeper than official, diplomatic pronouncements can express." Ambassador Jacovides conveyed the greetings of Cypriot President Spyros Kyprianou to the convention. Thanking the AHEPA for its support, Jacovides added: "Justice, freedom, the respect of human rights and the rule of law, these are the very principles at stake in the extremely difficult situation we are currently confronted with." At that point the banquet viewed a 20-minute multi-media show on the history of the AHEPA and its varied activities titled "The Ripples Will Not Cease." After a review of her administration and the achievement of the Daughters offered by Lillian Demitry, Grand President of the Daughters, diplomat Nicholas Veliotes discussed recent political developments in the Middle East. Among the presentations made at the banquet were ones to Cleo Deoudes, who had recently retired after working for 34 years at AHEPA National Headquarters; to Peter Agris, publisher of the Hellenic Chronicle; and to AHEPA President George Gabriel, for his outstanding leadership during the year.

The evening's principal speaker was Helen Boosalis, the Democratic Party Candidate for Governor of Nebraska. Alluding to the odyssey of the early immigrants, she noted that "it's a measure of the effective work of AHEPA that Greek Americans became a seasoning ingredient in this great melting pot called America, blending into this nation of diversity, yet holding out the values, the heritage, the true 'greatness that is Greece' as cornerstones for the foundation of our nation." Boosalis had been elected as the first woman mayor of Lincoln, Nebraska in 1975 and served until 1981. She was unsuccessful in her bid to be elected governor, losing narrowly in what was the first ever gubernatorial election in which the candidates both major parties were women. Outgoing Supreme President Gabriel spoke of his experiences during the last 12 months, and how, with each chapter contributing its share, the organization continued to be the major force in Greek American life. He reiterated the main theme of his term of office, that the organization offered many opportunities for leadership and that the development of leadership qualities was one of the most important benefits of participation in AHEPA.

At the conclusion of the 64th Supreme Convention on August 16, John Plumides was elected Supreme President. It was his second term as AHEPA Supreme President; he had also served in that office in 1963–1964, after being elected to several terms on the Supreme Lodge. Plumides was also well-known in Greece and Cyprus for his activities on behalf of AHEPA's Cyprus and Hellenic Affairs Committee since 1974. He had served as president of the Greek Orthodox community and Holy Trinity Church in Charlotte, North Carolina, one of the largest Greek American communities, for the last six years. He was a member of the Greek Orthodox Archdiocesan Council as well as a member of the regional diocesan council. The other AHEPA officials elected were Supreme Vice President Nicholas Strike; Supreme Vice President of Canada Peter Anas; Supreme Secretary James Scofield; Supreme Treasurer Thomas L. Chase; Supreme Counsellor George Pahno, and Comptroller George C. Drivas. The Supreme Governors elected were Michael Firilis; Nick T. Georges; Dr. Steve G. Kirkilis; Dr. Spiro J. Macris; Spero S. Margeotes; George J. Pappas Jr.; C. Peter Stath; and Anthony Topougis. Monthe Kofos continued to serve as Supreme Athletic Director.

Plumides immediately launched into action over the question of aid to Cyprus and appealed to President Reagan and Secretary of State Shultz to withdraw the State Department's proposed $12 million cut in US aid to Cyprus, stating that the aid cut "sends a very negative signal to the people of Cyprus and undercuts the efforts of the U.N. Secretary General to seek a negotiated settlement." Plumides added that "such a severe cut in economic support funds will be interpreted by the intransigent party in the negotiation, Turkey and the Turkish Cypriots, as a lessening of American interest in a solution." Plumides concluded by stating AHEPA's belief that "if the level of foreign aid must be reduced to meet the budget deficit reduction levels mandated by the recent legislation, it should be cut from Turkey, which uses its military and economic aid to continue its occupation of 40% of the Republic of Cyprus." A letter along the same lines was sent by the AHEPA President to all members of the Senate Foreign Relations and House Foreign Affairs Committee.[116] Plumides embarked on a policy of providing "a more visible and continuous thrust" to AHEPA's efforts for Cyprus and Greece. He appointed a new chairman of the organization's Cyprus and Hellenic Affairs Committee, Michael Savvides.

AHEPA's visit to Greece and its meeting with Prime Minister Papandreou in January 1987 was noted by the British Broadcasting Corporation that reported it as follows on January 16: "The Prime Minister received the AHEPA Executive Committee, headed by John Ploumidis, President of the Greek American organization… After the meeting, the Prime Minister issued a statement to the press stressing the inestimable services which AHEPA is offering to the USA, where it is striving for the defense of our country's national independence and territorial integrity. At noon the executive committee of the Greek-American organization visited President Sartzetakis." AHEPA's presence in Cyprus was also covered by the international media. On April 28, 1987, China's Xinhua News Service reported that "Cyprus' president Kyprianou said the responsibility and the ability to play a decisive role in the Cyprus problem, an official press release said today. Kyprianou made the remarks yesterday when he met some 30 leading members of the American Hellenic Educational Progressive Association (AHEPA) who were here for a three-day seminar on the Cyprus problem. Kyprianou rejected the claim that the US could not put pressure on Turkey and make Ankara change its policy toward Cyprus. He also rejected statements by some US officials that Turkish troops stationed in the northern part of Cyprus were for defensive purposes or for the security of the Turkish Cypriots. John Ploumides, supreme president of AHEPA promised the Cyprus government to try to make the Cyprus problem an issue to be discussed from party platforms during the next US presidential election campaigns in

1988. Ploumides said AHEPA had brought up the Cyprus issue with Jimmy Carter and Ronald Reagan, but he blamed Carter and Reagan did not keep the promises they had made when they were elected.

One of the more tangible positive outcomes of AHEPA's role as a bridge over the Atlantic was the restoration of the statue of President Truman to its original place in Athens. The statue had been knocked down by a bomb in March 1986 and the Athens Municipal Council, controlled by PASOK, had not wanted to restore it to its place. But after the socialists were defeated in the municipal elections in the fall of that year the way opened up for AHEPA to request its reinstatement and for the Greek government to agree. A report published in the New York Times leaves no doubt about the influence AHEPA and its president Plumides exercised in Athens, noting: "Analysts saw significance in the fact that on his mission to 'resurrect' the statue, Mr. Plumides was received almost like a head of government, meeting the Prime Minister and President and given a luncheon by the Foreign Minister... Mr. Plumides and his delegation came here after having exerted constant pressure on the Greek Government..." The report also mentioned that "Mr. Plumides said he had expressed concern that Greece might draw nearer to the Communist bloc, but Mr. Papandreou assured him that this would never happen. 'He said, "Greece will always be with the West,"' Mr. Plumides reported."[117]

Chapter 9: Honoring the Immigrant Roots

AHEPA has been closely identified with Greek America's immigrant heritage arguably more than any other organization. Although it is known mostly for promoting Americanization in the interwar period, it did so by also acknowledging the difficult journey from the homeland to America that all Greek-born immigrants experienced and the ways they built the foundations that enabled their children and grandchildren to achieve a great deal in America. Their trajectory went from struggle to success, although that phrase hides how difficult the process was for many, especially women, and in any case was not necessarily the experience of all Greek immigrants. Like all other European ethnic groups, the Greeks in America had to become accepted and established before they could turn to their origins and honor their pioneers. And by the same token this became even more significant when America as a nation paid tribute to its immigrant roots. The 1980s was one of those times, because it witnessed the restoration of the Statue of Liberty and Ellis Island, the point of entry of thousands of Greeks between 1892 and 1954, and a four-day celebration in New York harbor attended by millions surrounding the reopening of the Statue of Liberty to visitors in 1986. The main building at Ellis Island reopened as a museum in 1990.

While AHEPA pursued its broad range of activities during that time, it made a special effort to contribute to the work of the Statue of Liberty–Ellis Island Centennial Commission that President Reagan had formed in 1982 and was led by Chrysler Corporation chair Lee Iacocca, the son of Italian immigrants who had settled in Pennsylvania. Indeed, AHEPA would distinguish itself by the fundraising it engaged in and its donations for which AHEPA received special recognition by the Department of the Interior. Moreover, in 1987, Greek American Michael (Mike) Dukakis was chosen as the Democratic party's nominee in the 1988 presidential elections, and Dukakis' campaign which mobilized Greek Americans stressed his immigrant roots and the fact his parents were Greek immigrants to America. Although support for Dukakis was not unanimous among Ahepans, or the one million ethnic Greeks in the country, nonetheless the Order did a great deal to support his campaign. Thus from 1986 through the early 1990s that witnessed special events on Ellis Island, AHEPA honored the immigrant roots of Greek America in several important ways.

Dukakis and AHEPA

Dukakis announced he would be running for the Democratic nomination informally in March and officially began his campaign in May of 1987. During his announcement speech he said, "My mother and father summed up the American dream for me in 11 words: much is given to you, and much is expected of you." He further evoked his heritage by comparing the presidential campaign to a marathon race, an allusion to the race's ancient Greek origins. Dukakis himself had run the renowned Boston Marathon in 1951.

In August Dukakis, who was a member of AHEPA, appeared at the 65th Annual Supreme Convention which was held in New Orleans. At the convention, Supreme President Plumides' report was primarily focused on the Order's efforts to prevent a reduction of US aid to Cyprus and the successful restoration of the Truman statue in Athens. Those initiatives included a new, well-attended seminar on the Cyprus question held in Nicosia in April 1987. It was an opportunity for AHEPA's leadership to have a more systematic exchange with officials in Cyprus than it did during regular and necessarily brief visits. During the week the convention issued a strongly worded resolution that condemned Turkey's continued violations of the rule of law. The events that AHEPA had initiated over the past months were indirectly connected to its efforts on the international front that the convention showcased. In September 1986 AHEPA presented its Periclean Award to retiring Missouri Senator Thomas F. Eagleton at an event in St. Louis. AHEPA developed the Periclean or Pericles Award to honor individuals in government both on the national and local level. Eagleton had been one of the strongest supporters of the campaign to implement the rule of law with respect to US aid for Turkey after 1974. Indeed, Eagleton had been one of the "gang of four" legislators who helped impose the arms embargo on Turkey between 1975 and 1978, along with Congressmen Brademas, Benjamin Rosenthal, and Paul Sarbanes, who in the meantime had been elected to the Senate. At the same event Archbishop Iakovos presented Eagleton with the Cross of St. Andrew. The following month, in Washington, DC AHEPA presented its Aristotelean Award to Greek Cypriot businessman and philanthropist George Paraskevaidis. Another activity Plumides reported on was the aid AHEPA gathered and sent to Greece to aid the victims of an earthquake in Kalamata that had struck on September 1986.

The convention opened on August 16, 1987, with a welcome from local officials and the organizing committee and an invocation from Archbishop Iakovos. Dukakis attended an evening reception hosted by a group that called itself "Ahepans for Brother Dukakis." The event raised almost $50,000 for Dukakis' campaign. Dukakis was also the keynote speaker at the Awards Luncheon that honored outstanding athletes. He spoke about the Greek values of love and family and the pursuit of excellence that the honored athletes had demonstrated. As always, the social high point of the convention was the grand banquet. Greek American Congressman Gus Yatron of Pennsylvania, an Ahepan, was the keynote speaker. He referred to the Greece- and Cyprus-related foreign policy concerns previous speakers had mentioned and stated that those were not exclusively Greek but also American concerns. He urged AHEPA to continue its work and to broaden its scope so as not to be misrepresented as a Greek lobby. He added: "As you convey your concerns, do not be put off by accusations of ethnic bias. Instead, make it very clear to whomever your audience happens to be that you are speaking as an American citizen who has a unique understanding of how best to preserve our great country's interests. We must remain committed to righting the seemingly unnoticed wrongs suffered by peoples throughout the world, and those suffering include our Greek brethren in Albania, Turkey and Cyprus."[118]

At the conclusion of the convention, voting took place for the officials who would lead the Order over the next 12 months. Elected along with Supreme President Nicholas L. Strike were Supreme Vice President A. Steve Betzelos, Supreme Vice President of Canada; Anthony Vlassopoulos, an engineer from Toronto, Supreme Secretary; Dr. Andrew Karantinos, Supreme Treasurer; George Papuchis; and Supreme Counsellor Manuel P. Scarmoutsos. Also, Kaliope Xenakis was elected Grand President of the Daughters of Penelope, George Ioannides of the Sons of Pericles, and Kathy Kallas of the Maids of Athena. The new Supreme President, Nicholas Louis Strike, was born in 1916 in Salt Lake City, the oldest child of Greek immigrant parents, Louis Nicholas Strike and Christina Chipian Strike. He attended Stanford University and graduated from Westminster College and the University of Utah. He served as a Westminster Trustee for 16 years. In 1939–1940, he served as National President of the Sons of Pericles. His son Louis followed in his footsteps in 1965. They were at the time the only father-son team to do so. Strike served as a Navy officer in the South Pacific during World War II. After the war, he returned to Salt Lake City. From 1946 to 1972, with the efforts of his brothers, John and George, they owned and managed Ajax Presses and Laundry Machinery Co., an invention of their father's. During those years, he held numerous civic, church, and business positions. He was also a lifetime member of the Masonic Order and a Shriner. As a result of his civic involvement, he was drafted by the Republican party of Utah to run—ultimately unsuccessfully—for governor in 1972.

Strike's election was somewhat controversial due to an undercurrent of tension within AHEPA which appeared at times, and which was not always visible to outsiders. AHEPA was and still is reluctant to openly discuss its internal alignments, but on occasion these surfaced usually in the form of complaints about too much politicking. By the late 1980s there was growing discontent with the AHEPA First Party's dominance in the election of Supreme President. This was made public by George T. Douris, in an article in the NEA YORKH magazine that appeared in 1987. Douris was an Ahepan who had distinguished himself as the founder and chairman of the Hellenic American Neighborhood Action Committee which catered to the housing needs of Greek immigrants, especially the elderly, in Queens, New York. Douris wrote that there had been an agreement brokered between former Supreme Presidents Louis Manesiotis and John Thevos that would have ensured the election of Charles M. Georgeson as Supreme President at the 1986 Convention. This would have ended a 20-year-long monopoly over the presidency exercised by the AHEPA First Party. But that party according to Douris ignored the deal and went ahead and elected its own candidate, John Ploumides, with a narrow vote difference. Douris called for Georgeson's election in 1987 because he would provide "enlightened ideas that would move AHEPA into the new century."[119] Georgeson announced he would be running again, and he was endorsed by the New Horizons party but was unsuccessful for a third time. However, he would be elected Supreme President in 1994.

Dukakis' presence at the AHEPA convention in 1987 generated several news stories about how he was trying to capitalize on his ethnic roots and succeeding. Fundraising among Greek Americans was partly responsible for the impressive $4.6 million Dukakis had raised in his first three months as a candidate, far more than any of the other Democratic hopefuls. The related news coverage of this indirectly provided national media exposure to AHEPA. AHEPA's information director Elias Vlanton was quoted in an Associated Press wire: "A lot about the Dukakis candidacy stimulates Greek-Americans. He invokes his Greek heritage and the values that Greeks hold dear, love of family, the need and importance of public service. He projects integrity." Vlanton also said Dukakis had frequented AHEPA's conventions and events for years, adding: "People are just proud of the fact that he is a candidate and a viable candidate."[120]

AHEPA held its 28th Biennial Congressional Banquet for the presentation of awards honoring excellence in March 1988. Dukakis did not attend because he was in the thick of important primary battles, which he would win. The banquet was an occasion that highlighted AHEPA's role as a bridge between the United States and Greece. The program began with the presentation of the colors by the Hellenic Presidential Guard and the Marine Corps Color Guard. The Hellenic Presidential Guard, evzones dressed in the traditional

Greek costume, had specifically travelled to the United States to present the colors at the banquet. The master of ceremonies was Tom Korologos, a second-generation Greek American who was born in Utah, who had worked for Presidents Reagan and George H. W. Bush and had subsequently co-founded an important lobbying firm in Washington, DC. Korologos announced that all banquet proceeds would go to the newly established George J. Leber Memorial Scholarship Fund established in honor of the man who served as Executive Secretary of the AHEPA from 1958 until his death in 1976. The first speaker, Ms. Nancy Risque, Secretary of the Cabinet and the highest-ranking woman in the Reagan administration, described AHEPA as "the most important people-to-people bridge between the land of your forbearers, Greece, and the land of your children, America." The next speaker, Congressman Jim Moody of Wisconsin's Fifth Congressional District, spoke of his living in Greece for four years and referred to the significance of ancient Greek civilization. The Aristotelian Award was presented to John Kapiolatas, chairman, president, and chief executive officer of the Sheraton Corporation. In accepting the award Kapioltas spoke of many types of freedoms that constitute the essential bond linking Greece and America. The Solon Award was presented to Chief Justice William Rehnquist, who in his acceptance speech spoke about Solon's philosophy being guided by a sense of moderation. Supreme President Strike then took the podium to introduce the Socratic Award recipient, Archbishop Iakovos. The Archbishop in his speech said: "The Socratic Award should be given to the founders, leaders and members of the AHEPA who have departed from this world, because they were the ones who gave us the great blessing of Greekness, of identity, of Orthodoxy, and of integrity."[121]

Dukakis won the important New York and Pennsylvania primaries and was well on his way to winning the Democratic nomination, which he did officially at the Democratic Party National Convention on July 21, 1988. One of the earliest public statements of what this meant to all Greek Americans came from Ahepan James S. Scofield, a future Supreme President. Scofield, a columnist for the St. Petersburg Times in Florida, wrote about how Dukakis' nomination was a moment of validation for Greek Americans including himself who had, in the past, faced considerable discrimination. It was a subject he would elaborate on in a few years as AHEPA's Supreme

President. In his newspaper column that appeared a week after Dukakis' nomination, he wrote: "It was a magic moment of victory, pride and fulfillment which brought tears of joy. There was hardly a dry eye among Americans of Greek heritage when Michael Dukakis accepted the nomination of the Democratic Party for the presidency of the United States. Even those who do not agree with his politics and who will not vote for him in November were moved because they now know that the American Dream is real, not just mythology. Not that they ever really doubted it, but now it had been validated and endorsed by their fellow Americans—elite and ethnic, native-born, and foreign-born—who accepted one of them for national leadership. It was a truly symbolic triumph for those of us, and there are many more than is generally believed, who had to change our names in decades past. We changed them because we could not get job offers, were denied available jobs and had to prove we were better than the best to hold the jobs we had. When a man bearing the name Dukakis can be nominated for the presidency, win or lose, that means that we and our parents before us have succeeded in proving that we are worthy of acceptance in the American mainstream. Michael Dukakis says he never remembers being discriminated against. Maybe things were different in upper-middle-class Brookline. Or maybe he would rather forget. But those of us who had to battle up the economic ladder elsewhere remember it quite differently. Finishing at the top of your college class in the '40s and '50s usually didn't mean much if your name was different. The big job offers too often went to the people with easy-to-pronounce, easy-to-spell names which looked good on the corporate nameplate. When the generation of my mother and father was not hired, it created business ventures. When my generation was not hired, it went into business or entered professions where ability was more important than who you were. Or the family name was Americanized, reluctantly but realistically. When my name was legally changed, on the advice of a sympathetic college adviser and the permission of my understanding parents, from Skufakiss to Scofield, the whole job picture changed for the better. Doors that had been closed were opened. For the first time, I was judged completely on my ability, not on the sound and spelling of my name. But I never denied my Greek heritage, as those who know me personally can readily attest. Only the label was changed to make the package more attractive. My fond hope is that Michael Dukakis has done for names what John Kennedy did for religion and what someday a black presidential candidate will do for race and a Hispanic presidential candidate will do for origin. Then the American Dream will finally be fully realized for all. Skufakiss and Dukakis always sounded good to me, but they sound good to almost everybody now."[122]

The 66th Supreme Convention, 1988, Miami

When AHEPA met for its 66th Supreme Convention in August in Miami, Dukakis had lost the lead in the polls he had established in July, thanks to his opponent's hard-hitting campaign ads orchestrated by Bush's campaign manager Lee Atwater. A few years later while in the throes of a terminal illness, Atwater apologized to Dukakis for the "naked cruelty" of the campaign he had conducted. Despite Dukakis slipping in the polls, there was still a lot of time left in the presidential race and his presence in Miami was the highlight of the convention. More than 7,000 members and their friends gathered in that popular resort city to take part in a week-long series of social and athletic events. It was the largest convention in AHEPA's history. Archbishop Iakovos gave the keynote address at the convention's opening. Dukakis had to interrupt his campaign schedule to make a special visit to the convention. Following a meeting and reception with AHEPA leaders, Dukakis was enthusiastically received by many thousands of Ahepans and friends in an open session of the convention. Delegates chanted "Duke, Duke, Duke!" and "Let's Go Mike," the phrase that his cousin actress Olympia Dukakis had uttered at the end of her speech accepting an Oscar earlier that year. In his speech, which was frequently interrupted by applause, Dukakis spoke the policies he would pursue as president, the greatness of American and Greek democracy, and about his Greek roots and the support he had received from the Greek American community. He said he hoped that the following year on March 25, Greek Independence Day, Greek Americans could celebrate American and Greek values at the White House.[123]

At the Grand Banquet in Miami those attending heard speeches by author and journalist Nicholas Gage; Bill May, chairman of the Statue of Liberty–Ellis Island Foundation; Antigoni Karali-Dimitriade,

General Secretary for Greeks Abroad of the Greek Ministry of Culture; and Cyprus Ambassador Andreas Jacovides. The banquet witnessed the premier of an impressive audio-visual presentation, created by the Statue of Liberty–Ellis Island Foundation, which traced the history of Greek immigration to America. At the conclusion of the convention A. Steve Betzelos of Chicago, Illinois was elected Supreme President by more than a 75-vote margin. Also elected to the Supreme Lodge were Supreme Vice President Charles P. Tsaffaras, Supreme Vice- President of Canada Anthony D. Vlassopoulos, Supreme Secretary Andrew Banis, Supreme Treasurer John Mandros, Supreme Counsellor Manuel Scarmoutsos, and Supreme Athletic Director Monthe Kofos. Elected as Supreme Governors were Ted Boyce, Sam Kiriazis, Christ N. Kontenakos, Christ S. Manes, George Papageorge, John D. Sakona, Dr. Harry Torney, and John Vusikas. Chris Economides Jr. was to continue to serve as Sons National Advisor.

At the same time AHEPA was meeting in Miami, the Republican Party held its National Convention in New Orleans, where as expected, it nominated Vice President George H. W. Bush. What was a surprise about that convention, at least to Greek Americans, was that Bush mentioned AHEPA in the speech he made accepting the nomination. It came at a point when he described America as a community and employed the words "a thousand points of light" which became one of the signature phrases of his speech: "For we're a nation of community, of thousands and tens of thousands of ethnic, religious, social, business, labor union, neighborhood, regional and other organizations, all of them varied, voluntary and unique. This is America: the Knights of Columbus, the Grange, Hadassah, the Disabled American Veterans, the Order of AHEPA, the Business and Professional Women of America, the union hall, the Bible study group, LULAC [League of United Latin American Citizens], Holy Name, a brilliant diversity spreads like stars, like a thousand points of light in a broad and peaceful sky." Unsympathetic observers described that section of the speech as a political ploy but irrespectively, it was significant was that Bush chose AHEPA as the representative organization of Greek Americans, and also that this gave the Order an unprecedented moment of national exposure.[124] And in terms of the Greek Americans, Bush did not need to pander to them, because several of the leaders of the community, while acknowledging the pride involved in having a Greek American presidential candidate, stated clearly that they would be voting for Bush in November. Former Supreme President William Chirgotis was included in a list of prominent Greek American Bush supporters and was quoted as saying: "While many of us of Hellenic origin are proud to see one of our heritage running for President, I believe that ethnicity alone is not a good reason to support a candidate for any office, especially that of President of the United States."[125] Ultimately though no reliable figures exist, one can assume a majority of Ahepans, maybe not a vast one, voted for Dukakis, who in the end lost the election.

Addressing the Order's Internal Workings
There are moments in AHEPA's history when the Order, while continuing to pursue the broad range of activities it is involved in, also needs to find time to discuss its internal workings. In his report to the 67th Supreme Convention that took place in 1989 in St. Louis, outgoing Supreme President Steve Betzelos devoted a great deal of time to discussing the optimum relationship between the Supreme President and the Board of Directors. The Board had been created in 1986 to help AHEPA's leadership to operate with checks and balances. The rest of the report referred to AHEPA's activities during the past year, including a successful trip to Greece and Cyprus, both of which received extensive coverage, and a moving visit to the Ecumenical Patriarchate in Istanbul. At the time of the visit to Athens in May, Greece was gearing up for elections that were scheduled for June and Prime Minister Papandreou's standing was in question because of government scandals and doubts about his health. Betzelos deftly commented in his report that AHEPA did not get involved in Greece's internal politics and remained focused on its role of providing a bridge between the United States and Greece. The Supreme President's domestic trips included a visit to the St. Photios National Greek Orthodox Shrine in St. Augustine, Florida to which AHEPA was the largest contributor, and a visit to St. Basil's Academy in upstate New York where the Order had funded the Hall for Boys and the school. The 67th annual convention was completed with the election of Charles Tsaffaras as Supreme President. Charles P. Tsaffaras was the younger brother of William P. Tsaffaras, who had served as Supreme President in 1973-1974. Charles was a decorated

World War II veteran and an attorney who practiced in his hometown, Lowell, Massachusetts. Also elected to the Supreme Lodge were Vice President James Scofield, Vice President of Canada Peter Zegouras, Secretary Dr. Harry Torney a microbiologist from Indiana, Treasurer William Mackrides, Counsellor George Platsis, and Athletic Director Monthe Kofos. The Supreme Governors elected were John Alatis, Gus Aretos, Christ Kontenakos, James Pappas, Ralph Potter, Alex Rigopoulos, John Sakona, and George Zarafonetis. Elected to the AHEPA Board of Directors were John Deoudes, Dr. Gus Constantine, Harry, and Manuel Scarmoutsos. In 1989 the Order also inaugurated the Academy of Achievement Award to honor academics, scientists and public figures for their contributions to Hellenic culture and education.

Remembering Discrimination
At the first Supreme Convention of the 1990s, the Order's 68th which took place in Hollywood, Florida, AHEPA elected James S. Scofield Supreme President. Scofield, an information specialist with the St. Petersburg Times in Florida, had served as Vice President the previous year. Scofield's service in AHEPA had included extensive involvement with the Cyprus issue, including authorship of reports in 1974 and 1977 on the AHEPA Humanitarian Missions to Cyprus and co-authorship of an AHEPA documentary film on the Turkish invasion of the island nation in 1974. The other officials who were elected were John T. Pappas, Supreme Vice President; Peter Zegouras, Supreme President of Canada; Franklin A. Manios, Supreme Secretary; C. Peter Strath, Supreme Treasurer; Manuel Scarmoutsos, Supreme Counsellor; Monthe Kofos, National Athletic Director. The Supreme Governors who were elected were Gust M. Aretos, Perry D. Kallis, Michael J. Kavoulakis, Demitrios Nakos, Ralph Potter, James A. Poll, and Thomas A. Stamatis. William Mackrides was to serve as the Sons of Pericles Advisory Board chairman.

In his speech to the convention, newly elected Supreme President Scofield spoke about how his experience as a journalist would help the Order do a better job of publicizing its good works. He also mentioned that Greek Americans and Greek Canadians were still discriminated against, not in the blatant ways their parents and grandparents had been in the past, but in other more subtle ways. The immigrant background and the issue of discrimination was of great concern to the new president, who, as a young man with a university degree in Illinois in the 1950s, could not find a job until he changed his name from Skoufakis to the English-sounding Scofield, an issue he had made public during Dukakis' campaign. Scofield, who would be awarded the Ellis Island Medal of Honor in 1994, would keep the issue of immigrant contributions alive throughout his tenure and would raise the issue of past discrimination at the Supreme Convention held in Atlanta in 1997 to commemorate AHEPA's 75th anniversary.

Meanwhile, and within a few weeks of his election, Scofield was able to express his pride in the Greek American spirit, both its immigrants and ancient Greek roots, in an article he published after Greek American tennis player Pete Sampras won the Men's US Open Tennis Championship. Scofield wrote: "Pistol Pete Sampras, the son and grandson of Greek immigrants, won the US Open tennis tournament convincingly against overwhelming odds to become the youngest men's winner in the 110 years of the tournament. And all the more than 100 million living descendants of those heroic immigrant voyagers who journeyed across the wide sea to Ellis Island once again are reminded that it can happen only in America. The tall, cool, and composed 19-year-old son of Soterios Sampras, a Greek-American whose father immigrated to Chicago, rules his sports kingdom with the same domination as the Grecian gods who reigned over ancient Hellas. Modest and unassuming, Pete is not as flashy as Zeus, but appears to be as powerful as Hercules, as fleet as Hermes and as wise as Athena. The gods of Olympus are merely a memory, and Pete's tennis triumph may or may not be remembered even a century hence, but the values of the quality he exhibits are eternal."[126]

The Ellis Island Immigrant Celebration in 1991

It was during Scofield's tenure that AHEPA organized a major event on Ellis Island in April 1991 to honor the early Greek immigrants to the United States. In a moving celebration of the Greek immigrant experience, more than 1,200 Ahepans and friends gathered on Ellis Island on April 20 for the benefit of the AHEPA Charitable Foundation. The "AHEPA Evening on Ellis Island" specifically honored several prominent and successful Greek Americans, but the evening also served to honor the courageous immigrants who came to America.

For the entire evening, everyone was caught up in the emotional experience of being in those immigrants' footsteps. The evening began as they stepped off the specially chartered boats from Manhattan's Battery Park to the "Isle of Tears, the Isle of Joy." In the large Baggage Room, prior to an awards ceremony, all were greeted with the sounds of Greek period music that the immigrants had brought with them. The ceremonies were opened with an invocation by Bishop Isaiah, the Chancellor of the Greek Orthodox Archdiocese of North and South America, and the hall was then filled with 1,200 voices singing "Christos Anesti," the Greek Orthodox Hymn of the Resurrection. Sevy Phalangas, a 28-year-old Greek American composer and performer, sang the national anthems of the United States, Canada, and Greece. Ms. Phalangas then sang "Elpida," a song commissioned by AHEPA for the event, which she had composed. Speakers included Supreme President James S. Scofield; Past AHEPA Supreme President, and General Chairman of the AHEPA Evening on Ellis Island, Nick Smyrnis; and AHEPA Executive Director Constantine W. Gekas. Smyrnis noted that the original Ellis Island complex had cost $1.5 million to build in the late 19th century but cost $80 million to restore. He also read a greeting from the evening's honorary chairman, Angelo Tsakopoulos. Several particularly outstanding Greek Americans were awarded the "AHEPA Ellis Island Award of Distinction" for their achievements. In presenting the awards, Scofield said that the honorees had "kept the faith" of the immigrants who struggled toward America and the American Dream and they represented "the fusion of the greatness of the Hellenic spirit with the promise and opportunity of our sister North American nations." The honorees who received the specially commissioned AHEPA Ellis Island Award of Distinction included Lt. General William Gus Pagonis, whose father immigrated through Ellis Island from Chios in 1917, and who was born in western Pennsylvania in 1941. He had recently received his third star in a field promotion for his much-lauded work as logistics head for Central Command in the Desert Shield and Desert Storm operations during the Gulf War of 1990–1991. Pagonis, who had no West Point background nor family in the military, had worked his way through the ranks, including combat duty in Vietnam and the Persian Gulf, to become one of the highest-ranking Greek Americans in the US military.

Another honoree was Michael Dukakis, the most prominent Greek American politician in the United States. Dukakis proudly credited his immigrant roots throughout his political life and most notably during his recent candidacy for the presidency. Honoree Andrew A. Athens, a 27-year member of AHEPA, was President and CEO of the Chicago-based Metron Steel Corporation which he founded in 1958. Athens was prominent in the Greek Orthodox Church, an Archon of the Order of St. Andrew the Apostle of the Ecumenical Patriarchate, President of the Archdiocese of North and South America Archdiocesan Council, and National Chairman of the United Hellenic American Congress (UHAC) lobbying organization. Another honoree was noted oncologist Dr. George Peter Canellos, Deputy Physician-in-chief and Chief of the Division of Clinical Oncology at the Dana-Farber Cancer Institute in Boston and the William Rosenberg Professor of Medicine at Harvard University Medical School. Canellos' father was brought through Ellis Island by his own father, an immigrant from Vassaras in Peloponnesos. Honoree George Christopher, who was Mayor of San Francisco for two terms from 1956–1964, recalled being carried through Ellis Island at age two in his mother's arms. John Kapioltas, prominent hotelier, businessman, and community leader, was born in Akron, Ohio, to Greek immigrant parents. As chairman, president and CEO of the Boston-based ITT Sheraton Corp., Kapioltas had brought worldwide recognition to the global hotel company which comprises nearly 500 hotels, inns, and resorts in operation or in development in 67 countries. Kapioltas was an Archon of the Ecumenical Patriarchate and received the 1988 Aristotelian award from AHEPA. Also honored was Tom C. Korologos, President of the Washington-based consulting firm of Timmons and Co. Before helping to found Timmons, Korologos had spent four years in the White House as Deputy Assistant to the President for Senate Relations under Presidents Nixon and Ford. Korologos was very active in the Greek American community, and was a member of AHEPA and an Archon of the Ecumenical Patriarchate.

The others honored included: John G. Rangos is President and CEO of the Pittsburgh-based Chambers Development Co., the fourth largest environmental services firm in the United States. Chambers had operations in 21 states, and has had compiled an outstanding record of service, environmental protection, and cost effectiveness.

He has had also been cited for his tireless efforts on behalf of the Children's Hospital of Pittsburgh. Steve Stavro was president and founder of Canada's largest independently owned food chain, Knob Hills Farms, Ltd. Born in Greece, Stavro and his family joined their father in Canada in 1934. Stavro began his career in his father's food store. He started his own business with open-air markets and supermarkets in the 1950s. In 1986, he opened the world's largest food market. Stavro was also recognized in Ontario and Toronto as a generous humanitarian, patron of the arts, and sportsman.

Also honored were: George Vournas, who was Supreme President of AHEPA during World War II. Under his leadership, AHEPA raised over $500 million in War Bonds, an unprecedented and still unsurpassed service of an ethnic organization to the United States. Vournas was also a Captain in the US Army Office of Strategic Services (OSS) during the war. He served in Cairo and recruited many Ahepans and members of AHEPA's young men's auxiliary, the Sons of Pericles, into the OSS. He immigrated to the United States through Ellis Island in 1914.

Actress Betty White was starring in the top-rated television sitcom The Golden Girls. The four-time Emmy award winner had worked in television since the late 1940s and was a co-star on The Mary Tyler Moore Show. She had also worked extensively on the stage, often starring with her late husband, Allen Ludden. White had tirelessly crusaded for animal welfare and has devoted her time, energy and money to such organizations as the Fund for Animals and the American Humane Association.

Others honored included George D. Zamias, who was a Pennsylvania-based real estate developer and a first-generation Greek American. Zamias began his fulfillment of the American Dream working in his parents' hot cleaning and shoe-shine business. In 1961 he established his first real estate company and headed George D. Zamias Developer, ranked 11th among the nation's top shopping center owners. Charalambos A. Zarakiotis, a US citizen born in Greece, was President and CEO of the Atlantic Bank of New York. Zarakiotis had almost 30 years' experience in banking with the National Bank in Greece and its subsidiaries and affiliates.

Former San Francisco Mayor George Christopher, spoke on behalf of the honorees. In a moving speech, he called the evening "AHEPA's finest hour." Looking out on the audience of Greek Americans, one of the most successful ethnic groups in America, Christopher noted their humble origins. Where were, "the starry-eyed young men who came here long ago ... the peanut vendors, the pushcart vendors, the ditch diggers, the menial task workers and those who built the railroads..." he asked. "They are here—in every seat in this great hall," Christopher said. "The bootblacks, the ditch-diggers and the pushcart peddlers" had become attorneys, medical doctors, engineers, professors, and executives in business in what Christopher called "a great transformation." Christopher also urged the audience to "in the Athenian tradition, transmit our country even better than it was transmitted to us." He also said that now that the Greek Americans "have achieved this stature," that they "have every right to speak out for Cyprus" and to "differ with our president. "After the awards, those who contributed to the Ellis Island Wall of Honor through AHEPA were presented with a medallion specially commissioned and struck for the event.

The 69th Supreme Convention, 1991, Bahamas

At the very well attended 69th Supreme Convention in the Bahamas in 1991, outgoing Supreme President Scofield gave a very optimistic report, noting that AHEPA had experienced a year of rededication to its principles, rediscovery of its power, revitalization of its image, and "reglorification" of its substance in the eyes of all Greek Americans and the world. AHEPA, he declared, had emerged as the undisputable leader of all Hellenes. Indeed, AHEPA's eventful year had included a Unity Forum that brought together for the first time the leadership of all major Greek American organizations that had been active over the Cyprus issue, and a Charitable Foundation had been established, as well as a Hellenic Cultural Commission aimed at preventing the curtailment of the study of ancient Greek classics in colleges and universities throughout the United States and Canada. In the state of Georgia AHEPA joined in legal action to score an important victory over the Ku Klux Klan's challenge to a law banning the wearing of masks in public. Attorney and Ahepan William (Bill) Marianes represented the Order and was assisted by Supreme Counselor Manuel P. Scarmoutsos. AHEPA, having learned in September 1990 that the International Olympic Committee did not award the 1996 centenary Olympic Games to Athens, resumed its longstanding campaign to make Greece the permanent home of the Olympic Games.

At the conclusion of the convention in the Bahamas AHEPA unanimously elected businessman John T. Pappas as the next Supreme President. Pappas was born in 1915 in Lowell, Massachusetts, a town with a large Greek American population beginning in the early 20th century, where his immigrant parents owned a grocery store. The Pappas household was large with nine members, six boys and three girls. His family relocated to Washington, DC where job opportunities were greater, and he grew up in the shadow of the Capitol Building. He hawked newspapers on the corners of the nation's capital, and later entered the US Army at the age of 17 serving in the calvary. When World War II began, he was among the first 1,000 men to be recruited into the US Navy's "fighting Sea-bees," serving in the Pacific until the war ended. Shortly after he returned home from service in the Navy in 1945, he went to work for the late John F. McLaughlin, who operated a Washington, DC insurance agency which eventually became the largest insurer of labor unions in the United States and in which Pappas would become Chairman of the Board. Pappas' 50-year-long service to AHEPA had culminated in the previous year with his election as Vice President. In assuming the presidency Pappas spoke about AHEPA being on the threshold of a new era of unity in which the Order could and would "polish, strengthen and enhance every beautiful aspect" of the AHEPA family. He expressed the view that by pursuing its broad range of activities AHEPA had the opportunity to have the entire Hellenic American community rally to AHEPA.

The other officers elected at the Bahamas Convention were Dr. Gus Constantine as Supreme Vice President, Anthony Mavromaras as Supreme Vice President for Canada, Franklin R. Manios as Supreme Secretary, Peter Stamas as Supreme Treasurer, Manuel P. Scarmoutsos as Supreme Counselor, Monthe Kofos as National Athletic Director, and William Mackrides as chairman of the Sons of Pericles Advisory Board. Elected as Supreme Governors were James M. Broomas, George P. Kaffes, James Kaklamanos, Perry D. Kallis, George Paul, James A. Poll, George S. Spyrs, and Matthew G. Tsangarakis. Angelo Petromelis was elected as chairman of the Board of Directors, and Nick C. Demeris vice chairman.

At the Bahamas convention, the report offered by Phillip T. Frangos, the outgoing chairman of the Board of Directors was less optimistic in tone than the addresses by Supreme Presidents Scofield and Pappas. Frangos spoke first about how the action plan proposed by the Board at the 1990 convention had not been approved. He then went on to note that AHEPA needed to adopt a strategic plan and to reflect on why it existed and what form the organization would take in the near future. The key was to define AHEPA's mission and goals with the input not only of its members but also the broader Greek American community. Frangos also spoke about problems with the Order's financial affairs caused by the way the AHEPA Trust had been run. In an effort to maximize income, a decision was made to invest in corporate bonds. This, he noted, was in violation of the original agreement that stipulated investments should be made only in government or government guaranteed bonds. Subsequently that decision was ratified at the 1989 convention, but that also presupposed the sale of some corporate bonds which indeed were sold, but in a down bond market which meant a financial loss. He recommended that the Order adhere to the controls the Board was trying to introduce and concluded by saying AHEPA "must avoid the danger confronting it—of becoming a social club rather than the great multi-purpose association it must remain."[127] Frangos' candid report was indicative of how the leaders of the Order were concerned about ensuring that AHEPA's principles and values be upheld and also that it would adapt to the changing circumstances. One must not underestimate the organizational complexities of running an organization the size of AHEPA. Within a few years AHEPA would demonstrate its resilience by experiencing a crisis and managing to come out of it able to build on its past successes.

Chapter 10: AHEPA Recalibrates 1993–1999

AHEPA's history in the 1990s was one of crisis and recovery. Part of the crisis had to do with the overall social dynamics in the United States, another part was the Order's own responsibility. American political scientist Robert D. Putnam published a survey in 2000 that demonstrated the decline of civic, political, and social engagement in the United States since 1950. Among the many examples of a growing individualism and withdrawal from communal activities, Putnam noted the decline in membership in many fraternal organizations such as the Lions Clubs, the Benevolent and Protective Order of Elks, Freemasonry, Rotary, and Kiwanis. The causes Putnam suggests were responsible for this phenomenon included the intensification of work, the increase in dual career families, suburbanization, and the greater choice and individuation of the media, through the availability of cable television and more recently the internet. While Putnam was not especially concerned with ethnic fraternal organizations in America, his conclusions also applied to those organizations, including AHEPA. The other Greek American institution with a comparable size, the Greek Orthodox Church, also experienced declining membership.

Arguably, maintaining and increasing its members has been a major AHEPA concern throughout its history, but the challenges were even greater given national trends throughout the United States. Historically, AHEPA confronted the problem of sustaining and renewing its membership by adapting to the changes around it and especially those affecting America's relationship with Greece, and by responding to events it managed to mobilize and enlist Greek Americans in its campaigns. Occasionally, the need to overcome internal problems functioned as a catalyst and energized both leadership and members. This was the case in the 1990s, when in 1994 it became known that there had been serious financial irregularities over the previous few years. The need to put AHEPA's house in order was a motive for reform and regeneration. It did not come easily, and the rest of the decade was fraught with internal party divisions and budgetary issues.

What helped AHEPA find its footing in the late 1990s, aside from its own efforts, was the enhanced role diaspora communities began to play in the immediate post-Cold War era of globalization and transnationalism. AHEPA maintained its American character firmly throughout its history, but those conditions also favored its advocacy and concern over US foreign policy in the Eastern Mediterranean. Although this would become more apparent in the following decade of the 2000s, it did help AHEPA move forward in the late 1990s. Earlier that same decade the Order became active over the Macedonian question. Following the breakup of Yugoslavia into several independent nations, a process laden with a great deal of ethnic strife and suffering, the Socialist Republic of Macedonia declared its independence and changed its name to "Republic of Macedonia." Greece reacted very strongly to this, declaring it would not recognize any state with the historically Greek name of Macedonia. Segments of the Greek public became instantly mobilized in opposition to Greece's neighboring country, including the word Macedonia in its official name, and there ensued several of friction between the two countries until a compromise was struck in September of 1995.

There was one aspect of the enhanced role of the Greek diaspora that AHEPA treated cautiously and was ultimately justified in its attitude. In 1995 the Greek government formed the Council of Greeks Abroad, known by its Greek acronym SAE. Its purpose was to bring together the Greeks of the diaspora, creating a global network aimed at planning and materializing programs that would be recommended for implementation by the Greek government. AHEPA and other Greek diaspora organizations and individuals had not been consulted prior to the formation of the Council. Moreover, rather than the purely advisory role that was originally envisioned, it soon became apparent that SAE was closely linked to and dependent on the Greek government. At that point AHEPA switched its affiliation to one of observer status and continued to be indirectly involved through cooperating and exchanging information with SAE. Soon, SAE itself ran into many operational difficulties and ceased to function on a regular basis.[128]

In 1995 a bipartisan group of members of the US Congress established the Congressional Caucus on Hellenic Issues. Its purpose was and remains to this day to work to foster and improve relations between the United States and its allies, Greece and Cyprus. The Caucus brings congressional attention to key diplomatic, military, and human rights issues in a critical part of the world. The Hellenic Caucus also provides frequent updates from foreign ministry officials on the state of Cypriot reunification negotiations, as well as a focus on religious freedom issues of the Ecumenical Patriarchate. As the organization grew and increased its activities over the decades that followed, AHEPA would work closely with this group and especially its co-chairs, US representatives Carolyn Maloney and Gus Bilirakis.

AHEPA's 70th anniversary

AHEPA marked its 70th anniversary by holding its Supreme Convention in Washington, DC in August 1992. It was a happy occasion for many reasons, not least because the United States' relations with Greece were especially close. The previous year President Bush had made the first official visit of an American president to Greece in 32 years, and Greece's President Constantinos Mitsotakis had visited Washington and fostered close relations between the countries and expressed great appreciation for AHEPA and its work. A dispute between Greece and the former Yugoslav Republic of Macedonia over the name it would adopt as an independent nation was brewing, but there was optimism among Greek Americans that the issue would be resolved in Greece's favor and ensure stability in the region. On all other fronts AHEPA could look back with satisfaction on its achievements since its founding in 1922. The Winter 1992 The Ahepan magazine listed them as maintaining a well-structured international family organization, acquiring international headquarters in

Washington, DC, pursuing generous civic participation which included a seniors housing program, promoting loyalty to the United States, education of its members in the principles of government and working toward the betterment of society, opposing tyranny and evil, promoting Hellenism and education, and fostering morality and good fellowship. Major business concluded at the convention also included the inauguration of an AHEPA "Plant Your Roots in Greece" campaign, which would facilitate Greek American participation in the reforestation of Greece. AHEPA planned to develop a medical personnel exchange program with the AHEPA Hospital in Thessaloniki. Democratic presidential candidate Bill Clinton, in a message to outgoing AHEPA Supreme President John T. Pappas, gave his strong support for Greece on the Macedonia issue.

At the Convention's Banquet, noted philanthropist and benefactor Mary Matthews of Yorktown, Virginia, received the coveted AHEPA Socratic Award. Matthews pledged $125,000 to AHEPA in memory of her late husband, Nicholas Matthews. The first Greek woman to win an Olympic gold medal, Voula Patoulidou, was also honored at the Grand Banquet and received a prolonged standing ovation. The AHEPA Academy of Achievement also recognized five accomplished Greek Americans at the Grand Banquet for their work. The 1991 award in the field of medicine was won by cardiologist Dr. Peter C. Gazes, Distinguished University Professor of Cardiology and former Director of the Cardiovascular Division at Medical University of South Carolina. The 1991 award for business and commerce was won by Williams S. Stavropoulos, President of DOW USA. The 1991 award for natural science was won by John G. Rangos, of Pittsburgh, President and CEO of Chambers Development Company, one of the largest and fastest growing waste management companies in the United States. The 1992 award for medicine was given to radiologist Dr. Panos G. Koutrouvelis and the 1992 award for education was presented to Dr. Dimitri Basil Kececioglu. Other social events included a Greek dance night, a 70th Anniversary Ball, an athletic awards luncheon, and the Miss AHEPA Pageant won by Mary Mavromoustakos of Astoria.[129]

The convention capped off a week of business and socializing by electing Dr. Gus A. Constantine, a retired educator from the Chicago area, as Supreme President. Anthony Mavromaras of Agincourt, Ontario, was reelected as Supreme Vice President for Canada.

Also elected to the AHEPA Supreme Lodge were John Economou to the office of Supreme Vice President; Dr. Spiro Macris, Supreme Secretary; Fred Iconos, Supreme Treasurer; John Sakona, Supreme Counselor; and Monthe N. Kofos, Supreme Athletic Director. Elected Supreme Governors were Dr. Jim Dimitriou, John Herron, Chris Johns, James Kaklamanos, Panagiotis Karounos, Peter Masters, Matthew Tsangarakis, and Chris Zazas. New Supreme President Gus Constantine, the son of Greek immigrants who had settled in North Dakota, had started his service in AHEPA in the 1940s, in Chapter 11 in Wilson, North Carolina. His wife Julia had served as Grand President of the Daughters of Penelope in 1989–1990. Constantine's emphasis as president would be to mobilize the grassroots of the Order, the local chapters, to enact a vigorous membership drive with Supreme Vice President Economou and plan a simplification of the initiation process in the hopes of attracting new members more easily. Yet despite the urgency of those issues, during his year-long tenure Constantine oversaw the establishment of an AHEPA fund to assist the victims of Hurricane Andrew in South Florida, and the continued progress of AHEPA's National Housing Corporation, which at the time was serving 1,500 elderly and held dedication ceremonies in Niantic, Connecticut and Mobile, Alabama, and a groundbreaking ceremony in Merriville, Indiana.

A Fiscal Crisis Looms
By the time AHEPA held its 71st Supreme Convention between August 8–14, 1993, in Pittsburgh, the Order's financial difficulties had become acute, and measures were taken to address the problem. A decrease in membership brought in less income, and low interest rates on AHEPA's investment reduced cash flows. This had meant operational cutbacks, reduced philanthropic contributions, and very little spending on outreach and public relations. AHEPA had reached "a point of serious fiscal crisis" according to the Board, which believed the decline in membership was due to the overall drop in engagement in fraternal volunteer organizations throughout America, and also because of the steady assimilation of Greek Americans and especially the declining number of intermarriages and the different experiences of third and fourth generation Greek Americans who were no longer growing up in Greek neighborhoods and within a heavily Greek family environment.

Yet the Board believed that those Greek Americans for those reasons would have a thirst for things Hellenic and that AHEPA should address those needs. They echoed what many others also believed, to the effect that the more assimilated Greek Americans would search for their roots, the more they would find they had in "Hellenism" the most exalted cultural heritage available to them. That was something AHEPA could capitalize upon and regenerate itself.[130]

The convention, which opened with an invocation from Greek Orthodox Bishop Maximos of Pittsburgh and was coordinated locally by Past Supreme President Louis G. Manesiotis, a Pittsburgh native and long-time convention organizer, duly adopted several budget cutting and revenue raising measures. And in a sign of AHEPA and the Daughters of Penelope concerns over sustaining the significance of ancient Greek culture in America, the convention included a lecture by De Paul University professor Andrew Kopan, who spoke of the threat new trends in American higher education posed to the position of classical studies in the curriculum. The convention banquet featured the usual array of awards bestowed on worthy persons at that event each year, along with two new awards. One was the AHEPA Lifetime Achievement award presented to former two term president Nick Smyrnis for his work in establishing the AHEPA National Housing Corporation, the other was the AHEPA Olympic Award that went to Dan Rooney, the president of the Pittsburgh Steelers football team. The Rooney family had sponsored exhibition football games in the 1940s for the benefit of the Greek War Relief Association.

Toward the end of its week-long proceedings the Pittsburgh convention elected as Supreme President John Economou; Supreme Vice President Charles Georgeson; Supreme Vice President of Canada John Giourmetakis, a businessman from Edmonton; Supreme Treasurer George Pappas; Supreme Counselor Ike Gulas; Supreme Governors: Theodore Kyrkostas, Louis Peron, Angelo Pappas, Dr. Alexander Xenakis, Graig Clawson, Frank Gramas, Dr. Jim Dimitriou, and George Marmas; Athletic Director Monthe Kofos; and Sons of Pericles National Advisor Nicholas Karacostas. The new Supreme President, John N. Economou, a businessman from Akron, Ohio, acknowledged the difficulties AHEPA was facing, but he struck an optimistic note, saying that the decrease in Greek American intermarriages and the corresponding mixed marriages meant that

AHEPA could potentially attract more families. And he called on all chapters to redouble their efforts in recruiting new members. Another optimistic moment in the convention came when Senator Paul Sarbanes spoke at the banquet, accepting the Order's Socratic Award, praising AHEPA for its extraordinary contributions. It was a reminder of what AHEPA had achieved and its potential for the future notwithstanding the problems it was facing at that moment.

In the months ahead the Order's activities included the very successful 31st Biennial Congressional Banquet which coincided with the commemoration of Greek Independence Day. The weekend of the banquet included a well-attended major conference on Greek American issues, including a panel of experts on the Macedonian issue and talks with members of the National Security Council. AHEPA had responded negatively to the Clinton administration's announcement that it would be recognizing the Former Yugoslav Republic of Macedonia, which it did in February 1994. AHEPA decided not to attend a briefing organized by the White House. Very importantly, at the conference a State Department official in charge of southeastern European affairs assured everyone that Washington was not going the next step after recognition, namely establishing diplomatic relations with the newly independent nation, until the dispute with Greece was resolved in a way satisfactory to both sides. At the banquet itself there were 40 members of Congress in attendance, including Senator John Glenn who was honored. There was a mass initiation of new members at the banquet, an event designed to spark broader interest in the Order and attract new members. Nonetheless, the need to attract more members would remain and would be raised at the next Supreme Convention which took place in the summer of 1994 at Las Vegas. There had been one notable absence at the banquet, that of Archbishop Iakovos, and Supreme President Economou expressed concerns about AHEPA's relations with the Greek Orthodox Archdiocese in his report at that same Supreme Convention. While relations between these two major Greek American institutions have remained historically close, there have been moments when that closeness was not apparent, but this had to do more with circumstance than any fundamental differences. That year, the Archbishop's efforts were absorbed by the preparations for a major American Pan-Orthodox meeting that would take place in Ligonier, Pennsylvania at the end of 1994 and would subsequently generate a great deal of controversy.

Indeed, relations reverted to normal the following year, and at the 1995 Supreme Convention, Supreme President Charles Georgeson stated as much in his report describing his cordial meetings with the Archbishop. Georgeson had been unanimously elected Supreme President at the 1994 Supreme Convention in Las Vegas, along with Spiro Macris, Vice President; John Giourmetakis, Supreme Vice President for Canada; James A. Poll, Supreme Secretary; Steve Manta, Supreme Treasurer; Ike Gulas, Supreme Counselor; Monthe Kofos, Supreme Athletic Director; Nicholas A. Karacostas, Sons National Advisor; and Filippos Diamantis, Dimitri Karadimetris, Don Kibler, Thomas Kress, Theodore Kyrkostas, Tim Mavrellis, Louis Peronis, and George Tassos as Supreme Governors. Georgeson, of Clinton, Massachusetts, a retired businessman whose parents emigrated from Lagadia, Arcadia in Greece in 1912, had served as Vice President the previous year. Georgeson had a particular interest in youth development programs. In AHEPA he had led the Sons of Pericles National Advisory Board. A long-time member of the AHEPA Cyprus Committee, he had been on three fact-finding missions to the island. He stressed the need for AHEPA to continue its ties to Greece and Cyprus and expressed his support for continuing the very successful AHEPA exchange program between Deborah Hospital and the AHEPA Hospital in Thessaloniki. Georgeson had graduated in business management from Tufts University and served three years in the US Navy. His wife Joanne Nicas was long active in the Daughters of Penelope leadership and scholarship work.

Crisis Management
In December of 1994, Bob Leckrone, the chairman of the AHEPA Audit Committee, informed Georgeson that there had been serious financial irregularities at the Order's Headquarters. An investigation was launched immediately and AHEPA entered a period of turmoil and self-examination and of searching for ways of restructuring and improving its practices to stay true to its principles. The 73rd Supreme Convention that met in Miami addressed the ongoing situation with the thoroughness it deserved. Outgoing Supreme

President Georgeson opened his report by referring to the financial irregularities, and Supreme Counselor Ike Gulas in his report dealt with the issue in greater detail. He stated that in December there had been financial improprieties with the accounts owned by the Order of AHEPA and there would be an investigation to reveal the truth. In January 1995, two key individuals entrusted with the protection of AHEPA funds were replaced and subsequently released of their duties and faced criminal charges for fiduciary improprieties. Gulas expressed his thanks to all those Ahepans who had worked diligently for the investigation to be effective and systematic. Another report that detailed the events that took place during and after the uncovering of the accounting mishap was that of acting Executive Director Basil N. Mossaidis, who was one of the persons publicly thanked by Gulas.

Even though the financial problem cast its shadow over the convention, the proceedings were also focused on the wide range of activities AHEPA had engaged in over the past months. The Supreme President referred to the cordial meetings he had with Archbishop Iakovos throughout the past year and how the Archbishop had requested that AHEPA eliminate the perceived Masonic elements in its rituals and not hold events around the date of August 15, when the Greek Orthodox Church celebrates the dormition of the Virgin Mary. The climate of closeness between AHEPA and the Archdiocese came at a good time, because Iakovos was preparing to step down the following year. Georgeson's report also showcased those activities and paid special attention to the Order's work in promoting Hellenic causes through the lens of American interests and values. The outgoing Supreme President rebutted views that AHEPA should be doing less in that sphere or even step back and let other Greek American organizations to do that type of work. Instead, Georgeson asserted, even though AHEPA was going through a difficult period it had a duty to be active in trying to shape US policy with regard to the issues related to Cyprus, Macedonia, human rights in Albania, and the status of the Ecumenical Patriarchate. He went on to report on several successes that AHEPA had achieved in terms of legislative initiatives on Capitol Hill aimed at curtailing aid to Turkey. A report by George Savidis, the Director of the AHEPA Office of Public and Government Affairs, elaborated on those and other related activities.

The election of Spiro Macris as Supreme President was widely regarded at the time as the beginning of a new era in which AHEPA would recalibrate and move forward, and those hopes were to be confirmed over the next few years. Macris, who was 56 at the time, was a dentist based in North Carolina. He campaigned on a platform of reform. His calm and measured demeanor helped his candidacy; he was the type of leader AHEPA needed at that moment in its history. Macris, the son of immigrants from the town of Trikala in Thessaly, graduated Phi Beta Kappa from Davidson College and earned a graduate degree from Columbia University. He was commissioned a lieutenant in the US Army and served a tour of duty in Vietnam. He graduated with a doctorate in dentistry from the University of North Carolina.

Reflecting the reverberations of Macris' elections was the fact that the Greek language daily Ethnikos Kyrix reported the event on its front page, describing the election result as a surprise and an end of an era in which Louis Manesiotis was the dominant personality in the Order. After a few days it published an interview with Macris which also made the front page. Macris had the opportunity to pay tribute to Manesiotis' service and to talk about the course he wanted to follow, which entailed a thorough introspection following the embezzlement scandal, an acknowledgement of the Order's Greek roots, and a continuation of the efforts to engage with the issues affecting US policy in the Eastern Mediterranean. The reporter also posed questions about AHEPA's rituals, and Macris responded that they were rooted in the era the Order was formed and that there were ongoing discussions within the organization about their relevance. The other officers elected at the 1995 convention were Steve Manta, Supreme Vice President; James Anas, Supreme Vice President for Canada; James F. Dimitriou, Supreme Treasurer; E. P. Terry Mitchel Secretary, John K. Antholis, Supreme Counselor; Monthe Kofos Supreme Athletic Director; Nicholas Karacostas Sons National Advisor. The Governors who were elected were Harry Cavalaris, Jim Gaz, Paul Pappas, John G. Pappas, Michael Papanu, Constantine Rizopoulos and John E. Tsimekles, [131]

Macris had produced a straightforward solution to what was a complicated problem. The establishment of the organization at the time thought it best to conceal the embezzlement, he and others opposed that effort. They believed it was imperative that the membership and the community at large be informed of all the facts as to what had occurred. Macris viewed his responsibility as president as an endeavor to rally the membership and to assure them, through his presence, his enthusiasm, and his energy that the organization, though wounded, would survive and thrive once again. [Insert Endnote: Personal Communication from Spiro Macris]

The Olympic Games Tribute in Atlanta

Several major events in 1996 tested AHEPA's ability to operate its wide-ranging set of programs, with the Order being able to respond successfully. While AHEPA was still in crisis management mode, in early 1996 there was also a crisis in Greece's relations with Turkey. It occurred when the ailing Andreas Papandreou stepped down from his position as prime minister and was replaced by a more technocratically minded politician, Costas Simitis. The year 1996 was also the year the centenary Olympic Games took place in Atlanta. An important event related to this happened in June 1996 which reflected very positively on AHEPA. Back in 1989, a group of Atlanta members of AHEPA conceived of the idea to honor the 100th anniversary of the Olympic Games by commissioning a work of art sponsored by AHEPA and with funds raised from the Greek American community. The assumption at the time was that the centennial Olympics would be awarded to Athens and the work of art would be presented to the city of Athens in 1996. But in 1990 the International Olympic Committee in what was a surprise decision chose to award the 1996 Summer Games to Atlanta rather than Athens. The Greek actress and politician Melina Mercouri reacted by saying: "Coca Cola won over the Parthenon temple." In the words of the initiators of this project: "The Atlanta Hellenic community was caught in the middle—torn between their allegiance to their home city and their love of the home of their ancestors. Passions ran high in all Hellenic communities, and the pain that Greece experienced as a result of the I.O.C. decision was manifesting itself in adverse feelings toward the City of Atlanta. It became apparent to this group of Atlanta Ahepans that something had to be done to convert any hurt or anger into a positive act."[132]

Their solution was to work through AHEPA, which had a special relationship to Atlanta because it was founded there, to raise funds to create a sculpture that would pay tribute to three cities, Olympia where the Olympics had begun in ancient Greece in 776 BC, Athens where the first modern Olympics had taken place in 1896, and Atlanta, the venue of the centenary Games of 1996. The AHEPA Centennial Foundation, as the group was called, secured the approval of AHEPA at the 71st Supreme Convention that was held in 1993 in Pittsburgh, and that of the Atlanta Committee for the Olympic Games. There ensued a huge effort in time and money, and it included shipping over to Atlanta stones from Olympia.

Finally, on June 1, 1996, the unveiling and dedication of the sculpture took place in the presence of Archbishop Iakovos; Andrew Young, the Co-Chairman of the Atlanta Committee for the Olympic Games, former US Ambassador to the United Nations, and former Mayor of Atlanta; Senator Paul Sarbanes; Bill Campbell, the Mayor of Atlanta; the Consul General of Greece, Dionysios Sourvanos; George Devves, the Mayor of Olympia; AHEPA Supreme President Spiro Macris; and Johnny Economy, the president of the AHEPA Centennial Foundation. The master of ceremonies was Atlanta attorney Nicholas Moraitakis. The event was followed by a Gala Grand Banquet that evening at which Bill Marianes was master of ceremonies. The Tribute project which was successfully carried out represented yet another significant AHEPA achievement. It reflected the Order's roots in Atlanta, its commitment to its Hellenic heritage, and the ways it has consistently supported the universal values represented by the Olympic Games. The officers and directors of the AHEPA Centennial Foundation were Johnny Economy, Bill Marianes, Victor Polizos a pediatrician based in Atlanta, Steve Manta, Lou Zakas, Lee Durbetaki, Tim Maniatis, and Tom Rakus.

The 1996 Supreme Convention and the AHEPA 2000 Proposal

Macris was reelected at the Supreme Convention the following year, 1996, that was held in Houston, Texas. All the other members of the Supreme Lodge were also reelected. There was a greater sense of normality at that Supreme Convention because the embezzlement investigations were in the hands of the FBI and the justice authorities while delegates were presented with a comprehensive account of how the events transpired. Clearly this was a crisis the Order had faced which was dealt with a head on manner and in a way that would enable it to move forward. One of the highlights of the Houston convention was the presentation of a new strategic plan for AHEPA. The "AHEPA 2000" proposal aimed toward reorganizing the association toward the future. The AHEPA 2000 proposal was presented by Bill Marianes, the Atlanta attorney, to a joint session of Ahepans, Daughters, Sons, and Maids and garnered a strong vote of approval. According to the AHEPA 2000 working document, AHEPA planned to rearticulate its primary goals as Hellenism, Education, Philanthropy, Civic Responsibility, Family, and the Pursuit and Recognition of Excellence. The paper foresaw AHEPA restructuring itself strategically and operationally to serve these goals using modern organizational models. The meetings also served to fully inform the delegates on the financial and other issues arising from the late 1994 discovery of irregularities which resulted in the loss of substantial AHEPA assets. All delegates received a detailed 16-page briefing, as well as additional material, covering that issue. The briefing material was gathered by AHEPA Controller Aggie Capsalis, Finance Committee Chairman George Gabriel, Board Chairman Sam Nakis, and Counselor John Antholis. Capsalis had volunteered over a year and a half of full-time work at AHEPA Headquarters to put the organization back on its feet financially.[133]

Along with the information about the Order's finances that was presented, the setting out of AHEPA's positions on foreign affairs was also another important feature of that convention. There had been several important initiatives taken over the issues relating to US policy in the Eastern Mediterranean. In January 1996 the ongoing tensions between Greece and Turkey that arose whenever Turkey made revisionist claims in the Aegean became exacerbated over the issue of the sovereignty of the small Imia islets located east of the island of Kalymnos. Supreme President Macris had made a special effort to enhance AHEPA's engagement with US foreign policy issues. He had long been active in AHEPA's work on the Cyprus issue and under his guidance AHEPA published the first ever grading of members of Congress based on issues concerning Greek Americans. Macris met with US Ambassador to Greece Tom Niles, US Ambassador to Cyprus Richard Boucher, Assistant Secretaries of State Richard

Holbrooke and John Kornblum, and National Security Director Anthony Lake. As part of AHEPA's continued work on foreign policy issues the convention in Houston also issued resolutions concerning US policy in the Eastern Mediterranean as well as on organizational issues within the community. AHEPA Public Affairs and Government Director George Savidis and Cyprus and Hellenic Affairs Committee Chairman John Sitilides led several substantive meetings on policy issues. The convention approved a resolution emphasizing the positive role of Greece and Cyprus and the negative moves of Turkey in the region.

The reelection of Spiro Macris as Supreme President in 1996 was a sign of approval of the reforms he was introducing. "This is a time of great change in the Greek American community and a time of great change for AHEPA," he said upon his election. The other officials who were elected to serve alongside Macris were Vice President Steve Manta, Canadian President Anthony Mavromaras, Secretary James F. Dimitriou, Treasurer Michael D. Papapanu, Counsellor John Antholis, Athletic Director Monthe Kofos, and Governors George Anagnostos, Dr. John Grossomanides, Jr., Ike Gulas, Nicholas A. Karacostas, James Katramadros, James Miller, Paul G. Pappas, Byron Smyrniotis, and Sons of Pericles Advisor James Lolis. The AHEPA Board of Directors, a new body introduced to monitor the Order's internal workings for 1996–1997, would continue to be led by Chairman Sam Nakis. Serving on the AHEPA Board of Directors with Chairman Nakis were Vice Chairman A. Jack Georgalas, former AHEPA Supreme President A. Steve Betzelos, James Anas, Spiros "Sam" Arfaras, Thomas Lukas, Steve Moskos, Ernest Tsaptsinos, and Secretary George Paul; Supreme President Macris and Supreme Vice President Steve Manta also served on the AHEPA Board.

As always happened in an election year in the United States, the delegates at the Supreme Convention had the opportunity, away from the convention floor, to discuss the candidates. With incumbent Bill Clinton being challenged by Republican candidate Bob Dole there was certainly no argument about which of the two would support Hellenic issues better because both Clinton, who would be reelected in November, and Dole had a positive record in that respect.

AHEPA and the Changes in the Church
The other important event of that year that affected the Greek American community was that Archbishop Iakovos stepped down after 37 years as the leader of the Greek Orthodox Church in the United States. During that time Iakovos did a great deal to shape the present and future of Hellenism and Orthodoxy in America. He was a strong and popular leader who combined authoritarianism with charisma, who had managed to guide the Church during a period of many changes that Greek America had experienced. Throughout that time, he had recognized and valued AHEPA's role and its support of the Church, and this was shown by conferring the honorific status of Archon of the Order of St. Andrew the Apostle upon Supreme Presidents and other leading Ahepans. Iakovos' successor, Archbishop Spyridon, had a relatively short tenure, from 1996 to 1999 when he was replaced by Archbishop Demetrios. The end of the Iakovian era brought an enhanced role for the Ecumenical Patriarchate of Constantinople in the affairs of Orthodoxy and Hellenism in the United States. This change dovetailed nicely with AHEPA's longstanding commitment to defending the rights of the Patriarchate which are perennially under threat, and the Order's relationship with Ecumenical Patriarch Bartholomew has grown steadily since his election in 1991.

AHEPA's 75th Anniversary
AHEPA's 75th anniversary year was approached as an opportunity of reenergizing the Order. The Summer 1997 issue of The Ahepan magazine had three important articles that reminded members of the history of the Order and the need to continue its work in the future. The first was by Sam Nakis, who wrote that AHEPA had experienced a tumultuous time dominated by financial and legal concerns but that the anniversary was a time "to stop, step back and reflect on the best aspects of the AHEPA and its accomplishments." He listed the establishment of the organization, the role it played in integrating Greeks into American society, its philanthropic and athletic activities, its work in the sphere of US foreign policy, and the aid it had offered Greece and Cyprus.[134]

In the second article, former Supreme President James Scofield addressed the foundation of AHEPA and explicitly the way it was established to protect the Greeks from the Ku Klux Klan. This historical fact was not frequently mentioned in accounts of AHEPA's history, but Scofield's article was a turning point after which this issue became part of the Order's narrative. Interestingly, Scofield included references to the Klan's activities in Canada. In November of that year, Senator Paul Sarbanes entered the article in the Congressional Record, an important tribute to AHEPA. Sarbanes remarked: "As part of this 75th anniversary commemoration, James Scofield, a Past Supreme President of AHEPA, prepared an article on the early origins of AHEPA entitled, "Forgotten History: The Klan vs. Americans of Hellenic Heritage in an Era of Hate." This piece, written by Mr. Scofield, recently retired after 30 years as a senior executive at the St. Petersburg, FL, Times, has appeared in the AHEPA magazine and many Greek American publications. It records the struggle which Greek Americans encountered in their effort to participate fully in American society. AHEPA's history, as presented by Mr. Scofield, also reminds us of the extraordinary progress which our country has achieved in providing opportunity for people of all races, religions, and backgrounds. We are most appreciative to Mr. Scofield for his unique contribution and admonition to continue our efforts to ensure justice and respect for all. I ask that his article be printed in the Record."[135]

The third significant article published in the summer edition of the magazine was made up of three views on the future of Hellenism in the United States by sociologist Charles Moskos, the new Greek Orthodox Archbishop Spyridon, and Spiro Macris. Moskos suggested that although Greek Americans and especially the younger generations were becoming more and more assimilated, the Greek Orthodox Church in America would be able to preserve a form of Greek American identity if its influence could be complemented by trips and educational programs in the old country. Spyridon echoed Moskos' views about the central role that the Greek Orthodox Church in America could play, adding that it could benefit from close collaboration with organizations such as AHEPA. Macris focused on AHEPA's future role, posing the question of whether it would remain a fundamentally philanthropic institution or become the secular voice of assimilated Greek Americans and work toward preserving their ethnic identity. Macris outlined the way it could combine both those functions. As he correctly noted, on its 75th anniversary,

AHEPA had come full circle of sorts, from a beginning that sought to fuse Greekness with Americanization to a moment in which it had the responsibility of fusing Americanness with Hellenic culture.

AHEPA's 75th Convention in 1997 was held in Atlanta in honor of its founding in that city in 1922 75 years earlier. The Atlanta Journal-Constitution marked the occasion which described the Order's establishment. The obstacles it faced at the outset were described by a member of the original Mother Lodge, Nicholas D. Chotas, who was quoted as saying: "Lacking experience and capital we found our path strewn with the almost insurmountable obstacles of political prejudice, mercenary suspicions, and lack of interest..." The article went on to say that nonetheless AHEPA survived and flourished, noting that it shifted its early emphasis on assimilation over to focusing on its members' ethnic roots only after "more and more Greek-Americans have melted utterly into the melting pot." And it recognized AHEPA's contributions, noting: "This country's Greeks have done well financially, educationally and otherwise. They're influential in foreign policy beyond their numbers, and AHEPA, which retains quaint clubby features such as secret passwords, has branched out into all manner of good works: managing homes for the elderly poor of all backgrounds (such as the new 68-bed facility in DeKalb County that will be dedicated Sunday); promoting Greek art of every age (including the handsome fan-shaped bronze sculpture in Centennial Olympic Park); financing scholarships, orphanages, hospitals, disaster relief and more."[136]

The convention began with the dedication of a multi-million-dollar local AHEPA housing project. Cyprus was represented at the convention by Ambassador to the United States, Andros Nicolaides. Over 1,200 guests, including His Eminence Archbishop Spyridon of America, Senator Paul Sarbanes, and former Congressman Brademas, attended later in the week the organization's Grand Banquet. AHEPA honored at the Grand Banquet leading US scholar Mary Lefkowitz with its Homeric Award for her published works debunking attempts to detract from the accomplishments of the ancient Greeks. The convention unanimously elected Steve Manta as the organization's Supreme President. Manta, who was 57, was a 31-year member of the Milo Chapter 348 in Chicago and had served as the organization's Supreme Vice President for the previous two years. The new

AHEPA President was a leading businessman in the Greek American community and was Vice President of J. L. Manta Inc., one of the largest industrial painting corporations in the United States. The other officials who were elected at the 75th Supreme Convention were Supreme Vice President Lee G. Rallis, Canadian President Anthony Mavromaras, Supreme secretary Johnny N. Economy, Supreme Treasurer George J. Dariotis, Supreme Counselor Gus J. James II, and Supreme Athletic Director Monthe Kofos. The Supreme Governors elected were George Achedafty, Thomas Anastassiou, Vacilios "Likie" Beleos, Thomas C. Geanapulos, Ike Gulas, James Miller, Byron Smyrniotis, and Elias Tsekerides. James Lolis was elected as National Advisor to the Sons of Pericles.

The 76th & 77th Supreme Conventions, 1998, Orlando & 1999, San Diego

The 76th Supreme Convention held in Orlando in 1998 showed a continued effort to overcome AHEPA's financial problems and its aftershocks. The Convention adopted a resolution calling for unity, lamenting political maneuvering over the elections of officers and mentioned that AHEPA was losing members and prospective members who were alienated by the infighting. The resolution called on the organized groups within the Order to rededicate themselves to the pursuit of AHEPA's goals and work toward finding qualified persons who could run for office irrespective of their affiliations.[137] The divisions were evident when the Board of Directors presented a set of solutions aimed at addressing the unbalanced budget that existed for the second year in a row. These included small constitutional changes that failed to gain the required 2/3 approval from the floor. There was an effort to undermine the process of deliberation and decision making. In the words of the Board's chairman Jack Georgalas, "because of constant interruptions, and what appeared to be an organized filibuster, the report was not presented adequately."[138]

The convention had an easier time dealing with issues such as membership, the financial health of the Order, and US foreign policy in the Eastern Mediterranean. A resolution on Cyprus that was approved unanimously called on the US government to acknowledge responsibility for the Cyprus tragedy and to recognize Cyprus' sovereign right to self-defense, pending demilitarization, and to help restore the status quo and the rule of law as it applied before Turkey's 1974 illegal invasion. The convention elected Lee G. Rallis Supreme President; George J. Dariotis Supreme Vice President; Jim Giannoulis, an accountant from Ontario, as Canadian President; Johnny N. Economy Supreme Secretary; Vacilios "Likie" Beleos Supreme Treasurer; Gus J. James II; and Monthe Kofos Supreme Athletic Director. The Supreme Governors elected were Thomas Anastasiou, Tasos Kalantzis, Ptolemeos E. Kotzambasis, Chris Peppas, John Rumpakis, Dr. Michael Syropoulos, and Elias Tsekerides. Georgalas was reelected to a three-year term to the Board of Directors and subsequently elected as chairman by his peers.

The last convention of the decade, the 77th, held in San Diego in July 1999, confirmed AHEPA's steady regeneration. The convention elected George J. Dariotis Supreme President; Dr James Dimitriou Supreme Vice President; James Giannoulis Canadian President; George Anagnostos Supreme Secretary; Vacilios "Likie" Beleos Supreme Treasurer; William Marianes Supreme Counselor; Monthe Kofos Supreme Athletic Director; and Steve Kafkis National Advisor to the Sons of Pericles. The Supreme Governors elected were Dino Basdakis, Peter Leasca, John Mehos, Ernest Mylonas, Chris Peppas, John Rumpakis, Dr. Michael Syropoulos, and Nicolaos Trintis. The new Supreme President, George Dariotis, a pharmacy manager in Alexandria, Virginia, at age 36 was the youngest Ahepan to be elected to the post for three decades. He had served as head of the Sons of Pericles while completing his studies at Ohio Northern University. Upon his election he spoke about how AHEPA had to modernize and become more attractive to a younger generation of Greek Americans, and how he believed that while AHEPA tended to pursue a wide range of projects it needed to become more cognizant of Hellenic issues. During his tenure, AHEPA raised over $200,000 to aid the victims of an earthquake that struck Athens in September 1999. Dariotis worked actively with other Greek American organizations and leaders to promote Hellenic issues and was in Athens in November of that year to welcome Bill Clinton during the President's historic visit to the Greek capital. Other initiatives taken under Dariotis' leadership were upgrading the Order's website and reinstituting the Congressional Report Card, the guide that rated congressmen and senators according to their votes on Hellenic issues.

Dariotis' focus on Hellenic issues was, in many ways, a continuation of the trend that was initiated by Past Supreme President Macris and which had helped regenerate the Order and overcome the difficulties it had encountered in the mid-1990s. It was a perspective that included a continuation of AHEPA's domestic programs but also a pronounced concern with preserving the core values of Greek American identity and fostering closer ties with the homeland. As Macris had noted, AHEPA had come full circle and from working toward Americanizing the Greek immigrants in its early history, it was now engaged in an effort to help Americans of Greek descent maintain a connection with their cultural heritage. The trend would become even more explicit over the next two decades as AHEPA grew closer to its centenary.

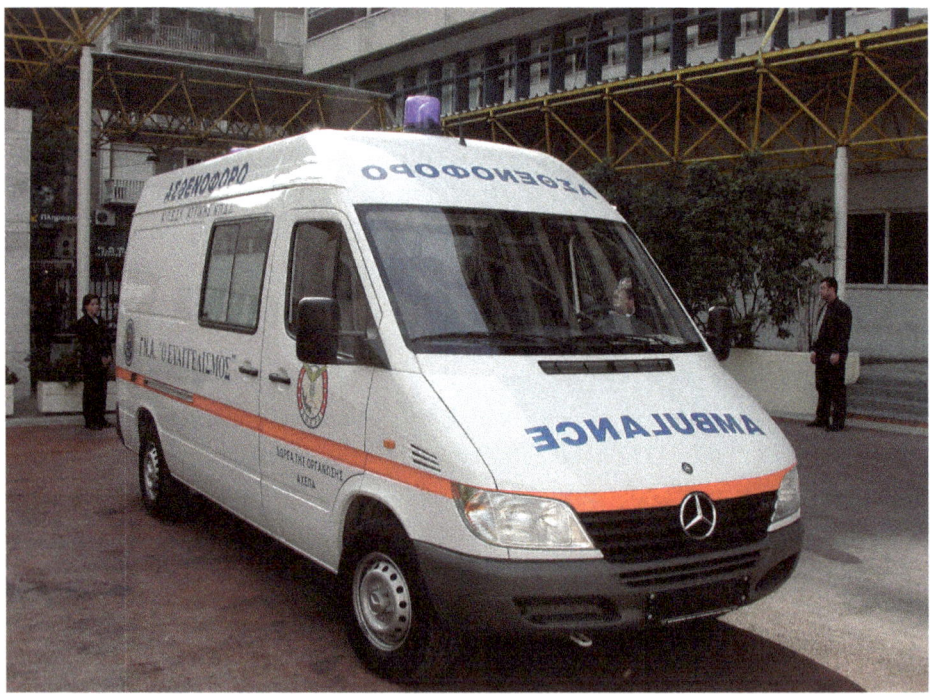

Part IV 2000–2022

CHAPTER 11: AHEPA ENTERS THE 21ST CENTURY 2000–2008

The dawn of the 21st century brought new challenges which AHEPA was able to respond to thanks to its ability to push ahead with all its initiatives, both international and domestic. A report on AHEPA's first Supreme Convention of the 21st century published in The Greek American, a weekly English language newspaper published in New York, stated that AHEPA was making considerable progress, and noted: "Party politics aside, the AHEPA, in the last few years has been undergoing something of a renaissance. Following a crippling financial scandal that drained the organization of both morale and much needed funds, the AHEPA has picked itself up by its bootstraps and forged ahead, endeavoring to initiate and continue programs that would both preserve Greek America's cultural identity and promote a positive relationship between the United States and Greece." It was a very fair summary of AHEPA's progress, all it had achieved over the previous years and all it still had to do, including the need to address its internal political dynamics and channel them for the good of the Order. Following the 2000 Convention AHEPA continued to grow stronger and signaled its strength and influence by holding its 2008 Convention in Athens.[139]

Entering the 21st Century & Responding to the 9/11 Events

The first AHEPA convention in the 21st century, the 78th in its history, took place between July 26–30, 2000, in New Orleans. The new Supreme President elected at the Convention was Johnny N. Economy, who successfully challenged incumbent president George Dariotis with the backing of the AHEPA First group. Dariotis had the support of the Reform Wing group. Economy was the son of Greek immigrants, Efstathios Economopoulos who was from Messenia in Peloponnesos and Evthoxia who was from Asia Minor, and was the founding president of a graphic design and apparel company in Atlanta. Economy evoked a sense of optimism and urgency about rising to the challenges of a new era, and the need for AHEPA to step up and protect, promote, and project Hellenism when he spoke about what lay ahead: bridging the gap between the second, third, and fourth generation Greek Americans, Justice for Cyprus, the 2004 Athens Olympics, the growth and protection of the Greek Orthodox Church, and the highlighting of US-Greek relations in the upcoming 2000 presidential election in the United States. But first, he noted, came the need to strengthen the AHEPA family by working on ongoing issues that involved initiatives such as Cooley's Anemia, Autism in Greece, the Bone Marrow Registry, and the campaign to return the Parthenon Marbles to Greece. In speaking about the promotion of Hellenism being the greatest challenge AHEPA faced going into the next millennium, Economy echoed what was becoming a consensus view among the leaders of the Order, irrespectively of whether there were different priorities and tactics in pursuing that strategy. The other officials elected at the Supreme Convention in 2000 were Supreme Vice President Andrew Banis; Canadian President Xenophon Scoufaras, a businessman from Montreal; Supreme Secretary Byron F. Smyrniotis; Supreme Treasurer Byron A. Argeropoulos; Supreme Counselor William Marianes Esq.; Supreme Athletic Director Monthe Kofos; and Sons National Advisor Steve Kafkis. Supreme Governors John N. Agnos, Louis G. Atsaves, Peter Baltis, Tasso Chronis, Peter Dress, Sayed J. Houssein, Alex Katsafanas, Thomas Rakus. Board of Directors A. Steve Betzelos Chairman, Franklin Manios Vice Chairman, Ike Gulas Secretary, and the governors elected were

Georgalas, C. Steven Georgilakis, Harry Lake, Nicholas Alexander, George P. Gabriel, Nicholas Alexander. An important sign of AHEPA's resurgence came with the establishment of chapters in Greece and Cyprus. At the New Orleans Supreme Convention, Hellas District 25 received official approval and recognition. In October the First District Convention was held in Athens where delegates from both AHEPA and the Daughters of Penelope gathered to lay the foundations and begin working to build the District in Hellas and Cyprus. There were three AHEPA chapters, Athens HJ-1, Glyfada HJ-2, and Alexander the Great Thessaloniki HJ-3. The Daughters of Penelope chapters included Karyatides 271 Athens, Hesperus 359 Athens, Olympiades 393 Thessaloniki, Vergina 383 Veria, and Alasia 404 Cyprus. The total membership of the district was 600. In May 2001 when Supreme President Johnny Economy installed an AHEPA chapter in Cyprus, he delivered an impassioned speech describing the significance of the creation of a chapter on Cyprus given the island's history, and AHEPA's involvement in trying to find a solution to the issues the island was dealing with. The event took place during the annual excursion to Greece, Cyprus, and the Ecumenical Patriarchate in Istanbul. A smaller AHEPA delegation also made a visit to Ankara to meet members of Turkey's Ministry of Foreign Affairs.

The George C. Marshall Statue in Athens
In 1947 George C. Marshall, who had served as general of the Army and US Army chief of staff during World War II and then became US Secretary of State, proposed a wide ranged funding to help European postwar reconstruction, benefitting several countries including Greece. It was officially named the European Recovery Program, but it became known as the Marshall Plan. Marshall received the Nobel Prize for Peace in 1953. As part of its role as a bridge between the two countries, AHEPA and its affiliates raised $125,000 to erect his statue in Athens. The unveiling took place in October of 2000, in the courtyard of the American Embassy in Athens. At the unveiling, Archbishop Christodoulos, Minister of Culture Mr. E. Pangalos, Mayor Dimitris Avramopoulos of Athens, and Ambassador of the US Embassy Mr. Nicholas Burns, Supreme President Johnny Economy,

and many dignitaries from Greece and abroad were all present. In his address, the Supreme President said: "I find it interesting that we are honoring a warrior who could have taken the route of 'to the victor goes the spoils' but who instead embraced the Hellenic principles of philanthropy and philoxenia to help the world recover from the terrible years of war. In dedicating the statue tonight, we should pause and understand that our commitment to the things George Marshall has done should not end here. Perhaps we should recommit ourselves to those Hellenic principles of philanthropy and philoxenia in our everyday lives." The Ahepans who were members of the AHEPA Centennial Foundation who worked on the Marshall Statue project consisted of Supreme President Johnny Economy, Executive Director Tim Maniatis, Supreme Counselor Bill Marianes, Past Supreme President Steve Manta, Past Supreme Governor Tommy Rakus, Past National Education Foundation Chair Dr. Pandeli Durbetaki, Louie Zakas, and Dr Victor Polizos.

The 2001 Excursion to Greece, Cyprus, and the Ecumenical Patriarchate

The 2001 version of AHEPA's annual excursion to the Eastern Mediterranean began with a meeting with Ecumenical Patriarch Bartholomew, and was followed by a meeting in Athens with Greek Foreign Minister George Papandreou, Archbishop Christodoulos, and Ms. Gianna Angelopoulos, the head of the Greek Olympic Organizing Committee, to discuss the Athens 2004 Olympics. Several delegates visited Thessaloniki, and a small delegation traveled to Ankara to meet with Turkish foreign ministry officials, a visit designed to improve the understanding of all parties involved in the disputes in the Eastern Mediterranean. During the visit to Cyprus, a small number crossed over into the Turkish-occupied territory to visit the Apostolos Andreas Greek Orthodox monastery and to convey a message of hope and solidarity to the few Greek Cypriots that still lived in a UN-supervised enclave in that part of the island. Among the visiting Ahepans was Past Supreme Counselor Gus James, who was born in one of those Greek Cypriot villages.

The 79th Supreme Convention, 2001, Puerto Rico

The Supreme Convention of 2001, the 79th in AHEPA's history, took place between July 24–29 at a resort hotel in Puerto Rico, a venue that attracted many younger than usual delegates. This received favorable reactions from the Greek American media, who saw this as a way in which the younger generations could be drawn into the life of Greek American associations.[140] High on the convention's agenda were debates on an amended constitution and new by-laws. The delegates elected Andrew T. Banis as Supreme President. Banis was born in Sioux City, Iowa in 1932, the son of Tom and Olga Lazana Banis, who were immigrants from Greece. After four years of active duty in the US Coast Guard he was honorably discharged and returned to California where his family had moved, completing his college degree in accounting and business. He went on to become founder and president of Banis Restaurant Design, Inc. The officials who were elected were Dr. James Dimitriou, Supreme Vice President; Xenophon Scoufaras, Canadian President; Nicholas Alexander, Supreme Secretary; Christopher Peppas, Supreme Treasurer; Nicholas Karacostas, Supreme Counselor. The Supreme Governors who were elected were Nicholas J. Ballas, Constantine Calliontzis, Gus Cusulos, Domino Giallourakis, James Gounaris, Stan Lefes, Basil N. Mossaidis, and Tom Owens. Monthe Kofos was reelected Supreme Athletic Director, and Steve Kafkis Sons National Advisor. A. Steve Betzelos remained chairman of the Supreme Board of Directors and Franklin Manios the vice chairman.

The Events of 9/11

On September 11, 2001, terrorists hijacked four airplanes and carried out suicide attacks against targets in the United States. Two of the planes were flown into the Twin Towers of the World Trade Center in New York City, a third plane hit the Pentagon in Arlington, Virginia, just outside Washington, DC, and the fourth plane crashed in a field in Shanksville, Pennsylvania. Almost 3,000 people were killed during the 9/11 terrorist attacks, which triggered major US initiatives to combat terrorism and defined the presidency of George W. Bush. Among the victims were 38 Greek Americans. Two of the victims were crew members of the planes and the remaining were in the World Trade Center's Twin Towers which collapsed. Another victim of the attack in New York was the small Greek Orthodox Church of St. Nicholas which was at the foot of the towers, and which was destroyed completely. The Greek Orthodox Archdiocese, supported by AHEPA and other Greek American organizations and individuals, launched a campaign to reconstruct the church as a national shrine that would honor the victims of that terrible day.

In the immediate aftermath of the attack, Supreme President Andrew Banis addressed the following letter to President George Bush that expressed the sentiments of AHEPA and all Greek Americans: "Dear Mr. President, on behalf of the American Hellenic Educational Progressive Association (AHEPA), and the Greek-American community, I humbly extend our deepest condolences to the families of the innocent victims of the horrific and tragic events that befell our great nation on September 11, 2001. Our international headquarters, located in Washington, has been overwhelmed by statements of support from members of our organization and our community. I write to you today to offer the unwavering support of Americans of Greek descent and all philhellenes in your pursuit to find, capture, and bring to justice the perpetrators of these heinous and barbaric acts against humanity. The principles of democracy and freedom gifted to Western Civilization by our ancient Greek ancestors over 2,000 years ago will not be vanquished from this earth by the evil hand of terrorism. As Greek Americans, we condemn these despicable crimes against humanity whether they occur on American or foreign soil. As you are aware, Greece has been allied with the United States in every major conflict of the 20th century. As Greek Americans, we expect the government of the Hellenic Republic, as a member of NATO and the European Union, to wholeheartedly support and cooperate with the United States government in its effort to combat and eliminate terrorism in this the first 'war of the 21st century' as you described. This will have far reaching effects, including heightened security measures to deter similar deplorable acts when Greece will proudly host another one of its great contributions to Western Civilization—the 2004 Olympic Games. Over its 80-year history, AHEPA has answered the United States' call to civic responsibility, philanthropy, and patriotism at times of need. As the largest Greek-American organization of its kind, AHEPA led the way in US War Bond sales during World War II, selling $162 million.

This accomplishment earned AHEPA the honor of being named an official Issuing Agent for US War Bonds by the US Department of Treasury. In 1943, US Secretary of the Treasury Henry Morgenthau, Jr. said of AHEPA's war bond effort, 'May I extend to you... sincere congratulations... Your chapters and members ought to be proud of having oversubscribed your $50 million goal... Your government appreciates your patriotic services and your contribution to the war effort...' Mr. President, AHEPA stands ready to serve our country once again should the United States call upon us to aid with war or unity bond sales. The Greek American community awaits your call and will respond accordingly. Already, our AHEPA family chapters have mobilized, setting a goal to raise funds for disaster relief. As we did during our War Bond Drive, I am confident we will shatter this goal. We have started our outreach within the Greek-American community to help the healing process among our families affected by this tragedy. AHEPA looks to assist St. Nicholas Greek Orthodox Church, a little church established in 1916 that before September 11 stood amid the skyscrapers of the city before it was destroyed by the collapse of the World Trade Center buildings. Mr. President, AHEPA's patriotic and civic deeds are many, including the donation of a statue of the late Secretary of State and author of the Marshall Plan, George C. Marshall, in the chancery of the US Embassy in Athens in October 2000. A great philhellene, Secretary Marshall fought tyranny and evil as a general and as a statesman. Moreover, AHEPA raised over $400,000 toward the restoration of the Statue of Liberty and Ellis Island, both of which are constant reminders of our immigrant forefathers who courageously came to our country with a vision to seek a better life, relish in democracy and escape the evil of tyranny. Obviously, terrorists do not have the same vision. AHEPA is strongly committed to protect our American way of life that is rooted in a foundation that strikes at the heart of Hellenism—the basis for man's humanity to his fellow man—and democracy."[141]

AHEPA's Solidarity with New York City
In response to the terrorist attacks of 9/11 and as a sign of solidarity with New York City, AHEPA held its 80th Supreme Convention in New York City in July 2002, changing the original plan that was to hold the convention in Greece. It took place between July 16–21 in Manhattan.

An audience of 1,000 people attended the convention's grand banquet, and the highlight of the evening was a presentation of $50,000 made on behalf of the AHEPA family and the entire Hellenic community to New York City Mayor Michael R. Bloomberg. The donation was made to the September 11th Anniversary Fund, an entity created to help the families of the victims partake in the upcoming one-year anniversary of the events. Mayor Bloomberg thanked the AHEPA family on behalf of the city of New York and added that the AHEPA family did three important things by coming to New York for its annual meeting. "You are reaffirming the deep historical connection between this city and people of Greek origin; you are helping to revitalize New York's economy; and you are demonstrating unwavering commitment to democracy and freedom," the mayor said.

The US Ambassador to Greece Thomas Miller was the Keynote Speaker for the event and applauded AHEPA for moving its convention to New York City. In his first formal address at an AHEPA Supreme Convention, the ambassador provided a thorough and informative update on present events in Greece since he assumed his post 10 months ago. Miller described cooperation with Greece on the issue of global terrorism as "excellent" and called Greece's recent breakthroughs against the domestic terrorism group known as 17 November a "triumph."

In his response, outgoing Supreme President Banis stated that the Grand Banquet was not only the culmination of a successful Supreme Convention, but that it was also the climax of 80 years of demonstrated excellence to the communities AHEPA serves. He underscored the Association's commitment to Hellenism, assuring his audience that AHEPA had and would continue to remain vigilant through its excellent relations with elected government officials and the diplomatic corps, and also by keeping its pulse on the Greek American community through its vast grassroots network. Thea Halo, author of the critically acclaimed memoir Not Even My Name, received the 2002 AHEPA Homer Award, and her mother, Sano Themia Halo, was awarded the AHEPA Medal of Freedom; President of the AHEPA National Housing Corporation Nick Stratas announced over $100,000 in donations emanating from its management company; and AHEPA Past Supreme President Gus Cherevas was presented with the AHEPA Distinguished Service Award. At the conclusion of the convention, the delegates elected Dr. James F. Dimitriou, of Palos Verdes Estates, California, Supreme President for the 2002–2003 year. "AHEPA means to us the greatness of Hellenism and the greatness of the American Dream," Dr. Dimitriou said following his installation ceremony. Fittingly it was in New York where his grandfather arrived at Ellis Island 98 years earlier. The newly elected supreme president, a 32-year member of AHEPA, had served two terms as Supreme Vice President. He ran on a platform titled "Greek Fire: A 10 Point Strategic Plan for the Order of AHEPA 'Preserving the Spirit of Hellenism Within the Context of the American Dream.'" It was a vision that spanned the next five years. James Dimitriou had earned a Doctorate in International Studies, and two master's degrees, all from the University of Southern California, and at the time of his election was working to reestablish the study of Greece and Western civilization throughout the curriculum of public schools. Among the many positions he held in several Greek American organizations was long time president of the Marmarinon Benevolent Society, whose members were descendants of Greek inhabitants of the island of Marmara in present-day Turkey.

On AHEPA's 80th anniversary, Dimitriou stated: "On July 26, 1922, the American Hellenic Educational Progressive Association was born in Atlanta, Georgia. It was formed by eight visionary Greek Americans with a common vision and purpose: to establish an association of mainly, but not exclusively, American citizens of Greek descent that would promote education, high levels of citizenship, fraternal sociability, and to practice philanthropy. Today, it is my honor and privilege to serve as Supreme President at such a notable time in the history of our unique and special association. Although our mission has adapted to meet the ever-changing challenges of our dynamic world, AHEPA remains steadfast, strong and committed to the American Dream, to future generations of young Hellenes, and to Hellenism as we head into the 21st Century. Finally, on this momentous occasion, I salute and commend our dedicated volunteer members and resilient chapters, without whom our many accomplishments on behalf of the Hellenic communities to society could not have been possible." The other officials elected at the Supreme Convention in

New York were Jack Georgalas, Vice President; Lazarus Kalipolidis, a financial advisor from Laval, Quebec, as Canadian President; Nick Alexander, of Columbus, Ohio, was reelected Supreme Secretary; George Demopoulos, Supreme Treasurer; Nicholas A. Karacostas was reelected Supreme Counselor; and Monthe Kofos was reelected Supreme Athletic Director. The eight Supreme Governors elected were: Nickolas Ballas, Domino Giallourakis, Tom Owens, Stan Lefes, Lyle Hochberger, Kostas G. Hazifotis, George Kalyvas, and Tom Pappas. Past Supreme President Lee Rallis was elected vice chairman of the Board, and Gud James was elected Secretary. In 2002 Basil Mossaidis was appointed Executive Director of AHEPA and remains in that position to this day. He was born to Pontian Greek parents who immigrated to the United States in the 1950s and settled in the expanding Greektown of Upper Darby, Pennsylvania. He received a bachelor's degree from Eastern University in Pennsylvania and his master's degree in international relations from Webster University, in St. Louis, Missouri. Mossaidis had served as Supreme President of the Sons of Pericles in 1989–1990, when the Sons' membership was at its greatest with 2,863 members.

Canada Issues AHEPA Postage Stamp
In 2003 the Canadian postal service, Canada Post, issued a commemorative stamp recognizing the 75th anniversary of the establishment of AHEPA in Canada. Prime Minister of Canada Jean Chrétien was present at the unveiling. According to Canada Post the stamp was issue to commemorate the help given from AHEPA to Greek families in their struggle to adapt to life in North America while also encouraging loyalty and patriotism to their new home. The design featured a figure releasing a bird in an artwork style that is similar to that seen on ancient Greek pottery. The bird, a metaphor of the journey many Greeks and other immigrants took to reach Canada, carries a 'maple leaf and an olive branch in its beak as a symbol of the intertwining of the two cultures and societies. The persons whose persistence and work led to the stamp becoming a reality were Canadian Ahepans Fotis Antoniou and Xenophon Scoufaras and Greek Canadian Eleni Bakopanos, a Member of the Canadian Parliament.

The Run Up to the Athens Olympics of 2004

In 2003, AHEPA held its 81st Supreme Convention for the first time in the city of Phoenix, Arizona from July 27 to August 1. Supreme President Dimitriou stated that the convention was a five-day event designed to offer attendees the opportunity to embrace their heritage through educational symposia and social events, featuring live Greek music and dancing. Dimitriou said AHEPA wished to contribute a sampling of Greek heritage to a city already rich with culture and ethnic diversity. At the Grand Banquet, at which documentary film producer George Veras acted as master of ceremonies, Phoenix resident George P. Kokalis was honored with the AHEPA Archbishop Iakovos Humanitarian Award for his decades of philanthropic service to the community. Additional honorees included: The Order of St. Andrew of the Ecumenical Patriarchate, a body of laymen who promote the mission of the Mother Church and the Holy Patriarchate of Constantinople, represented by its National Commander, Dr. Anthony J. Limberakis (Medal of Freedom); Erato Kozakou-Marcoullis, Ambassador of the Republic of Cyprus to the United States (Aristotle Award); Dr. Maria Pantelia, Professor of Classics and Thesaurus Linguae Graecae Project Director, University of California, Irvine (Academy of Achievement Award). Monthe Kofos received the Lifetime Achievement Award. There was, as usual, a distinguished list of guests and speakers. It included Archbishop Demetrios of America; Ambassador Kozakou-Marcoullis; Dimitrios S. Zevelakis, Consul General of Greece; and Elaine Rogers, USO Metropolitan Washington President, who received a $10,000 donation for the "Operation USO Care Package" program.

At the conclusion of the convention in Phoenix the delegates elected Anastasius Jack Georgalas, of Seaford, Virginia, and of Cypriot descent, Supreme President for the 2003–2004 year. Georgalas, who defeated incumbent Supreme President Dr. James F. Dimitriou, spoke about aspiring to explore avenues that would lead to the organization's continued growth. The Supreme President emphasized that a "team plan" with precise execution would take AHEPA to new heights in vital areas such as membership development and long-term financial growth. At the time of his election the Supreme President was the

CEO of Tri-Cities Beverage Corp., was a Commissioned Officer of the US Marines Corps, and like almost all AHEPA Supreme Presidents also active in his local Greek Orthodox church. Georgalas had graduated from the University of Virginia with a bachelor's degree in commerce in 1952. The other officers elected were Canadian President Lazarus Kalipolidis, Supreme Vice President Franklin Manios, Supreme Secretary Chris Economides, Jr., Supreme Treasurer Tom Owens, Supreme Counselor Dean Selimos, and Supreme Athletic Director Dr. Monthe N. Kofos. The eight Supreme Governors were: Tassos Chronis, Anthony Drakos, Nick Matthews, Cosmos Marandos, Chris Peppas, George Scarveles, George Sinadinos, and Steve G Trent (Triantafel). Nicholas Karacostas, Alex Katsafanas, and E. P. Terry Mitchell were elected to three-year terms on the Board of Directors. Lee G. Rallis was reelected chairman of the Board. Gus J. James and Manuel Scarmoutsos were elected vice chairman and secretary of the Board, respectively.[142]

In December 2003, AHEPA donated $36,000 to St. Basil's Academy, Garrison, New York, a sign of its continued commitment to the Greek Orthodox Archdiocese's institution for young children. Over $1.8 million was donated to St. Basil's Academy during the 20th century for the construction of dormitories and a school building. This contribution would provide new windows for the boys' dormitory.

In February 2004 AHEPA held its 36th Biennial National Banquet in Washington, DC. The theme was "Honoring the Olympic Spirit" to recognize the return of the Olympic Games to Greece, their country of origin. World Decathlon Champion Tom Pappas, NASA astrophysicist Epaminondas Stassinopoulos, United States Agency for International Development Administrator Andrew Natsios, and Olympians of Greek heritage from different generations were honored at the Banquet. Peter Clentzos, the world's oldest living Olympian (Pole Vault), the brothers Petros and Nikos Spanakos (Boxing), Alex Ghanotakis (Discus), John and Andrew Kambanis (Bobsled), John Livaditis (Bobsled), Irene Aidinli (Gymnastics), and Michael Voudouris (Skeleton Slider) were also honored with the AHEPA Olympic Award. Senator Paul Sarbanes addressed the enormous challenges facing Greece on the eve of the 2004 Olympic Games. The Senator said he was confident that Greece would do the job and said he looked forward to Greece staging a wonderful Olympics. Alexander Kitroeff, professor of History at Haverford College and author of the newly released book Wrestling with the Ancients: Modern Greek Identity and the Olympics, was the Banquet's keynote speaker and stated: "The Greek Diaspora has played a crucial role in Greece's efforts to support the revival of the ancient games, not only off the athletic field but also on it." His Eminence Archbishop Demetrios of America told the audience: "We see the Olympics as an opportunity for projecting this highest possible human value. By dedicating this evening to the spirit of the Olympics, you honor the spirit of human excellence and the spirit of a constant unyielding pursuit of peace, here and everywhere." In his concluding remarks, AHEPA Supreme President Georgalas said that the evening's program, through its honorees, brought the invaluable contributions of the ancient Greeks to the forefront, adding: "We have, among us tonight, outstanding examples of Hellenes who represent the very best of what our ancestors contributed to Western Civilization."[143]

The 82nd Supreme Convention, 2004, Miami Beach

The 2004 Convention, the 82nd in AHEPA's history, was held in Miami Beach. Much of the proceedings were taken up by discussions about the upcoming Olympic Games in Athens which would open on August 13. The delegates elected Franklin R. Manios, of Warren, Ohio, a 48-year member of AHEPA, as Supreme President for the 2004–2005 year. In line with other presidential acceptance speeches, Manios expressed humility and pride for the opportunity to serve the Greek American community and to promote Hellenism. He said he viewed the glass three-quarters full for AHEPA and all had to strive to fill it and take AHEPA to new levels. The Supreme President emphasized that he would continue the ambitious and proactive membership development program, which was starting to yield positive results. Manios had graduated from the University of Pittsburgh School of Pharmacy in 1957. He enlisted and served in the US Marines Corps from 1953 to 1955. He was founder of Franklin Pharmacy, and in 1979, he expanded it to Franklin Pharmacy and Health Care, an innovative concept for its time. The other elected officials were Canadian President Nicholas Spillios a media executive from Edmonton; Supreme Vice President Gus J. James II; Supreme Secretary Ike Gulas; Supreme Treasurer Ptolemeos Kotzambasis; Supreme Counselor Dean Selimos; and Supreme Athletic Director Dr. Monthe N. Kofos. James and Gulas served the previous year on the Board of Directors. The eight Supreme Governors elected were: Demetrius Alexander, Nick Dixie, Anthony Drakos, John Grossomanides, Cosmos Marandos, Harry Psaltis, Chris Rockas, and George Sinadinos. Drakos, Marandos, and Sinadinos were reelected. Vasilios "Likie" Beleos, George Demopoulos, and Lee Millas were elected to three-year terms on the Board of Directors. Lee Rallis was reelected chairman of the Board. Manuel Scarmoutsos and Demopoulos were elected vice chairman and secretary of the Board, respectively.

Tensions over the Macedonian Question

The Macedonian question, the name of Greece's neighboring country, flared up again unexpectedly in November 2004, nine years after it had entered the United Nations under the provisional name "Former Yugoslav Republic of Macedonia" and was known by the acronym FYROM. Greece objected to its northern neighbor's use of the name "Macedonia" on its own, believing that it would usurp Greece's heritage as well as imply territorial ambitions at Greece's expense. On November 4, 2004, a few days before the scheduled referendum in Macedonia on decentralization which if approved would benefit ethnic minorities, the US State Department announced that the United States had decided to refer to Macedonia officially as the Republic of Macedonia. The State Department spokesman said the decision underscored the "US commitment to a permanent, multi-ethnic, democratic Macedonian state within its existing borders" and US support for the Macedonian government's "courageous decision to carry through with decentralization." He emphasized that the recognition decision was taken without prejudice to the UN negotiation process and was not directed against any other country, in other words Greece. However, the decision sparked bitter protestations from the government in Athens and Greek diaspora organizations. Greek Americans were especially surprised because the move came only two days after the US general election at which George W. Bush was reelected by defeating Democratic candidate John Kerry. Prior to the election the Bush administration had given no indication of its plan to abandon the term FYROM.

AHEPA naturally joined the protests. Supreme President Manios issued a statement criticizing the unilateral nature of the US action and said AHEPA would make formal inquiry with the State Department: "We are deeply disturbed to learn of these reports, and we are greatly concerned. Our position is that a final settlement of the name recognition issue must not contain the word, Macedonia, or any form of Macedonia, because it infringes on Greek history and heritage. Relations between Greece and FYROM have steadily improved in recent years with Greece becoming FYROM's largest foreign investor. Our concerns are that such a unilateral decision by the United States may create unnecessary tension in the region and will stymie progress made on the name recognition issue between the two neighbors. A formal inquiry will be made to the US Department of State."

The 83rd Supreme Convention, 2005, Boston
AHEPA's activities in 2005 began as always with the blessing of the waters ceremony in Tarpon Springs on Greek Orthodox Epiphany, January 6. At the formal banquet on the eve of the ceremony, Supreme President Manios, Supreme Board Chairman Rallis, Congressman Michael Bilirakis, and Archbishop Demetrios, jointly awarded Vice Admiral Michael Kalleres the third annual AHEPA National Medal of Freedom at Saint Nicholas Greek Orthodox Cathedral in Tarpon Springs. Vice Admiral Kalleres, the son of Greek immigrants, who grew up in Indiana, was a member of AHEPA, and was at the time the senior Greek American military officer. Manios cited Kalleres' outstanding leadership as Commander of the US Navy Second Fleet and of the more than 300,000 Atlantic US Navy Seaborne forces during Desert Storm, for which he was awarded a Defense

Distinguished Service Medal (second only to the Medal of Honor) and a US Navy Distinguished Service Medal. Also commended were Admiral Kalleres' humanitarian activities in Bosnia, Somali, and Haiti, for which he was awarded an almost unprecedented second Defense Distinguished Service Medal. President Manios also noted that Admiral Kalleres had served for the past three years, with great success, as the National Advisor for emergency disaster services for the Salvation Army.

In 2005 AHEPA held its 83rd Supreme Convention in Boston. The delegates unanimously elected Gus J. James II, of Virginia Beach, Virginia, Supreme President for the 2005–2006 administrative year. James' roots were in the northern occupied Cypriot village of Koma Tou Yialou where his father and grandparents are buried. He left Cyprus at the age of seven with his two sisters. At the time of his election James was CEO and President of the Norfolk, Virginia law firm Kaufman & Canoles. The new Supreme President thanked outgoing Supreme President Franklin Manios for providing a fine example for him to emulate, adding: "To be elected Supreme President is an honor that I can't express in words, my commitment to you, the member, is to do the best I can to work with the affiliated organizations within AHEPA for the betterment and growth of our Order." James announced an ambitious fundraising campaign called "Voice of Hellenism." The goal was to help AHEPA reemerge as a leading proponent of Hellenism in the country and worldwide. Also announced by James were campaigns that will focus on outreach to AHEPA's districts and chapters that would drive membership. It included four regional conferences during the fall of 2005. The other newly elected members of the Supreme Lodge included: Supreme Vice President Ike Gulas; Canadian President Nicholas Spillios; Supreme Secretary Gus Stefanadis; Supreme Treasurer Cosmos; and Supreme Counselor Arthur Dimopoulos. Dr. Monthe N. Kofos was reelected Supreme Athletic Director. Elected as the eight Supreme Governors were Anthony Capranica; Gust Christofides; John Grossomanides; Kostas G. Hazifotis; Anthony Kouzounis; James D. Selimos; Spiros Vasilakis; and Paul Angelson. Elected to three-year terms on the Board of Trustees were Tom Owens; James Scofield; and Steve Tripodes. Lee Millas was elected chairman of the Board, E. P. Terry Mitchell was elected vice chairman, and Owens was elected secretary. Newly elected to the Board of Auditors were Vasilios Albanos and Louis P. Peronis. Also announced at the concluding Installation Ceremony by outgoing Supreme President Manios was the selection of Nick T. Georges as the National Ahepan of the Year and Dr. Nicholas Matsakis as the AHEPA Medal of Freedom recipient. Georges was a 57-year member of AHEPA who had been instrumental in the revitalization of AHEPA in the Detroit area. Dr. Matsakis was well-known for his decades of advocacy for the Cyprus issue and for the preservation of Hellenism in the United States.[144]

Honoring Senator Paul Sarbanes and Congressman Michael Bilirakis
AHEPA has always maintained close ties with all Greek Americans elected to the United States Senate and Congress, as well as all other senators and congressmen who have supported issues for which AHEPA has mobilized. Many of them have become members of the Order, mostly in an honorific sense due to their busy schedules. Two such leaders who forged a special relationship with AHEPA were stepping down after decades of service to the nation and the Greek American community, Democratic Senator Paul Sarbanes of Maryland and Republican Congressman Michael Bilirakis of Florida. AHEPA held a special event in March 2006 to honor them. Each of those legislators was introduced by their sons who were continuing in their footsteps, and who were elected to the US House of Representatives that same year: John Sarbanes and Gus Bilirakis. The event was chaired by AHEPA leader Nicholas Karacostas, the master of ceremonies was George Stephanopoulos, the ABC network's chief Washington correspondent, and present were the Ambassadors of Greece and Cyprus Alexandros Mallias and Evripidis Evriviades and many Greek and Cypriot American leaders.

In June, a few weeks before the opening of the 2006 convention, AHEPA celebrated the opening of Odyssey, Delaware's first Greek language and mathematics immersion charter school, on Monday,

June 12, 2006. Supreme President James, members of AHEPA Wilmington Chapter 95, and state and local government officials marked this historic occasion with a ribbon-cutting ceremony and speeches at the school. James stated that education was a key element of AHEPA's mission and it was proud and excited that such a monumental task has come to fruition and that the chapter in Wilmington was a catalyst in making this happen. He encouraged our chapters to explore the prospects of establishing a charter school in their communities with the hopes that AHEPA could get more opened nationwide. The Odyssey Charter School was established to prepare Kindergarten through Grade 5 students for a lifelong enthusiasm for learning, a keen awareness of world citizenship, and an ability to think independently and creatively through participation in a focused foreign language immersion program. The curriculum integrated the learning of Greek as a second language, along with English, to teach a rigorous curriculum of reading, writing, math, science, and social studies.[145]

The 84th Supreme Convention, 2006, Hollywood, Florida

The 84th Supreme Convention was held in Hollywood, Florida. A local newspaper provided an interesting image of the way outsiders viewed AHEPA at the time. It mentioned AHEPA's origins in combatting anti-Greek sentiment and went on to note: "As generations of Greek-Americans forged on AHEPA's focus changed. Today about three in four Greek Americans are born here and AHEPA serves primarily as a social and business network. That includes building 74 senior home projects nationwide and raising more than $220,000 for victims of an earthquake in Greece. It also raised more than $150,000 for a relief fund after September 11th."[146]

The highlight of the convention's Grand Banquet was the award of the AHEPA Medal of Freedom to Vice Admiral James G. Stavridis, Senior Military Assistant to the Secretary of Defense. At the time, Stavridis was awaiting confirmation of his promotion to the rank of Admiral from the Senate, which happened soon afterward and led to him being appointed to the Southern command and taking charge of the Pentagon's operations in Latin America and the Caribbean. He would go on to be appointed as NATO's top commander. Stavridis was born in Florida in 1955. His paternal grandparents were immigrants from Greece. Stavridis recalled with feeling the fact that "the whole immigrant experience is very real to me, part of my life experience." Stavridis' grandfather immigrated to the United States in the 1920s, opening up a restaurant. His father George served as a colonel in the Marine Corps and was the US naval attaché in Athens where the family lived from 1962 to 1965. Stavridis always remained proud of his Greek heritage and made frequent references to ancient Greek bravery and military tactics in his presentations and writings.[147]

The delegates at the 86th Supreme Convention reelected Gus J. James II, of Virginia Beach, Virginia, Supreme President for the 2006–2007 year. James won a close race against Ike Gulas. "I am honored to be given the unique opportunity to serve as supreme president for a second consecutive term," said James. "I will continue to work hard promoting AHEPA and its mission domestically and abroad. This effort, I strongly believe, will help AHEPA grow." James was the first president elected to a second term since Spiro Macris who served from 1995 to 1997. The other elected officials were Canadian President Fotis Antoniou, a businessman from Dorval, Quebec; Supreme Vice President Gus Stefanadis; Supreme Secretary Nick Karacostas; Supreme Treasurer John Grossomanides; Supreme Counselor Chris Rockas; and Supreme Athletic Director Dr. Monthe N. Kofos. The eight Supreme Governors were: Mark Alevizos; Anthony Drakos; Anthony Kouzounis; Michael Manios; Harry Psaltis; James Selimos; Spiro Vasilakis; and Tom Cavalaris.

In early 2007, AHEPA announced a new educational program, the "AHEPAcademy," a leadership and professional development program that identifies, educates, inspires, mentors, advances, and networks exceptional Greek American high school students as they progress through their high school, college, graduate, and professional careers. It begins in the summer after a student's junior year of high school and continues throughout their senior year of high school, their application to and acceptance to college, their academic and pre-professional careers while in college, any postgraduate schooling, and eventually their entry into their professional careers.

Honoring AHEPA's 85th Anniversary on Capitol Hill
In 2007 AHEPA reached its 85th year of existence. In honor of that significant milestone Senator Olympia J. Snowe, R-Maine and Congresswoman Carolyn B. Maloney, D-New York introduced in their respective chambers identical resolutions "commemorating

the 85th Anniversary of the founding of the American Hellenic Educational Progressive Association (AHEPA), a leading association for the Nation's 1.3 million American citizens of Greek ancestry, and Philhellenes." The Senate resolution was co-sponsored by Sen. Robert Menendez, D-New Jersey. Its wording read:

"Whereas the American Hellenic Educational Progressive Association (AHEPA) was founded on July 26, 1922, in Atlanta, Georgia, by 8 visionary Greek immigrants to help unify, organize, and protect against the bigotry, discrimination, and defamation faced by people of all ethnic, racial, and religious backgrounds perpetrated predominantly by the Ku Klux Klan; Whereas the mission of AHEPA is to promote the ideals of ancient Greece, which include philanthropy, education, civic responsibility, and family and individual excellence through community service and volunteerism; Whereas, since its inception, AHEPA has instilled in its members an understanding of their Hellenic heritage and an awareness of the contributions made by Greece to the development of democratic principles and governance in the United States and throughout the world; Whereas AHEPA has done much throughout its history to foster patriotism in the United States; Whereas members of AHEPA have served in the Armed Forces to protect the freedom of the United States and to preserve the democratic ideals that are part of the Hellenic legacy; Whereas, in World War II, members of AHEPA were parachuted behind enemy lines in Nazi-occupied Greece to help liberate the country; Whereas AHEPA raised more than $253,000,000 for United States war bonds during World War II, for which AHEPA was named an official Issuing Agent for United States War Bonds by the Department of Treasury, an honor that no other civic organization was able to achieve at the time; Whereas the members of AHEPA donated $612,000 for the restoration of the Statue of Liberty and Ellis Island, New York, for which AHEPA received special recognition by the Department of the Interior; Whereas the AHEPA National Housing Program was awarded $500,000,000 by the Department of Housing and Urban Development for its Section 202 Program, which has yielded 4,370 units in 80 properties across 21 States and 49 cities and has provided dignified, affordable housing to senior citizens; Whereas AHEPA was recognized by the Department of State as an organization that has engaged in 'Track Two Diplomacy' to foster reconciliation and rapprochement in the Eastern Mediterranean, which is in the best interest of the United States; Whereas members of AHEPA raised $110,000 for the George C. Marshall Statue to be erected on the grounds of the United States Embassy in Athens, Greece, in celebration of the historic relationship between the United States and Greece, and in tribute to an outstanding statesman and Philhellene, General Marshall; Whereas AHEPA financially supports scholarships, educational chairs, medical research, and countless other charitable and philanthropic causes by contributing more than $2,000,000 annually from its national, district, and local levels collectively; Whereas, in the spirit of their Hellenic heritage and in commemoration of the Centennial Olympic Games held in Atlanta, Georgia, members of AHEPA raised $775,000 for the Tribute to Olympism Sculpture, the fan-like structure of which helped to save lives during the bombing at Centennial Olympic Park; Whereas members of AHEPA have been Presidents and Vice Presidents of the United States, United States Senators and Representatives, and United States Ambassadors, and have served honorably as elected officials at the local and State levels throughout the United States; and Whereas President George H. W. Bush cited AHEPA as one of the 'thousand points of light': Now, therefore, be it Resolved by the Senate (the House of Representatives concurring), That the Congress—(1) recognizes the significant contributions of United States citizens of Hellenic heritage to the United States; (2) commemorates the 85th anniversary of the founding of the American Hellenic Educational Progressive Association (AHEPA), applauds its mission, and commends the many charitable contributions of its members to communities around the world; and (3) encourages the people of the United States to observe the 85th anniversary of the founding of AHEPA and celebrate its many accomplishments."

Congressman Gus Bilirakis issued his own statement on the 85th anniversary noting he was proud to call himself an Ahepan, a devoted member of the Tarpon Springs, George Washington Chapter 16, and went on to say it was AHEPA that had helped to assimilate and educate Greek immigrants, like his grandparents, as they arrived in America. He wished AHEPA continued success and at least another 85 years of fruitful educational, philanthropic, and civic endeavors. Bilirakis addressed the US House of Representatives on April 16, 2007, during consideration of H. Con. Res. 71, legislation commemorating the 85th anniversary of the founding of the American Hellenic Educational Progressive Association. He outlined the long list of accomplishments AHEPA had achieved since its inception and highlighted AHEPA's patriotic endeavors such as raising more than $253 million in US War Bonds during World War II, helping restore the Statue of Liberty, and providing thousands of dollars during the 9/11 relief effort. Bilirakis, who replaced his father Michael as the US Congressman for Florida's 9th District (later he represented the 12th District) would remain closely involved in AHEPA's activities and continues to do so as a congressman to this day.

The 85th Supreme Convention, 2007, Denver

The 85th Supreme Convention meant the completion of Supreme President James' two-year tenure at AHEPA's helm. In reflecting on his two years of service as Supreme President in an interview, James noted: "I tried to cover all bases by visiting with government, business and media leaders, and by traveling across the country to meet with our members in various chapters at the local level. AHEPA has always done that, but it hadn't taken that extra leap to become the beacon once again for Hellenic issues, as it had been in previous years. So we focused much of our energy in visiting with leaders of the Greek Government—to reconnect with Greece a little bit, and to remind them that AHEPA is still here, and that Greece can count on us to take the lead on Hellenic issues here in the United States." In 2006, James pointed out, AHEPA honored Prime Minister Costas Karamanlis and Hellenic Republic President Karolos Papoulias during a special banquet in Greece, "and we also held a very successful biennial banquet, during which we honored Senator Paul Sarbanes of Maryland and Congressman Mike Bilirakis of Florida for their many years of distinguished service just a few months before they retired. All these things were intended to enhance our relationships—which is really what AHEPA is all about—propel our mission forward and elevate our image at the international level. So they were a step beyond our normal domestic activities." He went on to say his second year as Supreme President was "an opportunity to utilize that momentum in ways which could further benefit not only the organization, but also the community and Greece."

"Year two was a chance to step back and reflect on how we could translate our renewed image into action, so we focused on Greece's entry into the US Visa Waiver Program. Right now, Greece is the only one of the Schengen countries that's not allowed to participate in the VWP [the 1985 Schengen Agreement is an agreement among European states includes provisions for common policy on the temporary, trans-border entry of persons and the harmonization of external border controls]. So, we made our rounds on Capitol Hill and spoke to a number of members of Congress, both in the Senate and in the House of Representatives, as well as to members of the Administration in Homeland Security and the State Department, to plug for Greece's inclusion into this program," James said. "Ultimately, we tried to help them understand that this isn't just to Greece's benefit, but also to the benefit of the United States because it forges stronger bonds between America and its allies, and Greece is an important US ally." James also discussed AHEPA's annual visits to Greece, Cyprus, and the Ecumenical Patriarchate in Constantinople, noting that the State Department asked AHEPA to defer its visit to Ankara that year because of pre-election turmoil in Turkey. "That was unfortunate, but we remain concerned about the Patriarchate and the reopening of the Halki seminary, and so should the US, because fundamental issues of educational and religious freedom are at stake. We fully support efforts for the Turkish Government to officially recognize the Patriarchate's ecumenical status, and to ease pressure on Christian minorities in their country."[148]

At the convention in Denver, Ike Gulas of Birmingham, Alabama was elected Supreme President for the 2007–2008 year, outvoting his rival, Lee Millas. "I am honored to be given the unique opportunity to serve as supreme president of the largest association of Americans who share a common bond of ancestry," said Gulas. "As we are in the midst of our 85th year, I intend to help AHEPA grow in terms of membership and international influence as we approach our centennial anniversary." Gulas said he was particularly proud to have his father, who had been an AHEPA member for more than 60 years, participate in his installation by reading the president's charge. Gulas's family had been in the Birmingham area for more than 100 years and he was the founding partner of the law office

Gulas & Stuckey, P.C. of Birmingham. The other elected officers were: Canadian President Fotis Antoniou; Supreme Vice President Nick Karacostas; Supreme Secretary John Grossomanides; Supreme Treasurer Anthony Kouzounis; Supreme Counselor John Galanis; and Supreme Athletic Director Dr. Monthe N. Kofos. The eight Supreme Governors elected were: Charles Stamoulis; Colonel Nick Vamvakias; Lou Arvanitis; Connie Calliontzis; Phil Giavasis; George Pantazelos; John Georgifandis; and Nick Perderis.

During the convention in Denver, an interview by AHEPA Executive Director Basil Mossaidis to the National Herald newspaper conveyed a vivid picture of both the convention and where AHEPA stood at the time. About the convention, Mossaidis said: "Since we're not in a non-resort environment, I think we did excellent. The number of delegates is where it should be, and attendance is excellent. We have 276 delegates for the AHEPA and 215 for the Daughters of Penelope, so in total, we have close to 500 delegates... we're very happy, yes, very pleased, because a lot of people took time off their busy schedule to come to the convention this year. It shows commitment. We're pleased that there is continuing interest in promoting our ideals—Hellenism, education, family—the ideals AHEPA upholds... we had 1,500 people on welcoming night, which was a very pleasant surprise, because originally, I was expecting 750. The local community here in Denver was very supportive, and the grand banquet was a tremendous success. We have a large AHEPA chapter here in Denver. They have over 300 members," he added.

Responding to a question about AHEPA's mission, Mossaidis explained it had evolved over time: "The mission in 1926 was to protect Greeks who were immigrants. Our priests had beards and wore a kalimavchion, and they were persecuted by Ku Klux Klan and other racist organizations, so AHEPA was founded to bind Greeks in America together, and the concept was so good in Atlanta, where it began, that chapters began to spread all over the country... today's mission is an obligation to our forefathers to protect Hellenism in this country; to preserve the language and the culture, even if it is within our own community. It doesn't necessarily have to be throughout America, but in our community at least, we can find a place where we can still be good Greeks and good Americans at the same time." He added that preserving use of the Greek language was an integral part of that effort: "It's very important to continue speaking Greek, of course. America was created for Greeks, in my opinion. As a country, America was created specifically for the Greek mentality: hard work, strong work ethic, good ethics—all principles and the pillars of America—were started by us. The heroes of the American Revolution used the ancient Greeks as a foundation for what they were building not only in terms of architecture, legal structure and system of government—and all these things that we offered as a culture to the world—but I also believe our ethics are sewn into the very fabric of this country, and it's easier for us to be successful because of that, and I want to make sure that my son and his children benefit from the same things that I have." When the reporter, Theodoros Kalmoukos, posed the question "on a scale from 1 to 10, where does AHEPA rate today?" Mossaidis answered: "AHEPA is excellent in many ways, but still needs a lot of work in other areas, but overall, AHEPA gets a 7 out of a 10. We have many categories in which AHEPA gets a 10. AHEPA makes a conscious effort to educate members of Congress about Hellenic issues. We reach out as an organization, not a lobby group, to promote Greek American issues… AHEPA is not an agent of the Greek Government. We cooperate with the Greek Embassy; we are asked to assist on issues that they feel are important and necessary. If the Greek ambassador to the United States calls AHEPA and asks us to do X, for example, we try to do X and mobilize our chapters behind the effort if it's within the purview of our mission, and I think we're very good in doing that because our members really want to have some firm connection with Greece and its interests."

Asked what were some of AHEPA's most critical challenges over the next 5–10 years he answered: "In any membership organization, two things are very important: financial viability and the influx of new members to maintain that—like a tree needs water and sun to grow, an organization needs money and members to grow. These are areas that need to be worked on from the elected leadership of the organization. Membership is not something that you hire someone at the headquarters and tell him, 'Find me members.' It doesn't work that way. What attracts new members are the deeds you do, so people can say, 'I want to be a part of that, too.' AHEPA is in a unique position to create financial security through donations and gifts—other than, say, dues. I don't think we should tell our members we need more money. We should tell them, 'Let's work together on this program to see if we can create financial stability.' Although AHEPA is very stable, I think that, with additional funds, more good deeds can be done, and then it is a perpetual cycle: The more good things you do, the more members you get, and the more money you have… today we have 401 active chapters, and the Daughters of Penelope have 250. We also have Sons of Pericles and Maids of Athena chapters; Collectively, we have about 700 altogether, with a total membership of around 28,000. With 1.3 million Greek Americans, we have 28,000. We should have more, of course. My personal belief is, if you're a Greek American and you care about any Greek American issue, you should automatically be an Ahepan. We invite everybody."

As the interview wound down, asked what the initiation rite is, Mossaidis said: "It's nothing. It's just an allegiance to what AHEPA is about when it was founded, and what the objectives of the organizations are. It has nothing to do with any secretive mystery, or anything like that. There is a religious dimension to it. It does if you believe in God, but it doesn't have any type of Church affiliation. It's not an organ of the Church." And in response to a question about the organization's day-by-day operations, he explained: "We have an international office in Washington, which I'm the Director of, and we have a staff of six people who manage the day-to-day operation. We manage communications, the magazine, and the programs the Supreme Lodge and the Supreme President institute, which they have the mandate from the members to institute. The last two years, for example, our (now former) president, Gus James, traveled to Greece a few times for preparations for the convention in Greece next summer, so all that coordination stems from headquarters… AHEPA's operating budget is currently $1 million annually, and dues for membership is only $40 a year; it's more symbolic than anything else. It's immaterial if you pay a thousand dollars or ten dollars to be a member of something. What's important is that the people who pay dues feel a connection with the organization. I think it's an obligation of the organization to find revenue from other sources which will allow us to say, 'Are you a Hellene? Be a member of the AHEPA.'"[149]

At the convention's banquet, the honorees were Undersecretary of State John Negroponte and Greek Foreign Minister Dora Bakoyanni with AHEPA's Pericles Award for excellence in government service in absentia, as conflicting schedules did not permit either of them to attend the banquet in person. The Demosthenes Award for excellence in journalism went to the publisher of the Ethnikos Kyrix and National Herald newspapers, Antonis Diamataris. In his acceptance speech he said that AHEPA and the National Herald were the only Greek American organizations which had managed not only to survive, but also to thrive, on a national level for decades, and added that the Greek American community's future depended on two factors: getting closer to one another and getting closer to Greece and Cyprus. He concluded his speech by stating: "In 1922, AHEPA was formed for the purpose of 'Americanizing' its members. It certainly achieved this, but today, it is called upon to bring the Greek American community closer to Greece through more enhanced use of the Greek language and practice of the Greek Orthodox faith, and I am certain that AHEPA can achieve this goal." Several other speakers hailed AHEPA's work and contribution to the community, including Congressman Gus Bilirakis and the Ambassadors of Greece and Cyprus to the United States, Alexandros Mallias and Andreas Kakouris.

Soon after the end of the convention in Denver, AHEPA was back to work, sending the first installment of $250,000 worth of goods and an additional $250,000 in financial assistance to victims of Greece's wildfires which swept through Peloponnesos in August. The relief packages were to be picked up by AHEPA's chapters in Athens and sent to the victims in the stricken areas. And at the end of the year AHEPA announced the continuation of the Journey to Greece program it had launched in 2006 in tandem with the University of Indianapolis Athens campus.

The 38th Biennial Salute Banquet, 2008 Washington, DC

At its Biennial Salute Banquet in March 2008, AHEPA honored over 30 legislators from state and national government with the AHEPA Public Service Award. "Every day public servants sacrifice their time and energy to ensure our rights, issues and causes are represented across our nation," said AHEPA Supreme President Ike Gulas. "We are fortunate to be given an opportunity to say, 'thank you,' present them with a certificate of appreciation and offer AHEPA's grassroots network to help champion our respective issues of concern." That year, AHEPA awarded the Demosthenes Award to

George Bistis, Chief, Voice of America Greek Desk and the Aristotle Award to John Catsimatides, Chairman and CEO, Red Apple Group, Inc. After the presentations, they were afforded the opportunity to tell the attendees about their lives as Greek Americans and the Greek American influence in everyday American culture. Additional speakers included President Gulas; Daughters of Penelope Grand President Karen Stamatiades; Former Foreign Minister of Cyprus Erato Kozakou-Marcoullis; Ambassadors Andreas Kakouris of Cyprus and Alexandras Mallias of Greece; US Representative John Sarbanes (D-MD-3); His Eminence Archbishop Demetrios; and the emcee for the evening, US Representative Zachary Space (D-OH-18).

Supreme President Gulas addressed the attendees of the banquet on the issues AHEPA has been educating members of the 110th Congress about, such as the Visa Waiver Program, Cyprus unification and Turkish troop withdrawal, the Greek wildfires, FYROM, and the Ecumenical Patriarch and Patriarchate. Gulas challenged the attendees during the banquet: "We can do more," he said, an important and inspired statement addressing the standing room only crowd on AHEPA's achievements over the past 86 years and calling for the continued dedication to the association's goals. The following month, the President of Parliament of Greece, Dimitris Sioufas, and several members of parliament hosted a private meeting for Supreme President Ike Gulas on the sidelines of events surrounding the celebration of Greek Independence Day in New York City at the Mandarin Oriental Hotel. The parliament members represented a diversity of political parties in Greece. Gulas expressed appreciation for Mr. Sioufas' interest in AHEPA's programs, especially the upcoming convention in Athens. In New York, Gulas also attended the annual meeting of the Cyprus Federation of America and expressed AHEPA's unwavering support of its friends at the Cyprus Federation, adding that the Order would continue to work toward a just and viable solution to the Cyprus problem.

AHEPA's Supreme Convention in Athens

AHEPA held its 86th Supreme Convention in Athens in 2008, 35 years after the last time the convention met there. There was great anticipation prior to the event at a time when the Order's membership was increasing thanks to membership drives and internet development. And AHEPA had made important strides in terms of philanthropy, its impact on congressional legislation and US foreign policy with respect to Greece, the Greek wildfire and earthquake relief efforts, the legislation to award the famous Greek Italian artist Constantino Brumidi with the Congressional Gold Medal, and ongoing efforts to help Greece participate in the US Visa Waiver Program. There was an unusually high number of pre-registered convention participants two weeks before the convention opened. Scheduled events included wreath-laying ceremonies at the Tomb of the Unknown Soldier and the Truman and Marshall Statues; a basketball tournament between Greek American Division I players and the Greek national team; the "Reunification of the Parthenon Marbles" presentation at the University of Indianapolis' Athens Cultural Center; and the 4th of July Barbeque at the Glyfada Golf Club.

At the convention, which took place between in July, Minister of Foreign Affairs Dora Bakoyanni was one of the many Greek officials to speak and praise AHEPA's work. Supreme President Gulas was reelected, having run unopposed. The other officers elected—several of them were reelected—were: Supreme Vice President Nicholas Karacostas; Canadian President Nick Aroutzidis, an engineer in Ontario; Supreme Secretary John Grossomanides; Supreme Treasurer Anthony Kouzounis; Supreme Counselor John Galanis. The eight Supreme Governors elected were Charles Stamoulis, Seminole, John Mesogitis, Louis Arvanitis, Constantine Calliontzis, Philip G. Giavasis, Canton, Tom Gober, Highland, Peter Kaldis, and Nick Perdaris. Elected to the Board of Trustees were Past Supreme President James Scofield and Past Chairman of the Board Lee J. Millas.

Monthe Kofos was reelected as athletic director, marking his 39th term in that position and the last one, because he passed away later that year. He had spent a total of six decades promoting athletic competitions for Greek American youths. He created the AHEPA All-Star Basketball Program and the AHEPA Athletic Hall of Fame to recognize outstanding Hellenic athletes. The purpose of the Hall of Fame was not only to recognize outstanding athletes of Greek descent but also to encourage Greek Americans to play sports. The first inductions took place in 1975, and there were several because of the need to honor athletes of previous eras. They included Harry Agganis, college football player and coach Dee Andros, pole vaulter Peter

Clentzos, baseball second baseman Alex Campouris, football player and professional wrestler Alex Karras, the legendary professional wrestler Jim Londos, baseball pitcher Milt Pappas, football player Pete Pihos (a two-time NFL champion with the Philadelphia Eagles), Boston Celtics basketball player Lou Tsioropoulos, and Gus Zarnas, the first Greek to play in the National Football League. A full list of those honored by inclusion in the Hall of Fame is available on AHEPA's website.[150]

AHEPA's return to Athens was a successful one. In the words of the Supreme President: "The convention served as a platform to explore and showcase how the AHEPA family can be a dependable, vibrant, and sturdy bridge between North America and Greece," said Ike Gulas. "I am confident we succeeded in meeting our goals. We exceeded our expectations for attendance, and we were also able to organize cultural and educational programs that featured our youth. Many participants, young and old, visited Greece for the first time, or became re-acquainted with the Greece of the 21st century."[151]

The Visa Waiver Program

The US government's Visa Waiver Program enables citizens of specific countries to visit the United States for 90 days without having to obtain a visa. Greece had not been included in the program even when other European Union members had been by 1999. Inclusion of Greece into the Visa Waiver Program was a significant initiative championed by AHEPA because of the organization's historical role as a bridge between the United States and Greece for 86 years. Since January 2006, AHEPA worked with Congress to introduce legislation that designates Greece as a visa waiver nation, sponsored by Hellenic Caucus Co-Chair Carolyn Maloney, the New York City Democratic Party congresswoman, and hosted a public policy forum with leading administration, congressional, and policy experts to create awareness of the subject. AHEPA worked with the Departments of State and Homeland Security to present the position of the Greek American community on the issue. In November 2008 several eastern European countries were included in the program, but Greece remained excluded because Greece had vetoed FYROM's entry to NATO because of the name issue. Supreme President Gulas sent a letter to President George W. Bush expressing AHEPA's discontent, stating the Order deemed the obstruction in Greece's roadmap to become a visa waiver nation as an act by the United States that was unacceptable and extremely disconcerting to the American Hellenic community. It appeared this was an act in retaliation to a Greek policy that has no bearing on Greece's well-documented merits to join the Visa Waiver Program. Gulas asked all AHEPA family members, and the Greek American community, to unite and let the White House know they found that act unacceptable, and furthermore, respectfully requested that Greece be allowed to continue its rightful path to become a visa waiver nation.

Although the year 2008 ended on a sour note, this did not detract from that year's achievements, and especially the successful Supreme Convention in Athens. The convention was the exclamation point at the end of several years of development and progress for AHEPA. And if anything, the issue of the Visa Waiver Program, which would be resolved in 2010, and the continued impasse in Cyprus were reminders that there remained the need of a strong organization to work toward bringing the United States closer to Greece and Cyprus.

Chapter 12: AHEPA Stands by the Homeland 2009–2014

From 2009 to 2014 Greece experienced the effects of what is known in the country as "The Crisis," a sovereign debt crisis in which the government was unable to continue to pay back its foreign debt. It began in late 2009, triggered by the worldwide recession of the previous years, and was deepened by the structural weaknesses in the Greek economy and its lack of monetary flexibility as a member of the Eurozone. In practice, the country's population saw a series of reforms and austerity measures that led to widespread impoverishment and loss of income and property. The crisis continued for almost a decade. AHEPA steadfastly stood by Greece by continuing to provide aid throughout that period, while at the same time it entered a new era in its involvement on the diplomatic front thanks to the emergence of a new alliance with the major Jewish American organizations.

The 87th Supreme Convention, San Francisco, 2009

In 2009 the 87th Supreme Convention was held in San Francisco. The delegates unanimously elected Nicholas A. Karacostas as their Supreme President. Karacostas ran unopposed, a sign that AHEPA was overcoming any issues generated by competing groups within the organization. "Words cannot express how humbled and honored I am to be elected AHEPA Supreme President," said Karacostas, who emigrated from Kyrenia, Cyprus as a three-year-old with his family. "It is the culmination of 30 years of service to the organization, dating back to my membership in the Sons of Pericles." He continued, "I look forward, to working with our new Supreme Lodge, and entire membership, to keep AHEPA on the steady path set forth by my predecessors. There are many challenges facing the community, and new ones will emerge. However, I'm confident we will strive to overcome them together in true spirit to our mission." Karacostas, from Flushing, New York, was at the time a 25-year member of AHEPA and had served in numerous leadership positions including Supreme Vice President, two terms as Supreme Counselor, and on its Board of Directors. The newly-elected Supreme President was born in Cyprus in 1963. The inter-communal fighting between Greeks and Turks on Cyprus caused his family to move to the United States in 1966. He told the National Herald newspaper they took a plane to Piraeus and then came by boat on the famous Anna Maria ocean liner due to the then-prohibitive cost of air travel. He was raised and studied in New York, where he attended the day school of the Church of St. Nicholas in Flushing and later law school. Karacostas, an attorney, received his JD from the City of New York Law School and was a graduate of New York University. The other officials elected to the 2009–2010 Supreme Lodge included Supreme Vice President John Grossomanides; Canadian President Nick Aroutzidis; Supreme Secretary Anthony Kouzounis; Supreme Treasurer Col. Nicholas P. Vamvakias (ret.); Supreme Counselor Anastasios Konstantin; and Supreme Athletic Director Spiro Siaggas. The eight Supreme Governors elected were Peter S. Sergis, John Mesogitis, Theodore Manolios, Alex G. Geourntas, Chris D. Kontos, Tom Gober, James J. Peros, and Peter T. Triantafyllos. Elected to positions on the Board of Trustees were Franklin R. Manios and John Galanis. Manios, a Past Supreme President, was reelected. Nick Dixie, of Dallas, Texas, was elected to the Board of Auditors.

One of the highlights of the convention in San Francisco was a presentation by Professor Speros Vryonis Jr. on the subject AHEPA and the Greek American community. Vryonis was the recipient of the Academy of Achievement Award in Education, an honor that Supreme President Gulas noted was overdue given Vryonis' contribution to Byzantine and Hellenic history. Professor Vryonis was professor emeritus of history at the University of California Los Angeles; founding director of the Alexander S. Onassis Center for Hellenic Studies at New York University from which he retired as emeritus Alexander S. Onassis Professor of Hellenic Civilization; and former director of the Speros Basil Vryonis Center for the Study of Hellenism.

National Regional Salute Banquets

In November 2009 AHEPA honored excellence in several professions at its "National Regional Salute Banquet" held in Flushing, New York. In the words of Supreme President Karacostas, those being honored "inspire and serve as a fine example for all of us to emulate in our everyday lives. Their work on behalf of the community, and within society, is reflected in the worthy mission of the AHEPA family. The American Hellenic community can be proud of their fine accomplishments." The honorees for the evening included US Senator Robert Menendez and Congresswoman Carolyn Maloney, who received the Pericles Award; Dr. William J. Tenet, a New York cardiologist, AHEPA Academy of Achievement Award in Medicine; Dimitrios Kaloidis, a restaurant owner, businessman, and philanthropist from Brooklyn, Archbishop Iakovos Humanitarian Award; Colonel Mark D. Gatanas (ret.), AHEPA Medal of Freedom; Captain Dimitrios G. Roumeliotis, AHEPA Presidential Certificate of Honor; Nick Manos, AHEPA Hellenic Award.

More than 300 persons attended this sold out gala affair which was the first of four AHEPA National Regional Salute Banquets to be held in 2009–2010.

Traditionally, AHEPA hosted a Biennial Salute Banquet in Washington, DC every two years. However, that year, the Supreme Lodge decided to embark on a new and fresh approach by taking this historically gala affair "on the road" to geographically dispersed communities. Future venues included: Portland, Oregon, and Chicago.[152]

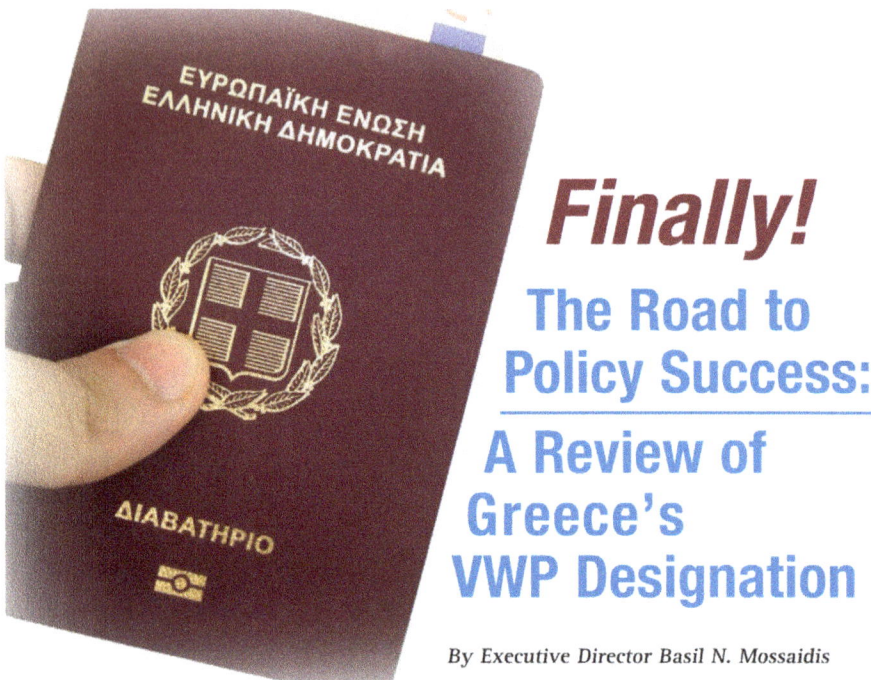

Finally!
The Road to Policy Success:
A Review of Greece's VWP Designation

By Executive Director Basil N. Mossaidis

A tremendous moment in U.S.-Greece relations was achieved when the United States designated Greece a Visa Waiver Program (VWP) nation on March 9, 2010. AHEPA Supreme President Nicholas A. Karacostas immediately hailed this announcement as one that will strengthen the long-standing strategic partnership between the two NATO allies. Greece's VWP designation means trade and commerce between the countries will flourish and tourism to the United States will increase. The strict security standards Greece had to meet, including passenger information sharing and screening, will help to protect our citizens. Finally, Greece's inclusion in the VWP is a tremendous source of pride for the Greek American community, making it easier for relatives to visit, especially at a moment's notice.

VWP travellers are required to have a valid authorization through the Electronic System for Travel Authorization (ESTA) prior to travel, are screened at the port of entry into the United States, and are enrolled in the Department of Homeland Security's US-VISIT program.

AHEPA championed Greece's designation to become a visa waiver nation. Beginning in April 2006, during AHEPA's annual excursion to Greece, AHEPA Supreme President Gus J. James, II, learned and identified that Greece's candidacy to become a VWP nation was ripe for resolution following meetings at the American Embassy in Athens and with Greek government officials. After all, at the time Greece was the only one of the original 15 European Union nations not to be a VWP member and Greece's passport biometrics were state-of-the-art, surpassing even the biometrics of passports of the original 27 VWP countries. Moreover, Greece's visa refusal rate of 1.6 percent was far below the maximum allowable rate by law.

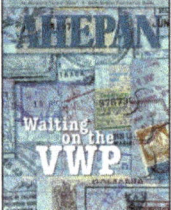

The Ahepan Spring 2007

The Resolution of the Visa Waiver Issue

In March 2010, an issue in US-Greek relations that AHEPA had worked on hard for several years was resolved. The United States designated Greece as a visa waiver country. As a result of this designation, Greek citizens would be permitted to travel to the United States for up to 90 days without obtaining a visa. Greece joined the 35 nations already participating in the Visa Waiver Program, established in 1986 to help eliminate unnecessary barriers to travel. In accordance with the visa waiver designation process, the Department of Homeland Security determined that Greece complied with key security and information-sharing requirements. Following his meeting with officials at the Department of Homeland Security, Supreme President Karacostas declared: "This is exciting and welcomed news Greece has worked extremely hard to meet, and in some cases exceed, the United States' rigid visa waiver program criteria. We also thank the efforts of officials at the Department of Homeland Security, the State Department, and our champions on Capitol Hill, especially the Hellenic Caucus, for working ceaselessly to see this process through to its proper completion." Karacostas added: "Greece's entry is a source of pride for the American Hellenic community. Now our relatives can visit us at a moment's notice if needed, commerce will flourish, and tourism to the United States will increase. Today, the long-standing strategic partnership between the United States and Greece becomes even stronger."[153]

The Onset of the Greek Debt Crisis
In October 2009 George Papandreou's PASOK socialist party won the election and he became prime minister, replacing New Democracy's Kostas Karamanlis. Papandreou revealed that Greece budget deficit was in reality double the previous estimates, and the country's borrowing costs spiked and by May 2010 the European Union and the International Monetary Fund provided huge loans to Greece in exchange for the prime minister's commitment to implementing a series of austerity measures. It was the first of three "bailouts" for Greece, which it earned by initiating some badly needed reforms but also took measures that severely affected the living standards of Greeks and would create great hardships. Papandreou would be forced to step down in 2011, to be replaced by a caretaker government made up of technocrats who it was hoped would help Greece manage what was becoming a worsening situation. As the effects of the debt crisis in Greece were becoming evident, AHEPA was preparing to offer its support. Significantly, at the time, the media reported that there was reticence among some Greek Americans about providing aid to Greece and suspicions about whether Greeks were aware

of their responsibilities. In contrast, AHEPA's early statements demonstrated a faith in the abilities of the Greek people. Executive Director Basil Mossaidis told the Voice of America in May 2010 that one should not write off the Greeks so quickly and pointed out: "They are very resilient people, they are very educated people, too. They are not fooling themselves into thinking everything is fine. They know what challenges they face. In every society, the media always accentuates the complainers. Not the hard-working people that go to work every day."[154]

The 88th Supreme Convention, 2010, Montreal

The 88th Supreme Convention was held in Montreal in July 2010. It had been 50 years since Montreal had the honor of hosting one of the largest gatherings of Hellenes in North America. The Montreal organizing committee was chaired by Xenophon Scoufaras and co-chaired by Frank Antoniou and Alexandra Vasilakopoulos, along with another 20 volunteers. On Wednesday of the convention week the attendees were treated to two compelling symposia. The AHEPA Educational Foundation sponsored author John Katsaros, who wrote the book Code Burgundy: The Long Escape. Katsaros provided a riveting account of survival after bailing out of his B-17 over occupied France during World War II. The second symposium featured Dr. André Gerolymatos, the Hellenic Studies Chair at Simon Fraser University. Dr. Gerolymatos spoke about the contributions of Greece to Western civilization. The AHEPA Hellenic Cultural Commission hosted this event. Metropolitan Sotirios of Canada gave the keynote address at the Grand Banquet. Before an audience of almost 600 attendees, the spiritual leader eloquently pointed out the three things he said he most admired about the AHEPA family: its discipline and respect, its work with the Church in the spirit of philanthropy and solidarity, and its faith and love. The metropolitan urged the crowd to "never, never give up!"[155]

The night of the Grand Banquet was also the occasion to honor: Professor André Gerolymatos, who received the Academy of Achievement Award in Education; Nick Stratas, Chairman of the Board of the AHEPA National Housing Program, received the Supreme President's Award of Excellence; Merrillville/Gary Chapter 78 received the award for Chapter of the Year; Costas Tsavellas,

Phoenix Chapter 219, received the award for the 2010 Ahepan of the Year. At the conclusion of the convention's proceedings elections were held and Nicholas Karacostas was reelected Supreme President, unopposed as he had been the previous year. Karacostas spoke about looking forward to building upon the significant grassroots momentum generated during his first term due to programs like the "United We Serve" Initiative. There were many challenges facing the community, he said, and new ones would emerge, but he expressed confidence the Order would overcome them in the true spirit of its mission. The other officers elected to the 2009–2010 Supreme Lodge were Supreme Vice President John Grossomanides; Canadian President Nick Aroutzidis; Supreme Secretary Anthony Kouzounis; Supreme Treasurer Col. Nicholas P. Vamvakias (ret.); Supreme Counselor Phillip T. Frangos; and Supreme Athletic Director Spiro Siaggas. The eight Supreme Governors were: Peter S. Sergis; Dr. Peter Nickolas; Andrew Zachariades; Kip Kyprianou; Chris D. Kontos; Louis Atsaves; Nick Dixie; and Peter T. Triantafyllos. Elected to positions on the Board of Trustees were Constantine Highland and Vassos Chrysanthou. Craig Clawson was reelected to the Board of Auditors, where he served as chairman.[156]

The Relationship with Israel

At a time when Greece was moving diplomatically closer toward Israel—politically and business-wise—AHEPA, wishing to contribute to the process, organized a one-day conference in October 2010 in Washington, DC called "Emerging Greek-Israeli Relations: What Are the Next Steps?" Congressman Gus Bilirakis welcomed guests at the Washington Club while AHEPA Supreme President Karacostas made closing remarks. The tone for the proceedings was set by the introductory remarks of Ambassador Vassilis Kaskarellis of Greece and Ambassador Michael Oren of Israel, and informative presentations were made by the Deputy Chiefs of Mission of the two embassies, Minister Ionanis Vrailas of Greece and Minister Dan Arbell of Israel. Although the speakers acknowledged that the recent developments were founded on years of initiatives, Oren stated that events such as the day's AHEPA conference were groundbreaking. The role of the Greek and Jewish communities in America was examined by Dr. André Gerolymatos, Professor and Chairman of Hellenic Studies of

Simon Fraser University, and Jason Isaacson, Director of Government and International Affairs for the American Jewish Committee (AJC). The moderator, Savas Tsivicos, who was born on Cyprus and became a construction business executive based in New Jersey, and a member of AHEPA's Cyprus and Hellenic Affairs Committee which presented the conference, pointed out that the two communities had much in common, which formed the basis for cooperation in their efforts to inform US foreign policy makers. At the conclusion of the conference, Supreme President Karacostas stated: "The Order of AHEPA will continue to encourage the strengthening and deepening of relations between Greece and Israel and to also bring the Greek and Jewish American communities closer together."[157]

Contacts between AHEPA and the major Jewish American organizations would continue, with mutual benefits for both sides. In December 2012 such a meeting was held in New York City. The AHEPA delegation, headed by the then former Supreme President Karacostas, was joined by two other Greek American leaders and fellow Ahepans, PSEKA's Phillip Christopher and AHI's Nick Larigakis.

The conversation was coordinated by Professor Richard B. Stone, the Chairman of the Conference of Presidents of Major American Jewish Organizations, and focused on the relations between Greece, Cyprus, and Israel. AHEPA was the first to recognize the importance of the trilateral relationship which was needed for stability in the region of the Eastern Mediterranean. The coalition building and partnerships made would last into the future.

The Supreme President Reflects

The year 2011 opened with an extensive interview that Supreme President granted to the National Herald's reporter Constantine Sirigos. In a wide-ranging but systematic way, the conversation covered all important topics in AHEPA's life and stands as an authoritative record of where the Order stood as it was entering the 21st century and its 90th anniversary.

Karacostas began by noting that much of his work involved "revitalizing and rejuvenating our membership base through our chapters and districts. We did this in two ways, through advertising and publicity, and by emphasizing public service and volunteerism by having our chapters go out and show who we are." The efforts included AHEPA's traditional and well-known philanthropic agenda, giving to charity, scholarships, as well as new initiatives. Karacostas said AHEPA reached out to its chapters and members "through regional banquets." He said they took "our show on the road and honored local Greek Americans, showing who we are." Under his leadership the biennial Congressional Banquet in Washington, DC was replaced by a number of annual regional banquets.

Karacostas said he was also excited about his outreach to young professionals, adding that "We have created a membership program that is online—Friends of AHEPA. They don't have to belong to particular chapters. People whose family and work commitments do not allow them to attend chapter meetings can be virtual members online, where they can get information about local events." The innovation acknowledged the transformation the lives of members of the Greek American community have undergone in recent decades as men and women entered professions with different work patterns and two-income families required fathers to spend more time at home, which is a challenge to all community organizations. Karacostas said he knew that the biggest value of membership organizations like AHEPA is the career and business building opportunities they offer. "We are in the process of creating a jobs program. Members can go into our database, where they'll see a list of positions available in their region. There is a committee led by our Executive Director Basil Mossaidis and we are testing it right now. All these things together have attracted a younger group of people. Those who want to network see that AHEPA is one of the organizations you should become a member of."

Karacostas said he was proud to be an American citizen and a Greek Cypriot. From his childhood, he said he knew he had to do what he could to help the land of his birth. He was 11 years old when Turkey invaded Cyprus, but he sought justice for Cyprus in any way he could with community organizations. Today he stresses that in AHEPA, "We do all we can to help with the Cyprus issue. We know it is and issue of illegal invasion and occupation," which means the key is "To push the US to help with the government of Turkey, which, as we know, pulls the stings of the Turkish Cypriots. They have moved in colonists and have built on our property," further disturbing the search for a solution. "Cyprus must be liberated and unified. AHEPA chapters and its headquarters fight for Greece and Cyprus by communicating with Congress, Secretary of State Clinton," and other major players, including the media, keeping them informed about key issues, he said. He said he is also proud of the success of AHEPA's Visa Waiver Campaign, which began under Supreme Presidents Gus James and Ike Gulas. "I was lucky that it finally happened when I was president. Now our friends and families don't need a visa to visit us. It was long overdue." He said he was also proud of AHEPA's 92 senior citizen facilities, which are located mainly in the South due to prohibitive real estate and building costs in other parts of the United States. AHEPA also takes pride in its presence in Greece, most notably the AHEPA hospital in Thessaloniki and the AHEPA Wing at Evangelismos Hospital in Athens.

Karacostas went on to say that AHEPA is looking to expand its bridge-building role between the United States and Greece and assist the homeland in rebuilding its economy. "We are waiting for the government to tell us how we can help. We have offered to link our website to tourism sites, and to help generate business in other ways," including having entrepreneurs invest in Greece. He noted AHEPA could help promote the upcoming Diaspora bonds. "We've offered our assistance but to this date we have not had a concrete request. Things are going slower than I expected," but he noted the government is focused on other aspects of the crisis. "We don't dictate policy we offer our assistance." There is one critical community issue, however, where AHEPA can and has applied political pressure. Regarding the delays in rebuilding the Church of St. Nicholas at Ground Zero, he said: "Sometimes the political process needs pushing. Our St. Nicholas petition drive has more than 20,000 signatures to show the states of New York and New Jersey that the Greeks of America our area want a solution and want the rebuilding to proceed." Karacostas said that AHEPA had communicated with New York's new Governor, Andrew Cuomo and said, "We believe there will be a meeting soon to reach a solution."[158]

Sending Young Greek Americans to Greece
The Annual AHEPA Journey to Greece Program, also known as The Journey, offered by AHEPA in collaboration with the University of Indianapolis in Athens, marked its sixth year in 2011. The Journey, a once-in-a-lifetime opportunity to earn college credit while learning about ancient and modern Greece, combining classes in Greek studies with excursions to places of interest, underlined AHEPA's commitment to bring young Greek Americans and other young Americans close to Greece and its history and culture. AHEPA was the first Greek American organization to institutionalize annual excursions to Greece in the 1920s and 1930s. For second, third, and fourth generation Greek Americans, such trips offered a unique opportunity to connect with their heritage. High level meetings became important Journey events, and each year the students were invited to visit the US Embassy, the Ministry of Foreign Affairs, and the Greek Orthodox Archdiocese in Athens. Special excursions included a visit to the New Acropolis Museum, a private tour of the Greek Parliament, the Benaki Museum, the Temple of Poseidon at Sounion, as well as an excursion to Corinth and Olympia, capped by a special five-day, four-night cruise of the Aegean Islands.

AHEPA & St. Nicholas Church
Affirming its commitment to the rebuilding of St. Nicholas Church, destroyed in the September 11, 2001 terrorist attacks, AHEPA took the rare step of organizing a small demonstration in July at Ground Zero in New York City calling for the process to regain the momentum it had lost. The rebuilding plans were stuck in a feud between the

church, New York and New Jersey Port Authority, and a lawsuit. AHEPA's initiative earned not only coverage but also praise from several Greek American media outlets including the Ethnikos Kyrix. The event gathered about 200 people in the square at Liberty Street and Trinity Place, just a block from where the church originally stood. Nearly a decade after the attacks, the AHEPA and some Greek American political leadership was onstage calling for the rebuilding, while a row of elderly female St. Nicholas parishioners silently held up signs.

Supreme President Karacostas underlined that AHEPA had sent Port Authority head Christopher Ward two letters and 20,000 signatures but had received no response. He said: "Shame on the Port Authority for taking this long to build our Greek Orthodox Church." Karacostas added: "I'm a native New Yorker. I walked by that church every day. I went in and lit a candle when I needed to." He emphasized the church's value to all Christian denominations, adding: "We will not rest until we have this church rebuilt, right on this corner here, 130 Liberty Street."

In town for the event were AHEPA leaders from around the country, including Supreme Secretary Anthony Kouzounis from Houston and Supreme Treasurer Col. Nick P. Vamvakias from Virginia. Kouzounis spoke for the members of the Annunciation Cathedral parish and Texan Greeks, noting: "We are totally behind the effort to rebuild St. Nicholas." Supreme Counselor Philip T. Frangos of Michigan added amidst the visible construction at Ground Zero behind him: "There is something missing... Mr. Governor, rebuild St. Nicholas!" Before a moment of silence, Ahepan Andrew Zachariades shared his memories of standing at the corner of Liberty and Broadway with "no place to run" on September 11, 2001.[159]

Within the next months the wish that St. Nicholas be rebuilt would be fulfilled. As the process regained momentum, and in marking the 10-year anniversary of the church's destruction, the Ethnikos Kyrix noted that AHEPA's energetic espousal of the cause of rebuilding honored Greek America and was to be commended. At long last, in October of 2011 Archbishop Demetrios and Governor Cuomo announced that the church would be rebuilt on the site of the old one.[160]

The 89th Supreme Convention, 2011, Miami Beach

AHEPA held its 89th Supreme Convention in 2011 in Miami Beach and elected Dr. John Grossomanides Jr., a senior clinical pharmacist at Advanced Pharmacy Concepts in Westerly, Rhode Island, to replace two-term leader Karacostas as Supreme President. Grossomanides' grandparents immigrated to the United States in a story familiar to many readers. His father's father came from Mytilene through Ellis Island in 1912, settling in Rhode Island. His mother's side came from Epirus around 1917 and settled in Massachusetts, attracted to that state's abundant mill jobs. His mother Celia (Vasiliki) grew up in Webster in Central Massachusetts. His father John Sr. was an active Ahepan, and John Jr. remembered going to district conventions as a four year old child. Grossomanides, who ran unopposed and stated he would try to pick up on Karacostas' legacy, spoke about the organization's recent program of outreach and efforts to attract the community's youth. In his final address as Supreme President, Karacostas remarked how he could never have imagined as an 18-year-old Son of Pericles—who joined because he wanted to play softball—that he would be standing before a large audience as the outgoing Supreme President.

Upon his election, Grossomanides said it was an honor to be elected Supreme President of AHEPA in a time of great challenges for Hellenism, including the Greek crisis, the Cyprus reunification talks, and the plight of the Ecumenical Patriarchate, but he added that "the need for community service is more in demand than ever." He spoke about living in exciting times for AHEPA after the Karacostas tenure and that AHEPA had been successful in attracting young people, especially through its athletic programs and internet endeavors. The Sons of Pericles had tripled their membership and chartered about 10 new chapters. The others elected to the 2011–2012 Supreme Lodge were Supreme Vice President Anthony Kouzounis; Canadian President George Vassilas, a business relations expert from British Columbia; Supreme Secretary Phillip T. Frangos; Supreme Treasurer Andrew C. Zachariades; Supreme Counselor George Loucas; and Supreme Athletic Director Spiro Siaggas. The Order also elected eight new regional Supreme Governors and a new Board of Trustees. The eight Supreme Governors were Sandy Papadopoulos, Dr. Peter Nickolas, Jimmy Kokotas, Nicholas Nikas, Dr. Mark Zigoras, Louis Atsaves, Nick

Dixie, and Alex Christy. Elected to positions on the Board of Trustees were Nicholas A. Karacostas and Lee J. Millas. Karacostas was elected chairman of the Board and Millas was reelected to the Board. The Board's remaining officers were Vice Chairman John Galanis, and Secretary Constantine Highland.

The Grand Banquet was the occasion for bestowing honors on numerous outstanding Hellenes. Greek American comedian Basile served as master of ceremonies, and the Keynote Address was offered by His Eminence Archbishop Demetrios, who conveyed the blessing of Ecumenical Patriarch Bartholomew, with whom he had just visited. Congressman Gus Bilirakis received the AHEPA Pericles Award. Vassilis Kaskarelis, Ambassador of Greece to the United States and Pavlos Anastasiades, Ambassador of Cyprus to the United States received the AHEPA Aristotle Award. Philip Christopher, President of PSEKA, received the AHEPA Freedom Award. Harry Lake of Dayton, Ohio received the AHEPA Lifetime Achievement Award, and Nick Aroutzidis, the President of AHEPA Canada, received the AHEPA Meritorious Service Award. In accepting the Aristotle Award, Ambassador Vassilis Kaskarelis said he would treasure it, adding that close-knit families, much like the AHEPA family, were the reason for the endurance of Hellenic culture. Cypriot Ambassador Pavlos Anastasiades thanked AHEPA for its demonstration of longstanding solidarity and support the organization had extended to Cyprus over the years. He dedicated the award to the memory of the 13 individuals who lost their lives in a munitions explosion that had happened in early July. Bilirakis accepted the Pericles Award, saying it was a privilege to represent the Greek American community in Washington and emphasized the importance of preserving the Hellenic heritage.

Grossomanides stated that the convention was one of the most successful and that rooms had to be booked in a second and then a third hotel to accommodate all the guests. The Educational Foundation sponsored several symposia on topics, including "Behind the Lens" by Pete Yalnis, which focused on the Parthenon Marbles; "Future of Hellenism" by sociology professor George A. Kourvetaris of Northern Illinois University; and "The Greek Language in the 21st Century" by John Papaloizos, an author of books on modern Greek. AHEPA's Executive Director Basil Mossaidis, a World War II history enthusiast, said he was especially enthralled by the book presentation offered by

George Blytas and engineer and founder of the Hellenic Professional Society of Texas which was based in Houston. His book First Victory details the account of the Battle of Crete and Greece's contributions to the war effort. Among the beneficiaries of AHEPA's philanthropic activities were the St. Jude Children's Research Hospital and the Archdiocese's Leadership 100, whose Executive Director Paulette Poulos received the Order's final pledge installment.

The Supreme President's Perspective
In an interview to the National Herald several weeks after his election, Supreme President Grossomanides outlined his and AHEPA's goals, underlining that continuing his predecessor Karacostas' focus on youth was of primary importance. Supplementing the Order's new message that it would recruit and promote younger members, the Supreme president said he looked forward to working with the Sons of Pericles—one of the AHEPA family's two youth organizations, along with the Maids of Athena—the Order's "farm system", to help them continue their outstanding recent success. In the past 12-18 months the Sons had tripled their membership. In addition to the permanent philanthropic ventures for which AHEPA is renowned—raising money for the treatment and cure of Cooley's Anemia and for the scholarships awarded by the AHEPA Education Foundation—the Supreme Presidents, Grossomanides explained, undertake initiatives that last for about a year, encouraging chapters to collect donations for other important causes such as Team USA, which is dedicated to giving scholarships to children of people serving the armed forces, and its current one, a special program for the children of armed forces members through the USO. Such charitable and community activities and networking were facilitated by the new social media such as Facebook, Twitter and LinkedIn which were popular among younger members of AHEPA just out of college and grad school. Grossomanides also said he was excited about the jobs board that was established last year. One must be a member to access job openings, but anyone can list a job. Executive Director Mossaidis, who was also at the interview, spoke about AHEPA's national membership program that began several years ago. People could join online directly to the Headquarters in Washington, he said, adding that "We are sensitive to the fact that professionals may not have time

at their disposal to attend chapter meetings or the other programs, but yet feel enough of a connection to AHEPA that they would pay dues and be connected with us that way, and that membership is steadily increasing." Grossomanides spoke about AHEPA's high-level concern about rebuilding the St. Nicholas Church at Ground Zero. For the commemoration of the 10th year after the 9/11 tragedy AHEPA placed ads in Greek American newspapers and in the New York Times. He also described how the Order also maintains its focus on the needs of Greece and Cyprus. Grossomanides also mentioned he was engaged to be married to Anna-Helene Panagakos of Brooklyn, whom he met at an AHEPA event in Tarpons Springs. She was at the time the national Grand Secretary of the Daughters of Penelope, so he had a better understanding than most past leaders of the needs and challenges the Daughters face, and their potential.[161]

Aiding Greece

As the economic crisis in Greece continued in 2012, AHEPA mobilized to help the homeland. In a newspaper article commentary, AHEPA Executive Director Basil Mossaidis wrote: "Homelessness and begging have become all-too-familiar in Greece, and the situation will get worse before it improves. AHEPA, through its chapters in Greece and in the United States, is one of the community organizations that has stepped up to the challenge of helping. Greece is facing its worst crisis since World War II. What can be done to help the country? As a Greek- American it pains me, and many like me, to see and hear of the terrible situation in Greece. Many people call and complain that we need to do more, we need to solve this, and we need to be vocal about what needs to take place. How can we (Greek-Americans) solve this problem? These questions are difficult to comprehend and more difficult to answer. All those who have been to Greece on a regular basis, and those of who have been active in trying to assist, understand that Greece is not a country that has many natural resources in order to create jobs and industry. Greece's sole natural resource is... its beauty...We can all work together to promote visiting Greece. We cannot necessarily fix the political problems Greece currently faces, nor is it our duty to fix those problems. Our concern is to assist the people. We can send food, we can send blankets, we can send medicine, but all those are like Band-Aids on a problem that is too big to fix. We can encourage business to foster in Greece, but the way Americans do business differs from how business is done in Greece. Our immediate and easiest impact is to promote visiting Greece... All Hellenes from around the world need to try to do their part to help Greece. The Greek people have undergone tremendous sacrifice and pain, forget placing blame, let's work to assist the people of Greece. Governments come and go, hopefully the need for the leaders in Greece to lead will make them take the necessary steps to solve their crisis, but we Greeks in the Diaspora should do our best to support the people. There are several ways to help, donate money, time, food, clothing, medicine, to name a few, but perhaps if all of us visited Greece to bolster the people in their time of need would be the best way to help. On our part the AHEPA will promote travel to Greece aggressively as a means of support. We are currently collecting funds to assist in sending food and medical supplies, but we will be promoting an aggressive tourism agenda in our efforts to assist. For 90 years the AHEPA has assisted our friends in Greece, we will continue to do so."[162]

The 2012 trip to Greece, Cyprus, the Ecumenical Patriarchate, and the Holy Land included the provision of aid to those in need. A check for $7,500 that Supreme President Grossomanides presented to the Church of Greece for its philanthropic work was a symbolic gesture, an indication of the various kinds of help AHEPA was preparing to offer the people of Greece during their time of troubles, but it sent a powerful message during the first days of the Order's visit to Greece. Aside from meeting with Archbishop Ieronymos, the delegation also visited with President of the Republic Karolos Papoulias and with Greek Prime Minister Lucas Papademos. AHEPA also met with Daniel B. Smith, the US Ambassador to Greece.

Papoulias expressed the motherland's pride and gratitude to the Greeks abroad, noting that they have two homelands, and thanked them for all they had done for Greece, in good moments and bad. He continued by saying he was not afraid for the future and, addressing the Greek American audience directly, asked them to remember what their grandparents had accomplished and where they started from. They had arrived barefoot on the shores of a great country, but their hard work led to the success of their grandchildren. He noted the presence of Greek Americans in academia, the arts, in science and medicine, in addition to the business world, where their achievements burnish the name "Greece" throughout the US and Canada. Papoulias spoke about his belief in the power of the Greek soul, noting that by having the courage to face difficult situations, the crisis would be overcome but that would only be done if the Greeks acted as a family. When the Greeks won battles in the past, they won as a family. When there was division and conflict they failed.

Grossomanides briefed Papoulias on AHEPA's undertakings for Greece, especially regarding the neediest. He noted that beyond the money they raise, AHEPA wants to show that there is more to Greece today than the disturbing images seen on television. He added that AHEPA encourages Americans and Greek Americans to invest in Greece, and recommended they visit and boost its tourism. He summed up his optimism by repeating the aphorism he heard often from his grandmother, "kathe embodio gia kalo (every obstacle is for the best)." The check that was presented was not the first instance of aid from AHEPA—numerous chapters in the United States and in Greece have been active in different ways—but it was an example of how Greek Americans who did not have faith in the Greek political system were seeking out established and trusted channels for their initial contributions. AHEPA expressed its wish to work with the Church of Greece and toward that end both parties hoped to sign a cooperation agreement with foresees the establishment of concrete programs. The archbishop thanked the AHEPA leaders for the contribution and its members for supporting Greece. Grossomanides responded by saying that by being united Hellenism would emerge from the crisis and find solutions to the problems that society faced. Grossomanides also said the problem for AHEPA was it did not know where to give the money we raise, "to be sure that we make an impact." That is why they would continue to develop lines of communications with Greece with the aim of guaranteeing the effectiveness of their efforts. After the meeting with the archbishop, the leadership visited the offices of the Athens AHEPA chapter which celebrated its 50th anniversary that year. The chapter secretary, Dimitris Hondros, said that among other things the chapter helped provide meals for students in poor neighborhoods in Athens.[163]

The support offered Greece during the economic crisis conjured echoes of AHEPA's role within the Greek War Relief Association which aided Greece throughout the 1940s. Yet the circumstances were very different because this time around there was a Greek government in place to channel the relief materials arriving from abroad. Many organizations and individuals in the diaspora were uncertain about where to send the aid and how that aid would be distributed. Also, the Greek American community writ large was in generational terms further removed from Greece than it had been in the 1940s and this affected its response. AHEPA did its duty; it moved carefully at first, relying on its chapters in Greece, and then gradually accelerated it work. Along with the Archdiocese the Order was (and remains) one of the most effective conduits of Greek American aid to the homeland in moments of crisis.[164]

Supporting Cyprus

AHEPA expressed its continued commitment to a solution to the crisis in Cyprus when its annual overseas excursion arrived in Nicosia in mid-April 2012. Supreme President Grossomanides met with President of the Republic of Cyprus Dimitris Christofias on April 10. Also during the four-day visit to Cyprus, the delegation met with US Deputy Chief of Mission to the Republic of Cyprus Andrew Schofer, Cypriot Foreign Minister Erato Kozakou-Marcoullis, Archbishop Chrysostomos, President of the House of Representatives Yiannakis Omirou, Mayor of Nicosia Constantinos Yiorkadjis, Mayor of Famagusta and President of the Committee of the Cyprus Occupied Municipalities Alexis Galanos, and businessman, philanthropist, and AHEPA supporter Efthyvoulos G. Paraskevaides. Grossomanides noted that the delegation was briefed about the ongoing direct talks under the United Nations framework that seek to reunite Cyprus and its people. He reiterated AHEPA's commitment to keep the Cyprus issue at the forefront of the community and to America's policymakers remained unwavering. There was also an emotional tour of the Imprisoned Graves cemetery (Fylakismena Mnimata) and the delegation laid a wreath there. It is where 13 EOKA (National Organization of Cypriot Fighters) members, who fought for Cyprus' independence from the United Kingdom, are buried. Nine of the 13 EOKA fighters were executed there. Lastly, AHEPA's Cyprus District hosted a reception at which former European MP Yiannakis Matsis was honored with the 2012 AHEPA Aristotle Award.

Three more events that took place prior to the Supreme Convention of 2012 underlined AHEPA's continued involvement with Cyprus. In May it honored Nick Larigakis, the president of the American Hellenic Institute. Larigakis received the inaugural AHEPA Outstanding Public Advocacy Award at the AHEPA Salute to Civic Responsibility Dinner. The AHEPA Outstanding Public Advocacy Award, which was presented by AHEPA's Executive Director Basil Mossaidis, recognizes individuals who demonstrate unbridled passion in the course of advocating for a public policy issue or cause. AHEPA cited Larigakis' steadfast advocacy on Capitol Hill, in the grassroots, and in the op-ed pages of influential publications as the basis for his honor. In accepting, AHI President Larigakis spoke about the importance of defending "our proud Hellenic culture" and about the influence his parents had upon instilling those values in him as a teenager. He said he was receiving the award with exceptional honor and humility and that there was a special meaning for him "to receive this award tonight, the first of its kind, from AHEPA and to receive it on Capitol Hill because when the American Hellenic Institute was founded in 1974, its number one priority was that invasion of Cyprus. With AHEPA's money we were able to put into place an embargo against the Republic of Turkey for its illegal invasion of Cyprus against extraordinary odds at the time. It is not something anyone of us should take lightly that victory." Also honored along with President Larigakis were US Congressmen John Sarbanes (D-MD) and Ed Royce (R-CA), both of whom received the AHEPA Pericles Award; and Cyprus Federation of America President Panicos Papanicolaou, who received the inaugural AHEPA Excellence in Leadership Award.

The second Cyprus-related event was a meeting between Supreme President Grossomanides and the President of Turkey Dr. Abdullah Gül in Ankara, to continue dialogue on matters of importance to the Greek American community. AHEPA discussed relations between the United States and Turkey, Greece and Turkey, and religious freedom. Executive Director Mossaidis accompanied Dr. Grossomanides to Ankara for the meeting. In addition, American Ambassador to Turkey Francis J. Ricciardone, Jr. met with the delegation. AHEPA was the first Greek American organization to visit Ankara to meet with the Turkish government in May 1997. Subsequent visits occurred in April 1998, May 2001, and October 2011.

And finally, the third event was the 28th Annual Cyprus & Hellenic Leadership Conference. Dozens of senators and members of Congress with jurisdiction over the formulation of policy toward Cyprus, Turkey, and Greece, and key administration officials, met with Greek American leaders from across the country and around the world in Washington, DC. And as AHEPA did every year, Supreme President Grossomanides called for the removal of Turkish troops from Cyprus on the 38-year anniversary of Turkey's invasion in July.

AHEPA's 90th Anniversary & 90th Supreme Convention, 2012

Nine decades after eight visionary Greek Americans in Atlanta, Georgia established the Order of AHEPA to protect Greek Americans from the xenophobia that was sweeping the country, to promote the Americanization of the Greek immigrants and to highlight the compatibility of American and Hellenic values, the Order gathered in Las Vegas to mark its 90th anniversary at its Supreme Convention. The 90th anniversary celebration culminated in the Grand Banquet, which was held on July 26, exactly 90 years since AHEPA's founding. Earlier that same day, the delegates reelected Supreme President Grossomanides, who ran unopposed, confirming the internal cohesion AHEPA had now established. The others elected to the Supreme Lodge were Supreme Vice President Anthony Kouzounis, Canadian President George Vassilas, Supreme Secretary Phillip Frangos, Supreme Treasurer Anthony Drakos, Supreme Counselor George Loucas, and Supreme Athletic Director Ike Gulas, PSP, of Birmingham, Alabama. The eight Supreme Governors elected were: Dalton Respass,: Ed Guminski, James Kokotas,: John Tanionos, Socrates Kolitsos, Nick Kavadas, James Peros and Chris Mellas. Reelected to positions on the Board of Trustees were: John Galanis and Constantine Calliontzis. Christopher Gallas was reelected to a term on the Board of Auditors. During the installation ceremonies for new officers, Grossomanides said he was "honored and humbled to be re-elected supreme president of AHEPA" and looked forward to "working with our seasoned Supreme Lodge and our membership to overcome these challenges, address new ones that will emerge, and keep AHEPA on the steady path set forth by my predecessors in a spirit true to our mission."

At the banquet nearly 800 people were present, and Las Vegas TV news anchor Sue Manteris was the emcee. Newly reelected Supreme President Grossomanides spoke about the founding of AHEPA in 1922 and described what it was like to be a Greek immigrant in the American South during those times. Chairman of the Board of Trustees Karacostas offered a toast to the organization on its 90th anniversary and the audience enjoyed a video montage of interview clips of Past Supreme Presidents, who reflected on memorable moments during their AHEPA career, what it means to be an Ahepan, and how AHEPA could remain an important factor to the community in the future. There was also a special video presentation with 90th anniversary greetings from members of Congress, including: Senator Robert Menendez and Representatives John Sarbanes, Niki Tsongas, Gus Bilirakis, Carolyn Maloney, and local Congresswoman Shelley Berkley. Tsongas, the wife of Paul Tsongas who had died of cancer in 1997, was elected to the House of Representatives in 2006 representing the Massachusetts district held by her husband. Berkley had been elected to the House of Representatives representing Nevada's First District in 1998. Her mother's side of the family were Sephardic Jews who had lived in Ottoman-era Thessaloniki. She provided a moving account of her visit to Thessaloniki to find the street on which her grandmother grew up. She took soil from the great city, placed it in a jar, and gave it to her mother for her birthday. She concluded, "I am one of you. Thank you for making me a part of your family." Cyprus' Ambassador to the United States Pavlos Anastasiades congratulated the membership and leadership of AHEPA. He said they were right to celebrate and asked the audience to "redouble their efforts" to achieve justice in Cyprus. Metropolitan Gerasimos of San Francisco addressed the audience and acknowledged AHEPA's contributions to society not through words, but deeds.

Archbishop Demetrios provided the Keynote Address and conveyed the congratulations and best wishes of His All-Holiness Ecumenical Patriarch Bartholomew. He noted the special relationship shared between the Order of St. Andrew and the Order of AHEPA, which have many members in common. Noting the Order's charitable work performed in post-World War II Greece, especially the establishment of the AHEPA Hospital in Thessaloniki and the AHEPA Wing of Evangelismos Hospital, the Archbishop drew a comparison between that period and the current situation in Greece. He highlighted some ongoing efforts, but also suggested the community was capable of a much more "developed, sophisticated" response, including a more vigorous defense of Greece's honor. The Archbishop was passionate in speaking about how "Greece has been treated unfairly internationally" during this crisis, stating there had been an unfair focus on Greece which deserved respect and assistance. The philanthropic dimension of AHEPA was further spotlighted by a presentation made by AHEPA National Housing Corporation President Angelo Kostarides of Indiana. He announced $80,000 in grants to AHEPA family entities and $50,000 toward AHEPA's humanitarian campaign to help the people of Greece. In the last 12 years, AHEPA Housing had issued $710,000 in grants. Grossomanides presented $30,000 to Konstantinos Dimtsas, the Executive Director of Apostoli Mission, the philanthropic arm of the Church of Greece. Daughters of Penelope Grand President Nicky Stamoulis presented Dimtsas with an $11,000 donation, part of the ongoing monthly commitment to Apostoli Mission which would continue until the funds that had been raised were exhausted.[165]

Continuing to Aid Greece

In the months following its 90th Supreme Convention AHEPA redoubled its efforts to offer aid to Greece in collaboration with the International Orthodox Christian Charities organization (IOCC). In February 2013 medical equipment valued at $650,000 was sent to the AHEPA hospital in Thessaloniki and to the AHEPA Wing of Evangelismos Hospital in Athens. Earlier, in October 2012 another batch of medical supplies had been sent to the island of Chios. The total value of aid provided jointly by AHEPA and IOCC up to that point in early 2013 was $1.2 million. And in April 2013, AHEPA's annual excursion to Greece in April was focused on how to provide more aid. In Athens, President Karolos Papoulias received them at the Presidential Mansion before they went on to meetings with Prime Minister Antonis Samaras, Foreign Minister Dimitris Avramopoulos, and the leader of the Greek Parliament Evangelos Meimarakis. Papoulias thanked the AHEPA members for their work during hard times for their homeland. "It helps many weak compatriots in a very difficult period," he said. "These people have a lot of potential. Your grandparents and fathers left in difficult times, went to another country, and yet progressed and managed so much so that Americans say 'Bravo for Greeks.'" He told them he saw the celebration and parade in New York to celebrate Greek Independence Day. He added: "You will not abandon your effort. You will persuade Americans to come and invest in Greece, you will persuade Americans for more tourists to come to our country, and it seems like this year will be a good year for tourism for Greece and I believe that our friends the Americans will not find a more beautiful country than this," he stressed. Grossomanides returned the thanks to Papoulias and there was a brief discussion about AHEPA's charitable work in Greece. An important part of the conversations AHEPA had with Greek officials was about the obstacles in the way of making donations to Greece because of the restrictive regulations and intricate bureaucratic requirements that discouraged donors and investors. After additional meetings with Archbishop Ieronymos, Samaras, and US Ambassador Daniel Bennett Smith, the delegation went on to Thessaloniki as well as Cyprus to meet President Nicos Anastasiades, who was also dealing with a critical economic crisis. They then went on to Constantinople to meet Ecumenical Patriarch Bartholomew.[166]

The next event on the agenda was the annual Capitol Hill Day and its Congressional Banquet, the 40th it had hosted. AHEPA and the Daughters of Penelope brought their legislative agendas to the attention of Capitol Hill legislators and their staffs in May. Seventy congressional offices from the Senate and House sides were visited by AHEPA family members, who represented 18 states. "Our mission, which is strongly founded on our cultural heritage and our community service programs, guides our legislative agenda," said Supreme President Grossomanides, adding: "As such, we have a diverse set of legislative interests, both foreign and domestic, that reflect our mission. We believe this makes the AHEPA family unique in its approach to Congress." AHEPA family members who participated at the organization's annual Capitol Hill Day discussed issues ranging from religious freedom for the Ecumenical Patriarchate to ending the division of Cyprus to ensuring cost-effective, job creating, and lifesaving domestic programs are preserved and maintained in the federal budget. Domestic programs of interest to the AHEPA family include senior citizen housing, medical research at NIH, and domestic violence. Also included on the agenda was comprehensive immigration reform and provisions within that legislation that would allow Greek nationals to seek "highly skilled" worker visas. The day's events included a morning reception where the AHEPA family received remarks from Congressman Gus Bilirakis, who was co-chair of the Hellenic Caucus and the Congressional Hellenic-Israel Alliance, and US representatives Niki Tsongas, Frank Pallone (D-NJ), and Dina Titus (D-NV).

The Congressional Banquet returned to the nation's capital after a number of years which featured regional banquets designed to bring the national leadership into closer relations with its local chapters and to spotlight the organizations' vibrant regions. AHEPA family members and friends gathered to honor excellence in public service and the community, and Fox News Chief Congressional Correspondent Mike Emanuel served as the banquet program's master of ceremonies. Congressman Gus Bilirakis presented his colleague Albio Sires (D-NJ) with the 2013 AHEPA Pericles Award for excellence in public service. Ambassador Gianna Angelopoulos-Daskalaki, former president, 2004 Athens Olympic Organizing Committee, received the Daughters of Penelope Civic Responsibility Award from Daughters of Penelope Grand President Joanne Saltas. Andrew Manatos, former Assistant Secretary of Commerce and founder of Manatos & Manatos, was awarded the Outstanding Public Advocacy Award by AHEPA Chairman of the Board Nicholas Karacostas. Colonel Steve Pisanos (ret.), a World War II Flying Ace, was given the AHEPA Medal of Freedom by Colonel Nick Vamvakias (ret.) and Congressman Gus Bilirakis, a member of the Veterans Affairs Committee. Rev. Father Alex Karloutsos, Protopresbyter of the Ecumenical Patriarchate, was presented the AHEPA Excellence in Leadership Award by Supreme President Dr. John Grossomanides.[167]

The 91st Supreme Convention, 2013, Orlando

AHEPA began the ninth decade of its existence by holding its 91st annual Supreme Convention in Orlando, Florida, August 18–24. As was the case with all conventions, it mixed business with pleasure, in this case all that Orlando had to offer, as well as honoring worthy individuals. The AHEPA Cyprus and Hellenic Affairs Committee passed a resolution adopted by the convention body backing all of the legislation introduced thus far in Congress by the Congressional Caucus on Hellenic Issues, chaired by Representatives Gus Bilirakis and Carolyn Maloney. The Grand Banquet was a moving and entertaining affair. Basile the Comedian served up laughter as emcee and the guests also received inspirational words from His Eminence Archbishop Demetrios, Congressman Bilirakis, and His All-Holiness Ecumenical Patriarch Bartholomew via video clip. Also present were the Ambassador of the Republic of Cyprus, George Chacalli, and the Consul General of Greece in Tampa, Antonios Sgouropoulos, who offered remarks and briefed the audience on the latest developments in Cyprus and Greece. All invited speakers thanked AHEPA for its assistance and effectiveness as an organization over its 91 years, and Archbishop Demetrios said all were thankful to God for having this association of AHEPA existing in America. Chris P. Tomaras, the Chairman of the PanHellenic Scholarship Foundations, was honored at the Grand Banquet. Outgoing Supreme President Grossomanides presented Tomaras with the 2013 Academy of Achievement Award in Business. One of the many highlights of the week was the annual awards and scholarship luncheon of AHEPA's National Athletic Department. Nikko Koutouvides, who played for the New England Patriots, received the AHEPA Harry Agganis Award, and Toni Kokenis, a basketball player at Stanford University, received the AHEPA William Chirgotis Award. Diver and Olympic gold medalist Greg Louganis headed the list of inductees into the prestigious AHEPA Athletic Hall of Fame and the community's outstanding scholar athletes received scholarships. Through the fundraising efforts of Ahepans George Behrakis and Nick Tsiotos, a life size statue of Agganis had been placed at Boston University's Harry Agganis Arena.

The election of the officials who oversaw the organization's activities throughout the coming year took place on August 23. Anthony Kouzounis of Houston was elected Supreme President. Kouzounis had been born in Thessaloniki and had arrived in the United States with his family at age eight in 1945, right after the end of World War II. He graduated from the University of Houston and went on to pursue a successful career in real estate in that city, where he was a member of AHEPA's Alexander the Great Chapter 29. After his election, Kouzounis spoke about the honor of being elected, the ongoing challenges the Greek American community faced, and that the promotion of Hellenic ideals was always a priority. He said reaching out to young people would remain another priority but since it was not easy for the older generation to be on the same wavelength with them, even if they were young at heart, he looked forward to working with the new presidents of the Sons and Maids and the national advisor and chairman of the Sons of Pericles committee, Jimmy Kokotas of Brooklyn. Kouzounis also stressed he wanted to further deepen their humanitarian aid collaboration with Apostoli Mission in Greece and with the IOCC.[168]

Following the elections of all other officials, the 2013–2014 Supreme Lodge was comprised of: Canadian President George Vassilas, Supreme Vice President Phillip T. Frangos, Supreme Secretary John Galanis, Supreme Treasurer Andy Zachariades, Supreme Counselor Gregory Stamos, Supreme Athletic Director Louis Atsaves, and Sons of Pericles National Advisor James Kokotas. The eight Supreme Governors elected were: Nick Stathopoulos, Philip Yamalis, Ted Fanikos, Nicholas Nikas, Tony Manolias, Nick Kavadas, Nicholas Dixie and George Booras. Elected to positions on the Board of Trustees were George Loucas, Cos Marandos, and Nick Matthews.

In the round of interviews that followed his election as Supreme President, Kouzounis emphasized that AHEPA was an association that brought Greek Americans together socially, but that AHEPA's philanthropic activities were paramount. He spoke about how the Order distributed $1 million annually on the chapter, district, and national levels, based on need as well as merit. But "Hellenic Education" in the name meant more than scholarships. Through its sponsorship of lectures and cultural events, AHEPA exemplified Greek ideals of service and civic pride. Working with HUD, AHEPA owned 240 rental units for senior citizens in southwest Houston. The Daughters of Penelope sponsored Penelope House, a safe haven for battered women, with locations in Alabama, New England, and Greece. Working with the IOCC, AHEPA helped ship 40-cubic-foot containers holding at least $640,000 worth of medical supplies to hospitals in Greece.[169]

As the year drew to a close it was obvious that the economic crisis Greece was facing was dragging on and that AHEPA would have to address the hardships this created. In August, just prior to the Supreme Convention, Greek Prime Minister Antonis Samaras had visited the United States and made a direct appeal for help for Greece from the Greek American community. Samaras had narrowly won the Greek elections held in June 2012 and had replaced prime minister and banker Lucas Papademos, who had led a caretaker government installed in 2011 which was charged with dealing with the economic crisis. During his visit Samaras met with President Barack Obama at the White House. Obama's two terms in office from 2013 to 2019 coincided with the decade-long crisis Greece faced, and the president would speak publicly for the need for fewer austerity measures and more meaningful debt relief for Greece.

The 2014 Leadership Mission
In 2014 AHEPA continued building on its ties with the Jewish American community and contributing to ties between Greece and Cyprus with Israel. AHEPA and the American Hellenic Institute were joined by B'nai B'rith International in participating in a historic three-country visit to Israel, Cyprus, and Greece. Also participating were representatives from the Conference of Presidents of Major American Jewish Organizations. The purpose of the trip was to analyze the strategic and emerging relationship between the three countries. The delegation of American Hellenic and American Jewish community leaders aimed to explore the major political, economic, and security developments underway in the Eastern Mediterranean with high-ranking government officials from each of the three countries. The joint delegation was yet another affirmation of the broad diaspora support for the emerging trilateral relationship.

To sum up the leadership mission, the group issued a joint statement: "Our meetings made clear that the trilateral relationship between Israel, Cyprus, and Greece is vibrant and strong on all levels. We believe the relationship has developed to the betterment of the region and is on sustained course. In a region with so much instability, the trilateral relationship possesses the potential to allow the Eastern Mediterranean to become a community of nations based on shared common values and aspirations. We applaud the leaders of these three countries for their foresight in establishing this cooperative relationship which we hope other nations will join. The American Hellenic and American Jewish communities will continue to work to foster closer cooperation in the United States and support the trilateral relationship. We are grateful to the many leaders who afforded us the opportunity to exchange views and ideas. The friendship and hospitality shown to us made the trip all the more meaningful and productive." The leadership mission followed two previous roundtable discussions held between the two communities in December 2012 and August 2011. In April 2011, AHEPA had made a landmark visitation to Israel to meet with Israel government officials, and in October 2010, AHEPA hosted a groundbreaking conference on the emerging relationship between Greece and Israel.[170]

The 92nd Supreme Convention, 2014, New Orleans

AHEPA held its 92nd annual convention in New Orleans in 2014. It was the fifth time a supreme convention was being held in that city, but this was a symbolic year because the first Greek Orthodox church in America had been established 150 years ago, in 1864. The delegates elected Phillip T. Frangos, of East Lansing, Michigan, as Supreme President; Frangos had run unopposed. An attorney, Philip Themistocles Frangos at the time of his election was a former Chief Deputy Secretary of State and CEO of the Michigan Department of State. In this capacity he had also served as Executive Secretary to the Michigan Historical Foundation. Frangos had served AHEPA in numerous leadership positions including most recently Supreme Vice President and all offices at the district and chapter levels. He also served as chairman of the Board of Trustees in the mid-1980s.

In his comments Frangos mentioned: "The community continues to face a multitude of challenges that are important to address as the need for community service is relentless, both in the United States and abroad, and the promotion of Hellenic ideals will always be a priority for AHEPA. I am excited to work with our seasoned Supreme Lodge and our membership to address these challenges and keep AHEPA on the steady path set forth by my predecessors in a spirit true to our mission." The other members elected to the 2014–2015 Supreme Lodge were Canadian President Kenneth N. Matziorinis, an economics professor at McGill University in Montreal and management consultant; Supreme Vice President John Galanis, Supreme Secretary Andrew Zachariades, Supreme Treasurer Tom Gober, Supreme Counselor Gregory Stamos, Supreme Athletic Director Louis Atsaves, and Sons of Pericles National Advisor James

Kokotas. The eight Supreme Governors who were elected were: Demetrios C. Kirkiles, Robert Stepp, Philip Vogis, Frank P. Fotis, Costas Boutsikakis, Nick Kavadas, Timothy Joannides, and Robert Sexton. Elected to positions on the Board of Trustees were Nicholas Karacostas and Vassos Chrysanthou.

At the Supreme Convention's Grand Banquet, George Kalogridis, president of Walt Disney Parks and Resorts, as well as B'nai B'rith International, were honored. George Kalogridis was presented with the AHEPA Socrates Award for excellence in his profession. "I stand before you both as a son of America and a son of Greece," he said in accepting. B'nai B'rith International was the first organization to receive the AHEPA Archbishop Iakovos Humanitarian Award (previous recipients had all been individuals) for its 171 years of global humanitarian work, service to the community, especially to senior citizens, and unwavering efforts to combat intolerance and anti-Semitism. In accepting, B'nai B'rith International President Allan Jacobs cited a 1938 write-up in B'nai B'rith's publication that reported on AHEPA's passage of a resolution that condemned "the inhuman and cruel persecution of a race which has given so much to the world."

Archbishop Demetrios was the Keynote Speaker. Remarks were also delivered from the Ambassador of Greece Christos Panagopoulos, Ambassador-Consul General of the Republic of Cyprus Vasilis Philippou, and Philip Christopher, president, International Coordinating Committee – Justice for Cyprus (PSEKA). The Ahepan of the Year and the AHEPA Lifetime Achievement Award were presented to Peter Marudas and Alex Booras, respectively. AHEPA National Housing President Angelo Kostarides announced charitable contributions of more than $360,000 to national and local community service and charitable organizations.

In the first months of his presidency Frangos worked toward increasing the membership of AHEPA, which stood at the time at 16,000, and he presented the President of the Republic of Cyprus Nicos Anastasiades with a $25,000 donation to help feed Cypriot children in need. "We stand with the citizens of Cyprus, who have endured hardship, as the country strives diligently to overcome the financial crisis and works to restore economic and social stability," Frangos said. "We hope the donation helps in some small way to ease this hardship on families." In late November he led a trip, in conjunction with the Archons of the Ecumenical Patriarchate and the Greek Orthodox Archdiocese's Philoptochos, to participate in the historic Apostolic Pilgrimage to Constantinople in honor of Pope Francis' visit to meet with Ecumenical Patriarch Bartholomew.

Right at the end of December 2014 a shipping container filled with $821,257 worth of medical supplies and equipment arrived in Chania, Crete, Greece, thanks to the efforts of AHEPA, which donated $18,000 to secure the shipping container, and to the International Orthodox Christian Charities (IOCC), which worked to coordinate the assembly of the medical supplies. It was the eighth shipment of medical supplies AHEPA helped to deliver to Greece working in cooperation with IOCC. The medical supplies ranged from syringes and walkers to catheters and nebulizers—all materials needed to run and administer a hospital daily. All told, nearly $5.5 million in medical supplies had been donated and delivered to hospitals throughout Greece. Up to that point in time, the AHEPA family had raised more than $550,000 for humanitarian aid for the people of Greece. Meanwhile, a political impasse in Athens triggered by the inability of the conservative government of Prime Minister Antonis Samaras to secure the election of a new President of the Republic created the need for national elections. Greece and AHEPA's relations with the homeland were about to enter a new era.

Chapter 13: AHEPA Stands by Hellenism & Orthodoxy 2015–2019

The years between 2015 and 2019 were a period of further and spectacular development of AHEPA and its activities. This period offered both opportunities and challenges. The opportunities stemmed from a continued improvement in the relations between the United States and Greece, which was a credit to both the Obama and Trump administrations in Washington, DC and the Greek government under Prime Minister Alexis Tsipras. Credit should also go to Ambassador Jeffrey Pyatt who was confirmed as ambassador to Greece on July 14, 2016. Ambassador Pyatt continued the hard work of his predecessors and built on the close and cordial relationship AHEPA has enjoyed with the US ambassadors in Athens. The challenges of this same period included political polarization in both the United States and Greece, a culmination of the economic crisis in Greece, and increasing tensions between Greece and Turkey. On the Greek-Turkish border in the Aegean, Greece also faced an unprecedented influx of refugees from the Middle East and elsewhere. Within the Greek American community there were conflicts over how best to achieve the rebuilding of St. Nicholas Church in New York City, and the end of Archbishop Demetrios' tenure and the appointment of Archbishop Elpidophoros. This situation posed great challenges for AHEPA, but continuing to build on its strengths, the Order stood up to those challenges and fulfilled its responsibilities effectively and successfully. Most notably, AHEPA was true to its word that it does not take political sides and maintained close and proper relations with the left-wing government under Alexis Tsipras who won the Greek parliamentary elections that were held in January 2015. Although the victorious left-wing SYRIZA party formed a coalition government with the right-wing "Independent Greeks" party, the administration was considered the most radical one Greece had experienced in its modern history. All those challenges and especially the left-wing orientation of the Greek government did not prevent AHEPA from continuing its support of the homeland and its political representatives. In his congratulatory message to the new prime minister, Supreme President Philip Frangos stated: "As you strive to meet the challenges Greece faces, the entire AHEPA family of organizations, including the Daughters of Penelope, Sons of Pericles, and Maids of Athena, is committed to being the sturdy, dependable bridge that has solidified the United States and Greece relationship for nearly a century. For our part, the AHEPA family continues on a humanitarian campaign that provides medical supplies to hospitals all throughout Greece. We have also donated more than $500,000 to help feed Greece's most hungry citizens. Going forward, please consider the Greek American community, and of course, the members of the AHEPA family, as resources to help Greece continue its emergence from the depths of an unprecedented economic crisis."[171]

AHEPA's activities in 2015 began with a visit by Supreme President Frangos to the headquarters of the AHEPA National Housing Corporation (AHNC) and AHEPA Management Company (AMC) in Fishers, Indiana, which houses 21 employees of the AHNC and AMC. It was a way of recognizing the work of those involved in an important aspect of AHEPA's history that receives little publicity. Frangos said he was greatly impressed by the range of professional expertise and skills possessed by the outstanding staff. It was apparent why the AHEPA senior housing program was so resoundingly successful. Frangos was dismayed that so many Greek Americans were still unaware of the program and the difference it was making in the lives of low-income senior citizens. The AHNC was a not-for-profit 501(c)(3) organization formed in 1983 as a result of the success of the very first low income multi-family senior housing complex created by

AHEPA Chapter 53 in St. Louis, Missouri. The mission of AHNC was to provide affordable housing for the low income elderly and disabled, and to ensure that they receive services to meet their physical and social needs. Up to that point AHNC had assisted AHEPA chapters in creating 92 apartment complexes in 22 states. They had provided quality homes for over 5,000 seniors over the age of 62 who meet HUD income requirements. Frangos noted that on his travels as Supreme President, "I had visited AHEPA apartment complexes in Connecticut, Pennsylvania, Florida, Michigan, Indiana, Missouri and California. The apartments were well maintained and were an appealing place for seniors to enjoy independent living and interesting neighbors. There existed a true sense of community." In March AHEPA participated in the events held in Alabama to commemorate the 50th anniversary of the Selma to Montgomery civil rights march. That was the occasion when Greek Orthodox Archbishop Iakovos marched side by side with the Reverend Martin Luther King. AHEPA's delegation was led by Supreme President Frangos.

The Congressional Banquet of 2015

The first major event of AHEPA's annual calendar was the 41st Biennial Congressional Banquet, held in April in Washington, DC. Nearly 400 leaders of the Greek American community from across the United States and Canada were on hand to salute excellence and service in the community. The banquet was preceded by another annual event, also in Washington, DC, established in 2006. AHEPA and its affiliated women's organization, the Daughters of Penelope brought their legislative agendas to the attention of Capitol Hill legislators during Capitol Hill Day. AHEPA family members representing 20 states and the District of Columbia registered for the event. It was the most diverse geographic representation to date for Capitol Hill Day. They discussed issues that included: US–Greece relations; religious freedom for the Ecumenical Patriarchate; ending the 40-year illegal division of Cyprus and safeguarding Cyprus' sovereign right to explore and exploit energy finds within its exclusive economic zone; and ensuring cost-effective, job creating, and lifesaving domestic programs are preserved and maintained in the federal budget. Domestic programs of interest to the AHEPA family that were raised included affordable housing for the elderly, medical research at NIH, and domestic violence. The day's events included a morning reception where the AHEPA family received remarks from Congressman Gus Bilirakis, co-chair of the Hellenic Caucus and Congressional Hellenic-Israel Alliance, and Congresswoman Carolyn Maloney, co-founder and co-chair of the Hellenic Caucus.

At the official banquet its chairman Andrew Zachariades, Supreme Secretary, welcomed the audience. His Eminence Archbishop Demetrios provided the invocation and benediction. The honorees were: US Representative and civil rights icon John Lewis (D-GA), who received the AHEPA Pericles Award, presented by Congressman John Sarbanes; Ambassador Robert W. Peck, ambassador of Canada to the Hellenic Republic, received the AHEPA Aristotle Award, presented by AHEPA Canadian President Ken Matziorinis. The Stavros Niarchos Foundation received the AHEPA Archbishop Iakovos Humanitarian Award, accepted by Ambassador Vassilis Kaskarelis, senior advisor to the Board of Directors and member of the executive Management Team of the Stavros Niarchos Foundation; it was presented by AHEPA National Educational Foundation Secretary George Vorkas. Col. Alan C. Macaulay (USMC ret.) received the Military Medal of Honor, presented by AHEPA Public Policy Chairman Carl Hollister (Maj., US Army, ret). Ambassador Eleni Tsakopoulos Kounalakis received the 2015 Daughters of Penelope Civic Responsibility Award, presented by Daughters of Penelope Grand President Anna-Helene Grossomanides. Past Supreme President Gus James II received the 2015 Lifetime Achievement Award, presented by Supreme President Phillip. Frangos. In their acceptance remarks, the honorees shared their inspirational personal stories of triumph over adversity and reflected upon the importance of public service and community service. In his introduction of Congressman Lewis, Congressman Sarbanes described him as "a hero of our time and of all time." In addition to the Pericles Award, Congressman Lewis was presented with a custom-framed copy of the historic March 26, 1965 issue of LIFE magazine "Memorial at Selma" with Dr. Martin Luther King, Jr. and His Eminence Archbishop Iakovos on the cover. The inscription written on the frame stated in part, "In Commemoration of the Unity of the African American and Greek Communities." The banquet program included a Keynote Address from His Eminence Archbishop Demetrios and Response from Supreme President Phillip Frangos. Ahepan Jim Vlassopoulos, retired deputy fire chief, Washington, DC Fire & EMS Department; and Dianne Katsakis Quebral, corporate social responsibility program manager at Fairfax County, Virginia made a special presentation to support the participation of police officers and firefighters from Greece in the Fairfax 2015 World Police & Fire Games.

In May 2015, during the annual excursion, AHEPA leaders met with Prime Minister Alexis Tsipras in Athens. They had already met him once the previous year when he was still leader of the opposition in the Greek Parliament. Welcoming the delegation, the prime minister asked for the support of the Greeks abroad, underlining their importance particularly when the Greek American community in the United States has the possibility to intervene to a power that can play a decisive role. The delegation also met with the President of the Republic Prokopis Pavlopoulos and Alternate Minister of Tourism Elena Kountoura.

The 93rd Supreme Convention, 2015, San Francisco

AHEPA held its 93rd Supreme Convention on the West Coast, in San Francisco in early July of 2015. It was the fourth time AHEPA was holding its national meeting in San Francisco and the first time since holding its 57th Supreme Convention there, when Nick Smyrnis was reelected Supreme President. Right at the same time as the 93rd Supreme Convention was meeting, the Tsipras government in Athens was holding a referendum on July 5 to decide whether Greece should accept the bailout conditions in the country's government debt crisis proposed jointly by the European Commission, the International Monetary Fund, and the European Central Bank. There were many aspects of the referendum, including the hastiness with which it was announced and its wording, which the European agencies found extremely troubling. Moreover, the European Commission signaled that the referendum question, to which they would recommend a "Yes," from its viewpoint should be understood as whether or not Greece wanted to remain part of Europe and the monetary Eurozone, which included acceptance of receiving conditional bailout help on a set of mutually negotiated and agreed terms. In other words, the referendum was a vote over whether Greece would remain part of the European Union or embark on a course all on its own. Realizing the implications of leaving the European Union, the government decided to continue negotiating with the European agencies and the IMF even though the electorate rejected the bailout conditions by a majority of 61% to 39%. Unfortunately for Greece, the new negotiations resulted in a three-year bailout plan with even harsher conditions than the ones already rejected by the voters. With the government in disarray followed by his U-turn (described in Greek as a somersault, "kolotoumba"), the prime minister called snap elections in September and managed to hold on to power albeit with reduced margins of support.

In San Francisco, the convention had opened with Metropolitan Gerasimos of San Francisco offering the opening prayer and saying that AHEPA was a wonderful organization which promoted family values, on the very eve of the day of the referendum. AHEPA called on the Obama administration to step up its engagement on the issue of the Greek debt crisis. It also encouraged the entire Order to stay sensitive to the needs of the Greek people, who had suffered greatly during this crisis, and to continue with its humanitarian aid whenever possible. It expressed the hope that integrity of the European Union would be maintained, and the statement concluded by noting regardless of the outcome of the referendum held in Greece on July 5, 2015, what was crucial to the Greek American community was that US–Greece relations remain strong and certain and Greece's geostrategic importance and contributions to the security interests of the United States and NATO were valued and appreciated.

Delegates elected John W. Galanis, of Elm Grove, Wisconsin, as Supreme President. Galanis, a 47-year-member of Chapter 43, Milwaukee, Wisconsin, ran unopposed. At the time of his election, the new Supreme President, a founding partner of Galanis, Pollack, Jacobs & Johnson, S.C., a Milwaukee-based law firm, and a graduate of the University of Michigan Law School, had served as president of several community and charitable organizations. "It is an honor and privilege to be elected AHEPA supreme president," Supreme President Galanis said. "My sincere appreciation is given to the convention delegates who placed their support and trust in me to lead this vibrant, venerable, and unique organization in the coming year. I am excited to work with our seasoned Supreme Lodge and our membership to keep AHEPA on the steady path set forth by my predecessors in a spirit true to our mission." He added, "My parents were Greek immigrants, and I'm proud of my heritage and that is why I'm a member of AHEPA." At the installation ceremony, the Supreme President also discussed his goals and challenges. "Obviously, our immediate thoughts and concerns are with the people of Greece during this most difficult and challenging time in Greece's history," he said. "Also, we aim to complete our capital fundraising campaign to help rebuild St. Nicholas and focus our internal efforts on membership growth and retention. In addition, the community continues to face a multitude of challenges that are important to address as the need for community service is never ending, both in the United States and abroad, and the promotion of Hellenic ideals will always be a priority for AHEPA." The other officials elected at the San Francisco convention were: Canadian President Kenneth N. Matziorinis, Supreme Vice President Andrew Zachariades, Supreme Secretary George E. Loucas, Supreme Treasurer Carl Hollister, Supreme Counselor George G. Horiates, Supreme Athletic Director Louis Atsaves, and Sons of Pericles National Advisor Jimmy Kokotas. The eight nine Supreme Governors who were elected were: Demetrios C. Kirkiles, James Stasios, Christopher Gallis, Frank P. Fotis, George L. Kalantzis, Tom Gober, Timothy Joannides, Nick Perdaris and Nicholas C. Papadopoulos. Elected to positions on the Board of Trustees were Nick Aroutzidis and Lee Millas. Michael Papaphotes, was elected to the Board of Auditors.[172]

 At the convention's banquet philanthropist/entrepreneur George Marcus presented Theofanis Economidis, a fellow philanthropist with a distinguished career as an electronics engineer, with the 2015 AHEPA Aristotle Award, representing excellence in his profession and in service to his community. Archbishop Demetrios was the keynote speaker. There was also a commemoration of the Daughters of Penelope's 85th anniversary. The convention featured former US Ambassador to Hungary Eleni Tsakopoulos Kounalakis, the first Greek American woman appointed US ambassador, who presented her book Madam Ambassador: Three Years of Diplomacy, Dinner Parties, and Democracy in Budapest. The Daughters of Penelope had presented the ambassador with its Civic Responsibility Award in April. Archbishop Demetrios offered remarks, and a message from

Prime Minister Tsipras was read by Greece's Consul General in San Franscisco, Dimitrios Xenitellis. As he stated in his acceptance speech, Galanis was planning to focus his efforts on the goals of AHEPA, which were to complete AHEPA'S capital fundraising campaign to help rebuild St. Nicholas, to promote AHEPA's internal efforts to increase and retain AHEPA membership, to address the need for community service in the United States and abroad, and to promote Hellenic ideals, "which will always be a priority for AHEPA."

In October the Supreme President attended the AHEPA European chapter convention in Stuttgart in Germany. The convention involved not only Germany-based members but several others from the 50 chapters that AHEPA had established in Europe, including 30 in Greece and chapters in Belgium, Bulgaria, Cyprus, France, Germany, Romania, and Turkey. After his return he continued focusing on the goals set out at the convention in San Francisco: the rebuilding of St. Nicholas, aiding Greece and Cyprus over the issues they faced, and visiting chapters throughout the country to bolster their growth and the retention of members.[173]

Focusing on the Affairs of the Eastern Mediterranean

In January 2016 AHEPA was among several leading American Hellenic and American Jewish groups that participated in a Leadership Mission to Greece, Cyprus, and Israel. The groups were AHEPA; AHI, the Greek American public policy center and think tank; B'nai B'rith International, a worldwide Jewish community service organization widely known as one of the world's most influential humanitarian, human rights, and advocacy organizations; and the Conference of Presidents of Major American Jewish Organizations, a central coordinating body for American Jewry, representing 52 national Jewish agencies from across the political and religious spectrums. Those groups embarked on their second Leadership Mission, which included stops in Israel, Cyprus, and Greece. The four organizations looked to build upon their historic, initial groundbreaking three-country Leadership Mission that occurred in January 2014. The purpose of the trip was to explore the major political, economic (business and tourism), and security developments underway in the Eastern Mediterranean with high-ranking government officials from each of the three countries and visits to military installations. The joint 12-member delegation also represented broad diaspora support for the trilateral relationship between the three countries.

Another one of AHEPA's earliest activities in 2016 was the Gala held annually to honor outstanding contributors to the community. Those honored that year included entrepreneur and philanthropist and Hellenic Museum of Chicago chairman John Calamos Sr., as well as Rev. Dn. Chris Avramopoulos, philanthropist Eleni Bousis, Northern District of Illinois Judge Honorable Charles P. Korcoras, and US Representative Peter Visclosky (First Congressional District of Indiana). Calamos' father Peter had joined AHEPA in 1928. John received the Aristotle Award for his contributions to the business community over the past 46 years. A few months later, in May, the annual trip to Greece, Cyprus, Turkey, and Jerusalem took place, where AHEPA met with political and religious leaders. As Galanis would note in his report to the Supreme Convention in the summer: "The most eye-opening part of the excursion to Greece was our visit to the island of Lesvos. We had the opportunity to visit two refugee camps. Needless to say the AHEPA was the only Greek American organization (up to that point) who met with the Greek officials… The mayor of Mytilene as well as the fisherman who saved people from the bay and the group of Yiayias (grandmothers) were honored by AHEPA. During our visit we saw the refugees who were in a 'halfway house' type camp which was a peaceful and humanitarian facility. The Moria (the second facility) facility on the other hand was filled with a different kind of refugee."[174]

This was AHEPA's first encounter with the thorny issue of the refugees from the war-torn areas of the Middle East. They had made their way north into Turkey, reached that country's Aegean coast, and then crossed over to the closest Greek islands, Chios, Lesvos, or Samos. They intended Greece to be their gateway to western Europe, but the countries in between closed their borders and the refugees became stranded in Greece. And an international agreement obliged Greece to contain the refugees at the points they had entered the country, pending an examination of their applications to be granted political asylum. Initially the local populations on those islands, especially Lesvos which received the greatest influx, welcomed the refugees. Three elderly ladies (the yiayias) became internationally known for the ways they helped, as did several owners of vessels who saved incoming refugees from drowning. Spyros Galinos, the mayor of Mytilene, the capital of Lesvos, and the other authorities on the island did their best to help the situation. But as the numbers grew and the camps the refugees were housed in became overcrowded, the refugee issue became very complex and required input from specialized agencies such as the United Nations High Commission for Refugees. Over the following years, the numbers would grow and the conditions on the islands would deteriorate. Nonetheless, at the outset of the crisis AHEPA's contribution was recognized and praised by Greek government officials.

In May, Congresswoman Maloney, the co-chair and co-founder of the Congressional Caucus on Hellenic Issues, met with AHEPA, the Daughters of Penelope, and the Sons of Pericles for the AHEPA Family Annual Capitol Hill Day to address US relations with Greece and Cyprus and the efforts to support awarding Greek American and World War II veteran James "Maggie" Megellas with the Medal of Honor. Lt. Col. James "Maggie" Megellas was a 99-year-old decorated World War II veteran who was recommended for the Medal of Honor based on his actions during the January 1945 Battle of the Bulge in Herresbach, Belgium as an officer in the 82nd Airborne Division. Megellas led his platoon in an attack killing over 100 enemy troops and capturing 180 Nazi SS troops without the loss of a single American life. He singlehanded destroyed a German tank armed only with his Thompson submachine gun and two gammon grenades. The records that accompanied "Maggie's" recommendation for the Medal of Honor mistakenly did not cite his individual act of valor, and the documentation was later destroyed in the 1973 Army records fire. Congresswoman Maloney and Hellenic Caucus co-chair Congressman Gus Bilirakis met with Acting Army Secretary Patrick Murphy to request that the Army reopen Megellas' case for the Medal of Honor. In February 2016, Representatives Maloney, Bilirakis, and Sessions wrote a congressional letter to Acting Secretary Murphy asking that this situation be granted another review. Maloney said all were inspired and humbled by Maggie's story that he shared with us during his Capitol Hill visit. They were working to make sure that the

Army sees any new information that would justify another review so that this American hero gets the recognition he so deserved.

The 94th Supreme Convention, 2016, Las Vegas

The delegates at the 94th Supreme Convention that was held in Las Vegas in late July 2016 elected Andrew Zachariades as Supreme President. Continuing the pattern of the elections that was by now firmly established, Zachariades ran unopposed in elections that were held July 28, 2016. In his acceptance speech Zachariades noted: "This is a critical year on many fronts. Elections in the United States will provide us with an opportunity to work with a new administration and Congress in 2017. Greece continues to deal with a gripping economic crisis amid an unprecedented migratory crisis; and in Cyprus, challenging issues such as property, territory and security need to be addressed as settlement talks proceed. In addition, the need for community service around the world is ceaseless and the promotion of Hellenic ideals and our Hellenic heritage will always be priorities for AHEPA. I am excited to work with our seasoned Supreme Lodge and our membership to address these challenges and keep AHEPA on the steady path set forth by my predecessors in a spirit true to our mission." Zachariades, a 25-year-member of Hudson Chapter 108, Jersey City, New Jersey, had served AHEPA in numerous leadership positions including most recently Supreme Vice President and the Fifth District's AHEPA Cancer Research Foundation. At the time of election Zachariades was an executive-level financial accountant and for the previous 15 had served as the CFO and Controller of FBE Limited LLC, a privately held investment firm located on Wall Street in New York City. He had earned an advanced degree in financial accounting from the New York Institute of Finance. The other officials elected to the 2016–2017 Supreme Lodge were: Canadian President Bill Bakalis, a financial advisor from Kitchener, Ontario who was born in Peloponnesos and had emigrated to Canada in 1987; Supreme Vice President George E. Loucas, Supreme Secretary Carl R. Hollister, Supreme Treasurer Jimmy Kokotas, Supreme Counselor George G. Horiates, Supreme Athletic Director Louis Atsaves, and Sons of Pericles National Advisor Sandy Papadopoulos. The nine Supreme Governors who were elected were: Gus Paras, Anthony Drakos, Chris Diamantoukos, Jack Isaac, George L. Kalantzis, Donald Vanover,

Timothy Joannides, George Booras, and Nicholas C. Papadopoulos. Elected to positions on the Board of Trustees were Cos Marandos, who was reelected, and Elias Tsekerides. Craig Clawson was reelected to the Board of Auditors.

About six months later, in an interview with Vicki James Yiannias of the Greek News newspaper, Supreme President Zachariades assessed AHEPA's ongoing projects while on the way to attend President Trump's inauguration in Washington, DC. Zachariades mentioned the perennial issue of how AHEPA could attract a younger demographic as members, saying: "How to draw youth to the organization is a big challenge, as is bringing youth to church. Millennials tend to not like institutions. We are discussing how to address these issues, taking to the next level how to identify the issue and the best way to approach it. We must do this. In 2017 the Board of Trustees will be interviewing Millennials for social media work." On the issue of how AHEPA could assist the Greek and Cypriot governments to attract investments from abroad he was very pragmatic, explaining: "When we were in Greece, we met with the secretaries of PASOK and New Democracy. They expressed their desire for AHEPA to bring new business to Greece. AHEPA can't endorse this until reforms are implemented. From November 16 to 20 we travelled to Brussels to meet with European Union officials about regulations and compliances, and representatives from AHEPA chapters in Europe. In the case of Cyprus, issues such as property, territory and security need to be addressed as settlement talks proceed. First, the Turkish troops have to be removed, then the property of the Greek Cypriots restored." Zachariades made special mention of a huge bequest to AHEPA in the will of Nancy P. Horton, saying he wished to "express our greatest appreciation and gratitude to Nancy P. Horton for the $1.25 million gift to the Charitable Foundation (Order of AHEPA)—the largest cash gift given at one time by a single donor in the organization's 95-year history... an annual donation will be made in her name in support of the AHEPA Hospital in Thessaloniki. As you know, Nancy Horton was a tremendous philhellene who was a philanthropist, author and poet, the daughter of George Horton, the former United States Consul General in Athens and Smyrna at the time of the September 1922 Catastrophe, an eyewitness to the Catastrophe, about which he wrote in his book The Blight of Asia. Nancy Horton's generosity will help to address the dire effects of austerity measures on Greece's public health sector where public hospitals' budgets have been slashed and medical supplies recycled. This bequest attests to the integrity of our organization... people trust us and give us money because they know where it's going." He followed that comment by describing AHEPA's upcoming events, including the Montreal AHEPA Family's annual Saint Valentine's Ball, a highly significant fundraising event for the benefit of various children's causes in Greater Montreal, with that year's beneficiary being the Neo-Natal Intensive Care Unit at Jewish General Hospital and Dr. Apostolos Papageorgiou, Chief of Neonatology, and his dedicated team and their ever-growing needs. This program was in its 17th year and had raised more than $740,000 in support of institutions that included St. Justine's Children's Hospital, the Shriners Children's Hospital, Giant Steps School for Autistic Children, the Jewish General Hospital Neonatal Intensive Care Unit (NICU), the Socrates/Demosthenes Schools, and Summit School. In response to a question about AHEPA's important housing program, Zachariades explained that the US Department of Housing Section 202 Senior Citizens Housing (HUD) had ended and that AHEPA's focus was now to develop assisted living for senior citizens, to support as many assisted living units as possible. AHEPA, he added, had been a leader in providing affordable housing for low-income seniors and disabled persons for over 30 years and had more than 80 senior citizen housing projects completed or in development. At the time AHEPA's National Housing Corporation, founded in 1983, had nearly 4,700 apartments within 95 senior apartment communities, spanning 21 states, with more in development. Other projects Zachariades mentioned were the "Journey to Greece" program, which was started in 2006, and the annual Hellenic History Tournament, which was unique to AHEPA, and promised to draw many young people. The Supreme President ended by returning to the issue of the membership's demographic profile: "I'd like to draw attention to the immediate need to draw Millennials into AHEPA. Since the organization isn't growing, and there is no new immigration, we have to understand how youth thinks, talks, the fact that they want change now, and that they are very democratic individuals... that's what matters. It's already in discussion. We're not waiting. We are being very proactive. We have hired a Communications Director who will handle only this aspect of growing the organization through social media and whatever other means will be explored, to expand the membership of AHEPA, thus its horizons for its success going the into future."[175]

The AHEPA Service Dogs for Warriors Program

The therapeutic application of human–animal interaction has gained interest over the past few decades. One form this interest takes is the use of service dogs as complementary treatment for veterans with Post-Traumatic Stress Disorder (PTSD). There are currently several programs that connect service dogs with veterans and there is a broad consensus about the benefits of this practice, especially among the veterans themselves. At the Supreme Convention in San Diego in 2016, Ahepan and Vietnam veteran George Karatzia, who himself had suffered from PTSD, successfully proposed that AHEPA create its own Service Dogs for Warriors Program. The program has grown steadily since then. Its mission statement states that it aims to match veterans with specially trained service dogs to help mitigate and assist them in their path to recovery and management of their disabilities; as well as provide the veteran with the companionship and therapeutic qualities of a specially trained service dog that was rescued from a dog pound. Beyond the undoubted virtues of this important project lies a much broader symbolism, that of AHEPA's displays of patriotism in honoring of its own and all of America's veterans throughout its history.

The 95th Supreme Convention, 2017, Orlando

AHEPA's schedule in 2017 included participation in a trip to Cyprus by the Conference of Presidents of Major American Jewish Organizations, along with AHI. This was a follow up to the January 2016 AHEPA, AHI, B'nai B'rith International, and Conference of Presidents of Major American Jewish Organizations Leadership Mission to Israel, Cyprus, and Greece, which had first taken place in 2014. The other activities were those that occurred regularly each year: the celebration of Greek Independence at the White House; the Annual Leadership Excursion to Greece, Cyprus, and the Ecumenical Patriarchate; and the public policy visit to Capitol Hill. Most notably, during AHEPA's stay in Athens, Supreme President Zachariades addressed the Greek Parliament, yet another significant recognition of AHEPA's importance on the part of the Greek government.

Carl Hollister of Mason, Ohio was elected AHEPA's Supreme President at the 95th Convention in Orlando, Florida. Hollister ran unopposed in elections, continuing the pattern of recent years. He said the need to provide community service was never ending, both in the United States and abroad. "I am eager to work with the Supreme Lodge, and our membership, to address this challenge, as well as others that may come our way," he said. "Of course, the promotion of Hellenic ideals will always be a priority for AHEPA, and I pledge to keep AHEPA on a steady path set forth by my predecessors with a spirit that is true to our mission." Hollister, of Icarian heritage, was at the time president of L.M. Kohn & Company, an investment advisory and brokerage firm in Cincinnati, Ohio, and a member of Chapter 209, Middletown, Ohio. Prior to his election, he had served as Supreme Secretary and as an executive board member on the AHEPA National Housing Corporation. Hollister was also a retired US Army Major with 21 years of active and reserve service, 17 of which were in Special Operations with tours of duty in Central America and Central Asia. As commander of the Khost Provincial Reconstruction Team, Afghanistan, he was awarded the Bronze Star in 2005 for distinguished achievement. The other officials elected to the Supreme Lodge were Canadian President Christos Argiriou, a businessman based in Winnipeg, Manitoba who was born in Kerkini near Serres in northern Greece; Supreme Vice President George E. Loucas, Supreme Secretary Jimmy Kokotas, Supreme Treasurer George Horiates, Supreme Counselor Demetrios C. Kirkiles, and Sons of Pericles National Advisor Sandy Papadopoulos. The nine Supreme Governors elected were Peter Nassos, Cleon Kordistos, Tom Duchas, Jack Isaac, Craig Theros, Don Vanover, Nick Dixie, George Booras, and Dr. Alfred Barich. Elected to the Executive Committee of the AHEPA Board of Trustees were Chairman Nick Aroutzidis, Vice Chairman Andrew C. Zachariades, and Secretary Cos Marandos.

At the Convention's Grand Banquet AHEPA honored the Minister of Defense of the Hellenic Republic Panos Kammenos and Chick-Fil-A President/COO Timothy P. Tassopoulos. Minister Kammenos, an Ahepan, received the 2017 AHEPA Pericles Award for excellence in public service. In presenting the award, Past Canadian President Nick Aroutzidis cited Minister Kammenos' diligent efforts to enhance relations between the United States and Greece, longtime NATO allies, especially in the areas of defense and security. Tassopoulos, an Ahepan from Chapter 519, Marietta, Georgia, received the 2017 AHEPA Aristotle Award for excellence in one's profession. In presenting the award, Past Supreme President Ike Gulas cited Tassopoulos' professional achievements, his commitment to the community, and appreciation for AHEPA's mission, including philanthropy and service. In accepting Tassopoulos noted that lessons he learned about service and generosity at Chick-Fil-A were also lessons shared by AHEPA. In reflecting about AHEPA's work in the community, he stated the organization's investment in education has "paid off," and he encouraged AHEPA to continue to "pay it forward."

In addition, an "Appreciation Presentation" was made to Walt Disney World Resort President George Kalogridis for the hospitality Walt Disney World afforded the AHEPA family conventioneers during the week. The AHEPA Veterans Committee, chaired by retired Col. Nicholas P. Vamvakias (US Army), made a special presentation of the AHEPA Medal for Military Service to approximately 200 veterans in the audience, which included His Eminence Archbishop Demetrios. Five AHEPA Past Supreme Presidents, each one representing a branch of the US Armed Forces, participated. They were Past Supreme Presidents A. Steve Betzelos, US Air Force; Andrew Banis, US Coast Guard; Franklin R. Manios, US Marine Corps; James S. Scofield, US Navy; and Nick Smyrnis, US Army. Defense Minister Kammenos and Congressman Gus Bilirakis, vice chair of the House Committee on Veterans' Affairs, also participated. Members of the Sons of Pericles and Maids of Athena assisted with the distribution and pinning of the medals upon the recipients.

In the fall of 2017, AHEPA demonstrated its close knowledge and involvement in US-Greek relations when Executive Secretary Basil Mossaidis made public the expectations the Order had from an impending visit of Greece's Prime Minister Tsipras. The statement, which opened with welcoming the visit and what it represented, went on to say that AHEPA expected the prime minister's visit would serve to build upon a sturdy foundation and bolster the US–Greece partnership in key sectors, including defense cooperation and security, energy, and business investment and partnerships. In addition, AHEPA expressed the wish that the Mutual Defense Cooperation Agreement (MDCA), which governs the United States'

Chapter 13: AHEPA Stands by Hellenism & Orthodoxy 2015-2019   337

use of the facilities at NSA Souda Bay, would be renewed on a long term basis. On the topic of Greece's economy, the statement mentioned that AHEPA's expectations were for the prime minister, and his accompanying delegation, to convey confidence that Greece was creating the proper business climate to attract additional foreign direct investment to support Greece's economy and Greek innovation. It was also AHEPA's expectation that the fragility of the EU-Turkey refugee deal be raised. The refugee/migratory crisis that had overwhelmed Greece could quickly escalate at a moment's notice should the deal fail to hold. The United States should continue to provide technical expertise from federal agencies such as the Department of Homeland Security, to help Greece manage the crisis. Finally, the statement reiterated AHEPA's commitment to serving as a bridge that ensures the US-Greece partnership flourishes.

AHEPA and the Macedonian Question

A misunderstanding over whether AHEPA would participate in a rally about the name issue of the Former Yugoslav Republic of Macedonia, scheduled in March in New York City at the UN Headquarters, gave the Order the opportunity to reiterate its support for Greece's demands. AHEPA's statement went as follows: "For almost a century, AHEPA has been at the forefront of championing and helping Greece here in the United States and in Greece. Since our very first official meeting with President Calvin Coolidge in 1923 when the subject of resettlement efforts was discussed to assist Greek refugees who fled Asia Minor—to the most recent humanitarian drives that raised more than $500,000 to feed Greece's needy and helped to deliver $12 million in public health assistance/medical aid to Greece. On the important name-recognition issue for the former Yugoslav Republic of Macedonia (FYROM), it is unfortunate to see misperception in the Greek American community about AHEPA's level of involvement. First, let's be clear: 'Macedonia' has been an integral part of Greece and Greek history for thousands of years. Further, let AHEPA be even more clear to dispel misinformation: AHEPA respects and encourages freedom of speech and people's rights to gather and demonstrate peacefully. AHEPA will be at the March 18 demonstration in New York. Our members will be part of this history. As an organization, AHEPA has discussed this issue with government officials in Greece—where this matter is being currently handled. Most recently, in January, the issue arose in meetings with Prime Minister Alexis Tsipras, President Prokopis Pavlopoulos, and Defense Minister Panos Kammenos. And AHEPA remains engaged. AHEPA will meet with Ambassador of Greece Haris Lalacos at the Greek Embassy in Washington, DC to discuss the matter next Friday. At AHEPA's Capitol Hill Day, the organization includes on its public policy agenda the need for congressional oversight of foreign aid to FYROM—that the aid must not be utilized to promulgate hate propaganda toward Greece or contribute to further provocations against Greece. AHEPA backed legislative language to this effect that passed the House Committee on Foreign Affairs in the 112th Congress. Also, in their meetings with congressional staff, AHEPA members present testimonials from NATO and US administration officials on when it will be acceptable for FYROM to join NATO.

"Moreover, AHEPA has cooperated with Greek American organizations on this matter. Do you know that the only outside organization to receive approval to have its policy resolution posted on the AHEPA website is the Pan-Macedonian Association? It can be found on AHEPA's public policy webpage, where, by the way, there's also access to information about statements made by FYROM government officials about that country's ethnicity. In addition, AHEPA has endorsed the policy statements of the American Hellenic Institute on the name-recognition issue.

"AHEPA is very engaged on this issue. Ultimately, it will be up for the people of Greece to decide via referendum. Recent reports cite a discussion in which AHEPA was accused of not promoting or supporting Hellenic issues, This Is False! AHEPA and members of AHEPA will be attending the rally March 18. AHEPA will be there, and our voice will be heard. AHEPA supports our Macedonia brothers, and we support Greece. Irrespective of the name-recognition issue, for individuals to state AHEPA is 'non-Hellenic' or 'not involved' is absurd, nonsense, and outright false. AHEPA's commitment to our founding principles which project Hellenic ideals, as well as fighting discrimination, bigotry, and hatred, are steadfast and true, today just as they were in 1922. For almost one hundred years AHEPA has not stopped supporting, defending, and promoting Greece, Cyprus and our Hellenic ideals and principles. Our long and dynamic history and track record speaks for itself."

The assertiveness of the statement along with the record of activities it listed was emblematic of AHEPA's deep involvement in the international issues the homeland was facing. As happens in any ethnic community in the United States, there are some who will on occasions make claims that persons or an organization are not fulfilling their responsibilities toward the homeland.

From the International to the Domestic
Two months later AHEPA was demonstrating its commitment to domestic as well as international initiatives when it and its affiliated women's organization, the Daughters of Penelope, brought their public policy priorities to the attention of congressional legislators and their staffs during their annual Capitol Hill Day, May 16, 2018. The AHEPA family's Capitol Hill Day has become an annual event since 2006. "Our mission guides our public policy priorities," Supreme President Hollister noted on this occasion, adding: "As such, we have a diverse set of legislative interests, both foreign and domestic, that reflect our programs and initiatives that serve our mission and community." According to Hollister, AHEPA family members who participated at the organization's annual Capitol Hill Day discussed issues that included: Greece's importance to United States defense and security interests in Europe and the importance of strong US–Greece relations, religious freedom for the Ecumenical Patriarchate, justice for Cyprus and Cyprus' sovereign right to explore for energy reserves, and ensuring cost-effective, job creating, and lifesaving domestic programs are preserved and maintained in the federal budget. Domestic programs of interest to the AHEPA family included: affordable housing for the elderly, medical research at NIH, and domestic violence. In addition, the participants' objective was to help to grow the Congressional Caucus on Hellenic Issues as well as other congressional caucuses of interest.

The 96th Supreme Convention, 2018, Atlantic City
The delegates at the 96th Supreme Convention in Atlantic City elected George E. Loucas, Esq., who ran unopposed as Supreme President. Loucas, a pharmacist and 3rd generation lawyer from Ohio came from an AHEPA legacy of leaders. His grandfather George served

as Supreme President in 1959. Lucas had gained degrees in law and pharmacy prior to becoming a registered pharmacist and was involved in fighting drug overdose death from prescription painkillers. After he expressed his appreciation to the delegates for electing him and the honor and pride he felt, Loucas spoke about AHEPA's overall goals and also more specifically how the Order intended to aid Greece in the aftermath, saying: "I am eager to work with our AHEPA family, and the diaspora, to address this crisis, as well as other challenges that may come our way." He added, "Separately, the promotion of Hellenic ideals will always be a priority for AHEPA, and I pledge to keep AHEPA on a steady path set forth by my predecessors with a spirit that is true to our mission." In addition to Supreme President Loucas, the persons elected to the Executive Committee of the 2018-2019 Supreme Lodge were Canadian President Christos Argiriou, Supreme Vice President James Kokotas, Supreme Secretary George Horiates, Supreme Treasurer George Booras, Supreme Counselor Louis Atsaves, Sons of Pericles National Advisor Sandy Papadopoulos, and Supreme Athletic Director Chris Atsaves. The nine Supreme Governors were: Peter Nassos, George Papaspyrou, George Karatzia, Jack Isaac, Craig Theros, Peter Lekas, Nick Dixie, Wynn Storton, and Phanos Pitiris. Elected to the Executive Committee of the AHEPA Board of Trustees were: Past Supreme President Nicholas Karacostas as Board chairman and Past Supreme President Carl Hollister as Board vice chairman.

At the convention's Grand Banquet two prominent Ahepans who were leaders in the community and within their respective professions were honored with the 2018 AHEPA Hellenism Award. They were Demosthenes Vasiliou, CEO/president, Astra Foods; and Dr. Spiro Spireas, founder, Sigmapharm Laboratories, both from the greater Philadelphia area. The honorees spoke with inspiration about the ideals and meaning of Hellenism and the importance of passing it on to future generations. They also conveyed appreciation for AHEPA, its mission, and its work in the community. John Vasiliou introduced his father, Demosthenes, stating, "My father is the first in line of people who stand up for Greece and Hellenic ideals." John called his father his hero and role model. In acceptance, Demosthenes dedicated the honor to his family, and he conveyed his delight because the award was a recognition of all the great people he had worked with over the years. "AHEPA continues to be, with our church, the leading voice of our Greek American community," Vasiliou said. "It has stood the test of time and has remained true to its ideals and its mission." He added, "We are here today because we believe in those ideals and that mission. We are here because our parents and ancestors believed in those ideals and the mission. They are the ones that reminded us, time after time, that we carry a very special cargo on our shoulders—Hellenism. Never lose it, they said. And make sure you pass it along to your kids. And share and give its fruits to this precious land they were lucky enough to come to and raise our families." Supreme Treasurer George Horiates, Esq., introduced Dr. Spireas. He described the honoree as a prominent member of the Omogenia with immense passion and a self-accomplished entrepreneur. "We are the beneficiaries of your excellence," Horiates said. In acceptance, Dr. Spireas stated the award is "very dear to my heart because it is a Hellenism Award." "The word Hellenism moves me," he said. "It's not Greece exactly; not Greeks exactly. Hellenism is an idea. And idea of enlightenment and civilization; of love toward country and to live and die with freedom… Hellenism is doing the right thing, the philanthropy, without wanting anyone to know… Giving from the heart without wanting anyone to know is a great thing. This is what builds civilizations." Dr. Spireas also noted that AHEPA had achieved a lot in the spirit of Hellenism, and he also spoke admirably about philhellenes and the hard work ethic they had brought to the community.

Archbishop Demetrios offered remarks and conveyed the love and prayers of Ecumenical Patriarch Bartholomew. The Archbishop also noted this was the 19th consecutive year he was joining the AHEPA family at its annual meeting. Congressman Gus Bilirakis, co-chair, Congressional Hellenic Caucus and the Congressional Hellenic Israeli Alliance, spoke about how the community's policy priorities were advancing through Congress. He also spoke of the merits of AHEPA's work with providing service dogs for veterans. "You have saved a veteran's life by giving him a service dog," Bilirakis said, adding: "AHEPA is incredible… $50,000 for wildfires… always there for Hellenes and Philhellenes, and that's what I love about the organization." Also, during the evening, the Pontian Society of Philadelphia entertained the audience with traditional dances.

One of the events of the day-time sessions was a panel on the topic of Turkish irredentism and the Finlandization of the Eastern Mediterranean. It was organized and moderated by Ahepan Lou Katsos, the president of the Eastern Mediterranean Business Culture Alliance, and included Ambassador Karolos Gadis, Former Hellenic Ambassador to Bosnia and Herzegovina and Deputy Ambassador to Ankara and Washington, DC; Alexander Kitroeff, Professor of History at Haverford College and Professor Emeritus; and Marcus Templar, National Security Advisor, Macedonian League, former cryptologic linguist and principal subject matter expert in intelligence. Its topic was the geopolitical situation in the Eastern Mediterranean with a focus on Turkey's policy claims.

Loucas Reflects

In November 2018 Supreme President Loucas was given the opportunity to assess AHEPA's work in an interview.172 It was wide-ranging, as any such interview by an AHEPA Supreme President would be. He spoke about the brotherhood of the fraternity's members and how the fraternity was bult by two brothers "rolling up their sleeves and working on principles founded in philotimo and Hellenism" and how "when Brothers work for the good of the community and charity together over time, they truly get to know one another and become like Brothers beyond an oath. Weddings, koumbari, and the such have been created through these relationships over dozens of years." He spoke about how all Greek American organizations should unite against the adversity of the day and age and that AHEPA was "a vehicle to teach philotimo and Hellenism to our future children and grandchildren," adding: "If AHEPA advertised one half of its good deeds, we'd have twice as many members. Homes for battered women; sandwiches for the homeless; truckloads of milk for children where the water supply contains lead; help to hurricane and fire victims; help to orphanages; dogs for warriors; jobs for vets… this is a but a fraction of by the AHEPA family: Ahepans, Daughters, Sons, and Maids." Loucas also referred to AHEPA's effectiveness in offering assistance in the wake of the wildfires in Mati and elsewhere in Greece, noting: "No other Greek American organization has the vast network of boots on the ground as AHEPA. The fires in Mati serve as an example. We were able to mobilize over 30 chapters in Greece in a blink of an eye to start investigating and helping. What better network to join when one decides it's time to start giving back to the community than AHEPA, where an idea can start locally, move to a district level, and then nationally and internationally."[176]

AHEPA Honors the Outgoing Archbishop and Welcomes the New One
The annual excursion to Greece, Cyprus, and the Ecumenical Patriarchate was unique in many ways. In Cyprus, at a ceremony at the presidential palace, International Coordinating Committee – Justice for Cyprus (PSEKA) President Philip Christopher received

AHEPA's highest honor, the Socrates Award, in the presence of the President of the Republic Nicos Anastasiades. President Anastasiades, AHEPA Supreme President Loucas, and Chairman of the Board Karacostas, presented the highest award of the largest Greek American organization to Philip Christopher "for his fulfillment of the American Dream, for his vision, passion, and determination to see peace, love and justice prevail and reign over a united Cyprus, and for his unwavering support for Hellenism and organizations such as AHEPA." "Philip's relentless passion to see justice for Cyprus is immeasurable," Executive Director Basil Mossaidis said. "He inspires those individuals who also make it their worthy mission to seek justice and peace for Cyprus. As an advocate, Philip has set the benchmark to which all others aspire." He added, "We also are proud to call him a Brother Ahepan. Not just for his advocacy. Philip Christopher embodies and exemplifies why AHEPA was founded nearly 100 years ago. He immigrated to the United States at the age of 10. Through a hard work ethic, and spirit of entrepreneurship, Philip ascended over a 30-year career to become a leader in the wireless industry—as President/CEO and Founder of American Network Solutions and serving on several trade association boards." Anastasiades remarked that Philip Christopher had helped and contributed to the greatest extent possible to the Greek Cypriot community of America and the work that it carried out, working with passion to protect and spread the Greek Christian ideals and to enlighten and promote the Cyprus problem.

From Cyprus the AHEPA delegation went on to Turkey to visit the Ecumenical Patriarchate, and this turned out to be a very special occasion. This was because it coincided with the Ecumenical Patriarchate's announcement of the election of Metropolitan Elpidophoros of Bursa as the new Archbishop of America. "We had the honor and good fortune to congratulate and meet with newly-elected Archbishop of America, His Eminence Metropolitan Elpidophoros of Bursa, soon after the announcement," Supreme President George E. Loucas said. "On our previous annual visits, His Eminence Metropolitan Elpidophoros graciously met with us and took the time to lead us on tours of the Theological School of Halki. We look forward to welcoming him to the United States. Axios!" According to Supreme President Loucas, the delegation took pride in being fortunate to be the first delegation to meet the newly-elected Archbishop. In a private audience with Ecumenical Patriarch Bartholomew, Supreme President Loucas reaffirmed the AHEPA family's unwavering support for the Ecumenical Patriarchate and presented His All-Holiness with a $25,000 joint donation from AHEPA and the AHEPA Canadian Foundation. Loucas added that AHEPA was steadfast in its support for religious freedom and human rights for the Ecumenical Patriarchate and all religious minorities in Turkey and would continue to press for these universal and fundamental rights and for the reopening of the Halki Theological School.

The announcement of Archbishop Demetrios' resignation had occurred only a few days earlier, and AHEPA expressed its gratitude for the prelate's service. AHEPA had enjoyed a close and warm relationship with the Archbishop, and this was evident in the statement which read:

"Since 1922, the Order of AHEPA has forged a strong relationship with the Greek Orthodox Archdiocese of America. This relationship has often been described as embodying 'The Twin Pillars of Hellenism' in America. For the last two decades, with the wisdom and guidance of His Eminence Archbishop Demetrios, AHEPA's relationship with the Archdiocese has grown even stronger. Since the moment of His Eminence's enthronement, he has walked side-by-side, hand-in-hand, with AHEPA family leaders at significant, even historical occasions for the community. His Eminence graciously and warmly received each newly-elected Supreme President for a private audience at the beginning of their respective terms. We cannot recall a major national AHEPA family event that His Eminence has missed—whether it was a Supreme Convention in Puerto Rico or Athens—or a Congressional Banquet in Washington. His Eminence also made it a priority to participate at events hosted by our junior auxiliaries, the Sons of Pericles, and Maids of Athena, investing the time to learn about the activities, projects and programs of our young leaders. His Eminence has provided the AHEPA family with many special moments, including when he accompanied His All-Holiness Ecumenical Patriarch Bartholomew on their historic first-ever visitation to AHEPA Headquarters, in Washington, DC, in November 2009. Or when he humbly revealed to our audience at the 2000 Congressional Banquet, where we honored our veterans, that he too, was a veteran.

We will always cherish these moments. Moreover, we were all proud to see Archbishop Demetrios comforting our fellow citizens of all faiths, races, and backgrounds, helping them to heal from a devastating event in our nation's history on September 11, 2001. He offered prayers and blessed the ground where so many innocent persons lost their lives. The image of His Eminence blessing a soldier amid the rubble, debris, and destruction comes vividly to mind whenever we think of this time. He conducted memorial services and funerals for the victims, and he met with Christian, Jewish, and Muslim leaders at an international conference convened by Ecumenical Patriarch Bartholomew to discuss the impact of September 11. Archbishop Demetrios has our sincere gratitude, appreciation, and love for his 20 years of untiring service to His Flock. He was an erudite Spiritual Leader. Our best wishes are with Archbishop Demetrios as he enters his well-deserved retirement."[177]

It was an end of an era for the Archdiocese and Greek America, and the beginning of a new one. AHEPA too was approaching the end of an epoch as its centenary year drew closer. No one could have guessed that the run up to the centenary would have been complicated by the emergence of a major pandemic a year later. Yet despite that huge obstacle, AHEPA steadily moved forward toward its 100th year.

THE AHEPAN

The Official Publication of the American Hellenic Educational Progressive Association
www.ahepa.org

SUMMER 2022

Centennial of Excellence

CHAPTER 14: AHEPA REACHES ITS CENTENARY

The summer of 2019 felt like a major turning point in the history of AHEPA and of Greek America. AHEPA began planning for its centenary which was two years away. The Greek Orthodox Archdiocese of America had a new leader, Archbishop Elpidophoros. In Greece, the country was emerging from the decade-old economic crisis and the conservative New Democracy party led by Kyriakos Mitsotakis won a resounding victory in the national elections. New ties between the Greek American and Jewish American community were being forged in tandem with the strengthening of the tripartite relations between Cyprus, Greece, and Israel. And in Istanbul, the stature of the Ecumenical Patriarchate continued to grow under the leadership of Patriarch Bartholomew, despite the many obstacles in its way. Some things remained the same—the continued Turkish occupation of the northern part of Cyprus—and an unexpected development would occur globally, the outbreak of the COVID-19 pandemic.

The 97th Supreme Convention, Chicago, 2019

AHEPA held its 97th Supreme Convention in Chicago from July 1–6. It was the fifth time in its history that the Order was meeting in the Windy City, which boasted one of the largest concentrations of Greek Americans in the country. At the grand banquet at the conclusion of the conference, outgoing Supreme President Loucas and Chairman of the Board Karacostas gave Archbishop Elpidophoros the remaining amount of $286,000, that fulfilled AHEPA's pledge to contribute $1 million for the reconstruction of St. Nicholas Shrine at Ground Zero. "Since 1922, AHEPA has stood by the Greek Orthodox Archdiocese of America thus creating the 'Twin Pillars of Hellenism' in America that we see today," Loucas said. "We are deeply grateful to the AHEPA family; to our amazing grassroots network of districts, chapters, and dedicated members, all of whom made this landmark donation a reality." Karacostas added, "We are proud to be the only secular organization to make and fulfill a one-million-dollar donation to this campaign. I echo the sentiments of Supreme President Loucas in conveying our sincere appreciation to all our donors." Additionally, Loucas and Karacostas expressed confidence that St. Nicholas Greek Orthodox Church and National Shrine will be rebuilt and both hoped AHEPA's fulfillment of its pledge would provide the springboard for the additional support the project needed.

Archbishop Elpidophoros conveyed to the Ahepans the greetings and blessings of Ecumenical Patriarch Bartholomew. "You are dearly loved by him as your support for the Church and the Ecumenical Patriarchate, your longstanding witness of philanthropy, your commitment to Hellenic ideals, and your service to those in need exemplify the exhortation of the Apostle Paul: …whatever is true, whatever is honorable, whatever is just, whatever is pure, whatever is lovely, whatever is gracious, if there is any excellence, if there is anything worthy of praise, think about these things (Philippians 4:8)… the AHEPA family affirms that you not only think about these things, but you do these things!" The Archbishop said the AHEPA Supreme Convention was a "blessed opportunity for fellowship in the bonds that we share through our faith, our legacy, and our service. It is also an opportunity to affirm the great potential we have before us… In your service as members of AHEPA and in our service to God as His Church, we know that this love is not limited by distance. This is why I can convey, and you can receive the love and blessings of our spiritual father, His All-Holiness Ecumenical Patriarch Bartholomew. We share this love with our brothers and sisters throughout this nation and around the world. It is the love that unites us in Christ. It is the love that guides and inspires us to address the needs of our youth, the elderly, the orphan and widow, and all who need physical and spiritual healing. It is the love that leads us in gratitude to offer all that we are and have as a witness of our faith and for the glory of God." Archbishop Elpidophoros also mentioned the Independence Day celebrated on July 4, as a celebration of freedom. "It honors the value of this ideal in providing a social and political environment where people can flourish and explore the potential of their God-created, human ability. As heirs of a noble Hellenic heritage that has cherished freedom and as the children of our Greek forbearers who sacrificed for independence, we know the value of freedom. We know that freedom is inseparably connected to the love of our fellow human beings and our love of God. We affirm that we have been called to freedom so that through love we can be servants of one another (Galatians 5:13); and because for freedom Christ has set us free (Galatians 5:1), we are called to use this freedom, as you the AHEPA family do so admirably, so that others may experience this love."

Archbishop Elpidophoros pointed out that in 2022 both the Holy Archdiocese and the AHEPA family would celebrate centennial anniversaries in this nation of freedom and hope. "These anniversary events are certainly times of remembrance. We will reflect on a century of faith and service. We will mark great accomplishments; honor the memory of so many who offered so much and give thanks to God for His many blessings. But we will also affirm that all that has been achieved has been through His love and the love we share. We will recognize that we are the benefactors of a legacy of love that has impacted innumerable lives. As we prepare for these commemorations, we share great joy in knowing that the Holy Archdiocese of America and the AHEPA family have worked together and shared this legacy."

The Archbishop went on to stress that over the past century, the members of AHEPA "have supported the sacred ministry of the Church through the establishment and growth of our parishes, through the support and leadership offered in our national programs and initiatives, and through the unwavering support for our beloved Mother Church, the Ecumenical Patriarchate… The Church has continued to recognize in love and gratitude the vital work of AHEPA in education, philanthropy, civic responsibility and in so many other areas of service, as well as in advancing Hellenic ideals which inspire and enliven our common humanity and enhance our witness of our

Orthodox faith. My hope and prayer is that this relationship will not only continue in the love that we share and that it will bear much fruit, but that it will also become even stronger as we prepare and commit for the work that is before us. Together, we can and will accomplish tremendous things that will reveal our love for God and our love for each other. Through our shared efforts in ministry and service, many more will experience God's transforming love. Together, we will honor the legacy of love that has been given to us by our forbearers, and we will bring honor and glory to God for the great and marvelous works that we will see. May His blessings be upon you and the vital work and service of AHEPA and the AHEPA family."[178]

At the Grand Banquet, as was customary, awards were presented honoring excellence in the community and saluting dedication and service to the Order. Two prominent Ahepans were honored with the highest award AHEPA bestows, the Socrates Award: Michael Psaros, co-founder and managing partner of KPS Capital Partners, LP, which manages a family of private equity funds, and Philip Christopher, president/CEO and founder of American Network Solutions and longtime PSEKA leader—the actual award had already been made in Cyprus. "I am proud to be an Ahepan because of its service to others and to the world," Psaros said in acceptance. "AHEPA is a selfless organization and the impact of AHEPA's 'philanthropia' over decades in our collective community is extraordinary." Psaros was on the Board of Directors of Georgetown University and was Vice Chairman of the Executive Board of Advisors of Georgetown University's McDonough School of Business. Psaros and his spouse created the Michael and Robin Psaros Endowed Chair in Business Administration at Georgetown University's McDonough School of Business in 2013. Christopher also conveyed his pride in being an Ahepan, saying "I have been a proud member of AHEPA for many years and always recognized the dedication and commitment of the organization to Greece, Cyprus, and Hellenism."

Publisher and philanthropist Gregory Pappas received the 2019 Academy of Achievement Award in Hellenism. Pappas, the founder of the news/blog site The Pappas Post and the Greek America Foundation charity, was introduced by Past Supreme President Ike Gulas. In addition, Leonidas Platanias, MD, PhD, director of the Lurie Cancer Center of Northwestern University, received the 2019

Academy of Achievement in Medicine. Lt. General Ilias Leontaris, chief of the Republic of Cyprus National Guard General Staff, was unable to attend to receive the AHEPA Military Medal of Honor and this was conferred at a later date.175

New Jersey lawyer and longtime AHEPA member George Horiates, a member of Chapter 69, Camden, New Jersey, was elected new Supreme President. Horiates, whose family originated from the island of Icaria, was born and raised in Cherry Hill, New Jersey and practiced law in nearby Pennsauken, New Jersey. During his remarks he thanked his family, and he paid tribute to his immigrant parents and especially his maternal grandfather Nicholas, who expressed to him back in 1972 his fear that the Greeks in America would lose their roots and would forget their language and history. "No grandpa! We will never forget our roots and Hellenism," George Horiates said at the banquet, giving a personal note to his call on all Ahepans to "Defend Hellenism." He had served as president of the Hellenic Federation of Greater Philadelphia, the Panicarian Federation, and the parish of St. Thomas in Cherry Hills. The other elected officials were Jimmy Kokotas, Vice President; James Stasios, Supreme Secretary; and Savas Tsivicos, Supreme Treasurer. Christos Argiriou was reelected President of AHEPA Canada, Louis Atsaves, and Chris Atsaves Supreme Athletics Director, and Nick J. Kavadas Sons National Advisor.[180]

Horiates Outlines His Vision

In an interview, Horiates discussed the state of AHEPA, its goals, and his vision as Supreme President. He spoke about how he was inspired by AHEPA, noting: "Two items have special meaning for me: first, the brotherhood and fellowship. The relationships forged around the world with fellow Hellenes and philhellenes are a treasure. Second, how AHEPA is truly woven into the 'fabric of America' and how it has nearly a century of service to the community. To travel and see firsthand the significant amount of volunteerism and community service Ahepans provide on an almost daily basis is what inspires me." On the issues AHEPA faced he said that "the challenges AHEPA faces are not unique to nonprofit, volunteer membership-based service organizations that resemble it—membership recruitment and retention and sustaining revenue streams. However, we are singularly unique in that we have almost 100 years of grassroots throughout the world, stated another way, it is not a replicable model as it would take almost 100 years to develop this amazing global organization that promotes and defends Hellenism."

Horiates also described AHEPA's projects: "Ahepans work on so many worthy initiatives that span the scope of AHEPA's mission. First, let me start by citing an initiative we have just proudly completed with the presentation to Archbishop Elpidophoros of America at our Supreme Convention in July of its $1 million commitment to the Greek Orthodox Archdiocese of America to rebuild Saint Nicholas Greek Orthodox Church and National Shrine at the World Trade Center in New York City. Our members, chapters and districts, in a true act of grassroots activism, fundraised and worked extremely hard to collectively raise the $1 million. It's a testament to AHEPA, and the AHEPA family's grassroots strength. AHEPA continues to address the public health crisis in Greece that was exacerbated during the economic crisis. In addition to getting a 'green light' to proceed with the establishment of a burn unit at Evangelismos Hospital in Athens, over a period of seven years, AHEPA partnered with International Orthodox Christian Charities (IOCC) to secure 10 shipping containers of medical supplies for delivery to as many as nine different hospitals all across Greece. Each shipping container was carrying between $650,000 and $850,000 in medical supplies. Ahepans are contributing in so many other ways—seven "Milk for Flint" drives to help victims of Flint's water crisis, raising tens of thousands of dollars for Thalassemia and cancer research, raising nearly $500,000 to sponsor 30 service dogs for veterans suffering from PTSD; and, of course, AHEPA is a primary source of scholarship awards for students from around the world through our chapters, districts, and national educational foundation."

Referring to AHEPA's work in the sphere of public policy, Horiates said: "America is second to none as the world's leading democratic power. However, the question needs to include all areas worldwide where the American Hellenic ethos, code for Western civilization, is apparent. Greece and Cyprus are the new Eastern front of Western civilization. Broadly, AHEPA works to bring the public policy priorities that impact its mission and programs to the attention of members of Congress. We always ensure opportunities are taken advantage to educate and convey the state of a strong US–Greece strategic partnership, the importance of bolstering US engagement in the Eastern Mediterranean, and all our policy priorities—whether that's through meetings, briefings, or other programs. Right now, it is critical we grow the Congressional Hellenic Caucus, which stands at 109 members, and we need the community's support to grow it. We also are proud of our annual Capitol Hill Day, which has been held annually since 2006. It is important for our community to bring its grassroots presence to the halls of Congress. We must continually build on this program. Additionally, AHEPA empowers its members to lead on an international stage to address issues of security, human rights, etc. Ahepans are problem-solvers, doers. Ahepans don't sit there from the comfort of a Twitter handle and troll foreign governments. Ahepans go and meet and have frank discussions with those with whom we have differences. Because Ahepans truly lead. These reasons and many more are reason enough to be an active, hardworking member of AHEPA."

AHEPA's global dimension was another topic the new Supreme President discussed, noting: "AHEPA has seen significant growth and expansion in Europe, and I believe that is a testament to AHEPA's mission and programs and the hard work of our brothers overseas. I look forward to working with them to fulfill our initiatives that will contribute to the strengthening of US–Greece people-to-people ties and relations as well as projecting our message in Brussels, London, Vienna, Stuttgart, and other major metropolitan cities in Europe. Our brothers in Canada also contribute significantly in leadership positions and to our public health initiatives in Greece. In sum, I foresee working in concert with Ahepans from across the globe to project and protect Hellenic ideals." And in concluding, Horiates spoke about the help AHEPA had offered Greece: "For nearly a century, AHEPA has been the bridge between our nations. Greece is a proud EU nation and invaluable NATO partner, and to its credit, has utilized and leveraged these meaningful relationships on an international stage when needed. However, AHEPA will always stand by Greece's side in times of crisis or great need."[181]

International Initiatives in 2020

In January 2020 AHEPA joined B'nai B'rith International, the American Hellenic Institute, and Conference of Presidents of Major American Jewish Organizations in issuing a statement on the trilateral pipeline agreement between Greece, Israel, and Cyprus. The statement welcomed the "agreement between Greece, Israel, and Cyprus to proceed with the 'EastMed' pipeline. The agreement demonstrates the significant progress the trilateral alliance has achieved in energy cooperation and the three countries' leadership in the region to provide energy security. We also are pleased the three countries are meeting for a seventh summit in Athens and that bilateral meetings also will occur between Israeli Prime Minister Benjamin Netanyahu and Greek Prime Minister Kyriakos Mitsotakis and Cypriot President Nicos Anastasiades, respectively. We anticipate the summit will yield further prospects for advances across a multitude of sectors. We applaud the commitment to fostering peace, security, stability and shared democratic values and ideals, in the region by all parties. We will continue to lend our broad diaspora support and encouragement for advancing the trilateral alliance." This was a continuation of the ongoing cooperation among Greek and Jewish American organizations. In January 2018, the four organizations completed their third Leadership Mission to Israel, Cyprus, and Greece. A fourth mission would occur in January 2020. The groundbreaking inaugural mission to the three countries took place in January 2014 and led to diaspora support for the tripartite, greater understanding between their communities, and the greater recognition of their common values, intents and aspirations. In December 2018, the organizations co-sponsored an international conference held in Jerusalem titled "New Realities in the Eastern Mediterranean."

A few months later with the world facing the spread of the COVID-19 pandemic AHEPA donated $30,000 to Support Public Health in Greece. The funds were earmarked for an Athens-based research center working to support the public health of the people of Greece in response to the coronavirus pandemic. Supreme President Horiates said that the donation to that center, known as the Center for Epidemiology and Outcomes Research (CLEO), would contribute to the development and implementation of a robust on-the-ground training program for healthcare professionals working in the newly established COVID-19 primary care centers and COVID-19-dedicated hospitals in Greece. In addition, AHEPA's donation would back time-sensitive and vital research on the spread of COVID-19 in Greece through data collection and biostatistical analysis performed at CLEO. Dr. Theoklis Zaoutis, a member of Hercules-Spartan Chapter 26, Philadelphia who founded CLEO in 2011, would lead the research. He was also a professor of Pediatrics and Epidemiology at the University of Pennsylvania School of Medicine and was a member of the Division of Infectious Diseases at the Children's Hospital of Philadelphia. He also served in an advisory role at Greece's Ministry of Health where he played an integral part of the ministry's outbreak management team and contributed to the government's response to the coronavirus pandemic. In Horiates' words: "AHEPA is proud to back his research… we were so impressed that Dr. Zaoutis would go to Greece and fill this vital role, he is one in a series of examples of Ahepans who are dedicated professionals, essential service employees, or volunteers worldwide that are working for the public good. This strong desire to help our communities is what drives Ahepans."

AHEPA & Aghia Sophia
Due to the ongoing COVID-19 pandemic AHEPA was forced to cancel the Supreme Convention scheduled for the summer of 2020. It was the first time a Supreme Convention had not been held since World War II, when smaller national conferences were held instead from 1943 to 1945. Before the war, due to the Great Depression AHEPA did not hold a Supreme Convention in 1933. Despite the cancellation of the convention and the pandemic, AHEPA was active in the summer months, especially in response to the conversion of the Aghia Sophia Church in Istanbul into a mosque. AHEPA released a commentary piece authored by Supreme President George G. Horiates titled "In Wake of Hagia Sophia's Status Change, A Need for Action. Let's Start with a Boycott." The proposal included various Made in Turkey imported products and the Turkish Airlines. It was not clear if traveling to Turkey was included in the list. AHEPA included the Ecumenical Patriarchate in Turkey every year in its annual trip to Greece and Cyprus. "The eradication of Turkey's religious and cultural

heritage, especially Christian and Hellenic, is alarming, disgusting, and has escalated with the demise of secular Turkish society and consolidation of Erdogan's power," Horiates wrote. "Hagia Sophia is the latest victim of his tyranny. It is hurtful to see one of the greatest monuments of Christian heritage used as a political ploy in what can only be described as a banana republic-style decision to convert Hagia Sophia to a mosque." Horiates' commentary called for a boycott of Turkish products and provided examples of Turkey's top imports to the United States, including hand-woven rugs and agricultural and animal products. He also renewed the call to press the US Senate to pass legislation that would impose sanctions on Turkey and reminded that the US House of Representatives had passed similar legislation. Further, Horiates noted the Trump administration was able to impose sanctions under current law, the Countering America's Adversaries Through Sanctions Act (CAATSA). AHEPA also organized a small protest outside the Turkish Embassy in Washington, DC.

AHEPA National Housing Corporation Donations
In response to a spate of natural disasters to strike the United States the AHEPA National Housing Corporation (ANHC) announced a $25,000 donation to the AHEPA Emergency Relief Fund at the ANHC's board meeting held September 19, 2020, in Nashville, Tennessee. Speaking at the event, Supreme President Horiates conveyed his appreciation to board members, and its president, Carl R. Hollister, AHEPA Past Supreme President, for the generous donation. Horiates stated AHEPA's affordable housing for the elderly program was the "crown jewel" of AHEPA. He commended the board for ANHC's, and its subsidiary, AHEPA Affordable Housing Management Company's, remarkable response to the COVID-19 pandemic and their care for the nation's most vulnerable elderly population during this critical time. Following the announcement, ANHC President Hollister said: "We all see the admirable job AHEPA is doing to help those in need during this most difficult of years through the AHEPA Cares initiative under Supreme President Horiates' leadership. The motion to make the donation was a unanimous one and one that made sense given the need and AHEPA's ability to go the extra mile to help individuals and families in these devastated areas. We are proud to assist, and we

encourage all chapters, districts and individuals, members and non-members alike, to donate too." In addition, ANHC President Hollister announced donations of $10,000 to each of the Junior Orders, the Sons of Pericles and Maids of Athena.

AHEPA & the Bicentennial of the Greek Revolution of 1821

In the first six months of 2021 AHEPA's Supreme Lodge organized several events to commemorate the bicentennial of the Greek Revolution of 1821, as did many chapters in the United States and abroad. In March AHEPA began the celebration of Greece's Bicentennial with a tribute to the best-known American philhellene, Dr. Samuel Gridley Howe. Howe, a Bostonian, was a Harvard-educated physician who became Surgeon General of the Greek forces. His work in raising monies for the heroic Greeks, tending to civilians and wounded combatants, and providing eyewitness accounts published in American newspapers helped the Greek cause in multiple ways. AHEPA first went to Brown University, the site of the flagpole and base dedicated to Dr. Samuel Gridley Howe, and Supreme President Horiates placed a wreath at its base. The monument was dedicated during the 13th AHEPA Supreme Convention in Providence, Rhode Island in 1935. Newspaper accounts indicate over 3,000 attendees were present at that time. Next was a commemoration with the AHEPA Bay District lodge, saluting and memorializing Dr. Samuel Gridley Howe at his graveside in Boston. AHEPA continued in its campaign celebrating the Greek Bicentennial in Annapolis, Maryland. There was a dual commemoration there, one that honored Constantino Brumidi who was of Greek and Italian descent and whose frescoes adorn the building of the US Capitol including the Rotunda in Washington, DC, and another that honored revolutionary hero John M. Allen, a midshipman of the United States Navy. Allen was one of many American philhellenes that went to Greece to assist the struggle for Greek independence. He served on Greek ships which blocked the port of Souda, Crete and was wounded in 1825 during the siege of Missolonghi while fighting with the Greek fleet.

The third of the major commemorative events took place in March in Astoria, at the Federation of Hellenic Societies of Greater New York's Stathakion Center, where AHEPA paid homage to the American support to the Greek War of Independence. Many fundraisers were made during the war to assist the Greek cause in New York and many other cities. This reenactment was of the Greek Ball of February 27, 1827. The original event had taken place in Manhattan, at the Park Theatre, which no longer stands. Thus, AHEPA took great care to replicate the Park Theatre of the times and many aspects of the evening from newspaper accounts. A large display of the Park Theatre circa 1827 was stationed at the entrance to the Greek Ball reenactment. In fact, the large hall had many displays designed to take the viewer back with historical accuracy. A newspaper display from the US Gazette of 1827 explained: "The ball given last night at the Park Theatre, for the doubly patriotic purpose of honoring the birthday of the great father of this country, and for contributing to the fund which our benevolent citizens are accumulating to alleviate the distresses of the suffering Greeks, and, if possible, to accelerate their march to freedom and independence, was all that could have been anticipated or desired." The company began to assemble a few minutes before eight o'clock, and continued to arrive until eleven, when the number of ladies and gentlemen was about two thousand. To the left and right of the staged reenactment were two large portraits of General Lafayette and George Washington. The Grecian Cross was on display as well, as it was during the evening of the actual event. The Grecian Cross was a symbol of the Greek struggle for years in New York. In September 1823, a huge cross appeared in Brooklyn Heights, raised by citizens at their own expense. It carried the wish, "May the Grecian Cross be planted from village to village and from steeple to steeple until it rests on the Dome of St. Sophia." The production included professional New York Broadway actors and actresses.

The next event took place in the town of Ypsilanti in Michigan. Originally named Woodruff's Grove, the Michigan community changed its name to Ypsilanti in 1829, to honor Dimitrios Ypsilantis, one of the generals of the Greek forces that fought in the revolution of 1821. At AHEPA's 6th Supreme Convention, held in Detroit in 1928, the Order unveiled a marble monument to Dimitrios Ypsilantis, his bust, that was placed on a column in front of the city's landmark water tower. In March 2021 AHEPA returned there to perform a commemorative ceremony that honored American philhellenes. The event was attended by His Eminence Metropolitan Nicholas of Detroit and Ypsilanti Mayor Lois Richardson. Supreme President Horiates spoke on the significance of AHEPA and its role in the alliance between the two nations, noting: "The forefathers of today's AHEPA understood the need to promote and preserve the contributions and sentiments of the American philhellene." He added: "To America, people like Demetri Ypsilanti were revered as defenders of Hellenism. To rename a town in his honor, and to have AHEPA forever memorialize this decision, is truly remarkable. AHEPA is here today in this the Bicentennial year of Greece to historically record and celebrate these stories—of heroism and of your most honorable residents of Ypsilanti of almost 200 years ago, which forever stands as a testament to the contributions of Greece to our culture and the inspiration Greece served during its heroic stance for freedom."

Amid the commemorations of the bicentennial of the Greek revolution, Supreme President Horiates also traveled to Wilmington, Delaware to visit the Odyssey Charter School. The school, created by AHEPA Wilmington Chapter and supported over the years by AHEPA, is a charter school that specializes in immersion techniques for Greek language. The Supreme President presented the administration at Odyssey with a $20,000 gift from AHEPA. Elias Rhigas, President of the Board of Directors, stated: "The school wanted to stay true to its roots of a Hellenistic education. We have seen AHEPA leading the diaspora in celebrating the Greek Bicentennial. We thought what a wonderful expression of gratitude in the Supreme President having come again this year like so many of his predecessors." Elias Pappas, Head of the school, stated: "These monies will go towards the building of a monument base and flagpole carrying the flags of the USA and Greece at the front of the school. A brick array and marble bases will also be created with AHEPA prominently displayed for our future students, parents, and administrators to know that it was AHEPA that assisted not only in the formative years but throughout with its dedication to Hellenism and education." In his remarks Horiates thanked the school and added: "The Greek Bicentennial year and the wind up to our AHEPA Centennial has been a wonderful time as AHEPA has highlighted and categorized its public works." The Supreme President cited AHEPA's first public work in Ypsilanti, its second work dedicated to Dr. Samuel Gridley Howe in Rhode Island, the Sons of Pericles memorial dedicated to the Exodus of Missolonghi in Greece, and AHEPA's support of the Brumidi statue in Annapolis as examples of statues recently highlighted during the Bicentennial. He emphasized that there were many others, and that "adding the Odyssey Charter School to this long and historic list during this Greek Bicentennial year will historically record the work of AHEPA on this campus with hopes for its future."

The 99th Supreme Convention, 2021, Athens

AHEPA took the bold decision to go ahead with its 99th Supreme Convention in Athens, and it turned out to be a historic accomplishment. It was a way to honor the bicentennial of the Greek Revolution and AHEPA's roots. AHEPA was the only diaspora organization that organized such a major event in the homeland. The response by Greece was an unprecedently warm welcome that demonstrated AHEPA had successfully established itself as the bridge between America and Greece. Preparations were especially challenging but the hard work paid off both in terms of the membership's response and that by the Greek authorities, the media, and the people of Greece. Both official convention hotels—the Grand

Bretagne and the affiliated King George next door—were sold out. There were about 500 paid delegates, part of a total of approximately 2,000 people who traveled to Greece. The first Supreme Convention held in Greece since 2008 began on a reverent note as leaders, delegates, and family members gathered at Syntagma Square in front of the Hellenic Parliament for a wreath-laying ceremony before the Tomb of the Unknown Soldier. The next day the business meetings began at the Grande Bretagne Hotel, chaired by Marshall A. Monsell.

There were several major evening events that took place after the convention's business sessions during the day and although it would be hard to single out the most important, perhaps the first among equals would be the reception hosted by Hellenic Republic President Katerina Sakellaropoulou in the grounds of the gardens of the Presidential Mansion. The first in that series of evening events was the AHEPA 99th Anniversary Event at the Greek War Museum. Defense Minister Nikos Panagiotopoulos and Chief of the National Hellenic Defense General Staff General Konstantinos Floros were the honorees, receiving the prestigious Periclean Award,. AHEPA's highest and most prestigious. Surrounded by the hardware of alliance—planes and weapons systems largely supplied by the United States—and the spirit of professionalism and dedication to shared values of Democracy and Freedom of Greece's national security leadership that is at the heart of the US–Greece, the The Greek officials, echoed by US Ambassador to Greece Geoffrey Pyatt, spoke of the remarkable recent strengthening of US–Greece military cooperation. Each emphasized Greece's bold efforts to strengthen its armed forces and the United States' commitment to supporting her in every way.

The next morning, Tuesday, July 27, parallel with general sessions for AHEPA and Daughter of Penelope internal business, there were special presentations on a variety of interesting topics. Dr. Peter Stavrianides, based on his research and Greek American community experience, spoke about "The Evolution of Greek America in the 20th Century and Its Struggle for Survival." Andreas Zapounides spoke about exchange programs, Elias Pappas spoke on the Odyssey Charter Schools, and George Protopapas addressed the delegates about the philanthropic work of the S.O.S Children's Villages. The AHEPA Family Awards Luncheon, which was held Tuesday in the Ballroom of the Grande Bretagne, featured speeches by Greece's

Deputy Foreign Minister for Hellenes Abroad Konstantinos Vlasis and Presidential Commissioner of the Republic of Cyprus Photis Photiou, who were presented the AHEPA Public Service Award. Carl Hollister, Past Supreme President, warmly welcomed the guests and acknowledged the presence of officials of the AHEPA National Housing Corporation (ANHC), who were honored with the AHEPA Excellence in Leadership Award. "The mission of AHEPA National Housing Corporation (ANHC)," according to its website, "is to provide affordable housing for the low-income elderly and disabled persons, and to ensure that they receive the services designed to meet their physical and social needs." Hollister declared the ANHC "the crown jewel of the Order of AHEPA."[182]

On Tuesday evening "Greek Night" was held on the upper-level terrace of the Stavros Niarchos Foundation Cultural Center (SNFCC), on the coast of the Saronic Gulf south of Athens, and hosted by AHEPA Supreme Treasurer Savas Tsivicos, Greece's Ambassador to the United States. Alexandra Papadopoulou accepted the Periclean Award on behalf of Greek Foreign Minister Nikos Dendias, who was unable to attend. But the foreign minister would be present at the important AHEPA Cyprus panel discussion "Trilateral Relations in the Region" later that week. The panel featured Greek Foreign Minister Nikos Dendias, Cyprus Foreign Minister Nikos Christodoulides, representatives of Israel and Jewish American organizations such as the B'nai B'rith and the Conference of Presidents of Major Jewish Organizations, and Cypriot American leader Philip Christopher. All emphasized the importance of the continuous strengthening and deepening of the "Trilateral" relations between Greece, Israel, Cyprus and the strong support of the United States, as well as of people-to-people relations in their respective diasporas.

On the Wednesday, the Cooley's Anemia Foundation meeting spotlighted the steadfast and noble efforts of Ahepans through the years to overcome the disease. This was followed by the athletic awards were held during the luncheon, an event emceed by Past Supreme Counselor Gregory J. Stamos. The inductees included Cypriot tennis star Markos Baghdatis. Also inducted but not present were Olympic weightlifting champion Pyrros Dimas, former NBA player and executive Kurt Rambis, tennis player and coach Stella Sampras Webster (sister of tennis great Pete Sampras), and TV broadcaster

Speros Dedes. Greek Minster of Culture and Sport Lina Mendoni was also honored. The Harry Agganis Hellenic Athlete Award was given to pro football player Ted Karas III, whose uncle Alex Karas was about to be inducted into the NFL Hall of Fame. Also honored was the family of Stylianos Kyriakides, on the 75th anniversary of his winning the Boston Marathon in 1946 against great odds. His daughter Eleni and granddaughter Maria Contos were at the event to accept the honor from Greg Stamos, Chairman of AHEPA's National Athletic Awards. Stamos mentioned that Kyriakides started the race with a handwritten note from Boston businessman and Past Supreme President of AHEPA George Demeter that read "E Tan E Epi Tas," the words said by Spartan mothers to their sons heading off to battle with their shields, told to come home "with it or on it." Demeter had written something on the back and told Kyriakides, who doctors almost forbade him from running, not to read it until he won. Kyriakides passed the defending champion and friend, Johnny Kelley, near the end and turned over the note to see "Nenikikamen." That word—"We are victorious"—was said to have been shouted by Pheidippides when he ran from the plains of Marathon to Athens in 490 BC to declare a Persian invasion had been beaten back. Panagiotis Giannakis received the Lifetime Achievement Award for his role on the Greek National Basketball team that won the 1987 European title, defeating the heavily favored Soviet Union in a thriller. Giannakis praised AHEPA for its public-spiritedness, lamenting that sometimes Greeks "have a voice in their head that tells them try shooting on your own rather than passing it." Khaliah Ali, daughter of boxing and civil rights legend Muhammad Ali, was honored—as was her father—with the AHEPA Humanitarian Award for their social activism. She was accompanied by Greek American and humanitarian advocate Christine Warnke. At the AHEPA Family Awards Luncheon Greece's Deputy Foreign Minister for Hellenes Abroad Konstantinos Vlasis and Presidential Commissioner of the Republic of Cyprus Photis Photiou were presented the AHEPA Public Service Award, which was also received by Secretary for Greeks Abroad and Public Diplomacy Dr. Yannis Chrysoulakis.[183]

 The convention's Grand Banquet was emceed by AHEPA Board chairman Nicholas Karacostas and featured both Greece's

Prime Minister Kyriakos Mitsotakis and the President of Cyprus Nicos Anastasiades. In introducing President Anastasiades, Philip Christopher spoke about the struggle for Justice in Cyprus—which continued with the recent provocations over Varosha—and thanked AHEPA as a reflection of the vital role of the diaspora, words echoed by the President, who in his speech emphasized the importance of the Greece-Cyprus-Israel Trilateral relationship. Antonis Diamataris, Advisor to the Publishers of Ethnikos Kyrix and the National Herald and past Deputy Foreign Minister of Greece with responsibility for Hellenes Abroad, said: "Kyriakos became Prime Minister almost exactly two years ago, on July 8, 2019. When I think of what he has accomplished in those two short years, I am reminded of a story Plutarch tells about the Athenian statesman Themistocles: One day as Themistocles was walking in the agora with friends, they encountered a skillful flute player, and one of his friends challenged Themistocles to play the instrument. Themistocles replied, 'I cannot fiddle but I can make a great state from a little city.' "Now, I have known Kyriakos for many years and while I have marveled at his many accomplishments, I can tell you that playing a musical instrument is not one of them. But, like Themistocles, he can take a beleaguered, disheartened, and disparaged state and turn it into a vibrant, hopeful, and respected nation, a country all Greek Americans and ALL Greeks everywhere can proudly call Patrida."

The Greek prime minister said he had prepared some speech points, but he would speak from the heart and began by thanking AHEPA for all it had done for Hellenism and noted that "AHEPA is always present in the fair struggles of Hellenism. We know we can count on you and you know you can count on us." Then, acknowledging that recent legislation granting expatriates the right to vote from abroad was just a first step, he pledged to continue the work of removing the "still significant restrictions that do not allow many of you to really participate in the political affairs of Greece," and to "simplify your dealings with the Greek state by digitizing government services." Praising the dynamism and contributions of the diaspora in general and especially AHEPA, Mitsotakis reiterated his joy in seeing the brothers and sisters in Greece. Anastasiades and Mitsotakis were presented AHEPA's Socratic Award. Mitsotakis dedicated the award "to our doctors and nurses and to all the employees of the National

Health System" on the front lines of the COVID-19 battles. National Herald reporter Constantine Sirigos, who was present, wrote: "Emcee responsibilities at events attended by presidents and Prime Ministers are not softball games. At the convention's podiums, home runs were hit by Past Supreme President and AHEPA Board Chairman Nicholas Karacostas and Executive Director Basil Mossaidis—both instrumental, along with Greece's Region 25 Governor Konstantinos Varsamis and their teams for the Convention's success—Supreme Counselor Lou Atsaves, and not least among them, Horiates, who also made a moving speech on 'why we are all here' at the Grand Banquet, giving the answer, about the threats faced by Greece, Cyprus, and the United States, 'because we are all in the Cyclopes' cave and we will only get out by working together.'"[184]

One of the concluding evening events of the convention was the "President's Reception" hosted by Past Supreme President Carl Hollister and his wife Cynthia. This was an occasion for honoring US Ambassador to Greece Geoffrey Pyatt and Greek Ambassador to the United States Alexandra Papadopoulou. The honorees took the opportunity to praise and thank each other, and the work of the Order of AHEPA. Hollister presented Ambassadors Pyatt and Papadopoulou with AHEPA's George Marshall and Periclean awards, respectively. Papadopoulou mentioned that her grandmother's sister immigrated to the United States, and remembered her talking about AHEPA. She later learned more through friends and personal experience about the Order's philanthropic and education endeavors and its support for Greece and Cyprus, for which she thanked them.

During his acceptance speech, Pyatt offered warm thanks for himself and on behalf of his wife Mary to Papadopoulou for the latter's moral support and advice when they first arrived in Athens. He went on to say: "I'm deeply honored to receive AHEPA's George C. Marshall Award, named for one of the greatest statesmen in American history. Thank you for this recognition, and for all of your support over the past five years. Strengthening our bilateral ties is a group effort, and I am very proud of our team at the US Embassy in Athens, our Consulate in Thessaloniki, and the State Department's European bureau who share in this honor… This bicentennial is a chance to recall how the flame of democracy that America's founders inherited from ancient Athens, 45 years later, fueled the American philhellenic movement. As our young country shaped its international identity, the American philhellenes argued that if our democratic experiment was to succeed, we had to stand behind the Greeks as they sought to break free from the Ottoman Empire… AHEPA has upheld these shared values for nearly a century, nurturing the bonds between our peoples, standing up for civil rights, and helping the United States and Greece advance our shared goals for peace, stability, and prosperity in this region and beyond… In the tradition of American philhellenic societies, grassroots civic organizations like AHEPA ensure that the flame of democracy born here in Athens 2,500 years ago continues to shine brightly in America, putting our democratic ideas into action… For me, this Marshall award, like the AHEPA-funded statue of Secretary Marshall standing outside my office, symbolizes the ongoing friendship between the United States and Greece. It reaffirms our commitment—from the Greek Revolution until today—to support each other through whatever challenges our democracies may face… Thinking back five years ago to my first meeting with Basil Mossaidis and then Supreme President Andy Zachariades, it's amazing to see how much progress we've made in the US–Greece relationship. Reflecting on President Obama's visit here in 2016, as Andy and I were doing the other day, it is apparent how far Greece, and our bilateral relationship, have come… As I detailed at AHEPA's War Museum event, US–Greece defense and security ties are growing stronger every day, and both our governments, at the highest levels, are committed to increasing the duration and scope of the MDCA to advance our shared security goals… In five years, I have seen Greece transition from being a problem for the European Union—a country where officials worried about the stability of the financial system, or Greece leaving the Eurozone—to an exemplar of vibrant democracy, good governance, and effective pandemic response, a trusted US partner in a challenging region, and a generator of stability, solutions, and shared prosperity… I also want to express my gratitude to AHEPA for its efforts to provide COVID-19 relief to Greece. At the start of the pandemic, Basil was one of the first people who called to ask me what AHEPA could do to help here in Greece… And of course, the AHEPA University General Hospital in Thessaloniki, founded in 1947 with AHEPA's support, became a lifeline for the residents of northern Greece when that region became ground zero for Greece's pandemic last winter."

On the last day of the convention, the delegates elected Jimmy Kokotas of Brooklyn, New York as Supreme President. Kokotas' family has been in the restaurant business for three generations. Within weeks of his election the new Supreme President was at work authorizing the opening of the Emergency Relief Fund in an effort to support the victims of devastating wildfires that struck Greece, including the Athens region, in August. Kokotas ran unopposed, which was the well-established norm in AHEPA thanks to an agreement between the two parties. But in 2021 the position of Supreme Vice President was contested. Lou Katsos, past District 6 Governor in New York, challenged Supreme Counselor Louis Atsaves, an attorney based in Wake Forest, Illinois. While most Ahepans, including the candidates themselves, acknowledged the good qualities of both, Atsaves prevailed, and immediately struck a note of unity and brotherhood while reinforcing the call for elevating the Order's younger members and letting them show the community what they have to offer. The other elected officials were Emmanuel Constas, a restoration services manager based in Toronto as Canadian President; Savas Tsivicos, Supreme Secretary; Emmanuel C. Kaitson, Supreme Treasurer; Demetrios C. Kirkiles, Supreme Counselor; Chris G. Atsaves, Supreme Athletic Director; Nick J. Kavadas, Sons National Advisor. The Supreme Governors who were elected were Kostas G. Sofikitis, James E. Gregorakis, Vassos Chrysanthou, Dalton Respass, Dimitris Papageorgiou, Sam Benjamin, Marshall A. Monsell III, Alexander Mallas, and Yiannis Mitropoulos. Outgoing Supreme President George Horiates was elected vice chairman of the Board of Trustees, Nicholas Karacostas was reelected chairman. With the election complete and the business sessions over, Chairman Karacostas found time to reflect on the huge effort made by many to make the convention in Athens not only happen but also be so successful. He spoke about the deep satisfaction gained by working so hard to give to the community and Hellenism and to all one could to improve people's lives, sentiments that expressed the core motivations of all Ahepans.

That same evening the convention ended with at the AHEPA Family Event at the terrace restaurant of the Acropolis Museum, with the Acropolis as an inspiring backdrop. Honored guests receiving awards expressed their appreciation to Ahepans from all over the world for all they do for their communities, Hellenism, and Greece and Cyprus, and their admiration for their successful convention that was planned and presented during a pandemic. The leaders of AHEPA in turn thanked Greek government officials for their substantial and vital help behind the scenes. The honorees included Athens' Mayor Kostas Bakogiannis; Gianna Angelopoulos- Daskalaki, President of the "Greece 2021" Committee for the celebrations of the Bicentennial; and Harry Theocharis, Minister of Tourism. Adonis Georgiadis, Minister of Development, was invited but could not attend due to illness.

The 99th Supreme Convention in Athens will go down in the history of AHEPA as the most symbolic as well as one of the most successful. It embodied the Order's commitment to defend Hellenism, and underscored its historical trajectory from its beginnings, and its commitment to defend the Greek immigrants and help them Americanize, through to where it stood a century later, calling on Americans of Hellenic descent to help each other, maintain their heritage, and defend their homeland.

The 45th Biennial Congressional Banquet

AHEPA held its 45th Biennial Congressional Banquet in honor of Ecumenical Patriarch Bartholomew, and to mark the commencement of his historic third Apostolic Visit to the United States, in Washington, DC, October 24, 2021. Metropolitan Emmanuel of Chalcedon represented the Patriarch, who felt unwell Sunday morning and was hospitalized overnight for observation. "AHEPA promotes all the values and principles that are the rich legacy of Hellenism—Ancient, Byzantine, and Modern," Metropolitan Emmanuel said during his toast. "And the Holy Archdiocese, as the daughter of the Ecumenical Patriarchate, embodies these values and principles as they have been baptized into Christ through the preaching of the Gospel. For the Omogenia, the Archdiocese and AHEPA are two hands of one body, and we are grateful for their cooperative spirit." In his remarks in honor of Patriarch Bartholomew, Supreme President Kokotas spoke about the effectiveness and meaning of the Ecumenical Patriarch's message of unity, love, and compassion, and he pledged AHEPA could do more to amplify the Ecumenical Patriarch's message. "Tonight, we celebrate the 30-year anniversary of His All-Holiness's election as Ecumenical Patriarch," he said. "Thirty years of service preaching love, unity and compassion to the world." Archbishop Elpidophoros of America received AHEPA's presentation of $100,000 to become a Founding Member of the Ecumenical Patriarch Bartholomew Foundation: For the Sacred See of Saint Andrew. Supreme President Kokotas and Chairman of the Board and Past Supreme President Nicholas Karacostas made the presentation, along with a gift to Metropolitan Emmanuel. Ahepan and prominent businessman Michael Psaros delivered the Keynote Address. Several members of Congress addressed the audience: US Senator Chris Van Hollen (D-MD); Congressman Gus Bilirakis, co-chair of the Congressional Caucus on Hellenic Issues and co-chair of the International Religious Freedom Caucus; Congresswoman Carolyn Maloney, co-founder and co-chair of the Congressional Caucus on Hellenic Issues; Congressman John Sarbanes; and US Rep. Nicole Malliotakis (R-NY). Malliotakis, whose father is from Greece and mother is from Cuba, was elected to the US House of Representatives in 2020 for a New York district that encompasses Staten Island and parts of southern Brooklyn, including Bay Ridge, which has a significant Greek American presence. Daughters of Penelope Grand President Kathy Bizoukas presented a gift to Metropolitan Emmanuel. Mike Emanuel, Fox News chief Washington correspondent, served as the master of ceremonies. Chairman of the Board Karacostas delivered welcome remarks.

AHEPA at 100
AHEPA's 100th year, 2022, began as usual with its presence at the Greek Orthodox Epiphany celebrations in Tarpon Springs, Florida in early January. In April and May an AHEPA delegation made visits to Cyprus, Greece, and Israel, as well as Brussels for meetings with representatives of NATO and the European Union. In addition to AHEPA, leaders from the American Hellenic Institute (AHI), B'nai B'rith International, and the Conference of Presidents of Major American Jewish Organizations, participated on the visit to Cyprus, Greece, and Israel. It was the fifth three-country Leadership

Mission since its landmark inception in 2014. The four participating organizations will build on the work of previous missions, which were widely recognized and praised as contributing to intergroup and international cooperation and friendship. The mission's purpose is to explore the major political, economic, and security developments underway in the Eastern Mediterranean and to advance the interests of the United States in the region.

On May 17, 2022, during an official visit to Washington, DC, the Prime Minister of the Hellenic Republic Kyriakos Mitsotakis presented AHEPA with the Grand Commander of the Order of the Phoenix, the highest honor Greece bestows, at a dinner held in concert with the prime minister's visit to Washington. "It is with an immense sense of awe, weight, and responsibility that I accept the Order of the Phoenix on behalf of the Order of AHEPA because this significant recognition is earned on the blood, sweat, and tears of generations of Hellenes, many of whom immigrated to the United States in search of a better life," Supreme President Jimmy Kokotas said. Supreme President Kokotas conveyed the Order's sincere gratitude to Prime Minister Mitsotakis and asked that he extend AHEPA's appreciation to President of the Hellenic Republic Katerina Sakellaropoulou, and the people of Greece, for the incredible honor bestowed to AHEPA. He also congratulated the prime minister for a successful historic visit to Washington, where the prime minister met with President Joe Biden and Speaker Nancy Pelosi, and delivered remarks to a joint meeting of Congress, a first for Greek premier.[185]

In June, a few weeks before the convention, there was a celebration of AHEPA's centenary in the city where it all started, Atlanta. Mother Lodge Chapter 1 hosted a centennial celebration tribute weekend, June 24–26. Atlanta's "Tribute to AHEPA" events included the dedication of the AHEPA Founding Monument at the Thalia N. Carlos Hellenic Center; a keynote address by Ahepan Tim Tassopoulos, who is president and chief operating officer of Chick-Fil-A; and presentations on early Greeks in America and on AHEPA's eight founding fathers by Stephen Georgeson and Dr. Victor Polizos, respectively. The audience included approximately 75 members of the extended families of AHEPA's founding fathers, including the daughter of a founder, George J. Campbell. Supreme President Kokotas and Daughters of Penelope Grand Vice President Georgette

Boulegeris unveiled the AHEPA Founding Monument and addressed the community. Chairman of the Board Karacostas, Supreme and Grand Lodge officers, and several Past Supreme Presidents attended. Also during the weekend, organizers facilitated visits to the Civil Rights Museum of Atlanta and to AHEPA's "Tribute to Olympism" sculpture in Centennial Olympic Park. The sculpture was dedicated in 1996 to commemorate the Centennial Olympic Games and absorbed shrapnel from the Olympic Park bombing.

The 100th AHEPA Supreme Convention

Attendees of the historic AHEPA Centennial Supreme Convention came from around the world to celebrate AHEPA's Centennial at Coronado Springs at Walt Disney World Resort. Spectacular fireworks, dazzling parades, and favorite upbeat Disney songs and lovable characters made AHEPA's celebration a magical one for conventioneers. Attending to the business of the Order, the AHEPA convention body reelected Jimmy Kokotas, Brooklyn, New York, as Supreme President for the 2022–2023 administrative year. Kokotas would have a seasoned Supreme Lodge serving with him as all but one officer would return. Supreme Vice President Lou Atsaves, Canadian President Emmanuel Constas, Supreme Secretary Savas Tsivicos, Supreme Treasurer Emmanuel Kaitson, and Supreme Athletic Director Chris Atsaves, were reelected. Supreme Counselor Themistocles Frangos was the lone newcomer to the lodge. Also reelected were Supreme Governors Kostas G. Sofikitis, James E. Gregorakis, Vassos R. Chrysanthou, Dalton W. Respass, Dimitris S. Papageorgiou, Sam Benjamin, Marshall A. Monsell III, Alexander Mallas, and Yannis Mitropoulos. Supreme President Kokotas reappointed Nick Kavadas as National Sons Advisor. AHEPA family organizations also held their elections. Georgette Boulegeris was elected Daughters of Penelope Grand President, Ryan Marinos was elected Sons of Pericles Supreme President, and Maria Ana Pantelous was reelected Maids of Athena Grand President.

The AHEPA Centennial Supreme Convention featured several memorable events to celebrate the Order's milestone 100-year anniversary and to honor excellence in the community. Delegates enjoyed a special Greek night dance at a unique venue, the American Dance Hall on the Disney Boardwalk. Conventioneers also enjoyed a unique event hosted by the AHEPA family of Florida, a 1920s-themed murder mystery. The fun continued thanks to the amazing hosts at Disney when AHEPA celebrated its 100th Anniversary at EPCOT's World Showcase Pavilion on July 20. Supreme President Kokotas, then-Grand President of the Daughters Kathy Bizoukas, and Chairman of the Board Karacostas welcomed everyone. They thanked George Kalogridis, president, Segment Development and Enrichment for Disney Parks, Experiences and Products, and his team, for hosting. Kalogridis greeted the conventioneers and congratulated AHEPA on its 100th anniversary. Participants enjoyed a spectacular fireworks display, plenty of food and spirits, and danced the night away at the pavilion. Past Supreme and Past Grand Presidents, Archbishop Elpidophoros of America, and kids and families of all ages snapped Insta-worthy pics with some very special friends—Mickey, Minnie, Donald, and Goofy—at photo stations that celebrated AHEPA's 100th. It was a unique centennial celebration that no one will forget.

There were other events that were part of the convention. The annual Athletic Awards luncheon hosted by the National Athletics Department honored excellence in athletics. They announced 10 scholarship awards to outstanding scholar-athletes and inducted six Greek Americans into the AHEPA Hellenic Athletic Hall of Fame. Former professional football player Tony Pashos, a Hall of Fame inductee, and former professional basketball player Enes Kanter Freedom delivered passionate speeches. Moreover, the AHEPA Marathon Team announced a $5,836 donation to the AHEPA Charitable Foundation, which 100 runners raised with the 100th Anniversary Virtual 5K. The AHEPA National Housing Corporation (ANHC) held its annual board meeting in the lead-up to the convention. The corporation, which would rebrand that year to AHEPA Senior Living, also sponsored the AHEPA Family Awards Brunch on July 20. Then-ANHC President Carl Hollister presented ANHC Board Member Mary Verges, president of Penelope 54 I and II, Inc., with ANHC's Lifetime Achievement Award. Hollister also announced ANHC donations and grants totaling upwards of $440,000 to charities and foundations for the year, including to the AHEPA Cooley Anemia Foundation and several AHEPA family entities. The AHEPA Service Dog for Warriors program also presented on its latest developments to help veterans who suffer from PTSD. The program was on the cusp of eclipsing the $1 million mark in funds raised to sponsor service dogs for 100 veterans. As part of the program's presentation, attendees learned firsthand how a service dog, Oscar, helped save Greek American Manny Koutalides and his family. The National Educational Foundation hosted its International Hellenic History Tournament. Five teams totaling 15 students vied for the coveted "Nikas Cup." Team "Disciples of Delphi" from Upper Darby, Pennsylvania, comprised of all siblings, Yianni, Nikolaos, and Liana Krontiris, came out on top. The Hellenic Cultural Commission hosted two informative panel discussions chaired by Lou Katsos. The first was on the topic of AHEPA's century-long history of service, "Order of AHEPA (1922–2022): A Century of Service to America and Hellenism," and the panelists included Past Supreme President Philip Frangos, who reflected on his experiences when he first joined AHEPA. The second, "Turkish Irredentism and Finlandization in the East Med Revisited," examined the geopolitical developments in Greece's geopolitical neighborhood.

AHEPA's Centennial Grand Banquet, complete with a Disney-inspired 100-year anniversary cake, did not disappoint those expecting something special at the centenary convention. The recipient of the 2022 AHEPA Socrates Award, Panos Panay, chief product officer for Microsoft, delivered an inspirational acceptance speech that visibly moved the audience. "There has been no other recognition in my life or career that has meant more to me," he said. "Not because of the prestigious nature of the organization, the award, or the previous recipients, but because this honor is so close to my heart as a Greek." Panay credited his wife, Mary, and family, especially his parents, for being the foundation upon which he built his life and career. "Both of my parents were born and raised in Cyprus," he said. "The truth is this award belongs to them. I would not be here without them, literally of course, but also because the risks they took and the choices they made gave me opportunities I never would have had otherwise." Like a master storyteller, Panay detailed his father Costa's journey from Cyprus to America. The narrative befitted the centenary celebration. It was a journey reflected in the essence of AHEPA and its image, an organization credited for helping countless Greek immigrants who took the same risks as Costa to pursue and fulfill the American Dream.

The banquet program's guest speakers included Congressman Gus Bilirakis, co-chair of the Congressional Hellenic Caucus, Greece's Minister of National Defense Nikos Panagiotopoulos, and Archbishop Elpidophoros of America. "You should take such great pride in the founding principles of this sacred brotherhood; for you uphold the traditions of what is best in Hellas, and what is best in America," Archbishop Elpidophoros said, adding that it was impossible to list what AHEPA means for the Omogenia in the time allotted. Congressman Bilirakis and Defense Minister Panagiotopoulos shared pride in their AHEPA membership. Ambassador of Greece to the United States Alexandra Papadopoulos, Ambassador of Cyprus to the United States Marios Lysiotis, and Leadership 100 Executive Director Paulette Poulos delivered congratulatory remarks. Ambassador Papadopoulos cited AHEPA's "valuable contributions" as the "brainchild of visionary Greek Americans." Poulos stated the country owed AHEPA a "profound debt of gratitude." Mike Emanuel, Fox News chief Washington correspondent, served as an excellent master of ceremonies for the program.

Special presentations included a commemorative 100-year pinning ceremony for Supreme Presidents in the audience by Executive Director Basil Mossaidis; the AHEPA Lifetime Achievement Award to Past Supreme President Anthony Kouzounis and former Board of Trustees Officer Lee Millas; an Appreciation Award to Grand President Bizoukas; Ahepan of the Year Award to Dimitrios Matthaiou, Chapter HJ-33, Rhodes, Greece; and a commemorative 100-year pin presentation to Disney's George Kalogridis in appreciation of his hospitality. Congresswoman Maloney, co-chair and co-founder of the Congressional Hellenic Caucus, and Democratic Congressman of New Hampshire Chris Pappas, submitted video presentations commemorating AHEPA's centennial anniversary and lauding its works. Special audience guests included former NBA Player and human rights activist Enes Kanter Freedom and NASA John F. Kennedy Space Center Director Dr. Janet E. Petro.[186]

The convention was another symbolic event among AHEPA's many initiatives during its 100th year of existence. In 2022 both AHEPA and the Greek Orthodox Archdiocese celebrated their centenary. It was not a coincidence that the two biggest and oldest Greek American institutions had been created at the same time. It was a moment in which the Greek immigrants were deciding in larger numbers than earlier to remain in the United States and build their future there. AHEPA emerged to protect them from racism and xenophobia and guide them toward becoming Americans, whilst the Archdiocese was formed to coordinate and inspire their spiritual lives. Thanks to the ability of both those institutions to adapt to the changing face of America over 100 years, they stood closer to each other than ever before as they looked forward to their next century. One can only wonder how proud the founders who gathered in Atlanta would have been, had they known the enormous achievements that were generated by their pioneering establishment of the American Hellenic Educational Association in July of 1922.

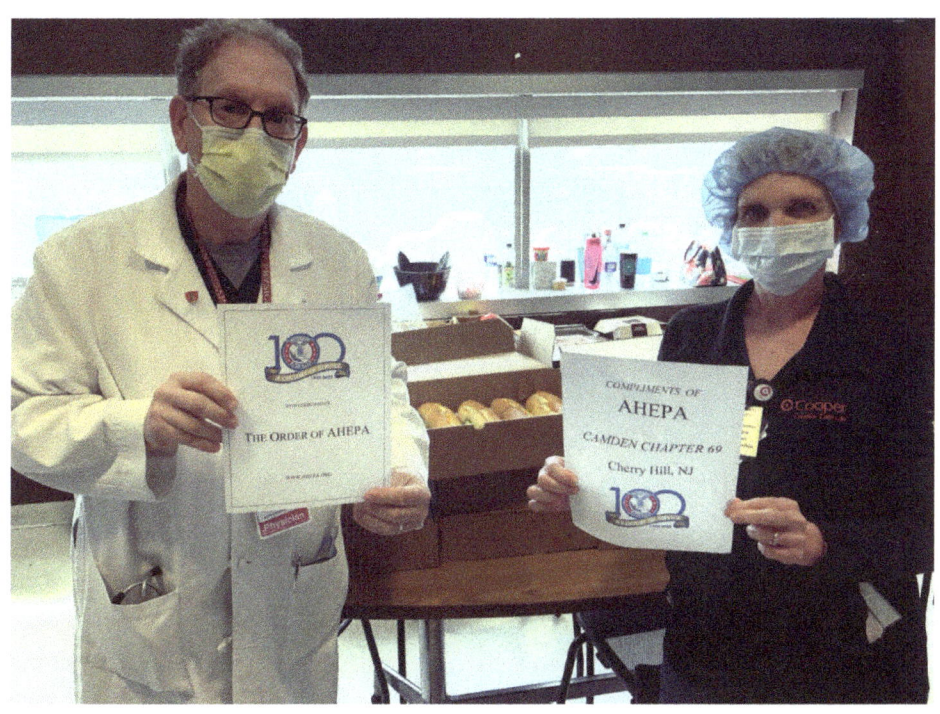

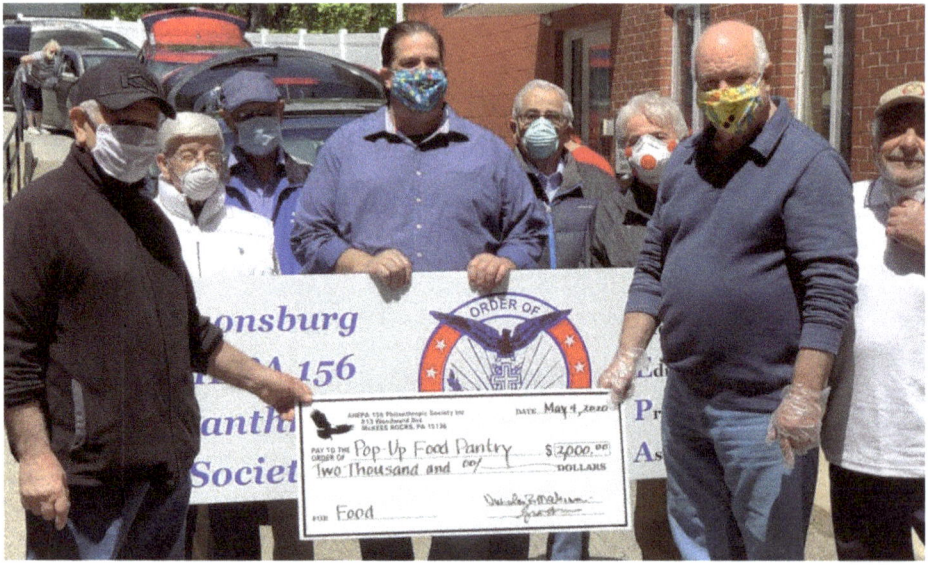

Endnotes

Introduction
1 George J. Leber. The History of the Order of AHEPA 1922-1972. Washington, DC: The Order of AHEPA, 1972.

Chapter 1
2 John Higham, Strangers in the Land: Patterns of American Nativism 1860–1925 (New York: Atheneum, 1963), 2nd edition; Madison Grant, The Passing of the Great Race (New York: Scribner's, 1936), 4th edition.
3 Grace Abbot, "A Study of the Greeks in Chicago," American Journal of Sociology 15 (1909), 373–393.
4 William Joseph Simmons, The Klan Unmasked (Atlanta: Thompson Publishing, 1923), 109, 126, 130.
5 Stephen P. Georgeson, Atlanta Greeks: An Early History (Charleston, SC: The History Press, 2015), Chapter 15, Kindle Edition.
6 Lazar "Larry" Odzak, "Demetrios is now Jimmy": Greek Immigrants in the Southern United States (Durham, NC: Monograph Publishers, 2006), 94.
7 Philip N. Racine, "The Ku Klux Klan, Anti-Catholicism, and Atlanta's Board of Education, 1916–1927," The Georgia Historical Quarterly 57, no. 1 (Spring 1973), 63–75.
8 Leber, The History..., 152–153.
9 Leber, The History..., 152.
10 "Atlanta Attorney is Honored Guest of Order of Ahepa he Helped Found," Atlanta Constitution, August 3, 1938.
11 Peter N. Mantzoros, AHEPA and I Across the Years (Glenview, IL: Pnyx, 1966), 9–11.
12 "Mr and Mrs Chotas Go on Honeymoon," Atlanta Constitution, September 19, 1922.
13 "New Organization Celebrates Greek Independence Day," Atlanta Constitution, April 12, 1923.
14 Mantzoros, AHEPA and I, 70.
15 Personal communication from Peter Senopoulos and Nick Tsiotos.
16 Leber, The History..., 173–174.
17 Alexander Kitroeff, The Greek Orthodox Church in America: A Modern History (Ithaca: Northern Illinois University Press, 2020), 49–57.

18 Odzak, "Demetrios is now Jimmy", 119; "324 Lawyers 20 Are Women Admitted to Washington Bar," Evening Star October 9, 1922; "$75 Given to Legion by Greek Veterans," Evening Star, May 28, 1923; "Private Dilboy's Rites Here Today," Evening Star, November 11, 1923.
19 "An Admirable Organization," St. Louis Star, June 23, 1925; "Greek Lodge Head Visits Local Body," Intelligencer Journal, March 17, 1927.
20 Leber, The History…, 182-183.
21 Carl Abbot, Stephen J. Leonard, and Thomas J. Noel, Colorado: A History of the Centennial State, 5th edition (Denver: University Press of Colorado, 2013), 276.
22 David R. Roediger, Working towards Whiteness: How America's Immigrants Became White (New York: Basic Books, 2005), 172.
23 "AHEPA Association to Meet Tonight," The Montgomery Advertiser, July 8, 1925.
24 "Homer Club Dinner," The Morning News, March 27, 1926.
25 "Assimilation is Need of Greeks," Charlotte Observer, August 25, 1925.
26 "Greeks Unite in National Civic Order," Press and Sun-Bulletin, October 29, 1925.
27 Theodore Saloutos, The Greeks in the United States (Cambridge: Harvard University Press, 1964), 252-253.
28 V. I. Chebithes, ed., "Quintessence of Hellenic Contributions," The AHEPA Pre-Convocation Number, August 1926, 11-12.
29 Yiorgos Anagnostou, "Forget the Past, Remember the Ancestors! Modernity, 'Whiteness,' American Hellenism, and the Politics of Memory in Early Greek America," Journal of Modern Greek Studies 22 (2004), 22-71.
30 "Greeks Unite in National Civic Order," Press and Sun-Bulletin, October 29, 1925; "Buffalo Greeks Organize Order of AHEPA Chapter," The Buffalo Times, August 8, 1926; Leber, The History…, 198; "Walker to Address Greek Order," New York Times, May 15, 1927.
31 Leber, The History…, 213-214.
32 "Greeks Unveil Statue of Ypsilanti Today," Detroit Free Press, August 28, 1928.
33 The Windsor Star, February 12, 1930.
34 "More than 200 Attend Annual Banquet of Order of the Ahepa Served in Arlington Hotel," Press and Sun Bulletin, November 16, 1928; "Better Citizenship Object of Association of Greeks," The Gazette, April 21, 1929; "President of Ahepa Visits," The Evening Journal, July 29, 1929.
35 Leber, The History…, 229-230.

Chapter 2

36 Guglielmo, Thomas A., and Earl Lewis, "Changing Racial Meanings: Race and Ethnicity in the United States, 1930-1964," in Race and Ethnicity in America, ed. Ronald H. Bayor (New York: Columbia University Press, 2003), 167-192.

37 "Buffalo Greeks Organize Order of Ahepa Chapter," The Buffalo Times, August 8, 1926; "George E. Phillies Dead at 85; Greek American Affairs Expert," New York Times Nov. 30, 1971.

38 "Kalos Ilthate" [Welcome], Akropolis, April 3, 1930.

39 Kitroeff, The Greek Orthodox Church, 51-61.

40 "Greek Orthodox Church Official Lauds Akronites," The Akron Beacon Journal, November 17, 1930.

41 "Dilboy's Memory Honored by Somerville and AHEPA," The Boston Globe, August 26, 1930.

42 Frank E. Hagan, "World War Yarns," The Brockway Record, September 25, 1931.

43 Leonidas V. Georgiou, Conversations with FDR at His AHEPA Initiation (New York: Knollwood Press, 2019).

44 "Jack Dempsey to Referee Benefit Card for AHEPA Sanatorium," The Albuquerque Tribune, October 12, 1936; Nikolaos Vavoudis, "To Axepikon Sanatorion en Albuquerque, N. M." [The Ahepan Sanatorium in N. M.], Miniaios Eikonographimenos Ethnikos Kyrix, December 1936.

45 Alexander Kitroeff, "Greek-American Ethnicity, 1919-1939," in To Hellenikon: Studies in Honor of Speros Vryonis, Jr., ed. Jelisaveta Stanojevich Allen et al. (New York: Caratzas, 1993), Vol. II, 353-371.

46 "Ahepa Group Eyes Grecian Situation," Spokane Chronicle, August 13, 1940.

Chapter 3

47 "Ahepas for Draft Plan," The News Tribune Tacoma, August 16, 1940.

48 "Van Nomikos Named Head of Hellenic Association," Chicago Tribune, August 19, 1940.

49 Alexandros Kyrou, "Greek Nationalism and Diaspora Politics in America, 1940-1945" (PhD diss., Indiana University, 1993); Louisa Karapidaki, ed., The Hour of Greece: Americans Respond to October 28, 1940 (Athens: Hellenic American Union, 2019).

50 Washington Times Herald, January 24, 1941; Tampa Bay Times, February 6, 1941.
51 Elias Vlanton, "Documents: The O.S.S. and Greek-Americans," Journal of the Hellenic Diaspora 9, no. 1 (1982): 45–47.
52 "Mayor of Athens is at Center of Storm at Ahepa Confab," The Cincinnati Enquirer, August 19, 1941; "Readers' Forum," The Ahepan 16, no. 1 (January–February 1942).
53 Ralph McGill, "One Word More," The Atlanta Constitution, September 15, 1942.
54 "Ahepa Leader Again Pledges War Support," The Atlanta Constitution, September 21, 1942.
55 Georgiou, Conversations with FDR.
56 Georgiou, Conversations with FDR.
57 V. I. Chebithes, The Order of AHEPA Under Dictatorship (Washington, DC, 1943[?]).

Chapter 4

58 The Ahepan 21, no. 4 (July–August 1947).
59 Peter A. Zervakis, "The Greek Lobby and the Re-emergence of anti-Communism in the United States after WWII," in Enemy Images in American History, ed. Ragnhild Fiebig-von Hase and Ursula Lehmkuhl (Oxford: Berghahn Books, 1997), 301–336.
60 "Bostonian to Lead First Coalition Administration," The Baltimore Sun, August 31, 1946.
61 Ioardanis Vlachopoulos, Ena Nosokomeio apo Allo Kosmo [A Hospital from Another World] (Chrysoupolis: Nestos Municipality, 2022).
62 "AHEPA Memorandum," in Hearings Before Subcommittee No. 1 of the Committee of the Judiciary House of Representatives on H.R. 1344, March 1949, 197–201.
63 Bella Kelly, "The Greeks Have a Word for It," Miami Sunday News, August 14, 1949.
64 "John G. Thevos Feted at Dinner," The News (Patterson, New Jersey), October 3, 1949.
65 Leber, The History..., 438.
66 Leber, The History..., 377–378.
67 "George Cazana, Veteran Sports Promoter," The Knoxville News Sentinel, December 4, 1978.
68 Leber, The History..., 385–386.

69 "Capital Leader, Restauranteur, Civic Leader," The Sacramento Bee, December 12, 1979.
70 Nick Tsiotos and Andy Dabilis, Harry Agganis the Golden Greek: An All American Story (Boston: Hellenic College Press, 1995).
71 "The Order of Ahepa," San Francisco Examiner, August 12, 1955.
72 "E Hellas Tha Symmetasxei Episimos Eis tin Pangosmion Ekthesi Tou Sikagou" [Greece will participate in the World's Fair in Chicago], Ethnikos Kyrix, May 13, 1934.

Chapter 5

73 "Cyprus Issue Looms at Greek Convention," St. Louis Globe-Democrat, August 19, 1957.
74 "Jim Verinis – Co-Pilot," Memphis Belle, https://memphisbelle.com/jim-verinis-co-pilot/.
75 Personal communication from James Verinis.
76 "Ahepa Delegates Enjoy a Suffolk Downs Barbecue," Boston Globe, August 19, 1958.
77 Jack Roth, "Scopas Arrested in Sale of Babies," New York Times, May 5, 1959.
78 Gonda Van Steen, Adoption, Memory and Cold War Greece: Kid pro Quo? (Ann Arbor: University of Michigan Press, 2019); Gonda Van Steen, "Of Foundlings and 'Lostlings': When the Scopas Scandal Rocked the Unstable Foundations of the First 1950s Intercountry Adoptions," Annales de démographie historique, special issue on the history of adoption, "Formes adoptives (XVIe-XXe siècles)," 141, no. 1 (January 2021): 123–155.
79 Alexander Kitroeff, "Greece's Forgotten Cold War Orphans and America's Responsibility," Pappas Post, May 5, 2021.
80 "Hellenic Group Honors Scientist, Mayor of S.F.," Los Angeles Times, August 20, 1958.
81 20,000 Expected at AHEPA Meet," Montreal Gazette, August 11, 1960; "Welcome Greetings Received," Montreal Gazette, August 15, 1960.
82 "Freedom Ideals Challenged," Montreal Gazette, August 18, 1960.
83 "Role of Greece Applauded by Goldwater," Chicago Tribune, August 23, 1962.

Chapter 6

84 https://ahepa.org/archive/ and https://ahepahistory.org/AHEPA-Awards/AHEPA-Socratic-Award-Socrates-Award.html.
85 "Leader in Greece Praised," Minneapolis Star, August 22, 1969.
86 AHEPA Resolution, "Military Aid to Greece," August 20, 1971.

87 https://ahepa.org/wp-content/uploads/2020/04/Harry-Agganis-Award-Winners.pdf.
88 "Rogers Vows No Pressure," Atlanta Constitution, August 25, 1972.
89 Letter by George Vournas to the Delegates of the AHEPA Convention in Atlanta in 1972, Theodore Saloutos Papers Box 49, University of Minnesota Archives.
90 Greek Orthodox Archdiocese of North and South America, 1973 Yearbook, 12.

Chapter 7
91 Orestis E. Vidalis, Confronting the Greek Dictatorship in the U.S. (New York: Pella, 2009), 231–241.
92 Vidalis, Confronting the Greek Dictatorship, 294–298; George Anthan, "Exiled Greek King to Give Talk in U.S.," The Des Moines Register, August 2, 1973.
93 "Goodwill to U.S. Fading Says AHEPA Leader," Boston Globe, August 15, 1974.
94 William G. Chirgotis, "Humanitarian Mission to Cyprus Special Report," The Ahepan 49, no. 5 (November 1974): S-1–22.
95 "AHEPA & Cyprus," The Ahepan 49, no. 5 (November 1974): 3.
96 Mary Russel, "Turkey Aid Terms A Victory for Greek-Americans," Washington Post, October 25, 1974.
97 William G. Chirgotis, "Special Report: AHEPA's Save-A-Heart Program," Ahepan Vol. 50 no. 3 May-June-July-August 1975.
98 Peter N. Derzis, "Final Closing AHEPA Florida Property," and William G. Chirgotis, "The AHEPA Florida Property," The Ahepan 50, no. 3 (May-June-July-August 1975): 27–31.
99 Gary Grace, "Greek Week in Cincinnati – Politics, Dances, Fun," Cincinnati Post, August 23, 1975.
100 "Ahepa Elects Chirgotis," Cincinnati Post, August 25, 1975.
101 Memorandum from Stuart S. Janney and Paul L. Ahern of the Office of the Deputy Under Secretary of State for Management to the Deputy Under Secretary of State for Management (Eagleburger) Washington, July 21, 1976, in Foreign Relations of the United States, 1969–1976, Vol. XXXVIII, Part 1, Foundations of Foreign Policy, 1973–1976, https://history.state.gov/historicaldocuments/frus1969-76v38p1.
102 AHEPA Yearbook 1976, 13–14.
103 Chris P. Ioannides, Realpolitik in the Eastern Mediterranean: From Kissinger and the Cyprus Crisis to Carter and the Lifting of the Turkish Arms Embargo (New York: Pella Publishing, 2001), 150–152.
104 Ioannides, Realpolitik in the Eastern Mediterranean, 347–352.

105 Weisman, Stephen R. "Olympians, Welcomed by Carter, Offer Petition Opposing the Boycott," The New York Times, February 26, 1980.
106 Kathleen van Nuys, "Hoosiers Participate in Olympic Ceremony," The Indianapolis News, February 11, 1980.

Chapter 8

107 Department of State Bulletin, April 1985, "Address before the American Hellenic Educational Progressive Association (AHEPA) on February 8, 1985."
108 Van Coufoudakis, "Greek Americans for Reagan Bush," Nea Yorki 33, no 384 (September 1980): 24–25.
109 "Report of the Supreme President Gus Coffinas," AHEPA 1982 Yearbook.
110 98th U.S. Congress Hearings and Markup Before the Subcommittee on Europe and the Middle East, Feb. – April 1983.
111 "AHEPA Acts Swiftly to Oppose Succession," Nea Yorki 37, no. 421 (January 1, 1984).
112 "Bob Hope Receives the Socratic Award," Nea Yorki 37, no. 428 (April 15, 1984).
113 "Report of Steve A. Manta, Supreme Governor," AHEPA 1985 Yearbook, 51.
114 "Report of Cleo N. Zambetis, Supreme President," AHEPA 1985 Yearbook, 3–9.
115 "Playing With Fire in Greece," Editorial, New York Times, March 14 1985; Shirley Christian, "Papandreou's Path Divides Greek Americans," New York Times, April 30, 1985.
116 "Plumides: Cyprus Aid Cuts Send Negative Signal," Nea Yorki 39, no. 463 (September 1986).
117 Henry Kamm, "Athens Said to Agree to Put Truman Statue Back," New York Times, January 15, 1987.

Chapter 9

118 "Yatron Speech at AHEPA Convention," The Greek American, August 29, 1987.
119 George T. Douris, "What is in Store for AHEPA?," NEA YORKH, June 1987 9.
120 Rita Beamish, "Democratic Hopeful Dukakis Capitalizes on Greek Heritage," The Associated Press, September 7, 1987.
121 The 29th Congressional Banquet," NEA YORKH (May 1988), 21–22.
122 James S. Scofield, 'Dukakis Bolsters the American Dream," St. Petersburg Times, July 26, 1988.
123 Ethnikos Kyrix, August 30, 1988.
124 Michael Kinsley, "The Book of Pander: A Tour of the Republican Platform," Washington Post, August 25, 1988.

125 Bernard Weintraub, "Campaign Trail Common Heritage Isn't Always Enough," New York Times, October 24, 1988.
126 Jim Scofield, "Champion Personifies Enduring Immigrant Virtues," St. Petersburg Times, September 21, 1990.
127 1991 AHEPA Yearbook, 27.

Chapter 10

128 Marina Frangos and Othon Anastasakis, "The World Council of Hellenes Abroad (SAE): From Great Expectations to Disillusionment and Crisis Irrelevance," in Disapora Engagement in Times of Severe Crisis: Greece & Beyond, ed. Othon Anastasakis, Manolis Pratsinakis, Foteini Kalantzi, and Antonis Kamaras (Cham, Switzerland: Palgrave Macmillan, 2022), 181–196.
129 "New Officers for the Order of AHEPA," Greek American Review 45, no. 544 (September 1992).
130 Constantine W. Gekas, "Report of the Executive Director," 1993 AHEPA Yearbook.
131 Theodoros Kalmoukos, "Vathy Nysteri stin AHEPA Yposxetai o Makris" [Macris Promises a Deep Scalpel for AHEPA], Ethnikos Kyrix, August 26–27, 1995.
132 AHEPA Centennial Foundation, Tribute (Atlanta, 1998), 55.
133 Personal communication from Bill Marianes.
134 Sam Nakis, "It's Time to Step Back and Take a Step Forward," The Ahepan (Summer 1997).
135 Paul Sarbanes, "The 75th Anniversary of the Order of AHEPA," Congressional record Senate S11892, November 1997.
136 Colin Campbell, "Greek Survival Southern Style," The Atlanta Journal-Constitution, August 7, 1997.
137 "Resolutions, AHEPA Unity," The Ahepan (Fall 1998).
138 A. Jack Georgalas, "High Expectations," The Ahepan (Fall 1998).

Chapter 11

139 Constantine N. Kolitsas, "Candidates Gear Up for AHEPA Elections," The Greek American, July 21, 2000.
140 "Nea Igesia stin AHEPA" [New leadership at AHEPA], Ethnikos Kyrix, July 30, 2001.
141 Greek-American Review 52, no. 647 (October 31, 2001): 7.
142 "A. Jack Georgalas Is New AHEPA President," Hellenic Times, September 4, 2003.

143 Revekka Papadopoulou, "AHEPA Banquet," Hellenic Times, March 18, 2004.
144 "Gus J. James Elected AHEPA President," Hellenic Times, August 5, 2005.
145 "The Odyssey Begins...," Greek News, June 19, 2006.
146 Ihosvani Rodriguez, "Greek-Americans Fraternize in Hollywood," South Florida Sun Sentinel, July 28, 2006.
147 "James Stavridis: A Greek-American Admiral Named NATO's Top Commander," Greek News, March 23, 2009.
148 Evan C. Lambrou, "AHEPA's Accomplishments Over the Past Two Years," National Herald, August 4, 2007.
149 Theodoros Kalmoukos, "AHEPA's CEO Shares his Outlook," National Herald, July 21, 2007.
150 https://ahepa.org/programs/halloffame/.
151 Hellenic Times, November 20–December 31, 2009.

Chapter 12

152 Hellenic Times, November 20–December 31, 2009.
153 "Greece Included in the Visa Program," Greek News, March 15, 2010.
154 Penelope Poulou, "Greeks in America React to Greek Financial Crisis," Voice of America News, May 10, 2010.
155 Beverly Gerolymatos, "A Week to Remember: AHEPA's 88th Supreme Convention in Montreal," National Herald, August 7, 2010.
156 "Nicholas A. Karacostas Re-Elected AHEPA President," Hellenic Times, June 25, 2010.
157 Constantine S. Sirigos, "AHEPA Hosts Ground-breaking Conference on Greece-Israel Relations," National Herald, October 16, 2010.
158 Constantine S. Sirigos "Karacostas Says The AHEPA Will Stay Young," National Herald, January 29, 2011.
159 Angelike Contis, "AHEPA: Rebuild St. Nicholas Now!," National Herald, July 2, 2011.
160 Antonis Diamataris, "Praktorika: E AHEPA sozei tin timi mas," [Praktorika column: AHEPA Saves our Honor] Ethnikos Kyrix, September 12, 2011.
161 Constantine S. Sirigos, "Tradition & Innovation at AHEPA – Interview With Grossomanides," National Herald, September 24, 2011.
162 Basil N. Mossaidis, "Will Greek-Americans Come to Greece's Rescue?," National Herald, March 3, 2012.
163 Vasilios Koutsilas and Gianni Sofianos, "AHEPA Arrives to Help Greeks in Need," National Herald, April 7, 2012.

164 Alexander Kitroeff, "The Greek Americans and the Greek Economic Crisis in Historical Perspective," in Disapora Engagement in Times of Severe Crisis: Greece & Beyond, ed. Othon Anastasakis, Manolis Pratsinakis, Foteini Kalantzi, and Antonis Kamaras (Cham, Switzerland: Palgrave Macmillan, 2022), 197–219.
165 "AHEPA Celebrates its 90th Anniversary in Vegas," National Herald, August 4, 2012.
166 Yiannis Sofianos, "AHEPA Members. From US / Canada Visit in Athens With Greek Government," National Herald, April 13, 2013.
167 "In DC, AHEPA Makes Greeks' Issues Known," National Herald, June 1, 2013.
168 Constantine S. Sirigos, "AHEPA's 91st Annual Supreme Convention Shines in Florida Sun," National Herald, August 31, 2013.
169 Constantina Michalos, "Supreme Philanthropy: Interview with AHEPA President Anthony Kouzounis," National Herald, November 30, 2013.
170 Andrew Kaffes, "American Hellenic, American Jewish Groups Hail Historic Three-Country Mission," The Ahepan 87, no. 1 (Spring 2014).

Chapter 13
171 "AHEPA Congratulates New Prime Minister," Greek News, February 2, 2015.
172 Constantine S. Sirigos, "AHEPA Hold its 93rd Convention," National Herald, July 11–17, 2015.
173 Vicki James Yiannias, "John W. Galanis and the Upward Path of AHEPA," Greek News, November 15, 2015.
174 "Report of the Supreme President John W. Galanis," 94th Annual AHEPA Family Convention, Las Vegas, NV, July 24–29, 2016.
175 Vicki James Yiannias, "Supreme President Andrew Zachariades' Plans for AHEPA," Greek News, January 23, 2017.
176 Vicki James Yiannias, "AHEPA Supreme President George E. Loucas Talks about AHEPA," Greek News, November 10, 2018.
177 AHEPA News Release, "Statement: Resignation of Archbishop Demetrios," May 4, 2019.

Chapter 14
178 "Address of His Eminence Archbishop Elpidophoros of America at the 2019 AHEPA Supreme Convention," Orthodox Observer News.
179 AHEPA News Release, "Grand Banquet Honors Community Excellence; Archbishop Delivers First Address to AHEPA Family," July 15, 2019.
180 Vicky James Yiannias, "AHEPA Sets a Goal," Greek News, October 5, 2019.
181 Constantine S. Sirigos, "AHEPA's 99th Anniversary Supreme Convention in

Greece is in Full Swing," National Herald, July 27, 2021.
182 Constantine S. Sirigos, "Vision of the New Greece at the AHEPA Convention," National Herald, July 28, 2021.
183 Constantine S. Sirigos, "AHEPA Convention in Athens a Celebration of Hellenism and Unity," National Herald, July 29, 2021.
184 AHEPA News Release, "Greece Honors AHEPA with Its Highest Accolade," May 20, 2022.
185 AHEPA News Release, "Centennial Grand Banquet Inspires, Moves Audience," July 22, 2022.

www.ingramcontent.com/pod-product-compliance
Lightning Source LLC
Chambersburg PA
CBHW042117300426
44117CB00021B/2977